I0750483

THE LIGHTNING AND BIN LADEN:

THE GENETIC TRAIL OF THE LIGHTNING

Dr. Julio Antonio del Marmol

The Cuban Lightning

ISBN: 978-1-68588-044-6 (sc)
ISBN: 978-1-68588-043-9 (hc)
ISBN: 978-1-68588-045-3 (e)

Because of the dynamic nature of the Internet, any web addresses or links contained in this book may have changed since publication and may no longer be valid.

Cuban Lightning Publications, Int
www.cuban-lightning.com

The events in this book arc true. Only the names of certain individuals, locations, and sometimes sequence of events have been changed to protect lives.

ACKNOWLEDGEMENTS

I am a very lucky man because I have a great group of people by my side that I not only consider my friends but also who are the most capable, sacrificing professionals equal to the ones I've risked my life with over the past 50 years in their dedication and values. This group has made possible the publication of this book. To them, with all my heart today, I give the best of my love, gratitude, and sincerest thanks to every one of these fantastic warriors. In order of seniority, I would especially like to thank O'Brien: a great friend, a great individual with extraordinary values, thank you for your contributions you have made in many different ways to this project, as well being loyally by my side and watching my back for almost all of my career. I know for a fact you have never done that before for anyone. To my right arm and great friend, Tad Atkinson: for your dedication to every detail in research and many hours of hard work with me, never hesitating to sacrifice even your personal and private family time in order to make this happen. To Steve Weese: thank you for the many pieces of computer and graphic work as well professional enhancement of photos to improve the quality of the book. To Carlos Mota: my thanks for your dedication and multiple contributions and sacrifices you have made in order to make this happen. To Gervasin Neto: for your constant loyalty and many hours standing on your feet or hiding between cars in order to maintain our security with your group of people you've coordinated to watch our backs, continually keeping us informed of any suspicious activity that occurs in our surroundings. To Chopin: for your great companionship, loyalty, and support for the last 50 years with me in our fight for freedom and that beautiful, generous letter you wrote in behalf of the project. To our editor, Jen Poiry-Prough: who managed to make this book as easy to read, using her magic touch to polishing this piece of coal and bring to you, the readers, what I consider to be a very rare diamond. It makes all of us very proud to be involved in this project. Your professionalism, vast knowledge, and dedication, has made this book a great piece for future generations. To all of you, my friends who remain in the shadows, who contributed in one way or another in making this book and help me to bring the truth to the public, you have given the best of yourselves, putting forth your best effort to educate future generations. God bless you all. I embrace you as the Christian warriors that you all are.

Dr. Julio Antonio del Marmol

THE AUTHOR

I have questioned many times whether it is my tenacity, personality, or character, especially in the most crucial moments of my life when I see immanent death so close to me, why I can maintain my eyes straight as I look into Death's eyes without him intimidating me. Even when he extends his rough hand so close to caressing the skin of my face, and I can smell his rotten, pestilent breath, I cannot explain to myself why, with my eyes dry of any tears, I can defy him and control my fear, screaming to myself from the depths of my insides, "que sera, sera."

Perhaps it is because I have completely convinced myself that this life is not forever, that it is only to be lived by the moment, taking whatever happiness out of it that you can for yourself. Maybe this irrational and incoherent attitude is very unusual in a typical, everyday man, but I, without wanting it, am able to impress Death himself, and so he allows me to live one more day, leaving me to look for the answer as to why I am who I am and different from everyone else I know.

I don't mean to say that I am better or worse, simply that I know and recognize that my personality, character, and reactions scratch the very border of insanity. Even though I love life, and I expect every comfort and splendor in life, I am willing to pack my bag and leave it at any moment. I know this as though I had lived a previous life and learned that any man should prefer to die a thousand times to living alive without dignity, in fear, or lacking freedom—that is not life!

That is the reason I made a very deep and exhaustive search of my genealogical tree for my past ancestors, looking for any answers for my reactions, character, and personality of who I really am and why I act the way I do. Deeply surprised, I discovered the extraordinary genetic connection that I did not understand before. With that clarity and a great deal of logic, now I can live with myself as I lived another extension in another life, full of peace and happiness, and I recommend every single one of my readers to make the same search I did. Until you know yourself, you will never be able to live with yourself without knowing where you're going, from where you come, and who you really are.

Dr. Julio Antonio del Marmol
"The Cuban Lightning"

INTELLIGENCE ANALYSIS BY "O'BRIEN"

I want to start the analysis of this book with one simple, concrete, and defined question: who is the Lightning, aka Dr. Julio Antonio del Marmol? What does he know about bin Laden, or for that matter any other subject of discussion anywhere in the world? We can only obtain the real answer from the horse's mouth. Of course, this can be done simply by reading his books. As we do, we must keep an open mind and use logic to put two and two together. Even the least educated among us and the most skeptical individuals will reach the clear conclusion that this man, the Lightning, is anything but the ordinary individual we encounter every day in our lives.

I always tell everyone that there is a very thin line that separates a hero from a villain. The reason for that is that human beings have their own ambitions, emotions, and political beliefs. These emotions can trick some men very easily. Worse, unless a person has very strong convictions he can be turned from hero to villain and become lost in the darkness through his own actions. He might not even realize that he is doing this. The reverse process can also occur, taking a man from the darkness and into the light; once more his actions can take him there without his even realizing it. Either process can send false signals to others.

Finding the details in the life of any spy is a very difficult task. I would say that it's almost impossible because the life of a spy depends on the discretion of each individual to maintain various identities and incognitos. He waits for the right moment when he will need it in order to save his life. When he is exposed, he will disappear like a magic act and reappear in another identity in order to conclude his mission without his enemies blowing his new cover. This is one more reason why this profession is very complicated. We are trained meticulously to not leave behind any trace. Any trace can take the form of documents, data, or even words on the lips of others which serve as witnesses later that the spy was in that place, in that country, at that time, wherever he has been before, following a plan and his work. This is almost impossible to achieve, because wherever there is a fire, there are always ashes left. Another highly skilled spy can trace those ashes, put the pieces together, and analyze them carefully to come to his best-educated guess in tracking the spy down and identifying who it is that was involved in that mission. We all have our individualized ways of working, modus operandi that leave a signature behind due to our individuality. It is not the sort of thing that everyday individuals will notice; but in this kind of work, we do not deal with everyday people.

I consider the Cuban Lightning, or Dr. Julio Antonio del Marmol, if you prefer, a very great friend—but who is he, in reality? We can start without having to go too far back in time, to October of 1971. The Lightning left Cuba with a small group of his best, closest friends. The U.S. government denied that these men, who were flown clandestinely to Miami, Florida, had been admitted into the country. The military plane left the U.S. Naval Reservation at Guantanamo without leaving any trace of this unusual event. The Lightning and his friends were accepted into the U.S. because they had established a long background of credibility with our government; they also did not have to go through normal protocols. Without hesitation, the U.S. government committed a flagrant violation of treaties and diplomatic conventions established under the contract the Navy base has with Cuba to not accept any refugee or grant any political asylum in that facility. They took the big risk of sparking an international incident without blinking an eye, protecting Dr. del Marmol and his friends, and went even further to relocate them within the soil of the continental United States, to California. There he disappeared in November of 1971 for over 17 years.

In silence, like a ghost, he created for himself a center for clandestine operations in Orange County with his team of Cuban freedom fighters. On Tuesday, September 27, 1988, the Lightning reappeared in Costa Mesa, California, before the public eye. This time, his cover was blown out of the water, ironically like 17 years before in Cuba, and once more through the error of his friends in the intelligence community. The last time, the vital mistake had led to him being extracted from the island. History repeated itself, but this time, the Lightning wound up occupying the front page of every newspaper not just in the United States but all around the world. His suffered the not-so-glamorous, embarrassing indignity of being accused as a counterfeiter with what appeared to be $23.5 million in his possession seized by the Secret Service. Dr. del Marmol maintained complete silence throughout the entire ordeal, even though the major headlines in the newspapers continued to speak of the seizure as being the greatest ever in the history of the U.S. If found guilty of all the counts of possession and transportation of counterfeit currency, he would face on all indictments of 75 years and 6 months in a federal prison.

However, all the front page articles vanished like smoke in a few weeks. After that, the case was sealed and classified. On the advice of the federal judge, Spenser Letts, Dr. del Marmol pled guilty and accepted full responsibility with the light sentence of one year, spending only six months in a federal camp. He was to report there whenever he had put his affairs in order and found it most convenient to serve the sentence. A few months after his release, he was authorized to leave the country to his vacation home in Baja, Mexico, indefinitely, while still under his three-year probationary period.

I ask all readers, especially the most skeptical of you, if after you completely read my analysis whether you could still have doubts about who this man, Dr. Julio Antonio del Marmol (aka the Cuban Lightning) really is. I also must ask all of you to take at face value his experience, his integrity, his courage, and his stories. There are not many things I can say of a certainty in my life, but one thing I can be sure of and wish to communicate with all of you is that I never once witnessed similar events. I can assure you that, as you study his books, you also will never read anything so vividly close to the truth. Even I, who was one of the participants, get chills at reliving how this man not only risked his life in all these operations but continues to further risk his life by telling these stories to the public. It is one more proof of his honesty, courage, and integrity. If it is not, I do not know what is! Please find me another person that is even close to this man.

"O'Brien"

AUTHOR'S PREFACE

When I was very small, just learning to walk and talk, I didn't have any idea the significance of the word "politics." I had something like an echo in my brain, the voice of my father that continually said, "Politics is filthy and corrupt."

Maybe that is the reason that my father never exercised his right to vote. Perhaps also it was why, as I grew up, when any one of my friends talked to me about politics, the word alone made me feel nauseous to the stomach. What my father didn't know or ignored all his life was that, in fact, like in other areas in life, it wasn't politics itself that was immoral—it was the men involved in the process who made it so.

In consequence, I never wanted to be associated with any of those who represented politics. It's simply what I heard from my father, who was always an honest and exemplary man in all aspects and expectations. Not only was he a decent, great, and dignified man, he was my major source of pride and my best example. As a young man, I always wanted to be, if not exactly like him, the closest I could possibly reach. Just as I matured into my preteen years and the years following, it was only time and my own experiences which made me understand the tremendous error committed by my father in his way of thinking.

Possibly it could have been his rebelliousness or his bad political decisions and deceptions practiced on him through all his life; but in the end, it gave him the worst disappointment precisely because he chose to not exercise his right to vote. He never wanted to get involved in a process he felt personal distaste for and proclaimed to every one of his friends with pride that he never in his entire life voted for anyone.

It was the worst mistake of his life. He embraced the worst radicals of the extreme Left wing, the absolute worst kind of politicians, those he despised and stayed away from all his life. Not only this time did he make the mistake for himself, he also dragged with him his friends and brother Masons, convincing them to follow this ideology and the false pretense of "nationalism." He took the entire Cuban nation down that path.

That right that he chose to never exercise completely disappeared for him and all his fellow citizens. The most important thing any human being can have in life was lost: the right to be free and live with dignity in joy, peace, and harmony, free of persecution and tyranny from any totalitarian government. Whether they call themselves "socialist," "communist," "fascist," or "Nazi," everyone at the ends of these extreme ideologies can be separated by a single hair, and hold hands with each other, like the same dogs with different collars. These filthy and corrupt extremist politicians inevitably take power without any scruples. They worm their way into authority, deceiving by making false promises to everyone, conquering many peoples' hearts with the promises of equality, all the while hiding their darkest ambitions and hunger for power.

They destroy from the ground up the established society, filling everyone with hatred and lies, until finally everyone has the rude awakening that the end of the road is not a garden of roses; it is hunger, misery, and a deep, deep cliff the edge of which no one can escape from. The youngest mind that follows that route due to inexperience as well as resentment toward those that have more now, eventually see with tears in their eyes the fraud they were sold right under their very noses.

They want to fight. Unfortunately, they will die, because now the extreme Leftist, totalitarian politicians who promised this great life where everything is free will now control the crowd. They will make them submit, without scruples, using violence against those who refuse to conform. These young minds now repent with no way out, because they willingly followed these extremists joyfully. They will ask themselves, "How could we have been so naïve to go and believe that everything in our future would be happiness and riches without any effort, work, or sacrifice in our lives?"

Only then will they see the cruel reality and look at each other to see the deception in everyone's eyes in this darkest night at that time when the hunger, misery, and the long lines for a loaf of bread have become reality. They will look to the past with sorrow at the freedom they left behind. Their full remorse will cause them to cry their eyes out as they remember the beautiful lives they had before, now gone beyond recall for the rest of their lives. They will then see this truth: that we never see the beauty of the things we have until they are no longer in our faces, out of reach of our hands, and forever gone from our lives.

INTRODUCTION

When we talk about bin Laden, the only thing about this man that people remember, unfortunately, is that dark day of September 11, 2001, and the worst terrorist act of the beginning of this century. We tend to forget who ignored this dangerous enemy and those who had inside information. We have many reasons to be upset that several Administrations in our country, for political and sometimes personal ambitions, embraced this macabre terrorist's ideas and helped to give life to this horrible monster, never imagining like Dr. Frankenstein that this monster would never be completely domesticated. They played with dangerous fire. We forget occasionally that violence creates violence and reproduces rapidly as a bad weed in the appropriate environment. Most of the time, the creators of such monsters end up being the first victims. Those bragging about their perverse creation and who claim to be its creators eventually lose control, and the reins cut loose when the beast is unleashed. They point fingers at each other, trying very quickly to disassociate and exonerate themselves from responsibility. They are now accountable for this horrible abomination.

I want to tell my readers that this, what you are reading today, does not come out of any book of tales. It is a product of my own experience and how, step by step, we tried again and again to send the signal to destroy this beast before it was too late. Some of what you read will be difficult to digest for any good, decent human being; my friend, atrocities, especially against innocent human beings, are not simple things to swallow. I don't want to point any fingers or to blame anyone. These monsters to begin with are not good human beings and are looking for the opportunity and power to kill, looking for any excuse to unleash violence and terrorism against men, women, and children that have nothing to do with the politics of any nation when they occur. The innocents die from the negligence of those politicians who have the power to prevent it, whether that neglect is due to avoiding international incidents or some other diplomatic impediment. In the end, however, the innocents are the ones who pay the price.

I will try to describe it all to you, without being a judge, just an observer, simply telling you the best truth I can discern from the facts in my grasp, with the proof of my eyes, the most accurate story possible. However, my hands are sometimes tied so that I don't reveal anything which could be detrimental to our nation. I am taking this opportunity to enlighten you with the best veracity as to why those who hold responsibility in the political, social, and historical events we live through sometimes try to pull the wool over your eyes and keep you in the dark.

PROLOGUE: RETURNING TO MY LINE OF WORK FOLLOWING THE ZIPPER

The lion is not always a lion. It can be a sheep dressed like one. The Bible tells us that the true Lion of Judah came as a child but will return not as a child, but as the King of Kings to rule in power and glory forever. The truth will always overpower lies with such force and glory that no evil can ever withstand it. The truth will endure, resisting every single force of Nature because it possesses the key to Mother Nature. With the force of lightning, the truth will destroy in the end all the lies, leaving a path of peace, love, and harmony for everyone.

Dr. Julio Antonio del Marmol

After the Zipper operation, my cover was entirely blown. My real identity had been exposed publicly. The scandal had been televised and printed in newspapers internationally. The largest seizure of counterfeit money in the United States—$23.5 million—had nearly cost me 75-and-a-half years in federal prison.

In the end, however, my sentence was reduced to a major personal embarrassment. The federal judge, the late Spencer Letts, handed me the lightest sentence—one year in federal prison—in order to appease the public that I would spend some time in prison. I only spent six months in a minimum-security institution, Boron Federal Camp.

My crime had been following the orders of President Ronald Reagan.

The judge and my associates in the intelligence community had both advised me to leave the country for at least a couple of years. This would allow the scandal to lose value over time, as current news cycles and events eventually buried the tremendous international success of the operation.

I always follow the advice of those who not only proved to me their loyalty but also made their best effort to protect me in the most difficult moments. I decided to take a break in my career as a freedom fighter and international spy. At the same time, why not take a long vacation, which I really deserved for keeping my mouth shut and maintaining absolute silence? I had been very careful to not expose President Reagan or involve him in anything that had occurred in that valuable and fruitful operation. It was painful to me due to the embarrassment of my friends and family. I also had the great satisfaction of seeing the Soviet economy collapsing and the Berlin Wall be torn down as a result of our great efforts and sacrifices. It not only wasn't something anybody expected would happen in the '80s, but it was also something never before seen in the history of the world.

And so, I took very seriously my retreat to my oceanfront vacation home in Baja California, Mexico. I arrived in 1990 and purchased another few acres of land, also close to the ocean, to keep active and protect myself against boredom. I established in that area a family farm, buying several pigs, cows, goats, chickens, and horses that very soon began to procreate. A few years later, the farm had become a very profitable business. I started to sell to the local markets the beef, pork, poultry, eggs, cheese, and milk that we produced on my ranch. The next four years passed rapidly, as they do when one has happiness, harmony, and tranquility.

During this, my second political exile, I had established myself in that small, civilized fishing town in Baja. It was a small corner of the world which I had almost forgotten and left behind. Now I had was trying to forget the intrigues and life of the world of espionage and their serious consequences.

That Tuesday morning of January 1994, I saw coming to the main gates of the ranch a Range Rover that I immediately recognized as the car that O'Brien had used several times during my exile to pay me a visit. I felt a mix of happiness and uncertainty. O'Brien was always welcome in my heart, but I knew also that he didn't come without a reason; he came because he had a problem. In the most diplomatic manner, he would either ask me to help him resolve it or to once more come back, as he had been doing during the past years.

My visits to Orange County in California, where we had our center of clandestine operations, had grown less and less frequent for various reasons. The most powerful one was the common contradiction between my way of thinking and the new Administration now occupying the White House. They did not represent at all the same values that my friends and I were accustomed to defending.

I glanced at the car as it drove up the sandy road while I continued my work castrating some small young pigs in the corrals. When the Range Rover came to the main gate, I had nearly finished my work. I instructed my assistants where to put the animals, separating them from the others in order to prevent the largest adults from abusing the wounded ones while they healed from the incision that I had made to extract their testicles.

O'Brien stopped the Range Rover close to the front gate. With his customary smile, he called, "Hey, how's the rancher's life going?"

I returned his smile and walked to the door of the corrals. O'Brien had been there before—he always wore expensive shoes and had learned from bitter experience not to come into the corrals wearing them. I saw another man getting out of the passenger side of the Range Rover. Olive-skinned from the semi-desert sun, black hair streaked with white at the temple, he appeared to be from Yucatan. He was perhaps about 5'8", had a small moustache, and was dressed in the uniform of the Mexican army. After we exchanged some greetings, O'Brien said, "This is my good friend, General Martinez Prieto."

I held my hand out to him. "Nice to meet you, General."

"The pleasure is all mine, as well as the honor of meeting such a great man who has done so much for freedom around the world, Dr. del Marmol. Or maybe, just between us in confidence, the Cuban Lightning."

I smiled slightly. "It's been a few years since I heard that code. It sounds to me a part of the past. As you know, General, we all are getting older, and we get rusty with time."

The General, in typical military attitude, grinned. "Men like us are not accustomed to anything, even time being capable of stopping us."

I smiled fully. "I'm truly sorry to contradict you, General—that's probably something you're not accustomed to. But to me, time has stopped me. You know what it is? Nothing less than seventy-five years and six months that I came so close to spending in a federal penitentiary in the United States of America, when virtually all of my friends ran away from me."

The General raised his right arm high dismissively, his expression deprecating. "Well, well—those are the small rocks that God puts in our road once in a while."

I frowned slightly. "Well, maybe God put those little rocks before you once in a while. But in my road, maybe it's because it's the first and only time, he set a rock bigger than that mountain!" I pointed to the mountain which backed against my ranch. We all laughed.

O'Brien had been keeping silent, but now he nodded his head and said, "All that you've said is absolutely true, and I'm one of your witnesses. But you have to take into consideration that with the help of God, you also got out from under that immense rock with only a few scratches."

I shook my head slightly, looking a little unconvinced. "Unfortunately, everything is relative. It all depends on the way you look at it and how you want to evaluate it. I cannot measure your pain because it's not mine. What might to you seem like scratches are to me very deep cuts, leaving equally deep scars for the next several years—possibly for the rest of my life."

O'Brien nodded. His demeanor changed; he knew what I meant. "You're completely right. I'm sorry for my insensitivity."

I smiled. "You don't have to apologize, please. You're my friend, but you didn't wear my shoes during that whole ordeal. It would be very difficult for you to understand the emotional effect that had on me as well as on my family and closest friends. They had no idea about my double life as a spy." I waved it away in dismissal. "That's all in the past. Let's forget about it. Let me ask you gentlemen what I can do for you today. That is most important. Let's forget the past, OK?"

"OK." O'Brien noticed my emotional state and put a friendly arm around my shoulders. "Let's take a walk around your ranch, show the General all the beautiful animals you have here as well as the genetic breeding you've been doing." He turned to the General. "The meat he produces is beautiful, like candy!"

I said, "Let's go walk to the well. We can work our way from there to the rest of the ranch."

We walked over to the massive water tank, perhaps 175 feet tall. That concrete tank stored all the water we drew from the well, which saved us from continually using the pump.

When we got near the well, the General said, "I won't beat around the bushes. I'm going to tell you the naked truth. The reason we are here is that I asked O'Brien for the best, and he said that is you. We, the Mexican people, need you, no matter what your price is." I had a small smile on my lips, but silently continued my walk with them. General Martinez took his hat off and scratched his head.

He continued, "I'm in charge of the entire counterintelligence network in Baja California. We have information about a huge conspiracy from the Cuban government with certain Mexican civilians, military, federal police, and politicians, all members of the extreme Left, to assassinate our candidate for President, Luis Donaldo Colosio Murrieta. On his next trip to the border city of Tijuana, we know for certainty based on the information we have from our agents, that at first the Cuban embassy offered two hundred fifty thousand dollars for this contract. They want a Mexican national to execute it, not a foreigner. That will prevent it from being an international scandal and keep it strictly within Mexico. The fresh information indicates that the price has been doubled to half a million. We believe that they have two prospects to execute this plan. Of course, this is the most recent information we have from our double agents. This concerns me very much; it's a lot of money here in Mexico. With that kind of payout in dollars, it won't take very long for many candidates in this profession to put themselves forward." He shook his head. "Half a million dollars! Someone would not only be capable of assassinating our candidate for President; they might even get someone to assassinate the President of the United States."

I smiled again and stroked my chin with my left hand. I looked doubtfully at him through my smile. I shook my head slightly. The General stopped. He looked a little irritated as he turned towards me. "This is the second time you've smiled. Do you know something I don't know? Or perhaps you find some humor in my serious words? This is nothing to laugh at. I can assure you of that."

I stopped as well. I turned and smiled without replying to him. I looked into O'Brien's eyes. "I believe you should take the General, with all my respect, into town to the medical doctor. Tell him I sent you. Perhaps he can prescribe some Valium or other sedative. He needs to calm his nerves. After you do that, maybe later we can have an intelligent conversation with humor not being a motive for irritation." I turned and started to walk back to the pigs' corral.

The General looked at O'Brien in astonishment. O'Brien spread his arms noncommittally. I listened to their conversation.

O'Brien said, "I told you to be careful in your manners. He's a nice man, but he's not one of your soldiers. If you want him to help you, you cannot talk to him like that."

I pretended not to hear the General's response, in a less authoritarian voice, "Please, Dr. del Marmol." I continued to walk, and he said a little louder, "Please, Dr. del Marmol. I beg you to forgive me; I've been under a lot of stress."

I stopped in the middle of the road, turned, and looked him in his eyes. I shook my head and looked at O'Brien next to him. He said nothing but gestured imploringly to me to give the man a second chance. I stood in the middle of the road silently, looking at both men. I shook my head in resignation and started to walk back to them.

When I got up to them, the General apologized once more. I raised my hand to stop him. "I don't really like to give explanations to anyone for doing what I do. But this time, as a courtesy to my friend O'Brien, I will break that rule. I will tell you, Mr. General, that my smile had nothing to do with the seriousness of the problem you have on your shoulders. The reason for my first smile is because you asked me what my price is. I tell you now that I have no price. I don't need money. As I told O'Brien's bosses in U.S. intelligence many years ago, nothing I do is done for money. Remember, General, those who do this work for money are untrustworthy. Somebody can always come to that person to pay a lot more than you are paying. Since he's working for money, he will follow the highest price."

The General started to apologize again, but I continued. "The second time I smiled is because you said that for two hundred fifty thousand dollars, someone would be willing to kill the President of the United States.

Do you know how much it cost the Cuban government to kill JFK?"

He grew pale and looked over to O'Brien for confirmation. O'Brien nodded. The General could only shake his head in reply to my question. My smile this time was one of satisfaction at the huge surprise in his face. "General—it cost them millions and millions and millions. I saw with my own eyes the briefcases filled with money, in bundles of ten thousand dollars each. My friend General Martinez Prieto, do you understand now the motive to my smiles when you were talking? That is only my silent expression, out of courtesy to not interrupt your conversation. Someone else might interrupt and correct you, because what you're saying is far from the truth. I only remember these things you were talking about, and all I could do is smile. That is no reason for you to get upset and think I wasn't taking you seriously. We have to be careful when we react in assumption, because when we assume something in life, ninety-nine percent of the time, we're wrong."

The General once more apologized and tried to correct what he was saying while preserving his pride. "Well, when I asked you what your price is, I wasn't referring to you personally. I was referring to the expenses you could incur in the operation. I am, on behalf of the President, authorized to pay whatever it is. A blank check. I will use any means to prevent the candidate from getting killed. My current President, Carlos Salinas de Gotari, considers Colosio Murrieta one of his best friends. This is the reason they gave me carte blanche and unlimited funds for this operation."

I could see the pride in his face.

"If you accept, Dr. del Marmol, all you have to tell me how much and where you want me to deposit the funds for this operation. I will personally deposit whatever amount you request without any intermediaries."

I nodded. "I understand perfectly. Before I make my decision to accept your proposition or not, I need to ask you a few questions."

The General nodded. "Whatever you need."

I pulled a small notepad and pen out of my shirt pocket. "What motive does the Cuban government have to plan an assassination, which would be a tremendous scandal?"

"Well, Colosio, our candidate, has expressed more than once that corruption exists within Mexican politicians in cahoots with communist Cuba, which uses extortion, blackmail, and tries to enrich themselves with public funds without any scruples at all. Colosio has also expressed that, if he gets elected, he will place sanctions against the Cuban government and dramatically reduce the diplomatic personnel in the Cuban embassy. Currently, there are over five hundred people there, and he considers the embassy a clandestine base for creating communist revolutions in Central and South America. Our candidate says that he has proof of Cuban involvement in the Chiapas conflict[1] and that Cuba has financed this, trying to destroy our constitution and bring a communist revolution into our country. This will allow them to continue their domination in Latin America and accomplish their golden dream of crossing the northern border to bring down the United States."

"It's OK, General. Thank you very much. This is more than sufficient motivation for the Cubans to assassinate a President. It's the same method the Cubans have used internationally for years. My other question: when are you guys expecting the candidate to come to Baja?"

"By the end of March. We don't know the exact date yet. For security reasons, nobody will know until a week before."

"We don't have very much time. Only two months. This is a real challenge. Another question, General Martinez: what do you expect me to do that you guys

---

1 Refers to the Zapatista uprising amid tensions between indigenous people and subsistence farmers in the Mexican state of Chiapas

cannot already do in your counterintelligence organization? Something out of your power? What exactly to you expect from me?"

"Very simple—the names and pictures of the people who plan to actually execute this assassination, and if possible, the details of how they plan to effect it."

"Very well. How will I communicate with you?"

The General smiled. "Does that mean we can count on you?" He held out a card to me. He turned it over. "On this card you have two numbers. You can call me twenty-four hours a day. If for whatever reason you cannot reach me at the first number, call my beeper, and I will call you back, no matter what time it is, day or night."

"Very well. Yes, I will take this assignment. However, I cannot guarantee much in this short time. One thing I can guarantee is that I will do the impossible now that I know the great qualities of your candidate to prevent his being killed. A man of that caliber has to live."

The General nodded. "He is a very good man and will be a great President. He might even be better than the one we have now."

"Be careful—you're still under his command," I said teasingly. "Make that 'as good as' the one we have now."

He grinned. "You would make a very good diplomat." He took a couple of steps forward and gave me a hug. "Thank you, and I apologize once again for my emotional outburst."

I smiled. "Who is perfect, General?"

He smiled. "Nobody." We both laughed. "Thank you again for your good manners and extremely good sense of humor. But you still haven't said how much it will cost us."

I raised my left hand. "Don't worry about it. It will be less than what it cost the Cuban government to kill Kennedy."

"Oh, *mi madre*! If I tell the President that, he'll pull out the last bit of hair he has on his head."

"We will let you know as we move forward. I will get in touch with my team. The first target will be the Cuban embassy in Mexico City. If this doesn't get the results we're looking for, we will move to Cuba and mobilize our contacts on the island. This will be more efficient, but it will be more costly. We might have to bribe some of the Cuban intelligence officers in order to obtain the intel we need to detour this assassination plot. Let's start with the exploratory surgery and not rush ourselves. If for whatever reason it's necessary, we'll move to the major surgery."

The General smiled and looked O'Brien, who had politely allowed us to finish our conversation. He took two steps, shook hands, and embraced him. "Thank you, my good friend O'Brien."

O'Brien smiled at the General. "When you called me and we had a delicious dinner at that restaurant and you confided to me your problem, I told you that you have in your country the best music for the whole orchestra. He is a virtuoso."

General Prieto grinned hugely and replied, "We have him right here on our patio, and I didn't even know."

O'Brien stepped forward and hugged me. He said to me, "This will be a good thing for you to weave back into what you're best at. You will refresh your memory and bring your good old times back."

I smiled. "The old times, really? I just remember all the work we did before, all the sacrifices we made. This new Administration in the White House now, like lambs, are allowing our enemies to run free again. Our enemies, like creatures in the jungle, smell the weakness in their victims, now regroup, get extreme, and take more and more territory, using this weakness and great opportunity. They are destroying in the process all of our work and sacrifice."

We said goodbye, and I watched them leave down the long road in the Range Rover. I thought, *I hope I'm not making a big mistake, accepting this delicate assignment with so little time to stop this assassination.*

Two months later, March 19, 1994
Golden Dragon Chinese Restaurant
Mexicali, Capital of the state of Baja California

I had in my hands all the details and even partial photos of the assassins who would be enacting this hit on their innocent victim. The names they were using were fictitious. Neither of these two individuals had criminal records under their aliases, of course. Even though counterintelligence had been distributing the photos, we only had three days before the candidate arrived in Tijuana. He was to speak at a public gathering, and General Martinez Prieto and all his intelligence and counterintelligence people were completely in the dark. I had confirmed with their intelligence that the target was indeed Murrieta. By bribing the elements involved in this plot, I had even provided to these individuals information about the weapons they were to use. The General sat at a table with me, discussing the final details. He had not even touched his food. He was filled with frustration and uncertainty with each passing day.

He asked, "Did you see them with your own eyes?"

"Yes, General. I not only observed them for a long time, recording their physical movement and behaviors, but they are extremely protected by Cuban security forces called the Internationalist Proletariats." I pointed at my forehead with my index finger. "I have a photographic memory for faces. It doesn't matter what disguise they use; I will recognize them from the way they walk, the set of their shoulders, or whatever—all the things that make each of us different. But you have to have the skill to pinpoint those things."

I stroked my chin with my left hand. "If you cannot convince the candidate not to attend this event, he will not get out of it alive. The saddest part is that we cannot do anything to prevent it. These sunglasses and broad brimmed hats that people like the FBI wear—they disguise their facial features very well. Unfortunately, we don't have many people like me around who have the gift and the training to pick these guys out in a crowd of thousands. My professional advice, General, and the responsible thing to do, is to stop this event and substitute it for another. Cancel this, please, and so give us time to find these two assassins."

The General shifted in his chair nervously. "Unfortunately, the candidate isn't listening to me. I spoke with him last night on the phone for over two hours. His last words to me were that nothing in this world would prevent him from attending that event. It is extremely important and decisive in his campaign against his opposition."

I raised both arms high. "Well, my General, the only thing I have left to say to you is that if this is the case, pick the phone up immediately we finish this lunch, and please call the President and tell him to look for another candidate. This one will not live longer than Wednesday, March 23rd unless a miracle occurs."

I shook my head sourly. I put all the conviction I could into my next words. "If you cannot find a way to change the candidate's mind, he will become another unsolved crime perpetrated by the Cuban government and organized by the internationalists who are trying to control our world, right in front of our eyes. It will be in the smoke for decades like John F. Kennedy's death, as well as similar crimes committed by the Cuban communists all over the world. I can assure you, General, that these Cubans have converted themselves into masters in this criminal profession. They know how to handpick men with the psychological problems or narcissism it takes to pull off these diabolical plans and assassinations. This is how they make utter fools of everyone and go beyond what any logical mind could fathom. They create the perfect distraction, getting everyone looking to the right as they perpetrate their crime on the left, right in front of thousands of spectators. That is why, my good friend General Martinez, my work is concluded today here and now. There is nothing more I can do for your candidate, and I don't want to give you false hope. Looking for two faces in a multitude of thousands, I can anticipate will be like looking for two needles in a haystack. It's something that is almost impossible and will take a lot of time, which we don't have in our hands today. For the good of your reputation, General, please talk to the candidate again and send him my regards. Tell him who I am, send him from me my most respectful greetings and complete admiration for his unnecessary braveness. But it's no less brave to exercise discretion. Tell him, please, that the probabilities of getting out alive from this gathering in Tijuana is like a fight between a monkey and a lion, but the monkey has been tied hand and foot to a pole. Guess who is going to win?" I breathed deeply. "Tell him this: the candidate might visualize how defenseless the monkey on the pole is." I stood up and held my hand out to the General in farewell.

"Will you come to the event on Wednesday?"

"I'm not a morbid person. I never like to assist in the execution of human beings."

He stood up. "I know exactly what you mean. Looking for these two faces in all those people is exactly like two needles in a haystack. But if I have you there on Wednesday, I will have a lot more tranquility, believe me."

I smiled slightly. "Thank you for your confidence, General, in this short time we've known each other. I've provided you a mountain of information, but that is all I can do. I don't have the time or the resources to stop this operation. As I said before, the probability of his getting out of this event alive are negligible. Even less than an innocent victim in a shopping mall where bin Laden sends his suicide bombers."

The General looked at me sadly. He had no further arguments. "Please, think about it. If you change your mind and decide to go, please communicate with me, and I will give you a walkie talkie with a secure frequency so that you can continue talking to us."

I nodded. "Thank you again. I promise nothing. If I change my mind, I will communicate with you."

We embraced. I walked out of that restaurant with a knot in my throat and a pain of frustration in my chest, knowing that the young man, a patriot and a decent human being who loves his country to death, would be sacrificed the next Wednesday that March. Nothing anyone could do to prevent it.

INSANITY: I LOVE IT

Somebody once told me I'm suffering from insanity. I replied with a big smile on my face, "Yes, I know. However, I might be on the border of it, but I don't suffer. I'm really happy and glad for being on that borderline. This is not only the fountain of my creativity but also the best cover I ever had in my life as a spy. This thought also makes me enjoy that stigma of insanity every single day of my life."

Dr. Julio Antonio del Marmol

Insanity: I Love It!

Music and Lyrics by:
Dr. Julio Antonio del Mármol
&
His Cuban Lightning Orchestra

INSANITY—I LOVE IT SO MUCH THAT I WILL TO THE END OF MY LIFE LIVE WITH IT AND LAUGH AT THOSE WHO CONSIDER THEMSELVES SANE

DR. JAM

CHAPTER 1: BIN LADEN'S MOST TRUSTED

Figure 1 Osama bin Laden with his trusted advisors

It was eight months and two weeks after the most devastating terrorist act in the history of the world: 9/11. To be precise, May 13, 2002, 5:30 am. We flew through a torrential thunderstorm in a private helicopter over Venezuelan airspace. The helicopter was completely painted in a translucent military thermal silver and bore emblems in black on both sides which read "Intercontinental Legal Affairs" surrounding the image of Lady Justice, bordered by olive branches. If one looked at it quickly, it appeared more like the official logo for any department of the United States government.

In the pilot's seat was a black man, Chopin, who was looking at the dashboard, reading the various gauges. In the co-pilot's seat was the beautiful red-headed Elizabeth, who for so many years had been fighting with us and risking her life around the world. In the back, Yaneba sat next to me facing forward, looking through the small porthole in silence. She looked out into the darkness of the night, watching the unsettling lightning display that came so close to our craft.

On the floor next to us, my dog, Rocco, lay at my feet. He did not look very happy at the turbulence which shook the helicopter, occasionally raising his head abruptly at the loud boom of thunder as a bolt of lightning struck too close to us. He was otherwise unaffected by the commotion, so accustomed was he to the craziness of our lives. He yawned and put his head back down to sleep. I reached out and patted his head.

To my right in the rear-facing seat, we had a new acquisition to the team: a black man who smiled at the gesture, his two gold-plated teeth shining in the glare of the lightning flash through the porthole. His name was Augusto Mayari; he had been the assistant in Cuba to my brother-in-law, Captain Canen of the Rebel Army. We had just taken him into the team to take the place of Hernesto. He had escaped from Cuba years before, taking one of the government's torpedo boats to Miami, where he gave it to the government to do research into the Soviet naval technology. My freedom fighters in Miami had introduced him to me when I was much younger, and we had just taken him into the team. He sat in his seat, cleaning his AK-47 with a small towel. I returned his smile with one of my own.

Figure 2 Rocco, the Lightning's companion

My mind at that moment was extremely distracted and saddened by the bad memories of the past months. I still could not get out of my mind the image of those innocent people jumping out of windows in despair, preferring falling to their deaths to burning alive in the fires. Even though it had been over eight months, and I had been trying to put it behind me, all these images repeated in my mind like a TV show each time I closed my eyes. They haunted me, for I felt guilty at not being able to prevent that barbarous attack.

I also had so many questions in my mind as to how our great friend and lovely individual, Hernesto, had spent the last minutes of his life on board Flight 93. All these questions were unanswered in my mind, including how he managed to rally the passengers on that plane.

It took my appetite away, and from that day I had even lost the palate to taste my food. It all tasted the same, and I could not sleep a single night in peace and tranquility following this horrendous incident. Guilt and many other emotions continually crossed my mind as I blamed myself unceasingly. If only I had not left those documents behind in the hotel room that night in Cuba, if only I had been able to talk to the terrorist, Abdul Hussein…

I wracked my mind to the point of mental torture. I kept asking how, knowing what I knew, I could have walked out of the Havana Riviera Hotel to meet him that night. I knew full well how in Cuba you can't move from one corner to another without an ID in your pocket, and yet I didn't once check my pockets before walking out into the street. All I did was give the police the opportunity to question me, arrest me, and frustrate my meeting with this important individual. He was supposed to provide me with such vital information that could have been the key to stopping that plan which had claimed so many innocent lives. Even though my friends tried more than once to convince me to the contrary, that I had done my best, it became a heavy weight on my shoulders, a massive package on my conscience. I was in the frame of mind to do whatever I needed to remove the burden and throw it far away from me.

The rain started to grow lighter, though the lightning continued to be violent on that dark night, continually illuminating the sky. The turbulence grew worse, shaking the entire helicopter. I continued deep inside my thoughts. I promised myself on that day of 9/11 to leave everything behind me and look for a place with peace and tranquility, far away from all the complicated, unstable world of espionage. It is a world where everything is uncertain and nothing is sure, where you could wind up with the greatest disappointment, even from those closest to you. All the information we sacrificed for that was only discarded at the uppermost levels by those who should have acted. I no longer wanted to be looking over my shoulder, and promised myself that even should the world end, I would, at least, not have a guilty conscience.

However, whatever one thinks yesterday, a different thought occurs today, and yet another occurs tomorrow. A few weeks before this flight, O'Brien came to me and told me that Abul Hussein wanted to meet with me and with me only. This was the only window of opportunity we might have for a long time to catch and kill Osama bin

Laden. Even though I hesitated as I had when O'Brien had first presented me with the plans for the Zipper, I didn't have any alternative after giving it serious consideration. I had to accept this opportunity to catch the man responsible for so many deaths. It wasn't only that—there was a personal satisfaction to obtain from the horse's mouth and clear my conscience of how much information he had before the terrorist attack. If this really, as I was always thinking, could be the key to stop future attacks, I would only find out by talking to him.

This man not only was involved in the past months of being a single courier and contact, but he had come to be one of the key most-trusted men in Al-Qaeda, close to bin Laden. I don't know if I was being a little selfish, but I thought it would be a tremendous relief to my mind if we could buy for a few million dollars the means to stop future attacks, whether that man had that information or not. With all this drama in my mind, I looked around the helicopter and saw a very thick wired attaché case, brown skinned like a crocodile hide, handcuffed to one of the handrails, laying in a side seat against the wall. I watched the briefcase as it swayed slightly in the turbulence.

Suddenly, there was a major explosion, much different than the thunder and lightning, and much closer to us. The helicopter shook violently as if struck directly by lightning, and the warning alarms started beeping as we started to go down. Everyone looked at each other, uncertain as to what had happened. Rocco stood up and started howling, an eerie sound to our ears. A dense, white smoke engulfed the entire interior of the helicopter. At the same time, we heard the screeching, terrified voice of Chopin exclaiming, "We're hit! We're hit!"

I took my seatbelt off, and hanging however I could to maintain my balance, even by some of the cargo nets near the ceiling, I made my way forward. "What's happening?" I asked.

Nearly simultaneously, Elizabeth and Chopin replied, "We've been hit by a rocket. It wasn't lightning."

"Sons of bitches!" I exclaimed indignantly.

Chopin managed to get the helicopter under control. "One engine is out. We're going to be very lucky if we make it even much further than here."

Slowly but surely, Chopin managed to control the situation. We still were shaking violently, but we were no longer losing altitude. The white smoke thinned from the cabin and the interior. Chopin crossed himself. "Let's all pray to God that this engine won't fail on us, or we're going down to Hell. There's no other remedy."

I touched his shoulder. "Well, you've so far managed to keep us in the air."

"Don't be so happy. We're losing a lot of compression. Some fragments of that rocket must have cut some of the hydraulic hose, and we're rapidly losing fluid."

I snatched up the map in my hand and spread it out near the windshield before them. I asked, "Do you think we can make it to this island? Santa Margarita? It's only twenty kilometers. It's perhaps fifteen minutes less. Can you keep this chopper in the air for that long?" I pulled out my compass and compared it to the gauge on the control panel, trying to show him the latitude and longitude of the island.

Chopin glanced at me doubtfully. He looked at Elizabeth, who had until now been silent as she tried to hold the wheel, helping him maintain lateral control. "We have no other choice," she said. "It's the only place we could crash land that's not in the water. There's no landing this safely. Instead, we might all have the opportunity, maybe, to dive deep into the ocean and find some of those black pearls this island is famous for." She crossed herself. "Jesus, please have mercy on all our souls."

Chopin gulped. "I advise you, my friend, with all my respect, go back to your seat. That is the most secure place in this craft right now, especially if we have to make a forced landing over the water."

I nodded and patted them each on the shoulder. "I have absolute and complete confidence in both of you guys. Besides, I know my guardian angel, Jesus Christ, is not going to let me die in this stupid way after He's saved me from so many other calamities. It would be a shame to die at the hands of that tiny, petty thief of a tropical dictator, Hugo Chavez."

They both forced small smiles at me. The turbulence grew stronger, the vibrations more acute, and it looked like the helicopter would fall apart in pieces at any moment. Both appeared not to have the strength to maintain the stability of the craft at the wheels. I walked as best I could back to my seat. I found to my surprise Yaneba smiling very calmly with a pleased look on her face. "Don't worry. They've kicked us out of worse places, and we always come back with greater strength to break their asses."

I couldn't contain myself and smiled. "For sure, you don't have ovaries. I believe you have testicles, and they're made of stainless steel. Make sure if we have to crash land in the ocean you have them completely covered so they don't rust."

She laughed loudly at that. Mayari had turned very pale by this point, almost white, and looked at us both laughing. He shook his head and said with a smirk, "I know now that both you guys are crazy, or you're made of the same wood."

He put his AK-47 into the net to one side and tied it down. He started rubbing both his arms, as if he were getting goosebumps. "Well, God forgive all us sinners and help us in this moment when we really need His help."

We all said simultaneously, "Amen."

The rain suddenly stopped completely. It was around 6:00 a.m., and the sunrise appeared, a beautiful multicolored sight over the ocean. A short distance away, we started to see through the breaks of the clouds and patches of fog down by the ocean beautiful green hills and the long, tall, tropical royal palms. As we moved forward, we could see the red glazed sunroofs of the village up ahead and a small construction of white color, like a hotel.

Figure 3 Isla de Margarita, Venezuela

Chopin yelled back from the cockpit, "Hallelujah! Hallelujah! Well, with God's favor, in a few more minutes, we'll be out from over the ocean."

I looked over at Yaneba and Mayari. "I don't know which is best—crash in the ocean, or crash on those hills in the jungle or the beautiful glazed roofs of those houses. At least the water is softer." I unfastened my seat belt, and as best I could with the turbulence still rocking us, made my way to the cockpit. I said to Chopin, "Try to find an appropriate place to land outside of the town—if you can make it. Put all the distance you can between us and that town. The more you can give us, the greater the distance there will be between us and the soldiers of this communist regime. Keep in mind as soon as we touch the ground, we must burn whatever is left of this helicopter. Take only what is necessary. Please establish contact with our travel agent and tell him we definitely need a secure house and transportation to get far away from the eyes of everybody."

Chopin didn't even open his mouth. He gestured to the hydraulic gauge and then to the gas gauge. Both were almost in red. He looked at me and rolled his eyes and shrugged. It was clear he was making no promises. I patted his shoulder. "You do the possible. We will leave the impossible to Jesus Christ."

Chopin turned around with a broad ear-to-ear grin. "Amen, brother."

I turned and went back to my seat. With a smile of satisfaction on my face, I told them, "Well, it looks like the probabilities of getting out of this alive are getting better and better. The level of possibility keeps raising up to probably a 65% in our favor."

Mayari frowned, not very convinced with that rating. Yaneba, full of optimism, gave two thumbs up and a grin. "I told you not to worry about it," she said. "You actually put worries in me, for a moment, when you told me that I had stainless steel testicles. If that statement is right, and we landed in the ocean, I wouldn't be able to float!" She crossed herself. "Thank God we're out of the water and those testicles can serve me like an anchor on dry land!"

I shook my head and laughed. Mayari kept frowning, as if none of this was funny to him. We could see through the portholes the land. First the beach, then the houses, then those glazed roofs of the coastal town we were flying over, and then the long, tall palm trees and vegetation, and finally, the hills.

Figure 4 Jungle in the mountains

Chopin screamed from the cockpit, "Prepare to crash! We're going down!"

I could feel my stomach churn at the rapid descent, and then moments later the violent impact as we crashed. We were tossed around like we were inside a blender as we rolled. Finally, there was another impact which sheered the tail of the craft completely off against a tree accompanied by the crash of fiberglass as broken shards and shrapnel-like pieces of metal flew over our heads. Then total silence, aside from the twang of cables as they parted.

In that stillness, some of the white smoke drifted upwards. Everything looked like it had all happened in slow motion, yet so fast that I thought I had lost consciousness for a few minutes. I realized that truth a little bit later as I heard screaming. I opened my eyes and touched my head, feeling a large bump there. The terrified screaming continued in Yaneba's voice. I could also hear Rocco barking and growling. I looked around and saw Rocco aggressively defending Yaneba, who had been dragged half out of the helicopter wreckage by a very large cougar, which held her fast by one of her legs. It was trying to pull her out through the hole in the fuselage left by the tail when it broke away.

Figure 5 Our crashed helicopter

I could see that everyone, without exception, was in varying states of confusion and surprise. They weren't moving, not realizing the gravity of the situation. If this mountain lion managed to get Yaneba outside, it would disappear with her body into the jungle, to be devoured later with the rest of the pride. Rocco, as dogs do, had rolled around to remain unaffected, and was the only one to realize the immediate danger. He was fully alert, and continually jumped at the lion, biting its paws. Guerrilla warfare-like, Rocco would jump back each time the cougar swiped at him with a paw, but then he would spring back in to bite some more. Occasionally, the lion would stop in a determined attempt to get Rocco with his long, sharp claws, trying to neutralize the only one confronting it.

Mayari finally found his AK-47 in all the debris, pulling out from beneath some shattered aluminum. He prepared to shoot at the cougar. As he started to aim, however, I brought my hand up. "Don't shoot!" I yelled. "You might hit her!"

I reached down toward my right leg and pulled up the hem of my pants. I unzipped the pouch to get the weapon I had fastened by leather straps, but I saw a pointed piece of metal sticking into my leg through the pants, just below my knee. I felt the blood, but the seriousness of the situation made me ignore that for the moment. I managed to raise my pants leg as high as the metal would allow me and pulled out a CO2 gun which shot a powerful anesthetic gas which combined Sulphur and rotten fish for a smell. I aimed for the best place I could find and shot out a capsule.

A green smoke, like Bengal lights, streaked forward in lines for a few seconds behind the capsule, which stuck like a barbed weapon in the shattered hull. The gas broke and began to spread. I yelled, "Cover your noses as best you can if you don't want to take a long nap!"

The lion immediately let go of Yaneba's leg and ran for its life out through the same place it had entered the wreckage. Not wasting the opportunity, Rocco ran behind it in full pursuit. Both left the helicopter. I pulled out a handkerchief from a side pocket and covered my nose and mouth. I yelled again, "Get out of here immediately, or we'll have to carry you out!"

I jumped up from where I had and went over to Yaneba. She grabbed my hand and pulled herself up. As we got out of the wreckage, I asked, "Are you OK?"

"Yes. Don't worry—he probably only scratched the skin. He had me by the khaki. I was only a little scared, if I must be honest with you. I thought it was very ironic, to have survived so many times and then this wrecked chopper, and only turn out to be a lion's breakfast. There was nothing cool in that, nothing at all."

"It would not be cool if it ate you. You would not digest well in his belly—in the best situation, you would give him indigestion. The worst-case scenario, you would give him diarrhea!" She slapped me on the shoulder indignantly. "If I must be honest with you, the only thing that crossed my mind is that if he managed to get you outside, we would never see you again. It would be in its natural environment, and we would never be able to catch it. Before we could find you, it would have taken you to the other members of its group, probably with knives and forks out on the table!"

She smiled. "Thank you for saving my life once again, and for remaining so calm and collected. But you are bleeding from your leg."

"It's nothing—just a piece of metal. I'll be fine." I looked around. "Is everyone else OK?"

Chopin replied, "Yes, everyone's fine. Some scratches and bruises. I've got a little bump on my forehead, but nothing serious. I already communicated with our travel agent by radio. I gave her our coordinates, and she will be in this location in about twenty minutes." He pointed to a precise spot on the map. "She will be waiting for us in a vehicle to transport us to a secure house, a nice place where we can put our plans in motion once again, far away from this place and the crash site."

"Thank you, well done," I said. "Take whatever is most necessary, and then burn everything else. We have no time to waste. With the noise we made with this chopper malfunctioning over that coastal town so early in the morning, we probably woke everyone back there up. The local authorities will be here very soon to investigate who we are and what we're doing here. From this minute on, we must improvise and reassess how we're going to complete what we're supposed to do and how we're going to do it, if we want to be able to accomplish to the optimum and take this operation successfully to the end."

Yaneba interrupted me. "I completely agree with everything you're saying. But first things first—and the first thing we must do is remove that metal fragment from your leg before it gets infected and we must amputate it. I don't think it would be too cool to see you with a wooden leg, and I don't think you will be able to function the same way."

"Very well," I replied, "but we have to move out of here *immediately*! We cannot allow the authorities to find us at the scene of the crime. Grab the first aid kit from the chopper, and at the first opportunity we have I will let you patch me up. But we first must put some distance between us and the chopper. Later I will let you play around with that piece of metal and make me suffer for a while."

"OK, whatever you say is fine with me. But at least let me put a temporary bandage so that you don't continue to bleed."

"Yes, and when you take that piece of metal out, I'll bleed more. It's blocking the blood flow."

"All right, *Doctor*, but let me wrap the bandage *around* the metal."

"Very well, but Chopin, Mayari, Elizabeth—please burn that chopper!"

While they worked, I let Yaneba put the bandage on my leg. We burned what was left of the wreckage down, consuming the tree unfortunately in the process. I crossed my fingers, hoping that we wouldn't start a forest wildfire with this. We then abandoned the area and tried to put as much distance between us and the wreck as quickly as possible. We walked for a while as far as we could, looking back at the long line of smoke emanating into the sky from the fire. As we walked away, Chopin maintained radio communication with our contact that was already waiting for us at the rendezvous point with civilian clothes to disguise us as tourists as best as possible. We were told that we would have to be prepared to spend some time to catch the local dialect so that if by any chance we were confronted we would not raise any suspicions.

I looked at Mayari. "Be sure to cover your weapon up. We need to make sure we look like campers and blend in."

"You got it, Chief," he said. He put his AK in a specially designed cover made of raincoat material that zipped up to one side. Once he had zipped it closed, it looked like he had some fishing gear with him.

We continued to walk and place as much distance between ourselves and the crash site. After nearly an hour, we were deep in the mountain forest. We arrived at a small town. Architecturally, it looked very much like it had been established during the 18th century Spanish Colonial period. There were very few people about—two men carrying bundles of wood on their shoulders and a small wagon pulled by mules with bales of hay in the back. We tried not to call attention to ourselves, but it was nearly impossible due to the emptiness of the town. As we continued walking, we saw two donkeys grazing in an empty lot, while a pack of dogs were trying to mate with a female in heat in the street.

Other than that, we saw no one. It seemed to me as if a plague had struck the town.

We needed to meet with our contact on the opposite side of town, so there was no other alternative but to continue crossing across the empty street, looking for the point of reference the contact had given Chopin.

Finally, Yaneba said in a low voice, "Somebody in this ghost town, an ancient lady, is coming towards us with a herd of sheep."

I touched Rocco's head. "Take it easy, boy." Rocco growled softly, but obediently calmed down and continued walking behind me.

Chopin smiled. "Man, you have this dog very well trained. Most dogs would go crazy with those animals."

The elderly lady continued on her way down the hill with her herd. She had a large stick of bamboo that she alternated between using as a cane and as a crook to keep her sheep together. When she drew close to us, she nodded her head in our direction without smiling. She was dressed all in white with a black turban covering her head. Slung across her shoulder was a long canvass bag with a pair of baguettes in it. I could swear I heard the electronic screech of a walkie talkie in that bag as well.

I raised an eyebrow. It occurred to me that it *could* simply be a means for her to communicate with her family—though it could also indicate that she was with the government somehow. Yaneba was closest to me. As I returned her nod, I murmured softly, "Did you hear that?"

"No. What?" Taking a cue from me, she kept her voice down as well.

"It sounded like a walkie talkie's frequency screech."

"No! That lady is almost dead—she can barely walk, and she has so many wrinkles on her face that there's no room for even one more. Calm down, calm down—everything will be OK."

"I know everything will be OK, but remember Cuba, and remember your family."

She looked me dead in the face. "You have to bring *that* up?"

"I'm sorry, but we have to be very alert."

Elizabeth was near enough to hear the conversation. "For God's sake—I agree with you, Yaneba. No space at all for one more wrinkle."

"*Claro, chica*—why do you think she doesn't even give us the gift of her smile?"

Mayari replied, "Maybe she doesn't want another wrinkle on her face. Did you guys know that the birth of wrinkles is both laughter and crying?" he continued, trying to sound very educated. "If we never laugh or cry, we never get any wrinkles."

I said, "That is a good one, Mayari. Now you are becoming a philosopher. But if you ask anyone who doesn't have a wrinkle that he must stop laughing or crying in order to never get one, he'll tell you to go screw yourself. Forget about the wrinkles."

We all of us were laughing, and Chopin interrupted. "My old friend, with all my respect, I want to know where the hell you got that Chinese tale. Did you hear it, or just create it?"

Mayari looked at Chopin seriously. "I'm going to tell you that you are extremely wrong, Chopin. It's not a Chinese tale—it's a fact. The reason I tell you that is because I read it in the *Reader's Digest* magazine. Let me inform you and bring you out of your ignorance. This magazine is one of the most prestigious magazines in the entire world for its accuracy in its reports. They don't print Chinese tales."

Chopin shook his head, unconvinced. "You all should be ashamed of making fun of that poor old lady. Remember, we all are going to get to that age eventually, if we're lucky. That is why we should respect and admire all our elders so that, when we reach that age ourselves, we'll receive the same respect from the generations coming along behind us on our heels."

He was about to say more, but then two loud, sharp reports rang through the air right behind us, perhaps half a block away, near where the lady had disappeared with her herd. They sounded like pistol shots. We all immediately reached for our concealed weapons under our clothes. There was a flash of light, and Mayari leaped behind a rock. As he did so, he unslung his "fishing kit" from his shoulder, unzipped it, and pulled his AK out.

I raised my hand high to calm everyone and shook my head. "Calm down—there's no reason to react like that for a few isolated shots in the distance. We're giving ourselves away that way for anyone who might be observing us in any of those shops. Unless we have a direct aggressor in front of us, we should never blow our cover. Let's keep walking, slowly, as if nothing has happened. Let's get to our point of contact and not allow anything else distract us. We have to maintain our equanimity and discipline."

I hadn't even finished when we heard the sound of a motor vehicle approaching us from behind at high speed. Everyone, even Rocco, turned around to look. There was an olive-green Range Rover, like the ones used by Chavez's Rebel Army; we could not see inside because all the windows were darkly tinted. The driver was flashing the headlights off and on, as if he was trying to signal to us. A dense cloud of dust trailed behind the vehicle, kicked up by the high speed as it traveled down the dirt road. It stopped near us, and the driver's side door opened.

A silhouette got out; it looked like a woman's, dressed in the military uniform of a *chavista*, the female members of Chavez's military. She looked at us and yelled, "Get in the car quickly! We have no time to waste—please get in, everyone! The rescue team you were expecting has been killed!" She looked at Chopin, who had his radio in his hand. She snatched it out before anyone could react and smashed it against the trunk of a tree. "Every conversation you have had on that device has been listened to by members of Chavez's intelligence forces. You all have to disappear, or you will be dead."

Everyone by now had their weapons out and pointed them at her. Mayari yelled, "How do you know about this?"

Before she could answer, I stepped forward. Even though she wore a broad-brimmed military cap and large sunglasses, her face looked familiar, and her voice had tints of Spanish with a slight Asian accent. It sounded familiar. I asked, "Who the hell are you, and who sent you?"

She smiled. "You don't recognize me, Julio Antonio?" She took the hat off and shook her long, black hair out. It was so black that beneath that sun it seemed to have blue highlights. Grinning broadly, she took the sunglasses off, and she said, "I am a Christian warrior, a freedom fighter to the death. Do you recognize now, Dr. Julio Antonio del Marmol—or, better yet, the Cuban Lightning?"

I returned her broad grin. It was a joy to recognize Chandee and see her with us once more. I could not contain myself further, and we ran to each other and embraced for a few seconds. She gently took my arm. "We only have minutes—*minutes*! We have to get out of her immediately, or you'll be killed like your extraction team."

I immediately understood her anxiety and urgency as well as the need to get out now. I turned to the others. "Get in the car. Questions and answers later!"

The others did as they were told. Chandee got behind the wheel. She floored the accelerator and headed for the forest. We bumped and jolted as we left the road. She continually checked a compass she was wearing on her left wrist while checking the time on a watch she wore on her right hand, coordinating between where she needed to go and some clear deadline.

"Looks like time is against us," she said, "if you take into consideration all the 'coincidences' against us in the last few hours." Everyone kept their silence, respecting my call for trust and allowing Chandee to do her job.

After several minutes of her navigating the forest by compass, I decided to break the silence. I was sitting in the front passenger's seat. Not even Rocco made a noise. "I heard, before you showed up, some pistol shots. Can I ask you a question—was that the government soldiers?"

Chandee shook her head. "No, those shots were from my pistol. Unfortunately, I had to shoot an old lady in the head. She had a herd of sheep. I had traced the signal to her. She had the radio to turn you guys in, not now, but several hours ago. She's been passing the signal to Chavez's intelligence. I checked her out, and found out that hundreds, if not thousands, of freedom fighters have been tortured and killed because that diabolic old woman was pretending to be an innocent shepherd. Until today, she was the one who controlled all the information for the Chavez intelligence for all of Margarita Island. She was like the madam of intelligence for the area. She was the one who communicated with the army this morning about the suspicious helicopter in this area."

Chopin's eyes went wide in disbelief. He sat between Yaneba and Elizabeth in the middle section of the three seating areas of the Range Rover, with Mayari and Rocco taking up the furthest back seat to themselves. He put his hand on the side of my seat. "Forgive me, Miss, but you want to tell us that the old woman with the sheep, who could barely walk, is working for Chavez's government and in charge of the intelligence network of this entire island?"

Chandee glanced back at him and nodded. "Was, yes. That damned old devil woman has held this entire island in panic, serving the communists for a handful of bolivars. All these communists are the same—they cut their own umbilical cord with the same pair of scissors."

Chopin stroked his chin. He shook his head and muttered to himself, "I'm thinking about how bad I felt when I saw her. I was reminded of my own grandmother, and nearly offered her the last bar of my chocolate to her, I felt so bad for her. Just shows that today we can't believe in anyone. These communists, socialists, progressives, whatever the hell they want to call themselves tomorrow, are all a bunch of hypocrites. All they do is speak about corruption, but they themselves are the motherlode of corruption that you could ever find in any part of the world. Not only do they corrupt the young generation, but now we see they also corrupt the elder generation. They indoctrinate through greed. Nobody is safe."

Chandee continued driving in silence, concentrating on coordinating her compass and watch. She was growing concerned as we started to run out of time. It looked like we might not reach our destination when we needed to. I put my hand on her shoulder. "I don't want to interrupt your concentration—I know you're trying to do the impossible to get us out of this situation. But I only want to know one thing from you: do you know where you're taking us, or are you improvising the same we had to start improvise the moment our helicopter got hit by that missile?"

She replied with a sarcastic smile and a quick glance, "Both."

"What?"

"I know exactly where I'm going and where I wanted to take you guys to keep you safe for the moment. But, yes, I am improvising, because this was not in my plans for today. Even so, I am at your disposal for whatever you need until you complete your task. According to my information, whatever you have on hand right now will have international repercussions. For me, it's always a pleasure and a source of pride to have the great opportunity to work with you again, like we did in the old days. Remember, in Cuba, the Havana cigar that Che gave you, and you inserted that diarrheic medicine? And how you arranged to give him back his present, but in a bigger package? You had him sitting in the bathroom probably for a whole week and his butt like a red *marañon*[2]." She gave me another quick glance, this time with a mischievous smile. She shook her head. "You are really something else—I have to grant you that. As your Mima would say: Julio Antonio del Marmol!"

We both laughed. Yaneba was sitting directly behind her, but out of sight from the rearview mirror. She put her

---

[2] Cashew apple

index fingers in her mouth and made an exaggerated, fake smile in mockery. Elizabeth put her right hand over her mouth to contain her laughter at that. Chopin and Mayari both noticed Yaneba's joke and burst out laughing. Chandee glanced up in the rearview curiously.

I pointed forward. "Keep your eyes on the road or we'll lose our lives in this crazy forest."

Chandee could only see Elizabeth trying very hard not to laugh. We came out into a small valley in the hills which held a tiny town of perhaps twenty rustic Spanish style houses. There might perhaps have been a total of forty or fifty people living in this small village. All the people looked like they had more indigenous blood with only a tinge of European influence. We could see the parochial church in the middle of the place. She pointed to the right of that church.

"The best friend you will have here is Padre Rodrigo. You can count on him unconditionally for anything, except killing someone. Let's make that clear. He told me when he embraced us that he would do whatever we needed, but he would not ever take a human life. He hates communists to the core, and he has gambled his life so many times to protect us and get us out of trouble."

I nodded. "It is very good to know that we have such a person in this town. That is difficult to find anywhere. You had a taste of that with the old lady you killed today. They'll sell their souls to the Devil for a handful of dollars—or, as you told us, a handful of bolivars."

Figure 6 Island retreat of Chavez

We drove through the town in a brief amount of time before leaving it, then drove for another three kilometers or so beyond. We crossed a small wooden bridge over a small stream. We arrived outside a gate in a large cement wall with a small code box on a cement pole outside it. Chandee pulled up next to it, rolled down the window, and entered a code on the box, and the gate opened. After we drove through, the gate closed automatically behind us.

It was a massive, heavy gate of double-wrought iron, and must have cost a great deal of money. I noticed that a crest was inscribed in the iron rails: HC. It looked almost like a military compound, with razor wire lining the top of the wall.

We arrived at a rustic cabin built from trunks of royal palm trees. It was clear that it had been built with pride. This cabin was in the middle of nowhere, surrounded by huge fruit trees: mangos, oranges, and lemons. Chandee stopped the Range Rover about fifty feet from the cabin. We got out of the vehicle and began to unload our stuff.

Chandee looked at the briefcase. "Let me guess—that's the motherlode you brought to bribe your contact."

"Yes," I said. "You're right."

The roof of the cabin had been made with the same red glazed tiles that seemed to be popular in this area. As we walked from the Range Rover and stepped up onto the porch that wrapped around the entire cabin, we could see a couple of men to the side feeding goats and pigs in some corrals.

Chandee said, "Well, I hope we can all stay here and be comfortable for the time you have to finish your work. Let me open the door for you." She reached beneath a large pot next to the side of the house and pulled out a key. I could see to the right side of the cottage a large multicolored hammock, while there were two hammocks on the left: one large and one smaller. On the far side of the porch there were a pair of rattan porch swings. The whole porch had wooden rails with small wooden gates at the top of the flight of six stairs, elevating the house in case of flooding.

When Chandee finally opened the door, we found we had a surprise waiting for us. The inside of the cabin looked like a giant suite from the Ritz Carlton hotel, with a large screen TV, radio, the whole works. I asked her, "Where do you get the electricity?"

Figure 7 Retreat interior from two angles

She pointed towards a large gas generator. Near it, at one corner of the house, we could also see some solar panels. We walked inside and found ourselves continually surprised by the luxury of the place. There were even a Jacuzzi, a sauna, and a hot tub. I said, "Please, tell us who lives here. Is this the home of the dictator Chavez?"

Chandee smiled. "You're right on the money. How did you guess?"

I replied, "I know these communists very well—I've been around them for a long time. They criticize the wealthy, but they love to have the wealth for themselves. How did you manage to get so close to this man? This is not an easy target."

She grinned mischievously. "I met him a few years back at a party in the Brazilian embassy. He was completely fascinated by my intelligence." To underline her sarcasm, she gestured over her body. It was clear that he hadn't been thinking of her mind. "You know these men—all they care about is whatever sexual favors they might be able to win. After we had a few one-on-one political discussions, which I of course I let him win while letting him know I wasn't fond of socialism, I became a challenge to him to convert. One thing led to another, and once we got to know each other a little more, he invited me to his house here on the island. After he brought me here a few times in order to bribe and impress me without me getting what he wanted, he went a step further by offering me a job inside his precious team of advisors. He gave me the key to this place and told me I could use it anytime I wanted and bring any friends along as well."

"Wow! *Chinita*[3], you hit the jackpot! You penetrated the disciple of the old Devil himself. Be careful, because you can end up smelling like sulphur, not expensive perfume. He'll take even that away from you."

"Don't worry—I've been dealing with the Devil himself. I've let him close, but not so close that his pestilent breath could even touch my skin."

"I always say that God works in mysterious ways. They shot us down, and we end up in the house of the 'President' of the country that we're trying to save." I shook my head in disbelief as I looked around. "All you have to do is look at the way these people live while at the same time the poor people can't even put a piece of bread on the table at night after a long day at work. They work for miserable salaries while at the same time these unscrupulous politicians enjoy the air conditioning and the best luxuries that money can buy. If these people only knew that it would be this way,

---

[3] Chinese woman

that their money would end up in the pockets of these politicians, while their life savings that they have guarded meticulously all their lives would be spent on luxury houses like this, they would probably want to kill themselves for believing in the false promises they fell for made by these Marxist communists."

Chandee nodded in agreement. "Yes, indeed. You know what the funniest thing is? What a woman can get out of a man in a very short amount of time, when these men are looking to impress her, even to try to conquer her sexually or to convert her to their own ideology. Or perhaps just to show her off like a trophy in his collection to demonstrate to his friends and associates his superiority. As a woman, I say that all communists are identical: ignorant fanatics."

"Yes, but remember, there are many of them that are just lazy opportunists, resentful because of their frustration with the capitalist system. Because of their laziness they cannot accomplish what they're looking for in life. They embrace socialism in order to live without working, living a good life off the sweat of the others."

Chandee looked down at my right leg and the improvised bandage there. It was soaked with blood. "I think you should sit down for a minute or two, please, and let me examine that wound of yours. You look like you've been losing a lot of blood and might collapse at any minute."

"Don't worry about it. It's only a piece of iron fragment that flew into my leg below my knee when we had that forced landing. The reason it's still there is because I don't want to pull it out until we find either a doctor that can look at it or at least I have the proper utensils, needles, and surgical thread. You know there are a lot of veins and arteries in the legs. If we remove this piece of metal without having that on hand, the remedy could be worse than the disease. My experience is that you can kill people even with the best intentions if you don't have the proper medical gear handy."

Chandee nodded as she listened to my explanation. "Are you telling me that you've been walking with that piece of metal all the way from the crash site to where you were to meet me? I knew you were crazy before, but I didn't know you were *that* crazy! You should have been carried by someone. And you're telling me this in that cold-blooded manner, like it's not a big deal?"

I smiled. "*Chinita, chinita*—in what other way did you want me to tell you? With chocolate or strawberry? I don't have either one here. The only way I can tell you these kinds of things is the way I know best, which is using my logic and my knowledge. With those facts in hand, without complaining or moaning about something I cannot do anything about, my only choice is to wait until I can resolve it the best way I can."

Yaneba came up to us with a few things from the car, including the first aid case. She stopped for a minute, placing the case on the sofa where I had been sitting, close by my feet. "Chandee, maybe you'll have more luck than I've been having. Can you convince him that if he doesn't do something about that piece of metal as soon as possible, he might not die from a hemorrhage—he might die of gangrene."

I smiled. "Thank you, Doctor, for your compassion."

Yaneba shook her head. "As you said before, Chandee, like Mima always would say: Julio Antonio del Marmol, you have the hardest head I have ever seen in my life."

Chandee shifted uncomfortably. "OK, guys—don't involve me in your discussion. I have no say-so in that. I can say this, without contradicting you, Dr. del Marmol, and the only thing I agree with you, Yaneba, is that last part about the hard head. The rest I cannot comment on, because I'm not a doctor and lack the knowledge he has to start a medical discussion."

I shook my head. "Ignorance dares." I lay back on the sofa. "As long as that ignorance isn't applied to me, I don't care. I'll let you live with that." We were the sitting room in the front of the house. The sofa I was on was very comfortable, upholstered in black and gold leather, covered with several pillows in tiger skin. I said, "This is the only thing I need now, after this turbulent day, to end it in such a precious way, that you both are conspiring against me." I raised both my hands. "Chandee—let's leave behind the blah-blah-blah, like communists, and look at things the way they are. Unwrap the bandage Yaneba improvised around my leg and bring me a hand mirror so that I can see more accurately my wound and diagnose what would be the best way to follow up."

Elizabeth had been listening and came over to sit down and be a part of the conversation. "Maybe we can find a doctor, or even a nurse in the town." She turned to Chandee. "Do you know anyone trustworthy that we can bring here to look at that wound?"

Chandee replied, "Yes, I know some people. But trustworthy? Hm. I don't know about that. There's a small polyclinic in town, but I don't know how many of those people are dependable. They all work with the government. But if you like, later, I can consult with Padre Rodrigo."

I nodded. "A good plan. Chandee, unwrap the bandage."

Chandee proceeded to slowly, carefully remove the bandage. Immediately, when she got to the last bandage, she shook her head before I could say anything. She clucked her tongue. "I don't think we can handle this ourselves. You're right—this wound is extremely deep, and I believe you will need several stitches. We should be prudent. It might be safer getting a doctor here."

I said, "Give me the mirror. It all depends on how large this object is. Whether it's iron or fiberglass, we definitely need needles and surgical thread." I looked at the mirror and used it to look as I pulled on the piece slightly. Immediately, blood started to well out of the wound. "It could be nothing, but there is a possibility that it's punctured a vein or artery."

All three women smiled at my expression. Yaneba nodded. "Yes, yes—once more, you're right. I might have killed you if I took that out, eh? Don't worry, I won't let you die, even if I must put my finger in the vein to keep it from spurting. I couldn't live with that on my conscience. What are you going to do? You can't leave that in your body much longer."

I said, "Why don't we resolve this the most simple and calm way?" All three women looked at me.

Chandee replied, "What is your recommendation, Dr. del Marmol?"

"Very simple," I said. "I'm going to make you a small list. You go with Padre Rodrigo, so that it looks like you're buying things for him or charity and buy all the things I ask you to bring. That way I'll have the necessary medication and tools I need to disinfect the wound. I'll stitch myself, with your help, of course, and we'll resolve the problem without putting ourselves in the hands of a stranger. Don't you think that is the best and most educated way to resolve this problem?"

Elizabeth shook her head unhappily and grimaced. "Are you telling me you will stick that needle into your skin yourself and sew yourself up like a pair of pants?"

"Why not?" I asked with a smile. "Don't worry—this won't be the first time, and let's hope it won't be the last. The last time I won't be around for. Besides, I'm not doing this by myself. Luckily, I have three assistants right here in my hands. Believe me, that will be a tremendous help."

Elizabeth muttered, "Oh, God."

Chandee got up. "OK. There's nothing more to discuss. This is an excellent idea. Write out that list for me, and I'll leave at once to contact Padre Rodrigo. It won't take me too long." She looked at Elizabeth and Yaneba. "Will you please put some water on to boil in the kitchen and take some small washcloths from the master bedroom closet, and prepare the patient?"

I smiled at that and gave her the list I had written out while she was speaking. She left and we heard the Range Rover pull out in a hurry. I saw it flash by the large window of the sitting room as it disappeared.

CHAPTER 2: THE MAIN CONNECTOR

My Cuba brought misery and suffering to the beautiful Venezuela

Please forgive my Cuba's enslavement, my brother Venezuelans

It matters not now many efforts we made to make you realize

To prevent in vain the bullying tyrant to catch you by surprise

But unfortunately, you never heard our anguished screaming

Exactly like our Cuban brothers before

Then as a thief in the middle of the night the odious tyrant bully

As he stole my Cuba also steals from you your beautiful Venezuela

Dr. Julio Antonio del Marmol

I could not thank God more to be sitting on that luxurious sofa. If I was going to die, for whatever reason, I would be going out with a bang and in the high life. Mayari and Chopin had finished taking the luggage from the car and up to different rooms and came in to join us. Each one had a sweaty beer in his hand. I smiled. "Hey, guys—are you enjoying the mini vacation?"

They smiled and sat down in overstuffed leather armchairs. Chopin asked, "Do you want a beer for yourself?"

I smiled. "Not now on an empty stomach. Maybe a little later, after I finish the ordeal of cleaning this stupid wound. It might wind up being nothing more than a superficial injury—that is my hope. I'm going to be optimistic, since I'm the patient. But if I must be honest, I'm just a little, *little* worried, because things could be more complicated. The only thing that really concerns me is that it's disrupting our plans."

Yaneba nodded understandingly. She had known me for so many years and knew that my "little" was an indication of my level of true worry. "I have faith that you'll resolve this as soon as Chandee gets back. I don't think one beer will be bad for you. It will help you relax with what you're about to do to yourself. I'll drink one." She looked at Elizabeth. "Do you want one?"

"OK," she said. "Why not? We have two huge refrigerators in the back filled with all kinds of food, beer, and wine. Evidently Mr. Chavez does a lot of entertaining here. He must love beer a lot, since he has over fifty boxes of the most expensive German beer I've ever seen."

I smiled. "Have you guys been doing an inventory? You planning to stay here for an extended vacation and making a survey of the provisions?"

Elizabeth said, "Of course, *chico*, we might be here at least a week, in a mini forced vacation."

Yaneba smiled. "Yes—forced all the dimensions of the word!" She walked into the swinging doors to the kitchen which connected with the sitting room.

A little while later, she came back with a large platter of ham, cheese, slices of roast beef, and crackers, and three beers. She smiled splendidly. "Now you have no excuses. Your stomach will no longer be empty, so I've brought you your beer."

I shook my head. "Well—since you insist so much, I'll sacrifice myself. I don't want to spoil your party, guys, while at the same time letting you have all the fun. Let me partake so that we are all in perfect harmony. We all will have joy that way, like a great family, and not leave anyone out in agony like the communists do."

Elizabeth asked in concern, "What do you think? Is Chandee going to have any problems by having us here? I'm concerned if someone blows the whistle to Chavez. The last thing I want, after she's saved us, is to abuse our welcome."

I shook my head. "Elizabeth, it's a great pleasure to listen to your worry and concern. That tells me the level of your class and manners and the good person you are. I assure you that Chandee, who I've known all my life, will have no problems. If she thought there would be any problem, she would never have brought us here. Believe me, she knows what she's doing and how to manage any situation, just like you guys. No matter what, though, whatever we eat or drink, we must replace before we leave. We also must leave everything as we find it. In no way do I want to compromise her security." I pointed to the case that I had handcuffed to one of the legs of a wine rack next to the wall. "Remember, Elizabeth—that money is not just to negotiate with the terrorist. It's also part of the operation to cover any necessities or unexpected expenses we need it for, at my discretion."

Elizabeth nodded. "OK, I get it. Thank you for taking that worry out of my mind."

I said to them, "You guys eat and drink, enjoy however you want to, until we resolve the situation we have at hand. We'll take care of it, one way or another."

They started to pick at the platter and drink their exquisite beers. In the end, though, I never told Yaneba I was glad I had that beer. It relieved the tension and stress I had felt that day. She smiled, seeing my state of relaxation. She stood up.

"I'm going for seconds. Anyone want any?"

Everyone nodded or chorused their desire for more. Elizabeth stood up and helped Yaneba pick up the empty bottles. They left the sitting room to get the second round of beers and food. A little while later they returned and spread the food and drink around to everyone gathered there. We could hear the motor of the Range Rover approaching and crossing over the wooden bridge over a small creek which bisected the driveway to the cabin. It cascaded out of the hills and surrounded the property.

When the Range Rover pulled up outside the large cabin, we could see through the window that Chandee parked the car a little closer to the building this time and brought two strange companions with her. They were middle-aged and looked as if they had come out of a horror movie. The woman had a pronounced hunchback and looked very muscular. Half of her face was covered by a large birthmark, covering half of her nose and continuing past her ear until it was lost in her hair near the back. She was helping Chandee to unload some grocery bags from the back of the Range Rover. The man was not as corpulent as the woman and seemed to have one leg shorter than the other, was completely bald, and almost all his face was covered with large moles. He gave the impression of having leprosy.

She evidently was used to them and spoke with them in a very respectful manner. They conducted themselves very humbly, even bowing and curtseying to her occasionally. We saw the man nod occasionally with a huge smile, revealing tobacco-blacked teeth. He grabbed a bound, live pig of about 70 or 80 pounds and threw it over his shoulder, revealing that he also was quite strong. Evidently the wood was soundproofed and the glass of the window quite thick, as no sound penetrated. They disappeared into what appeared to be a service door to the kitchen, a double door in the back for the unloading of supplies. The man returned a few minutes later to where Chandee waited, his strange limp reminding us of Quasimodo. He pulled out a string of good-sized chickens, perhaps ten or fifteen, tied by their legs, and threw them over his shoulder.

After they finished, Chandee took the plastic from the back of the vehicle, shook it over the ground, and rolled it up. She handed it to the woman who stood patiently behind her and gestured away. The woman put the roll on her shoulder and disappeared through the same service door. When it looked like they had finished, Chandee went to the front passenger door, opened it, and picked up a bag. She closed it and walked into the cabin through the front. She was smiling as she came into where we were still eating and drinking our beers.

She noticed our beverages and joked, "Is this a private party, or can I join in?"

We laughed, and I replied, "You are the hostess, and you didn't even know!"

She said, "I know. Everything here is for you—we're all brother and sisters as freedom fighters."

I said, "Shhh—the walls have ears." She smiled again. "I see that you not only brought food, but some more help. Very interesting characters—maybe we can cast them in the films we might do in the future."

"Shh—they're very nice people."

I laughed. "I never said they weren't nice people—shhh."

"They are Camile and Trabuto. They are the caretakers in charge of maintaining this property. They're employees of the 'President,' Mr. Hugo Chavez." She lowered her voice. "Even though I've managed to get their trust, we have to be very careful about what we say from now on. Later, I will introduce them to you guys. For now, though, I don't want to interrupt them. Camile will prepare an excellent lunch, and Trabuto will help her with killing the livestock. They are extremely loyal people, but for a long time they didn't trust me that much. With the great care, love, and respect that I gave them, I have earned their trust. Now I've not only earned their trust, but also their love; Mr. Chavez doesn't exactly pay them very well for their work and doesn't treat them properly, either. He makes absurd jokes in front of his friends about their handicaps and appearance. That has slowly taken a toll on how they feel about him. But this is completely confidential, guys."

Elizabeth clucked her tongue as she shook her head. "Bad boy—bad boy, Mr. President."

We laughed with her joke. Chandee held up the bag she held and put it on the coffee table in front of the sofa. She said to me, "Here—I brought you everything you asked for plus another thing you left out: a local anesthetic. That way you won't suffer when you sew yourself up. But perhaps you don't need it, since I see your friends have been sedating you already. And since it only takes a couple of beers to get you drunk, you're probably already half sedated. How many beers have you had?"

"You know me very well." I held up my nearly full bottle. "This is my second, and I don't think I will finish it. You know I'm not a big lover of alcohol. Besides, local anesthetics don't last long for me, and I have a very high tolerance for pain. That is why I didn't include it on the list. Alcohol should do fine for that purpose. When I drink socially, I never cross the line."

Chandee smiled. "Yes, only when you pour too much Grand Marnier on your dessert, then you don't care."

I nodded. "I know, I know."

She shook her head. "I'm just joking with you."

Mayari came back from the kitchen with two more beers in one hand and two glasses. He handed one beer to Chandee. "Do you want a glass?"

She smiled. "Of course—that is the best way to enjoy that beer. Thank you. Well, I can see that, even though you're new to the team, you have been spending some time with the Lightning already. That is one of his customs." She pointed at me with my glass next to my bottle of beer.

I smiled and nodded. I raised my glass in a toast. "Like some people like the bottle, I prefer mine in a glass, especially if the glass has been in a freezer for a couple of hours."

Chandee smiled again and gave me two thumbs up. "I think I know you a little bit and your tastes, some of which never change at all."

Yaneba didn't like that too much and stood up abruptly. She picked up her beer and went towards the kitchen. "Well, happy hour is coming to an end. Let me bring the stuff from the kitchen." She also snatched up the bag without asking. "I'm going to sterilize the instruments. It won't take me five or ten minutes." She asked Chandee sarcastically, "Well that give you enough time to enjoy your *glass* of beer, Chandee?"

Chandee understood Yaneba's sarcasm and smiled in a relaxed manner. She nodded and took a sip of beer. "Ahhh, yes, yes. Sufficient, sufficient—more than enough. You should drink your next beer in a glass, Yaneba. Then you'll see that Julio Antonio is right, and it gives you more flavor and happiness. The bottle makes you angry and upset, because you cannot get enough." She looked me directly in the eyes with a seductive, mischievous expression.

Yaneba stormed off through the swinging doors without bothering to reply. Elizabeth rushed to apologize. "Don't take Yaneba wrong—she is an extraordinary girl. She's a little temperamental. Of course, also take into consideration the stress we all just passed through recently. Forgive her for her unfriendly attitude." She felt embarrassed by Yaneba and indebted to Chandee and so was trying to be a mediator.

Chandee waited for Elizabeth to finish her apology. She slowly raised her right hand. "Thank you, Elizabeth, for your beautiful manners. I understand perfectly what you're trying to say, and I appreciate your good intentions. But if I must tell you the truth, personally, I believe there's something more than the stress you guys went through today that could be provoking her to react that way. She was so very sarcastic only with me—that attitude has another name, and it's not precisely 'stress.' But let's forget those petty female things, and be adults and concentrate on our plans to move forward and be able to complete our work successfully. Let's do this efficiently and without creating any problems for anyone." She turned to me. "What is your next plan? By now I know you a little bit, after all the years we spent together in Cuba and elsewhere. After you drink nearly two beers, have you already a plan to follow? What's the next move?"

I smiled. "Yes, I have a plan. This is a good time to give you a little trailer for it." I pointed to her. "You will go to Caracas with Chopin and bring a contact, Abdul

Hussein—from now on, let's call him 'the package.' In a very short time, I'll give you all the details—place and time and code—so that you can identify him as coming from me. You will bring him back here, and I will handle him as well as the other details. After we finish with him and our business, you will bring him back to Caracas to the same place you contacted him."

Chandee replied, "Very well. Very simple and very efficient."

I turned to Chopin. "You will take with you the same exact coordinates to the hair from this place and do your job. You will contact our people in Caracas and provide to them the extraction point from there. You will give them this in code, so if anyone intercepts it, they will never know what those coordinates are and find us. Make it very brief; all we need is our center of operations to know where we are. This will be our point of extraction. If we are safe here, we have no reason at all to take any unnecessary risks to move ourselves to another location. Tomorrow morning early, you will leave. Let's hope that you guys have no unexpected problems on your trip." I looked at Chandee. "I'm pretty sure, if you drive a Range Rover registered to the President, you'll have no problems."

Mayari raised his hand. "What about me? Forgive me, but don't you think I should go with them to provide extra security?"

I shook my head. "I thought of that initially. But too many people in the Range Rover will call more attention than we need, especially when you come back with Abdul. If you go with them, it would be three men and one woman. It would be better if it looked like a personal bodyguard for Chandee, and it still wouldn't look too strange on the return trip."

Chandee and Elizabeth nodded in agreement. "Less baggage, more clarity," Chandee said.

Yaneba came back in through the swinging door with a metal tray still steaming from the boiling water. She said to Elizabeth, "Could you please put two of the large towels on the coffee table? I don't want this metal tray to damage the wooden border. It's probably very expensive."

Elizabeth rushed to go get the towels. She returned and Yaneba put the tray down. There were scalpels, scissors, clamps, and pliers on it. Yaneba said, "Well, let's start this party. Everything is ready." I looked at her a little angrily. She felt bad and put her hand on my right shoulder. "Cheer up—you'll see it's nothing. Just think of it as taking one rotten tooth that's been bugging you painfully."

"That's what worries most—I don't have any pain. Just occasional discomfort. The pain will probably come the moment I start to extract the metal from my leg and begin to seal the wound."

Yaneba tried to comfort me once more. "Don't worry. You'll see, it's nothing. It's probably a small piece of metal, and it will be very simple."

"Thank you, honey, but a small piece of metal doesn't make that kind of hole. It's wide and deep. Let's get ready to get rid of this as soon as possible."

They removed my boot and took off my sock. Yaneba put a small pillow on the table next to the instrument tray. I raised my leg and put it on top of the pillow, looking for the most comfortable position. I washed my hands with soap and water in a bucket that had been placed next to me in a wooden breakfast tray. I dried my hands and put on the surgical gloves Chandee had provided. She opened a towel and put it by my right side on the sofa. She opened a sterilized packet with the needle and surgical thread and put that within easy reach of me. I pointed at what I needed. She pulled the instruments out of the hot water and put them on the towel next to me. I picked up a syringe and injected the local anesthetic around the wound.

"Elizabeth, put on a pair of surgical gloves, in case I need you to help me."

Once everything was ready, and Elizabeth knelt to one side next to me. I picked up the forceps and set them next to me, since I knew I would need them to block a vein. I used them to make the sign of the Cross and then clamped them onto the metal fragment. "Well—here goes." I slowly, carefully, began to pull—and the metal fragment kept coming. It was perhaps six or eight inches long by the time I fully extracted the thing. I was the only one unsurprised by the length. A stream of blood gushed out, spraying Elizabeth's face and chest.

It took her so much by surprise that she couldn't help but screaming, "Oh, my God!" She started to clean her face and blouse, embarrassed.

"You have nothing to be ashamed of," I said. As quickly as I could, I unlocked the forceps, dropped the metal in the pan of water, and dug furiously into my wound, searching blindly for the blood vessel to clamp it off. The anesthetic was either of very poor quality or my adrenaline rush had completely negated it; and anyway, this wound was far, far deeper than any local could hope to numb. Even with my high tolerance for it, the pain was excruciating.

Poor Elizabeth tried to clean the hand mirror so that I could see better. I ignored the mirror and thrust in again. Still nothing. I blindly thrust them in a third time, found the vessel, and clamped it off. The flow of blood ceased.

Elizabeth helped me clean the leg of all the blood. I realized it was going to be very difficult to suture the vein without seeing it, so I picked up the scalpel and made an incision approximately one inch in order to open a space sufficient for me to see what I was doing in order to fully suture the ruptured blood vessel closed as well as to thoroughly clean the area before closing. The original wound was around two inches, so I now had a three-inch gap in my leg. My friends watched me as if they were watching a horror movie, flinching with each stitch I sewed.

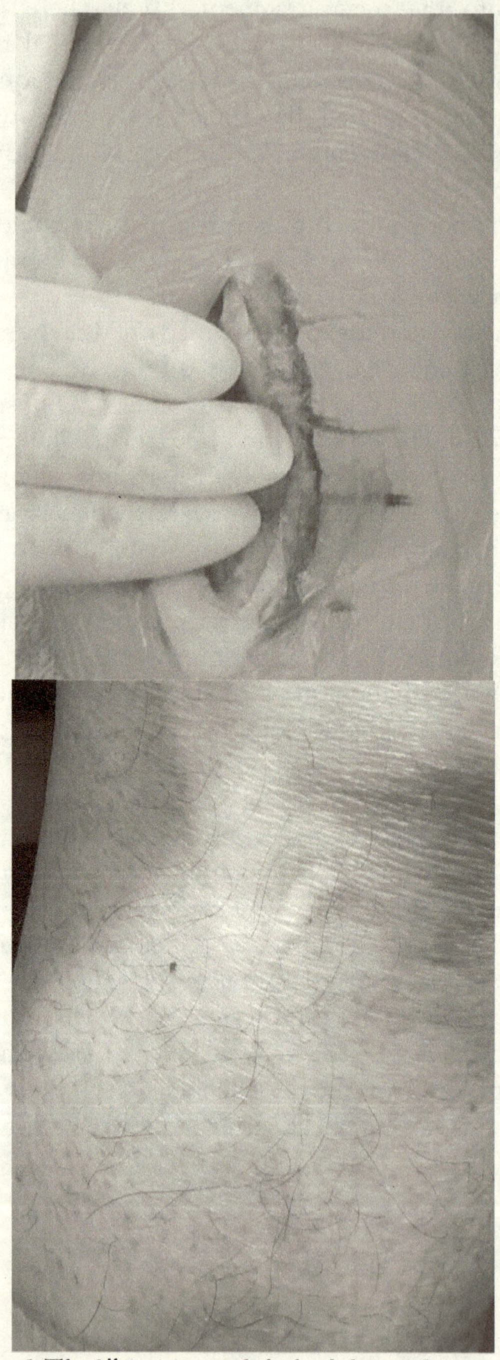

Figure 8 The 3" incision and the healed wound

After almost two and a half hours, I finally closed with six internal stitches and ten external ones. I disinfected the surgery site, applied an antibiotic cream, and wrapped my leg in a double gauze bandage with a hole for drainage. I then injected 500 mg of the intramuscular antibiotic that Chandee had brought and washed my leg with peroxide. When I was finished, I was utterly exhausted, between the loss of blood and the strain.

Elizabeth and Yaneba took all the towels to the sink in the restroom closest to the sitting room. They made sure everything was disinfected and immaculately clean. I pulled my pants leg down, and noticed that, except for the hole in the leg, you could not tell I had been wounded. I said to Elizabeth when she returned, "Save all these instruments and put them in the first aid case, just in case we need them again. At least until we leave Venezuela, anything can happen, and those instruments could save someone's life."

"Absolutely. I'll divide them up, so that they don't attract attention at any check. Some I'll put in my luggage wrapped in a towel, and the rest in the first aid bag."

"Good idea." She got up out of her seat.

The front doorbell rang at that moment. Chandee stood up to answer it. Padre Rodrigo was there, invited to have lunch with us while they were out. She introduced him to the group. He was a very short man, plump, about 50 years of age with receding hair. His expression was very pleasant.

Chandee said, "I'll go check on the lunch. You'll need a very good lunch, so that you can regain all the blood you lost this afternoon."

Mayari smiled at the mention of food. "I've been smelling such great odors from that kitchen, every time that door opens. It's way past my lunchtime, and it makes me very happy to hear that!"

Padre Rodrigo said, "I don't know what it is, but it smells delicious."

As she walked towards the door, Chandee said, "Camile is a great cook, a chef. You guys better loosen your belts a couple of notches, because you're going to have an unforgettable lunch today." She disappeared into the kitchen.

I tried to adjust my pants leg better. Curiously, I stuck my finger in the hole of my pants on one side to see how large it was—it fit perfectly. The other one wasn't as large. "It's strange—it's like a bullet hole."

Yaneba smiled. "If you want to, I have needles and thread in my luggage. After lunch, I can sew it for you."

"Absolutely, thank you. The last thing I want is some soldier looking at my pants and thinking I've been shot."

Yaneba smiled and nodded. "That really *does* look like a bullet hole. If they ask you to raise the leg and see that bandage, it could be difficult to explain without taking your pants off to see the actual wound."

Chandee reappeared at the kitchen door and signaled that things were close. "OK, the food is ready. Everything is served on the table. All we need are your mouths to liberate it."

We moved to the fancy dining room, which was splendid, practically a buffet that had been prepared by Camile and Trabuto. Chandee introduced us to the couple. "These are my best friends," she told them. "Even if I'm not here, please show them all the courtesy you can. When I get back, I will remunerate you properly."

Camile said, "There's no need, *mi niña*[4], don't worry about it. We do this with pleasure for you. Anyone who is your friend is our friend."

We sat down at that beautiful, luxurious dining room. I believe it resembled the Louis XVI style of dining table. It was vast, engraved wood, made of mahogany with the engravings of precious stones, forming a family crest at each place around it. The backs of the chairs were decorated not only the Chavez family crest but also the initials "H.C." The napkins and doilies were of a fine mesh material, making them nearly transparent. There was so much food on the table: several jars of orange juice, other

---

[4] My little girl

tropical fruit juices, a huge glazed *arroz con pollo*[5], a large platter of Australian lobsters, another platter with a pineapple and avocado salad, a platter with fried green banana and ripe banana plantains, yucca with garlic butter and fresh asparagus along the border, huge pork ribs with chunks of deep-fried pork and crackling, and stuffed potatoes with meat at the center. We opened our eyes in awe, and I said to Camile, "What a fabulous banquet you have prepared for us!"

Figure 9 The elaborate welcome dinner

We praised the couple highly and bestowed many compliments on them for such a sumptuous feast in such a short time, only perhaps three hours from killing the livestock to this point. I gave Chandee two thumbs up and said, "You went over the top!" The others agreed, and we

[5] Rice with chicken

sat down to eat and drink that fantastic banquet. Camile and Trabuto moved in and out, continually bringing us more beer. Camile came near to Chandee and whispered something in her ear. Chandee's expression changed from smiling to one of worried sadness. Chandee deposited her napkin next to her still full plate. With a slightly angered expression, she stood up and went over to Camile and murmured in her ear. The old woman nodded and politely went towards the front door, rather than the kitchen.

"Is everything OK?" I asked Chandee.

She took a deep breath. She fiddled with her napkin, stalling. "Yes, everything is OK," she said a little unhappily. "I'll be right back. It's nothing of importance." She left through the same door Camile had just gone through.

Enough time passed that we were almost done eating and ready for dessert when Chandee finally reappeared. This time, she came in through the kitchen door, now with a satisfied expression on her face. She shook her head. "There's always a hair in the soup, if not from your head, then an eyelash from the cook, but there's always one there." She sat down before her plate.

Before she could start to eat, Camile came and took it. "Let me warm it up, *mi niña.* It's not good to eat it cold." Chandee nodded and smiled. A little bit later, Camile returned with her plate covered with a steel cover like in a restaurant. Chandee bowed and thanked her for the service. Camile patted her on the shoulder. "It's a pleasure, *mi niña.*"

As Chandee finished her food, the dessert course arrived. Chandee nodded to me. "After we finish eating, I will debrief you about what happened a little while ago, but everything is fabulous, don't worry about it. We'll have to take a walk, so that I can go into greater detail about what I have to do in Caracas."

"Yes, finish your meal—no rush. When you're done, we'll take a walk, if nothing else, to work off this feast. It will also give you the chance to show me the whole property. This looks like a castle in the middle of a kingdom."

She smiled and nodded. "You're not kidding. This is one of Chavez's little kingdoms. Let's finish our food in peace. I will have another beer; maybe it will help me to relax as it does for you." She asked Padre Rodrigo. "Do you want another beer, Padre?"

He grinned broadly. "Yes, yes, yes, my angel! I want to be relaxed, too. I had a very busy, agitated day with that young Captain Augusto. He and all the commotion that he brought to our little town with his soldiers really stressed me out. But the worst is already over, thanks to the Lord." He crossed himself.

I smiled as I utterly enjoyed my dessert, which was a flan with crushed coconut and sugar, topped with Grand Marnier. "Don't bother me, anyone—I'm in heaven!"

Chandee grinned. "You're enjoying your dessert? Do you want another one? This is flan a la Marmol!"

I said, a little embarrassed. "No, no—it's fine. Thanks for remembering and making this for me."

"I didn't make it, I told Camile, and she made it. But you don't have to thank me, since this is my favorite! You stepped on the tail of two cats at the same time."

Yaneba shook her head, unnoticed by the others. Sarcastically, she mocked Chandee by mocking her head movements. I thought it was fortunate the others were distracted, and I was a little embarrassed.

It was by now 4:30 in the afternoon. We said goodbye to Padre Rodrigo, and Chandee gave us a tour of the interior of the cabin. It was immense, more like a hotel. She showed us the library, the ten bedrooms which were more like master suites with their own bathrooms, and then finally the game room. It had two pool tables, baccarat and card tables, even slot machines and pinball machines. Everyone was so fascinated by this and began to play some of the games. Chandee and I excused ourselves so that I could fully debrief her on her mission and left the cabin.

She said, "Come here, I want to show you something."

We went around a small hill. Almost imperceptible from the cabin was a large lake, almost like a lagoon. It was fed by a large waterfall coming out of the mountains. What took my full attention was the complete landing field, perhaps 150 feet from the river which flowed out of the lake. There were even containment walls between the field and the river to guard the airstrip against flooding. There were night reflectors, an independent generator, and solar panels. I rubbed my forehead.

"Oh my God! How much money did this cost? This must be his center of operations for many things!"

Chandee smiled. "I saw with my own eyes planes filled with cocaine, opium, all kinds of crap leaving from this airstrip over the past couple of years. I met virtually every single leader from around the world here at private parties. You see all this? Revolutionary money from the humble and needy—according to Chavez, of course. But it's for him, too, since he was poor."

I shook my head in disgust. "What cynics all these communists are!"

"If you want to see cynical, you just wait and see Captain Augusto. He came to visit me today while we were having lunch. He tried to blackmail me, but he left here like a dog with his tail between his legs."

This filled me with curiosity. "Blackmail you? For what?"

She smiled sarcastically and pointed at me. "For you guys. It looks like, according to him, that he has a witness which said my Range Rover was seen in the proximity of the crash near the forest. In the end, after all he was demanding from me, he only wound up with a plate of food and the worst bottle of wine from Chavez's stock, that I give to Camila to cook with."

"How did you manage to get this guy off your back? That is the reason you took so long—you almost took an hour!"

"No, no, no, no, no. I took so long because Captain Augusto, after I scared the hell out of him with my answer to his extortion, could not find any more apologies, one after the other. He wouldn't let me go, even to the point of shedding some crocodile tears to make me feel guilty, telling me about his family and kids when I told him what I was going to do. I told him I held no grudges in my heart and told him to go home and examine his conscience, and I would not denounce him to President Chavez nor ever mention his absolutely filthy blackmail attempt."

Chandee looked at me this time with a mischievous smile. "I did to him what you taught me. He'd come in with a very aggressive attitude, attempting to intimidate and threaten me. I will admit, I was nervous, but I never showed him any fear. I gave him all the rope he needed to hang himself. When he felt he had me in his hand, I asked the final, crucial question that you used many times to get out of major problems."

"OK, OK—stop it. What did you say?"

"Just a simple question: what do you want, Captain Augusto? What exactly do I have to do to keep you quiet? If you were going to call Chavez, you wouldn't be here, trying to extort me. He gave me his demand, which included the perverted condition of going to bed with me. The blood rushed to my head, and I had to control myself to not blow up in his face. What a villain—what a lowlife! Get in bed with me, and he's a married man with kids and everything!" Chandee tapped her chest. "OK, let's take the shaved lion out of the cage. Until now, we had an apparently innocent-looking *pollo.* I sang to him your 'Ave Maria de Julio Antonio.'"

"No!"

"Just listen to this—*this* 'Ave Maria' had a lot of obscenities and bad words. It was triple X. I pulled every obscenity out of my black book."

I put both hands on my face and shook my head. "I can only imagine the surprise this young captain had. He must have been completely frozen."

Chandee smiled. "I have his complete record in a file, the reason Chavez took him out of his personal escort, and the reason why he's right here on this island, far away from civilization and the glamor of the capital. When I pulled that file and showed it to him, he realized that I wasn't the mistress to the President—I was something more. I ended up by saying to him, 'When I'm finished with you, if you don't wind up in a military prison, you'll be in front of a firing squad for being a counter-revolutionary. The best that could happen to you would be to be in the big ship with black Cubans that Castro sends to Congo, Africa for the 'liberation' of that continent.'"

I could not restrain myself from laughing anymore. "You are something special—I think you're not just special, you are unique." I hugged her and gave her a kiss on the cheek.

She smiled. After we separated, she seemed a little confused by my spontaneous affection. She said, "You gave me goosebumps. It's been a long time since you hugged me like that and gave me a kiss. I hope you repeat it in the future."

I smiled. "Just remember, I always have great respect, love, and admiration for you."

We continued walking along the river, where she showed me all the details of how the generators, lights, and gear operated for the landing field. I fully debriefed her for her mission to Caracas. It was by now twilight, and so we walked back to the cabin.

Chandee said, "Don't think for a second that all the construction for places like this one came out of Venezuela." She shook her head. "They are all financed by the Tri-continental, the dream of Castro, Che Guevara, Mao Tse Tung, and Adolf Hitler. Those dreams were shared by many leaders around the world today, even though they may not show it to the public. Silently, though, they all want to be like these men. That is why Castro and his disciple Chavez, the Ortega brothers, and all the others, when they take the power, they build places like this to render awestruck these people. Some don't go along because of their egotism; they get killed. But others follow them and become their allies. I'm going to give you an example. These leaders have the potential to change the world today and bring it to the greatest darkness any human being could dream of seeing. The first one I met here was Khaddaffi, bin Laden, the Ortega brothers, the Ayatollah, Putin, an entourage of others, too many to mention right now. I can include Senators from the United States of America, to mention a few: George McGovern, Bernie Sanders, the Clintons, movie stars, major media figures, and many other high-profile figures in the corporate sector from the United States as well as other countries around the world. Every one of these people dreams to control the world under their ideology: socialist, communist, Progressive, whatever they decide to call it next."

I said with passion in my voice. "That will never happen so long as I remain alive on the soil of this earth."

She smiled. "I'm with you, and I say the same. But remember, years before we left it behind, we heard this same stuff in Cuba. Now Venezuela is gone, Nicaragua, what is going to be next? USA? We never dreamed these guys would be able to convert these countries to communism. I'm telling you right now that I'm scared. Every single democratic country in the world is in danger. Many of the people that are too young to know the consequences of this ideology are even voting for people with these ideas. Imagine what would happen if this occurs in the USA! It would be the complete destruction of democracy in the world."

I shook my head and put my arm around her shoulder. I gave her a squeeze, stopping her. "Listen to me very well: we have to remain optimistic and continue our fight to the last drop of our blood. That is the reason we will never, *never*, allow for as long as we live a system like that system of Cuba to continue. I would rather suffer a thousand deaths than deal with the uncertainty as to whether it will ever end. That is the reason you, I, and our friends will continue this fight while we have life, breath, and faith in God."

We had stopped right in front of the cabin. We stood looking at one another, our faces filled with frustration and concern, tears in our eyes. Chandee stepped forward and gave me a strong hug. She whispered in my ear, "I have a terrible fear that God has abandoned us to the hands of this horrible, poisonous serpent that sticks its fangs in everyone that comes close to it. Some they convert into allies through fear of being killed and then compel the fearful to submit to them. The ones they cannot convert, they kill."

I pushed her away a little. "Listen to me: God will never, *never* abandon us. Listen carefully: we are the only hope to save His creation. He will never let His creation be destroyed by his worst enemy, Satan."

Chandee looked at me intensely, with gratitude. She nodded. "Thank you for your words of hope and encouragement. Your optimism and tenacity are contagious." She took my hand. "Come to the library. I want to show you on the map the itinerary I will follow to go to the capital in greater detail."

"OK. Let's go into your castle, Princess." I bowed and gave her a reverence.

Chandee smiled. "I love your sense of humor. It's refreshing—even in the worst times, you can make me smile."

We went into the game room, collected our friends, and went to the library. Chandee opened a large map of the country of Venezuela over a baccarat table. She showed me where she would leave the Range Rover in the largest city on the island of Santa Margarita, Porla Mar. With the back of a pen, she showed us the great airport of Santiago Mariño. From there they would take a private plane to the capital of Caracas.

Chandee said, "If everything goes well, it should not take more than two or three days to pick up the package and come back to Porla Mar. From there we'll take the Range Rover once more to return here."

"Fantastic," I said. "Excellent idea. No one will bother you leaving the island in a private plane. We will be waiting for you here."

Chandee gave me a big hug and then went around the group, hugging each in turn. "Don't worry about anything. I have already given instructions to Camila and Trabuto. They will prepare meals every day for you guys, and I've already arranged for Padre Rodrigo to bring them in his car from town, even though it's only two or three kilometers. I spoil them; I don't like them walking that far. They'll be here from nine until five. You'll have an early breakfast, lunch, and dinner, so that they can get back to their family. I want to keep their loyalty—it's very important to my security. That's why I go the extra mile to give them as much comfort as possible. Now I'm going to take them home—that is why I'm saying my goodbyes to you now, since Chopin and I will be leaving very early in the morning. I might not be able to see you until I get back. Like I showed you before, this cabin has ten spacious rooms. Pick whichever ones you like the best for yourselves, be comfortable, and enjoy your stay here. This is a courtesy from President Hugo Chavez of Venezuela. We'll see each other very soon. God bless you." She hugged each of us again. When it came to my turn, she added a kiss on my cheek.

I murmured in her ear, "Take care of yourself, and good luck."

"Thank you for your optimism and strong character. You really, really made me feel a lot better. We'll see each other soon. Goodbye."

She turned at the threshold of the door and pointed upwards. "Remember what I told you—go to town only if it's absolutely necessary or an emergency. Do not go into town, please!"

"We will do as you have asked. Go, and don't worry about."

The first two or three days after Chandee left passed very fast. Because we changed my bandages frequently and continued to take the antibiotic, my wound started to heal rapidly. Followed by my loyal dog, Rocco, my friends and I constantly took walks along the riverbank out of the sight of casual observers. We enjoyed the beautiful panorama as a medicine and muscle relaxer, watching the beautiful flamingos flying away as they were chased by Rocco. He clearly was enjoying to the maximum this beauty, especially chasing the birds.

I asked myself why human beings couldn't live in peace and harmony as I looked around that the gorgeous scenery. This beautiful creation should be enjoyed in peace—and the answer came into my mind, the answer I always knew. It was the evil ambition of powerful men to enslave and control others without any scruple or sympathy for anyone.

The fourth day passed, and then the fifth day. I started to worry, and I discussed my concerns with the group. Because we had no idea what was going on in the outside world, we unanimously agreed that the best step for us as fugitives would be to remain in a secure place like where we were—even though it was one of the caves of the Venezuelan beast. He had many caves, and the best part of the whole thing in our favor was that the beast didn't know that we had been inhabiting one of them.

One week after Chandee and Chopin had left, the worry and uncertainty grew—not by days, but by hours and minutes. I took to staring out the window looking for the Range Rover. I started to consider other options, since I didn't want to be a sitting duck, waiting for the hunter to shoot us. I consulted once more with the others, and again we unanimously agreed to wait until Sunday—one more day.

We spoke with Padre Rodrigo, and he agreed to provide an appropriate vehicle by which we could leave the island. My greatest worry, after so many days, was that the authorities had investigated the wreckage of the helicopter. We didn't know how great their intelligence network could be, but all it would be a little clue for them to discover the whole thread. It occurred to me that by this time, Chavez's intelligence might even have pictures of each of us. Of course, these were only assumptions in my mind. But risk was part of our lives, and we got out of many bad situations based on such expectations.

Finally, Sunday came. No sign of Chandee or Chopin. We started to pack our things. We had decided to leave that night late, when everyone in town would be asleep. Sunday morning went by, afternoon lingered, and I was in the sitting room on my daily watch over the wooden bridge. My stomach was a huge knot, which prevented me from eating breakfast or lunch that day. All my friends sat in the room silently. The sun started its inevitable path towards the horizon. We all looked towards the bridge still visible in the gathering darkness through the glass of the huge window. I stood up, not able to take it anymore. Rocco followed me.

"I cannot stay here anymore. I'm going to walk for a while." Yaneba and Elizabeth asked for me to wait, because they wanted to come with me. While they changed their shoes, I touched Rocco's head. "Rocco, let's go chase the flamingoes."

As soon as I opened the door, he ran at once to the back yard of the cabin, towards the riverbank and his flamingos. The three of us walked out of the cabin. As we neared the riverbank, we heard the noise of a low-flying plane. We looked up. In the time we had spent here we had never seen a plane come to use the airstrip. The sun was still high enough to provide light, and so we could see clearly that the plane was dropping several small parachutes with packages. It looked, we thought, like an agricultural drop—food in cans to the most impoverished people on the island. But then the plane turned around and dropped almost right over our heads what looked like a larger box, heavier than the others. The vast parachute floated down and gently landed near where we were walking.

Figure 10 Surprise package drops

We went over to the large, wrapped bundle, filled with curiosity. Even Rocco was curious and ran ahead of us to inspect it. Sniffing it and finding nothing of interest, he raised his hind leg and marked it. The parachute was still floating in the breeze. We wrapped the parachute and secured it with rocks.

Something unusual caught my attention. All the bundles said everywhere "Fragile: Handle with Care." Why would such cargo be airdropped? Not only that, but the notices were also written in English, Spanish, and French. I was puzzled by this. The more I looked at it, the more I thought it looked like something military. I could not, however, figure out what it was. I looked at Yaneba and Elizabeth, a little worried.

"What do you guys think this is?"

They both looked at me in confusion and surprise and shrugged their shoulders. Yaneba said, "If I have to be honest with you, remember whose house we're in: Chavez's. This could be a bomb. It could be detonated from a distance. Or it could be a nuclear device that the dictator obtained on the black market, planning a terrorist attack somewhere in the world. That would explain why they dropped it here on his property."

That concerned me even more. This was a grave complication. Elizabeth shook her head. "You know what? I don't like this at all." She held up her forefinger and thumb. "Not even this much. I don't like your suppositions, either one. With the first one, we'll blow up with the bomb. The second means that the soldiers will be here quite soon to pick them up, like dogs taking a ball to their master. That means we cannot stay here one minute more. The best thing to do is get out of here right now and leave this place behind as soon as possible. Like they say in the States, let's cut our losses."

I scratched my head as I watched the plane rapidly flying away as nonchalantly as it had come. I stood there for a while in deep thought, silently trying to discern what this was all about. I analyzed the different possibilities. Without making any conclusions, I strove in my mind to determine what would be the most secure step we could take. These packages could literally represent life or death, especially regarding how quickly we moved from this point on. I thought the only possibility at that moment in relation to this was not the two negative possibilities Yaneba gave to us. It could have been the result of the strain she was under, a kind of natural panic. We had all endured a great deal of stress due to the overlong wait for the return of Chopin and Chandee, combined with the sensation of being trapped in that beautiful yet dangerous place. Perhaps God had decided we should stop. Chavez, after all, was the student of Fidel Castro, who himself modeled his behavior from Adolf Hitler—I started to recall the time I had actually caught him imitating Hitler in his office. Perhaps deep in my thoughts about my memories of Fidel Castro in Cuba, I did not hear the calls of Elizabeth and Yaneba, who were extremely worried by my prolonged silence.

I finally heard their voices like an echo: "Julio Antonio, Julio Antonio!" I felt a hand on my right shoulder, giving it a gentle shake. It was Elizabeth. I was so deep in my reverie in my attempt to discover a positive outcome for us in those packages. I took my commando knife out of my pants pocket. Both women stepped back a couple of steps from me with their hands held up. They both yelled, "Julio Antonio, it's us! We're not the enemy!"

I looked at them for a few seconds. I could not understand why they had such terrified expressions on their faces and why they were holding their hands up in surrender. I looked at the knife in my hand, and I all I could do was laugh. In a flash, I realized that I must have spaced out, and they must have believed I was having a nervous breakdown and had pulled my knife in response to my perceiving some threat and might cut their heads off. All I was thinking about was to cut the lines off the boxes. I had no time for explanation if what I thought might be in those packages. I had to get them open quickly.

I stepped forward to the large package and began to stab through the thick plastic covering it. My action probably looked to them irrational and threw them off. Both women stared at me stabbing away at the plastic. They were half-petrified, because I kept looking at them, which fed my laughter. I must by now have sounded like a maniac. I was ripping the pieces and throwing them away violently. I didn't have time to waste if I was correct. If I was wrong, we needed to get out of there immediately.

I stopped for a few seconds and yelled at them. "Are you going to help me, please?"

They had partially lowered their hands, but still appeared reluctant. Still slightly terrified, I understood their situation and tried to control my laugh. It was difficult, though, because of the combination of their comical faces and the situation. As I started to make headway with the packages, I could see I was right. I was filled with joy, and tried harder to tamp down on my laughter, producing a series of giggles. I thought to myself how God never abandoned us, and yet once again He provided us with help.

This time, more soberly, I yelled, "What are you waiting for? We have no time to lose, and if this is what I think it is, we have to get it unpacked at once!"

They came over hesitantly to help me rip the package open. Elizabeth remarked first, "I thought you were going crazy. Maybe you had gotten one of those bumps during the crash."

I shook my head, still smiling. Yaneba said, "I thought you were having a nervous breakdown and could not recognize us. It could happen to anyone, and such people could confuse friends for enemies. I won't sugar coat it; when you took that knife out with your eyes staring off into space, I soiled my pants. Knowing your skills, I figured we had no hope, and that you would filet us into pieces for Rocco on this beautiful summer afternoon."

I couldn't control it anymore and burst out laughing again without stopping. I finally gasped, "Girls, I can be accused of many things, but to think I'm completely insane like that? You, better than anyone, know who I am. I know we're under a lot of pressure, but to imagine me like Jack the Ripper? I've been your best friend and protector all my life." I decided to play around with their feelings a bit. "That really, really hurts me right in the heart."

Elizabeth replied with greater enthusiasm and energy as she helped me unwrap the plastic, "Remember, mental insanity is real. It can happen to any one of us at any moment from an emotional shock."

I smiled. "To everyone else it's possible; but to me, I lived all my life since I was a kid on the border of insanity. Since I knew her very well, I've learned to completely control my emotions."

This time they both laughed. Yaneba replied, "Yes, to that I can be a witness. It is true; but you cannot deny it to us, I think you enjoyed scaring the daylights out of us like that."

"No, no, no, no." I shook my head. "I only laughed by the look on your faces. You both turned lily white. The only reason I got my knife out because the idea to cut open that plastic was the last one through my mind before I spaced out to my childhood in Cuba and the memories of the dictator imitating Adolph Hitler."

Yaneba laughed. "You were going through all that stuff? You wandered really far with your mind—no wonder when you turned around your eyes were in La-la-land!"

I smiled. I had almost opened part of the wood of the box with my knife. "Bingo! Exactly what I was imagining in my positive possibility." I rapped on the box with my knife. "This is our ride back home."

They looked at me in consternation. Yaneba asked, "What is it? Would you please explain it to us?"

I put my knife away and embraced them both, one in each arm. "You guys have nothing to worry about anymore. We have here either a brand-new helicopter in pieces or perhaps something better. Until we get all the other pieces and put it together, we won't know exactly what it is, but it's not what Yaneba assumed."

Yaneba asked then, "Who is going to put it together? It's like a puzzle."

I replied, "Who better than Chopin?"

Elizabeth shook her head. "Chopin is not here! Are you OK? Or do you really have a concussion? We were supposed to leave today because they haven't shown up."

"In reply to your first question, Chopin will be here very soon. I assure you that, if he had done what he was supposed to, these things would not be here. In reply to your second question, no, I have no concussion." I pointed down towards my leg. "Only that stupid wound in my leg, which is getting better, thank you. Ladies, you have to learn from now on to have more faith, more optimism, and don't jump to conclusions so quickly, especially when this has happened so frequently for so many years."

Out of the blue, Rocco stopped chasing the flamingos. He raised his head and barked a couple of times and then howled. He came over to me. "Uh, oh—somebody's here." I patted his head. "Go find out." He loped away, his tiny nub of a tail wagging furiously. I turned to Yaneba and Elizabeth. "Speaking of the angels, I believe they have just appeared before us at last." They both looked at me curiously but did not dare to ask further questions.

CHAPTER 3: THE REPENTANT TERRORIST

We walked together over the small hill that Rocco had just disappeared behind, heading towards the cabin. The sun was just setting, a mist was rising from the ground, and the automatic lights on the patio started to turn on with the growing darkness. We could see in the distance the lights and silhouette of the Range Rover in the driveway. Yaneba and Elizabeth could not contain their happiness, and both jumped towards me to hug me with tears in their eyes. I was caught by surprise and almost fell face forward towards the ground.

"Hey, girls—I'm still a wounded man," I protested as they held me to prevent me from falling onto the brick driveway. "Remember, faith is the most important thing in the life of any human being." They nodded.

We were close enough to see that Chandee and Chopin were trying to help a wounded man with a very thick beard. He had a bandage extending from his neck into his thick hair. Rocco ran around them affectionately, trying to stay out of the way. The man was groggy and walked slowly and unsteadily. Chandee and Chopin saw us and nodded.

Chandee said, "There you go—you have your package here. A little damaged, but perhaps not too bad. I think we can repair the damage. Is everything fine here?"

"Everything is fine," I replied. "All in order."

Elizabeth released me and walked over to Chopin. "It's OK, I've got him." She took the wounded man. She turned to me. "Where did you want to put Mr. Abdul?"

I didn't even have to think twice. "The first room towards the back, close to the front door, in case we have to get him out of here quickly." Abdul appeared to be nearly unconscious. "What happened to him?"

Abdul groaned deliriously. Chandee and Elizabeth supported him between them. "We'll join you in the sitting room to discuss all the details in a bit, and you can bring us up to date."

Chopin asked, "Have you already received the other package?"

"Yes."

"Our people didn't fail, then!"

"No—in fact, I only just now opened the first box. What is it—a helicopter?"

"No, something much more sophisticated than that. Something that no radar on earth will be able to detect, something so advanced that they tell me it will blow your socks off! It will be a surprise especially for you." He said mischievously as he rubbed his hands together. "I will enjoy piloting this!"

Chandee started to take Abdul into the cabin with Elizabeth. "Do you need some help?" I asked.

She replied, "No, no—he probably weighs no more than 80 pounds. I don't know what these terrorists eat."

Yaneba said, "They probably fast for several days before they blow up innocent victims. That way the seventy-two virgins in their imagined Heaven won't smell the crap that these miserable, conniving terrorists are feeding them." She bit her lower lip, restraining herself from violence as she looked at him with disgust. "They don't even deserve to be living."

We walked into the cabin. I went into the kitchen and poured myself a glass of orange juice, since I hadn't eaten all day long. I went into the sitting room and joined the others as they waited for Chandee and Elizabeth to come back in. Rocco followed me as usual and lay down right in front of the wine rack—his favorite place, on top of the polar bear skin which lay on the wooden floor before the wine rack. A few minutes later, Elizabeth and Chandee reunited with us.

I asked Chandee, "How is the package?"

She shrugged uncertainly. "Let's hope in the end that all the work we've been doing will result in you getting the information you need. The way things happened was strange. He had to get shot precisely in the throat. I don't think he will be in any condition to negotiate anything with you, possibly not even able to speak at all."

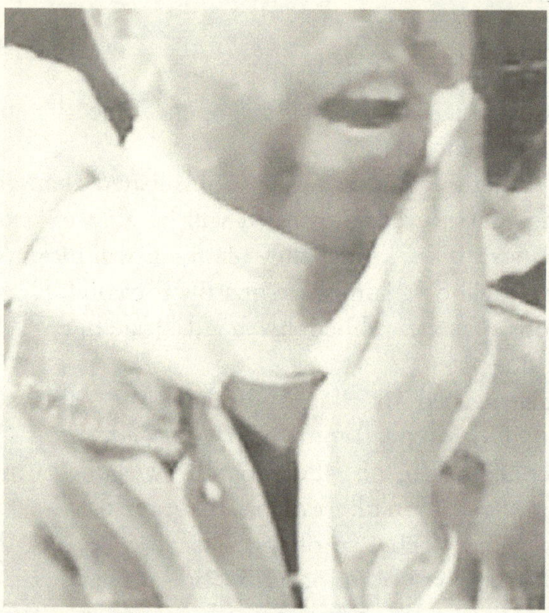

Figure 11 The shot terrorist

"You guys had us very worried. We almost left this place."

"Yes, I see—everyone is packed and ready to go, luggage in front of the room. Elizabeth already told me that Padre Rodrigo brought you the Bronco I saw parked in the driveway."

"Yes. We are ready to go. If it weren't for the cargo plane a few hours ago that parachute dropped the packages from the sky, we would be gone by now. We almost freaked out, but when I opened the first box, I realized you were OK and that we should expect you any minute. I know our people move fast, but not so fast that they could send such a large package over such a distance in a few days."

Chandee leaned back in her chair. "there's no doubt that God protects the innocent. I have not even the smallest doubt that we are all guiltless, trying as best we can to protect blameless lives in what we do. But let me get right to the point and debrief you as soon as possible."

"Take your time, relax. There's no rush here, and we're not going anywhere now. We're just glad to see you both back in one piece."

Chandee breathed a deep sigh and stroked her chin with her right hand. "Well, let's start by telling you that the trip to Caracas went beautifully, even better than we had planned. We had no interference of any kind. When we arrived, we rented a car and contacted Abdul. We followed your instructions, as always, and explained to him the rules and where the negotiation would take place. He accepted without any problem. We came back with no problem all the way to the Porla Mar. After we picked up the Range Rover at the Santiago Mariño Airport, we assumed the package was already safe and we were nearly home free." She looked at Chopin for confirmation.

He nodded. "Yes, exactly as she related. Everything went well until we came to a small town close to here. We decided to stop and refill the Range Rover's tank, go to the bathroom, and get some refreshments. My instinct told me, and I don't know why, that we weren't safe there, from the moment we entered it."

Chandee nodded. "It gave me a bad vibe." She rubbed the back of her neck nervously with her left hand. "It was like I could feel the eyes of the whole town on us, tracking all of our movements. I felt like someone was waiting for us. Thanks to our instincts, things didn't go worse. I took all normal precautions, parking the Range Rover in a secure place, everything I knew to do while we were in that town. I don't think the target was only Abdul—I think we are all the target." She tapped herself. "Including me. Everything happened so fast, but God protected all three of us. Not one of us should be alive. I was right next to Abdul. I put my hat on him and jokingly said that he looked good. As he took it off, a shot was fired. Instead of getting him in the head, it went from one side of his throat to the other. This happened at the cashier station, just as we were almost out of the door. Chopin was still behind us, looking for a specific brand of tomato juice, *El Monte.* Everything looked like it was happening in slow motion. I saw, a few moments before that shot, the truck that refilled the tanks for the gas station drove in and blocked the view through the store window for the shooter. That protected us against further shots, since the sniper must not have wanted to blow himself up by shooting the tanker truck."

We listened to Chandee's account with extreme attention, not losing a single detail of her story. She rubbed her forehead with her fingers.

"After I saw Abdul wounded, I yelled, 'Shooter! Everyone down on the ground!' Even the cashier hit the ground. There were two more shots, the second one striking a container of lemonade right next to me." She raised her arm, and we could see the bullet hole in both sides of her shirt under her arm.

Chopin said, "I hit the floor as soon as Chandee shouted. I heard the two shots, and both would have hit me in the head if I hadn't done so. They both struck the tomato juice cans that were at eye level to me." We could see the dark stains of tomato juice on him.

I stayed deep in my thoughts, wondering who would have known about this. Nobody, not even O'Brien, knew where we had been hiding—at least, not until Chopin contacted our people with his instructions as to where to send the package. A strange feeling went through my whole body. It all sounded very strange, a real puzzle. I asked Chandee, "Did you take him to a doctor? I assume so, because I see his bandage was done very professionally."

Chandee replied, "Yes. I took him to a veterinarian in that town. I didn't stop into the only doctor in town so that we wouldn't call any attention to ourselves."

"What did the veterinarian tell you? What is his condition? Will he be able to speak?"

Chandee shook her head. "No. The veterinarian said that the bullet had come under his mandible and exited through the neck. It's not a joke, but it's not a mortal wound, unless it gets infected or some other complication occurs after the fact. The worst, from what he could observe, was that the bullet had gone through the vocal cords and damaged some of them. Unless we take Abdul to a hospital, as soon as possible, there is a likelihood he will never talk again. At a hospital they could do reconstructive surgery. He was put under anesthetic in order to clean the wound as best as the veterinarian could." She held up a bottle of pills. "The only pain killer was morphine. He gave me another bottle of antibiotics. He assured me that Abdul will be in agonizing pain, and so not to fail giving him the painkiller on time. We'll use these pills to keep him sedated each day for several hours until the process of healing starts. Then I will withdraw them as soon as he no longer needs them."

I said, "Let me think about what we're going to do with him." I turned to Elizabeth. "Can you take care of him, give him his medication, and not let him out of your sight until we decide?"

"No problem."

"It's very important, Elizabeth, that you give him the medicine on time. If you must leave the room, come back as soon as possible and keep an eye on him."

"Don't worry—I'll take care of him and be in charge of him."

Chandee said, "OK, Elizabeth—catch!" She tossed first the morphine and then the antibiotics to Elizabeth. "He's your package now."

"OK," I said, "let's go to bed now. Early in the morning we should pick up those parachutes, open the packages, and help Chopin put everything together. We have the larger package closest to the cabin, practically on the patio, but there are several smaller ones scattered around the property." I turned to Chopin. "Pick the best place where you can put it together and let me know what you need."

"OK," he said.

"Who is going to be on guard tonight?" I asked.

Elizabeth said, "Me, during the first four hours, and Mayari in the next four hours. And the last four hours, it will be me again."

"OK," I said. "Hold the medication for him until he wakes up in the morning, as long as you think is prudent. When he starts to protest because of the pain, wake me up, no matter what time it is, and then I'll want to talk with him. If you sedate him, he won't be alert, and I hate to sound cruel—but a little bit of pain will help me negotiate with him better."

"How are you going to question him?" she asked.

"He cannot talk, but he can hear, and he can write. He speaks several languages perfectly. That's why he's so close to bin Laden."

Elizabeth smiled. "Very well. I'll have a tablet with pen or pencil available in the room."

"Thank you," I replied. "Well, if there's nothing more to discuss, I will retire and rest. Tomorrow morning will be busy."

Chandee touched my arm. "Thanks for your trust in us and your patience to wait until the last minute. I love your beautiful and great faith."

I smiled. "I know you cannot live without us—no one could keep you from coming back."

She returned my smile. I stood up and patted her shoulder. "Thanks to both of you guys. Not only can you come back in one piece with that valuable package, but you made us secure for our exit from this place, at least seventy-five percent alive. We all, without exception, owe a debt of gratitude to you guys." I bowed to her. "Thanks for a good job well done, and welcome back. Thanks be to God for bringing you back, safe and sound. We should not lament the little hairs in the soup that we can correct, one way or the other. Again, if we have nothing else to discuss, I will retire now." Everyone nodded. "OK, good night, everyone."

A while later, I woke up and checked one of my watches. It was 4:30 a.m., and so I got up, brushed my teeth, and washed my face. As I got dressed, someone entered my room. It was Elizabeth.

"Well, I see you're up. I was waiting for you. Abdul asked me to take him to a hospital. He's in very bad pain and cannot take it much longer. He's crying like a baby."

"OK, let's go. Hurry up—this is the precise moment to interrogate him. Get there now and let him know I'll be there in a second."

"OK." She left in a hurry.

I went to the sitting room and removed the keychain from my pockets. I walked over to the wine rack and unlocked the handcuffs on the briefcase there. I went to the first bedroom and rapped on the door with the back of my knuckles.

Elizabeth's voice answered, "Come in."

I walked in and had to control myself upon seeing him in so much pain. I really wanted to be kind and instruct Elizabeth to give him his pain killer. He was on his knees in bed in prayer, swaying back and forth as he asked Allah to take him out of his agony. When he saw me, he stopped. His eyes were red from crying, and he pointed at his wound with his right hand. He opened his hand and looked towards the ceiling, imploring me to help him with an agonized expression.

I signaled with both hands to calm him down. I picked up a tablet. "Everything will be fine, don't worry. What language are you most comfortable in, and you can write your answers on this tablet: English, Spanish, Portuguese, Italian—I'm giving you a variety so that we can fully communicate."

He wrote in Spanish, "Hospital. Agony. Please." He thrust the tablet at me.

I signaled to him to calm down again. I opened the briefcase with the money. I took bundles of $10,000 out of it. "How much do you want for the information you're going to offer me today?"

He waved his hands agitatedly and shook his head. He wrote, "Money later. Hospital now."

I thought perhaps that he was considering the possibility that we had arranged for him to get shot, so that he would be more preoccupied with his pain and not the money. It might also explain to him why we, who were his enemies, were being so considerate to him.

He wrote once more, "Please. Pain unbearable." His shaking hands held the tablet to my face, his eyes pleading.

I realized that the man was in agony beyond his ability to bear. I no longer needed to delay his relief. I had no desire to make him suffer unnecessarily. I said to Elizabeth, "Give him his medication."

If I moved fast, I could probably get my information before the sedative took effect. I figured it would take at least half an hour before he would be too drowsy to answer my questions.

Abdul eagerly grabbed the pill like a child grabbing candy. Panting, he sipped water from a straw to wash it down. After he took his pill, I gave him reassurances that I would take him to the U.S., the Hoag Hospital in Newport Beach, to the best hospital in California. There they would do whatever was necessary to reconstruct his vocal cords. He looked at me gratefully, clasped his hands together before him and bowed to me. Once he grew more relaxed, he wrote down the name and telephone number of his contact with a small smile on his face this time. The address and phone number he wrote down was in Newport Beach. He then wrote down a code so that his contact would know I was sent by him and give me a package. It would contain all the details, safe houses, and movements not just of bin Laden but also all the members of al-Qaeda. The name of the individual was supposedly Brenton Cooper.

Finally, after a while of communicating with him, I believed I had all the information I needed for the moment, and he was growing groggy as the morphine took full effect. The last thing he wrote was that if anything happened to him, I should give $1,500,000 to his friend

Brenton Cooper to help Abdul's family. I gave him reassurances that everything would be OK and provided him with moral support as well as making my best effort to show him that I cared.

I told him that the doctor who had examined and treated him had informed us that his wound was not a mortal one and had not done major damage. As soon as we took care of it, even though the area was a delicate one to treat, he would recuperate well with intensive care. I left out the fact that the doctor in question was a veterinarian. Even though he was an associate of terrorists, it was never my custom to obtain satisfaction by being emotionally cruel to any human being—including my enemies.

We finished. He was practically asleep by now. I told Elizabeth to keep her eyes on him and to give him his fluids until his condition improved.

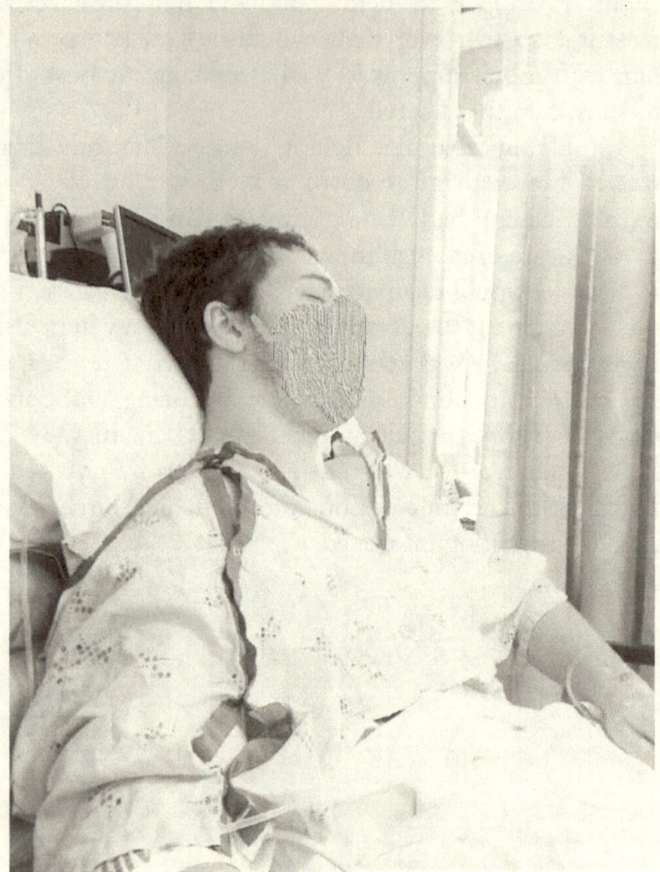

Figure 12 The terrorist under sedation

She said, "Don't worry—I'll take care of him. You made this my job now."

I left the room and returned to my own. I took a shower and then headed to the dining room to eat something. My stomach had been crawling like a cat and a dog in a fight, complete with some very unpleasant howling. I had eaten virtually nothing in the last 24 hours. I found Yaneba in the dining room, who greeted me and asked, "How is your terrorist doing? Did you obtain the information you expected from him?"

I nodded. "Yes, yes—I believe a lot more than I was expecting."

She smiled with satisfaction. "Very good. I'm glad. Then our job has been successful and not in vain. I was thinking that for a while over the past few hours."

"No, no—our work has been extremely productive. It's not complete just yet, at least not until we get out of here and safely back in California. Until then, we cannot count on victory. But at least we know we got it right on the patio. Let's hope everything continues as now, even though we have some small difficulties. I think, very soon, we'll be able to celebrate another triumph against our enemies."

Yaneba asked, "What do you have in mind to do with Abdul? If you already have all the information that we need, shoot him in the head and drop him in the river."

"No, no, Yaneba!"

"Yes," she said emphatically. "You cannot leave him alive. He might go buy more bombs with the money you gave him for the information. He'll enable them to kill more men, women, and children in shopping malls." Her tone was harsh and resentful, but her words were true up to a point.

"Come on, honey," I said, "you're better than that. Don't talk this way. We cannot lower ourselves to their level. Remember what Mima always said to me, and probably your mother said to you: if a dog bites you, and you get on the floor and bite it back—you are nothing more than another dog. Also remember you are a woman. You should give life, not take it away. You are better than them. Don't let your hatred and desire for revenge convert yourself into a dog or a terrorist like them. They are actually wild animals; it's not fair to call them dogs." I patted Rocco's head. "I'm sorry, Rocco. Look at how loyal and noble Rocco is." At the mention of his name, Rocco wagged his nub of a tail so violently his whole rear wiggled.

Yaneba had grown teary-eyed at my words. "Forgive me—but today is the anniversary of the deaths of my mother, father, and little sister at the hands of the Cuban communists. My mood has not been good because of that. This has been a sad, ugly week for me."

I put my hand on her shoulder. "I'm sorry, honey. You know in your heart that I loved them, too. For a long time after the Cuban military planes shot your family's little boat to pieces in the ocean, I believed I had lost you as well. I cried like a baby many times. I thought I would never see you again."

She stood up next to the table. We embraced each other hard. I had tears in my eyes as those memories flooded my mind, the kind that are so sad they never truly leave you. She was the only survivor in one of the many crimes against humanity committed by the communist Cuban government every day in the Gulf of Mexico.

Mayari entered the dining room. When he saw us in a tight embrace, he assumed the wrong thing. "Oh, Dr. del Marmol! Excuse me!" He turned to leave.

"No, stop," I said. "What's up?"

"Oh, Chopin wanted to see you. He has a few important questions about the prototype airplane for you."

Yaneba tried to dry her eyes. He noticed that and saw my own tears. "What happened, guys?"

"Yaneba is extremely emotional. Today is the anniversary of the deaths of all her family. I knew them, too. I'll be back in a few minutes. Do you mind, Yaneba?"

"No, no—go and see what Chopin wants. It must be important."

"I'll be right back. Don't go away—would you please stay with her, Mayari?"

"Of course, with pleasure," he said.

"I don't want to slow Chopin a single moment in his work. I don't have a good feeling about this attempt on Chandee and Chopin's life on the return trip. I want to get out of here as soon as possible."

Mayari touched my shoulder. "Don't worry—go, go. Take care of whatever it is, and I will not leave until you return."

"Thank you."

Yaneba was still sniffling. "Are you sure you're OK, honey?" I asked.

"Yes, yes—go, please."

I left the cabin, crossed the patio, and walked over to where Chopin was working. As I approached the hill and walked around it, I could see by the landing field that Chopin had all the frame of the prototype placed together, though not yet assembled. It looked like a spaceship from the future or from a science fiction movie. He had been using the cement ramp that was normally at the beginning of a landing field. It was a massive circle of concrete, and it was there he was putting it together.

"My God!" I exclaimed. "How quickly you've been putting this together."

He smiled with pride. "Thank you, with the help of everyone, but especially Chandee." He pointed to Chandee, who held one of the wings, trying to balance it as Chopin tied it against the body. He looked at me seriously. "Really, you should send Chandee to learn piloting and aviation mechanics. She's a natural—even the pieces I could not find, she was able to locate in those boxes."

She smiled. "He's only telling you this because he had me working since five a.m., working me like a slave driver."

Chopin laughed loudly. "Hey—you came voluntarily. I never recruited you."

Chandee smiled. "Voluntarily—you mean like the Chinese in Cuba?"

We all laughed at Chandee's implication regarding what the communist government in Cuba referred to as "voluntary work."

"I was told you had an important question for me—what is it?"

He should his head as he continued to work. "I only wanted to know how many passengers you wanted to carry with it. It's built for six passengers, not including the pilot and co-pilot. If possible, it's best if I can leave some of these seats here on the ground. I will only install as many seats as you direct. According to the manual, we can only carry a hundred pounds of luggage per passenger, taking into consideration the average weight of a person is two hundred pounds. Any more than that and we'll have to redistribute weight to follow the instructions exactly. If we overdo it, we will cause the plane's performance to worsen, while if we go lighter, we'll improve things. Bear in mind that these engines are electrical. I want to follow these suggestions to the teeth to avoid another forced landing."

My face grew long. "That is the last thing I wanted to hear. I don't believe anyone would survive another forced landing in this plane of fiberglass, and Heaven and the Devil know whatever plastic components this thing has."

Chopin dropped the manual and crossed himself. "God forgive him for mentioning the Enemy! *Chico*—how could you mention both him and the possibility of a crash?"

"I'm sorry, but the mention of a crash put my neck hairs to stand on end. But let's correct who mentioned a forced landing first, Chopin!"

He nodded his head, "Yes, 'forced landing'. Not *'crash'*—there is a tremendous difference, *chico*! And then to overflow the glass of my nerves, you mentioned my enemy—the Enemy!"

I grew serious this time. I could see how stressed out he was. "Calm down, *chico*. I'm sorry—I just noticed how much anxiety you have. Take a break. You have been working too many hours and then the shooting you survived yesterday. You're probably on the verge of a nervous breakdown."

"*Chico*! I have had to change my undies many times! I never wanted to tell Chandee, but while we were driving back, my rear end turned into a garden's automatic sprinklers. And as I slid around on the leather seat, the cracking of the leather made me think back to the shooting, and the sprinklers shot off on a timer. I don't even know what I have in my shirt, but on my pants was either the tomato juice or the diarrhea. If you don't want to believe me, ask Chandee. I asked her ten times to stop, and I finally threw away my undies so that it would be easier to relieve myself. She asked me what was wrong with me, and I just told her that I only needed to pee a lot and asked her to pull over once more." Chandee burst out laughing. "I have to thank her for telling just her side of the story, since I didn't want to bore you with my problems, which weren't exactly heroic. Not everyone is born to be one, but even with my rear end full of caca, I made it over here with my tongue on the ground, like you say the Fords always bring you home. And not one single complaint—isn't that true, honey? With the favor of God, we might manage to leave this beautiful but dangerous place tonight." He crossed himself. "Let's pray that no other problem comes up and that the engines function as expected. They're brand new. If we take off tonight, perhaps by tomorrow we'll be drinking piña coladas in the bar at the Hilton Hotel on Bristol, in Costa Mesa."

"I want you to remember that you have no pressure. If we don't leave tonight, we'll leave tomorrow. Let's not create problems by rushing."

Chopin smirked. "I think you're forgetting something. I'm the pilot, and it's my duty to take you guys safe and sound to our destination, and not to Hell."

I pointed at him. "Ah! I got you—you mentioned the Enemy!"

He dropped the wrench and laughed. "You always get me." He clasped his hands together and looked toward Heaven. "Please, God, forgive me."

"Well, I said, "it makes me feel better to see you're not losing your sense of humor."

Chopin pointed to himself. "Me, never, never—but you haven't told me yet how many passengers you plan to bring on this prototype."

"Put five seats, just in case Chandee decides to come with us."

Chandee smiled beautifully. "I think you have ESP, because you read my mind. After what happened yesterday, I think the intelligent thing would be to put some distance between this place and me. At least for a while. I know how beautiful California is currently. I believe that I will accept your offer and hospitality."

Chopin and took the pliers and yelled, "Whoo-hoo!" The pliers came down and nearly hit him in the back of the head.

"OK guys," I said, "I'm going back into the house, and check on our patient's condition. If you see Yaneba in a bad mood, today is the anniversary of the death of her family."

"Oh, God," Chandee said, "that is bad. Poor girl—I'll be extra careful with her today and give her all the love she deserves."

"Thank you. I will send Mayari back to help you guys."

Chandee said as I walked away, "Don't send Yaneba, OK? She's not normally in a good mood, so she won't be a good help to us today."

Chopin and I looked at each other and smiled. "What? What are you two smiling about?" She shook her head and said, "No, no—it's not what you're thinking." She pointed with the index finger of her right hand. "Let's go, let's go—we have a lot of work to do. You guys stop fooling around."

I said, "OK, *chinita cubanita*—we'll see you later this afternoon, flying from here to California."

"You have to give me some time to pack," she said.

"Remember what our friend, Chopin said. Very light, no more than 100 pounds, OK?"

"OK, OK," she laughed.

I looked at Rocco, tirelessly chasing the flamingos. "Hey, Rocco, I'm leaving." I turned and walked back to the cabin, followed by my loyal dog. Inside, Yaneba was sound asleep, and Mayari was sitting in a chair, nodding off.

He jumped up from the chair. "Oh, she fell asleep. I didn't want to leave her alone—I didn't mean to start falling asleep myself."

"It's OK. Where is Elizabeth?"

"She is in her room, sleeping. She took the last watch last night."

"Yes, I know. I practically made that watch with her to question the package."

Mayari smiled. "Do you need me for anything, or do you want me to back to help Chopin and Chandee?"

"Yes, go help Chopin—they need you there. I'm going to go take a nap. I got up at four a.m., and I hardly got any sleep. Don't hesitate to wake me if anyone needs anything."

"OK," he said, and left the cabin.

I looked around, found a blanket, and covered the sleeping Yaneba. I then went to my own room to get some more sleep. As I passed Abdul's room, I paused and opened the door to look in. He was sleeping deeply under the influence of the morphine. I continued to my room, entered, and sat down on the edge of my bed. I took off my boots and shirt but kept my pants and T-shirt on. I got into the comfortable, very expensive bed, a lot more relaxed with the tranquility in my mind that we would finally take off from that place in just a few hours without any further problems.

Several hours passed, and I felt something wet on my face. When I opened my eyes, I saw my dear friend Rocco was licking my face. Elizabeth was only a few feet away. She said, "Forgive me for waking you, but your friend Abdul wants to see you. It looks like you earned his trust and sympathy in a single interview. Congratulations."

I smiled, trying to rub the sleeping sand out of my eyes with my knuckles. "The first impression with anybody in life is the most decisive in all aspects." I sat up in the bed and began to dress. I had placed both pistols on the nightstand before I went to bed, but they were no longer there. They had been placed on the chest at the end of the bed. I looked questioningly at Elizabeth.

She smiled when she noticed that my weapons had moved. "Don't worry—I did it. I didn't want you to get confused like you did with that knife. I didn't want to have to run out of the room just because you pulled those guns on me."

"Oh, you think you disarmed me, eh? Look." I pulled up both pants legs, revealing two more concealed weapons there. I smiled mischievously. "Evidently you forgot the best part: I put those pistols on the nightstand to make an intruder assume that I'm disarmed. You had better be more careful when you approach someone you want to disarm. In this case, you don't have to worry, since I'm your friend."

Elizabeth nodded in agreement, smirking slightly. "I assure you that, next time, I will have that in my mind. This will never happen again."

"I know. But don't take it so seriously. I'll repeat it: I'm your friend. OK?"

"OK." She grinned back at me.

We left the room, followed by my Rocco. We entered the hallway and walked down to Abdul's room. On the way, we met Chandee, who joyfully said with a grin, "It works! It works! And *how* it works—this experimental airplane is *amazing*! It must cost a fortune—it's a combination of a helicopter and an airplane."

I said in surprise, "Have you tested it already? How long have I been sleeping?"

They both smiled mischievously. Elizabeth said, "You've been sleeping for seven hours."

"Oh, my God! I must have been very tired indeed!"

Elizabeth said, "We didn't want to wake you up. You were snoring so deeply that we decided to let you rest so that your mind is clear when we take off."

I looked at both of my watches, still disbelieving that I had been asleep for so long. "Thank you for being so considerate. Evidently, I needed it. I completely lost any perception of time with all this craziness. I don't even know which day I'm in right now." The two of them giggled. Apparently, there was something they didn't want me to know.

"Literally," they both said in unison.

"Hey!" I said. "What kind of conspiracy are you two brewing behind my back?"

Chandee said rapidly, "Oh, no—don't take it wrong. There's no conspiracy. You slept through lunch, but if you're hungry now, I advise you to eat something light.

Camila and Trabuto have prepared a tremendous farewell feast for us. I told them both that I'll be leaving with you guys for a while. I asked them for a simple dinner, but they wanted to make an elaborate meal for us. I tried to not only be on good terms with them, I also wanted to make sure they knew how they were going to answer if anyone questioned them about who was staying here." Chandee gave me a reassuring nod for emphasis. "At this point, I don't even know how much cover I still have to blow, after what happened yesterday. But I always do what you trained me to do, and you taught me to never close any door behind me, nor burn any bridges unless it's absolutely necessary."

I nodded in agreement. "Of course, but I'm going to tell you what O'Brien told me several times. I've taught many people how to do things, and they don't always follow it. But what you did was absolutely right, because you never know if you'll have to cross that bridge again in the future."

Chandee raised her right arm, looking at her watch. "Uh, oh—I have to leave. I've invited Padre Rodrigo to our dinner, and I told him I would pick him up early this afternoon so that he can take the Bronco with him when he goes back."

"An excellent idea. Just so you know, I already gave my sincere thanks to Padre Rodrigo and paid him the price he asked for that car, plus a little bonus. Tell him, for my part, to take that car as an extra bonus to fix the church in whatever way he needs."

Chandee grinned broadly. "Yes, yes—he's already told me you were very generous."

"I only wanted to let you know so that we keep the accounts clear and the communication between us open, for the good function of our team."

She was already at the door to Abdul's room. She pointed towards it as she spoke. "When you're finished with him, Chopin told me to let you know that he's waiting for you. He wants to give you a short ride in the new toy so that you will be giving the green light that everything is

OK and the time we'll be leaving, whenever you decide." She smiled broadly in satisfaction. "This time you will be the last, not the first, in breaking in the new toy. Chopin has already given the rest of us an incredible ride earlier, while you were sleeping."

I pointed at Elizabeth, my brows furrowed in surprise. "Everyone? You were supposed to not leave Abdul alone and keep your eyes on him all the time."

Elizabeth nodded guiltily. She shrugged. "Abdul is completely sedated, but even though I had just given him his medication at that moment, I asked Camila to stay with him until I got back. She did very well, even better than me. When I came back from the ride, she was sitting in the exact same position in that chair."

I smiled and patted her shoulder. "You guys—you just wanted to play in the new toy. Did you like the ride, Elizabeth?"

"Oh, my God—there's no word to describe it to you. All I can say is that in all my life, I've never seen anything so fascinating."

I spread my hands. "What's so fascinating? It's just a plane."

"Oh, no—I'm not spoiling it for you. When you get back, you tell me if it's just a plane."

"It sounds like great sex!" I said. They both nodded with huge grins. I couldn't help but smile and shake my head in confusion. Before I entered the room, I added, "I've always said that if sleeping weren't a physiological necessity, this might be the most absurd way to burn the valuable, short time we have on this earth." Both women smiled, and we entered the room.

As we entered the room, and the bed was empty. We exchanged glances with each other, but before we could say anything, the sound of a toilet flushing immediately caused us to relax. We thought for a fleeting second that Abdul had taken off, which would have been a complete disaster for our mission, especially given his current condition. The worst part was that if the man could negotiate with us, his supposed enemies, then what would he be able to do with his friends?

He opened the bathroom door and came out. I couldn't answer for Elizabeth, but my stomach turned in joy and complete release. The first thing that came out of my mouth was, "I have great news for you." He nodded slightly to avoid causing himself pain. His face remained serious. "This afternoon, after the sun sets, we will leave from here to California in our private plane, which is in the backyard waiting for us. As I promised, you will come with us." He started to smile, but he clutched at his throat as even that caused him pain. He sat down on the bed. "It looks like you're getting better and that wound is healing. Elizabeth told me that, since she's changed your bandages several times, the scars show no signs of infection and that you'll be well very soon. Of course, we must give thanks first to the antibiotic and second to Elizabeth, who has not left you alone for a single minute." I threw her a sly sidelong glance at that. "She kept your medication religiously on schedule, giving you those morphine pills in time to prevent you from suffering unnecessarily." He gave two thumbs up to signal he agreed with me.

He motioned to Elizabeth to give him the tablet. She handed it to him, and he wrote: "Thanks to all of you. First, Elizabeth for her dedication and care. And to you for being a man of integrity. I knew from the first time I met you that you were a true gentleman. Now I know I was not mistaken. You are a man of honor who would never betray me."

After I read it, I said, "Thank you for your beautiful description of me. I promise you that neither my friends nor I, despite our differences in ideology, will ever let you come to harm, unless you make a fool of me and break our commitments. If you make any kind of physical aggression against any innocent human being in front of me, I will not hesitate to take your life."

He rushed to take the tablet. "I'm an intellectual, a man of peace and God. My wife is a Christian. We have two sons, Abdul, Jr and Aryan, and a daughter, Paquita, in La

Guaira. They are the light of my life. I fell in with this organization by mistake, and by the time I realized what they were doing, I could not get out. I had become bin Laden's most trusted man, fluent in 12 languages and dialects, and so was able to move millions of dollars around the world for his al-Qaeda with little risk. I had no idea what that money was being used for until 9/11, when I saw with my own eyes on television those people jumping out of those buildings or burning alive in that inferno we created."

I read that. I looked at Abdul and could see a few genuine tears rolling down his cheeks. He ran his hand across his cheeks to try and stop them, and I realized how valuable he could be for our intelligence. He could be called a repentant terrorist, a man who embraced the wrong ideas without considering how those leaders were going to take him. For one reason or another, this ideology took away his faith in this act of indiscriminate violence. He realized for himself, perhaps, that the violence was not against any government or political system, nor even an ideology or religion, since in that horrible 9/11 terrorist act, people of all races and religions were killed who had only shown up for their daily job to put bread on their table.

I went to the side of his bed and opened my arms. "You're welcome, brother, to the broken heart and betrayed deception of political ideas. The pain in your writing made me remember the words of my father when he cried on my shoulder in the airport in Los Angeles, filled with pain and deception like you are, and so remorseful with the wrong ideology he had embraced to such a point that he called me, his golden son, a traitor. He didn't want to hear the truth of the political leaders in his revolution. All I was trying to do was warn him and was condemned by his silence for years because of my good intention."

As I remembered that whole episode, I was the one who had to contain my tears. I still carried that pain, even though he had apologized by weeping on my shoulder. I tried to quickly wipe them with the sleeve of my shirt.

Abdul, completely remorseful, broke down and cried like a child as he embraced me. Even Elizabeth started to weep as she witnessed the scene. After a few minutes, we all composed ourselves and sat down. I gave him a pat on the back. "We all make mistakes."

After this affectionate expression, he broke down once more. A few minutes passed, and we let that moment pass and recuperated ourselves. From my chair, I said, "I have one last question to ask you before I leave the room." He nodded and gestured for me to go ahead. "Remember, when you were in Cuba before 9/11 and we were supposed to get together? Unfortunately, our meeting had been frustrated when the local Havana police arrested me because, by a fluke, I didn't have my documents when I left the hotel." He nodded his recollection. "OK, my question is, did you possess at that time the complete information of the exact location of the terrorists, the exact time and place they would make this happen, and the ways they were going to tear down those buildings?"

He reached for the tablet again and began to write. He handed it to me. "No. No one had that information but bin Laden. The men assigned to the mission were not permitted to communicate between themselves. The targets weren't given until the last minute. Bin Laden didn't trust anyone and didn't want to waste the millions of dollars the operation cost. His heart is full of hatred. He told me the Yankees used him to get the Russians out of Afghanistan. After his rebel fighters finished and hundreds of his friends died, the CIA broke every single promise. Every one of the survivors were practically flushed down the toilet. From his point of view, the CIA are personal emissaries from the devil over the earth."

I digested that for a few seconds. "The CIA, first, is not the entire U.S. nation. The men responsible and leaders in the CIA are just a single group of bureaucrats. No one, not bin Laden or anyone else, can blame an entire nation for their broken promises. Not even the CIA or the entire organization; it's the individuals in charge of that entity. They're all temporary positions within the government of course. Nothing in this world, nothing, can justify what bin Laden did. It was the worst crime of the twenty-first century, and not against the USA or the CIA. That is a flimsy excuse. It was done against innocent people, defenseless people. It makes him the worst coward. At the same time, he earned for himself a position as the worst, most notorious criminal in the pages of history, putting himself to the same category as Hitler, Stalin, Mao Tse Tung, and others." I shook my head and smiled slightly. "Thank you very much for your information. You lifted a huge weight from my conscience. Now I understand that nothing would have been different if you and I had met at that time."

That missed meeting in Havana had bothered me so long, but Abdul had had no idea what was going to happen until the last minute, either. I felt much better about myself. I leaned over and returned the tablet to him. He hurriedly wrote out something more to show me before I left.

"Thank you for your generosity and care."

I smiled once more. "You're welcome. Try to rest, because we have a long trip to make."

Elizabeth gave him another dose of painkiller and antibiotic. As I left the room, I felt such a release from the nagging conscience which had plagued me.

CHAPTER 4: A GHOST PLANE FOR THE GHOST SPY

I double-timed it out of the room, anxious to cross the patio and finally see the prototype on the landing field.

"Oh, my God!" I said softly as I got close. Rocco ignored the beautiful aircraft to chase the flamingos. Elizabeth and Chandee were not exaggerating in the slightest. It looked like a spacecraft, but its beauty and design surpassed a Lamborghini or La Voiture Noire Bugatti; it was reminiscent of the Horten Aircraft GmbH.

Figure 13 Similar prototypes of escape planes

Flanked by Yaneba and Mayari, Chopin greeted me with a wide grin. He had a document in his hand. He shook it as I approached and said, "Somebody loves you so much and must really appreciate your work! Or perhaps they're gratifying you with over $1 million for every attempt on your life. I found this invoice inside the dashboard box. They must have forgotten it was there because they removed all the price tags everywhere else. But one always forgets something."

"They probably didn't do it with that intention, Chopin."

He shook his head. "Like the French say, ooh-la-la. With this I could retire and buy myself a private island." He gave me a rough pat on the shoulder and hugged me joyfully. "Come on, man, my greatest and best friend. Even James Bond doesn't get expensive toys like this."

I smiled and replied, "I think you're happier than anyone else. You'll be the one piloting it!"

"Hey, *claro, chico*—but you're going to be happier than me when I take you up for a few minutes in this plane. I'll tell you all the beautiful and unbelievable things this toy does. You'll be even happier when I tell you a small secret." He held a small device and pressed a button. The entire plane disappeared from sight.

"No!" I exclaimed. I walked up to touch where it had been in disbelief. As I touched the area where the plane had been, Chopin pressed the button; like a magic trick, the plane reappeared. My expression must have been incredulous, because everyone watching started to laugh.

Chopin pushed another button, and the wings of the plane retracted into the body of the craft.

He explained, "With this feature, you can park this plane in any normal car garage."

After demonstrating all the features, Chopin was grinning widely at my expression of surprised wonder. "Saved the best for last. Let's go for a little demonstration ride in our new toy."

"I cannot wait any longer! I'm bursting with curiosity—what is so great that these girls nearly had an orgasm? They didn't even want to tell me."

Chopin asked Mayari and Yaneba if they wanted to come along. They both accepted his invitation with the greatest enthusiasm. To my surprise, after we were seated, the plane, instead of taking off horizontally, lifted off vertically. It hovered for a second, then like a car which had shifted gears, swept forward at extremely high speed. It made no sound, just a buzzing like several bees flying together. To me, that brand new plane could be the 9th Wonder of the New World in technology. There was air conditioning or heater climate controls; it had even seat temperature controls. I didn't even feel the motion of flying forward—it felt like we were just floating through the air. The aerodynamic design made us feel like we were sitting in the air like a cottony cloud.

Chopin took us in a large circle, from the mountains to the coast, and so avoiding the town, just in case someone with a telescope was watching. After that, he showed us his skills as a pilot, even performing some barrel rolls, dive bombing runs, flying low to the ground, power climbing, and zig zag maneuvers.

We finished our ride and returned to base. Even as we had taken off, he landed us vertically. It was like we were in a UFO from deep space, landing on the Earth. As he landed, we could see through the windows Rocco continuing his harassment of the flamingos. By now, they looked more like they were playing with him, jumping only a short distance away and then returning to the spot he had chased them from, paying him scant attention.

Once we had landed on the concrete platform, Chopin turned off the engines. We deplaned with huge, satisfied smiles on our faces. We had been laughing and enjoying ourselves thoroughly the entire ride.

"Satisfied, Doctor?" Chopin asked me.

I gave him a military salute. "Aye, aye, Captain! Green light for departure, and congratulations on your great navigational skills as well as the fantastic work you managed in putting all those pieces together. Be ready—we will depart tonight. I'm going to take a shower, and then after the dinner—which Chandee tells me will be better than our welcoming dinner—we will all board and leave."

Chopin nodded. "There are supposed to be all kinds of surprise recipes. Camila and Trabuto will do everything in their power to impress you. They want all of us to have a good impression of them because they're thinking of getting out of Venezuela if this political system continues much longer."

"Well, well, well—there's no doubt that Chandee has done a tremendous job educating these people and opening their eyes to reality."

Chopin nodded. "Yes, she has, my great friend. Always remember there's no better way to communicate love and no other way to get to know the beast that lives close to you."

I nodded in agreement. I turned and made my way back to the cabin. I told the others, "I'll see you guys later in the cabin. I advise you to have all the luggage or whatever you want to take with you ready as soon as possible and already loaded into the plane. If anything unexpected happens, all we'll need to do is jump into our new toy and get out of here."

"Very well," Yaneba said. "I will make sure of that. Take your shower in peace and don't worry about anything."

I waved and headed to the cabin. "Come on, Rocco—they're going to drop an egg on your face!"

When I entered the cabin, Chandee had already returned with Padre Rodrigo. They both sat in the sitting room, deep in conversation. We exchanged greetings, and Padre Rodrigo asked, "How is your wound? Are you better?"

I smiled. "What wound, Father? Who has any memory of that?"

He smiled and shook his head. Chandee nodded and pointed to her chest. "Maybe you want to forget, but I will never forget that experience in my life."

I placed my left index finger to my lips for silence and gestured to them to lower their voices. I pointed to the door leading into the kitchen and then to my ear. Chandee smiled. "I already told you that you have absolutely nothing to worry about with those two."

I repeated my desire for them to lower their voices. I looked straight into her eyes and replied in a very soft voice, "I know you've told me many times, and I believe you, but there's no reason that they need to know about my wound. It doesn't bring us any benefit to give them that information, which maybe could be the only connection between all of us and that chopper crash. I remember O'Brien always tells me, 'Don't tell me what I don't need to know.' All we're doing is giving them information they could reveal if they are squeezed for it."

Chandee understood at once and her face grew serious. "I'm sorry. I understand you perfectly. We won't discuss that subject anymore but follow the rule we know is best: keep your mouth shut."

"Thank you for understanding."

She raised her right hand as she stood up. "You're welcome. Do you want a beer?"

I looked at the two sweaty glasses they had. "OK. I will be with you in a little while and have a beer with you guys before I take my shower."

She paused on her way to the door, turned, and looked at me in surprise. "Didn't you already take a shower this morning? When you met me, your hair was still wet."

"Yes, you're very observant, and yes, I took a shower. But I feel like I need to take another one. I want here to leave clean and not take any of the dirt of Venezuela into California. Besides, I have no idea when I'll have beautiful bathing facilities like you have here—I might be in the middle of the jungle next! Let's hope the next one, if God helps us, will be in California."

Chandee disappeared through the swinging doors. Padre Rodrigo said quickly, "You are one hundred percent correct in taking Chandee away from this country. She's in a great deal of danger—she's compromised her security more than she should. She's already spent a few years playing with fire. If we examine the developments over the last few days, this young Captain Augusto has his eyes right on Chandee's back. Last night, he came to the church and asked me all kind of questions about Chandee and all of you guys."

"What kind of questions?"

"Like how many of you there are, if I noticed if any of you was wounded, if I noticed anything suspicious. Of course, I tried to throw him off as best I could, but I'm not very good at lying. He might have noticed."

"Don't worry, Father. They're all professional liars and do it some much themselves that they can no longer distinguish the truth for themselves."

Padre Rodrigo looked at me humbly. "Of course, as a man of God, I tried to answer his questions as truthfully as I could without admitting anything that could harm you guys. Of course, I never saw any weapons here, because you guys were careful never to show any, so I didn't lie to him there. And when he asked me how you guys got here, and I told him that Chandee had of course mentioned to me over a week ago that she had some friends coming into Porla Mar and was picking them up at the Santiago Mariño Airport. She told me that they were friends of President Chavez and that you guys were visiting her. Even though I think he believed me and was calmer when he left, he came back this morning to the church with more questions. He wanted to know, when Chandee came in last night, if I had seen a man with a thick beard and a wound in the neck."

I leaned back and looked at him grimly. "Father, are you *sure* that he said a man wounded in the neck?"

"Yes, my son." His face showed absolute certainty. He pointed to where Augusto told him the man was supposed to have the wound. "He told me to keep my eyes open, because he wanted to know if I see anyone here, especially the man with the beard. He wants to know immediately—it's the only thing he needs to raid this place. He's been in contact with the President frequently, and because you haven't left here that much, there's nothing he can relay to Chavez. He said he would be back late this afternoon or tonight for more information."

I looked at him intensely in the eyes. "Padre Rodrigo—have you shared this information with Chandee?" He shook his head emphatically. "Why?"

He took his glasses off and shrugged noncommittally. "I'm sorry, but if I answer your question properly, I will betray my promise to Chandee."

"What?" I looked at him in wonder, without understanding. "What in Heaven's name is going on here?"

He looked at me compassionately, understanding my confusion. "I only can tell you one thing: please don't betray me. I can only tell you that, in all the time I've known Chandee, I have never, never seen her so happy as I've seen her now, with you guys around. I don't know if it's you in particular or what it is. I know she put so much effort into the dinner tonight, and I don't have the heart to break that beautiful, legitimate joy I saw in her face when she came to pick me up in the church."

I shook my head and said abruptly, "Father Rodrigo, I cannot understand whatever you promised her, but whatever it is, I ask you only one single question: is it more important than the lives of all of us, including hers? Do you not realize how irrational this sounds?"

At that moment, our conversation was interrupted by Chandee coming through the swinging doors with three beers and one glass in her hands. She had a big grin on her face. "Here's your beer with the sweaty glass from the freezer, and a new beer for both me and the Padre." She looked into my eyes, and looked at Padre Rodrigo's face, and asked, "What is going on? Why are you so serious on such a beautiful day? Considering today is our final day and our exit is completely assured."

"I'm sorry, Chandee," I said, "but things aren't how you are portraying them."

"What? Is there a problem?"

"Yes, we have a problem. And it's a big one."

Her eyes went wide in surprise. She asked, "What's happened, Julio Antonio?"

I glanced at Padre Rodrigo. "Father, do you want to tell her, or shall I?"

He looked at me in resignation. "Very well—I'll explain it to her later."

"No, Father—either you explain it to her now, or I will. Please make up your mind. I don't think we have too much time to waste. If what I have imagined is correct, we could be in great danger at any moment right now."

"OK, OK," Rodrigo said. He related to Chandee what he had just told me. When he finished, I was surprised to hear Chandee laugh.

She said, "I've already explained to you that that imbecile doesn't have the guts to move against me or any of you guys. Relax, take it easy, take your shower—just please don't take too much time. Camila just informed me that the dinner will be served in less than an hour. I put several bottles of the most expensive champagne I could find in Chavez's cellar to celebrate your success in your mission."

I raised both hands on high to stop her. "I have one question for you, Chandee. How in the hell—excuse me, Father—did you think that the young captain knew that the man with the thick beard has a bullet wound in the throat? Either he knows who took those shots at you guys, or he was one of the shooters. Either of these reasons means that it's possible that this individual, for a little while or even for a long time, has the trust and confidence of Chavez. He's trying to weave himself in to re-establish what he lost, and using those old, friendly connections, telling whatever lie comes into his mind, creating whatever that imbecile Chavez believes, and maybe, *maybe*, Chavez gave him the green light to discretely investigate the friends you have in his house, drinking his beer, and now his best champagne. I'm just exaggerating a little bit, Chandee, to get your attention so that you can figure it out. My last question for you is whether or not it worries you just a little bit, that maybe, just once, those suppositions from this old Lightning could possibly be the reality?"

Chandee smiled and shook her head and replied calmly, "From anyone else, yes. I will admit to you that I've been a little worried, and I've taken that into consideration. But from this cowardly, extorting low-life rat, I can assure you that he is not going to raise a finger as long as I'm here on this property to even get close to this cabin. He knows very well what I am capable of doing. Unless he got complete clearance from Chavez, which would be very solid evidence and proof for Chavez to act that way, he can investigate and suppose, but do nothing physical."

Her last words carried such assuredness and conviction that I could not argue with her. I could be wrong. My assumptions were, to a certain extent, baseless. "Well, let's hope that you prove me wrong. But this cowardly bootlicker of a tyrant, I believe, will try to do something tonight or tomorrow, and get some kind of backing from the President in order to prove to him his loyalty. He's desperate to come back once more into the inner circle."

Chandee's eyes got teary. "Please, I beg you—don't allow the suppositions you have of this coward run away with you and ruin this beautiful meal and farewell party. It's so special tonight, since we'll all return together to California."

"OK. But I want to ask you a little favor."

"Tell me, whatever you want, whatever it is, it won't be a problem."

Yaneba and Mayari entered the room at that moment. Mayari asked, "What is going on? I could hear you guys arguing from outside."

"No, no, *chico*—we're only exchanging opinions. You know how loud we Cubans can get when we get excited, especially when it's above ninety like it is today."

Everyone laughed at my joke. I turned to Chandee and asked, "Who has the key for the metal door communicating from the kitchen to the outside door? I checked it, and it's double locked."

"Nobody has a key. That door is only used by Chavez when he's here, to come in and out, because he doesn't want anyone to see him when he comes and leaves. I'll ask Camila, just in case."

"Please do. If she doesn't have the key, we'll have to make one."

"Very well." She got up and went into the kitchen.

Elizabeth came in from the living quarters section of the house, rubbing the sleep from her eyes. "What's going on, guys? Is there a problem?"

I took a deep breath. "I hope not, but I'm taking precautionary measures, just in case one of the suppositions I have in my head becomes a reality. I don't want to be a sitting duck for our enemies."

Chandee came back in through the swinging door with a huge grin. She held a key in her hand, which she held up for us all to see. Elizabeth said, "Oh, no—when you have bad suppositions in your mind, they always become a reality, because you are an unbridled optimist."

"Let's hope not this time, Elizabeth. Would you please take Father Rodrigo into the dining room? I don't want him to lie to Captain Augusto in response to any question posed to him. He cannot lie about what he doesn't know. Come back right away so that I can ask you something important."

"Very well," Elizabeth said. Without saying a word, the Padre picked up his beer and went out with Elizabeth.

Chandee handed me the key, and I put it in my pants pocket. "What are you thinking of doing?" she asked.

"Don't worry about it," I said. "The farewell dinner that you've prepared will not be spoiled by anyone." I patted her on the shoulder. "It's a simple thing, just ensuring our security. I'm merely taking some precautions, just in case, so we can get out of here without any problems."

"Very well," she said in a blend of resignation and pleasure.

I told Mayari. "Go and look for a key position for a sniper. That will be you. Monitor the bridge. You have to make sure that your exit from that key place will be unobserved. I don't want anyone sacrificing themselves. I want you to come back with us to California. Just go and explore to find that strategic position, then come back here. Dinner will be in one hour."

"More than enough time for me. I'll be back before then."

Elizabeth had returned. I asked her, "You already got Abdul all his medications?"

"No—it's still a little early."

"Forget about the old schedule. We're on a new one now. I'm going to take a shower. Make sure that he's gotten his meal, medications, everything, and then take him to the plane. I want him already sleeping there in comfort. I don't want to drag him at the last moment if there's a problem. Put him in the last seat, close to the tail of the plane."

"OK."

"Chopin, please help Elizabeth with the package."

"OK, no problem."

"Yaneba?"

"Yes?" She was already waiting for her assignment. "What do you want me to do?"

"You will be in charge of checking all the luggage for all of us. Make sure nothing is left in any of the rooms, not even a hair from you girls. When Mayari comes back, help Yaneba with the luggage. Bring it all to the plane—and repeating again, make sure not even a hair is in those restrooms. You are in charge of that."

"OK, no problem. My luggage and Chopin's are already in the plane."

"Very good. One less thing to worry about. I will go up there to make an exploration of the surrounding area. We'll see each other in one hour in the dining room. After dinner, we will all leave from here. OK?"

Everyone nodded agreement.

I went to my room and opened a box. I took out some packages wrapped in foil. I opened one of them and pulled out a backpack. I opened it and deposited the foil package inside. Out of the same box, I pulled out some plastic bags with different colored wires. I took several of them and put them in the backpack, as well. Then a remote detonator.

The loyal Rocco followed me as I left the cabin and went out to the wooden bridge. I gestured to Rocco to "stay" and "watch." I went under the bridge and looked for the main support posts of the bridge. I ripped open the foil package and pulled out an amount of plastic explosive. I placed them on the supports. I measured with my arms the length of the bridge to calculate the distance between the supports needed. At each support, I peeled off a portion of the plastique and stuck it to the post. I then inserted a couple of wires for the detonator. After I was done, I carefully ran all the wires and connected them to the central detonator which would receive my signal. I hid them by putting them as close to the underside of the bridge's surface, as far out of sight as possible.

Figure 14 Bridge at the entrance to the retreat

When I was finished, I turned on the detonator. Three small lights, a green, a yellow, and a red, started to glow. I pushed the button of the remote control for a test. There was a beeping sound. It was working perfectly. I left it on and adjusted the settings so only the green light remained on. "Ready for the party," I said to myself. "The music is ready, if it is requested."

I returned to the cabin, followed once more by Rocco. I saw Mayari, and we greeted each other.

He said, "I have a fantastic spot along the fence. There is a great exit to retreat down without any harm to myself at all."

"That is the way I like it. Always have a secure exit."

Mayari went to find Yaneba. I went back to my room and took a short shower. My instincts told me we should already have left, many hours ago, and forgotten about the dinner. But I didn't want to spoil it for Chandee and break her heart. Like the Padre had observed, she was so happy and enthusiastic about it that, even against my instincts, I acquiesced. I could not understand why she was putting so much emphasis on it when she was probably never returning to this place. There was a very strong possibility that she would never again see Camila or Trabuto.

But in the end, it was the least I could do for Chandee. She not only saved our lives and created a major problem for herself, but also, thanks to her, we did not have to abort the mission. So far, we were nearly at the end of it with absolute success. I smiled and told myself that if Captain Augusto moved a foot against us to get some brownie points with his dictator, I would move both of my feet to be ready for him. I would play Jamba Rhapsody Number One, the music that will play at his funeral.

I got dressed, still lost in thought, and still worried. I went straight to the formal dining room to meet my friends. I looked first at one watch and then the other to corroborate the time. I was fifteen minutes early. As I approached the door to the dining room, I noticed something odd. Elizabeth was watching the door and stepped very quickly inside as soon as she saw me. She didn't wave or greet me in any way. It was very strange to me. I figured the food absolutely must be delicious, since she was so quick to get there. I smiled at that thought and went into the dining room.

I had quite the surprise. When I walked in, everyone was already there, and on a small, wheeled table was an enormous cake with candles on top. As they laughed, everyone sang "Happy Birthday," delighting in my genuine surprise. I looked at my watch and realized today was indeed my birthday. I will never, for the rest of my life, forget the mix of feelings that brought into my heart. I looked at Padre Rodrigo who was joining them in the song. I felt ashamed of my earlier harsh words, but smiled, my eyes moist with tears of gratitude and happiness. I looked over at Chandee, and then one by one at each of my friends, still feeling a mixture of surprise and joy. It is still difficult to express in words. The only way I could digest it was to go back into the past and realize the impact on my soul when I was thirteen to hear my father call me "traitor" when I attacked his cause, only to see the tears of sorrow and joy, years later, when I met him in the LAX airport, and his weeping as he asked for forgiveness for his harsh words to me. It was the only way I can describe the sense of guilt for my treatment of the priest and blend of gratitude and joy.

Figure 15 En Mi Cumpleaños, as Chandee sang to me

I went over and blew out the candles. Chandee murmured in my ear, "Why are you crying?"

I looked at her with a smile and replied in a voice choked with emotion, "Those are tears of happiness."

Chandee gave me the strongest hug she had ever given me before. She again said in my ear, "I love you and always will until I die."

I nodded. I looked deeply into her eyes. "I know. Me, too. Thank you for this beautiful birthday present."

She smiled and stepped back to allow the others to embrace and congratulate me. After I got cheered by the entire assemblage, even Camila and Trabuto, I gave my great, sincere thanks for that incredible feast they worked so hard to prepare. We seated ourselves at that large table.

Chandee had not exaggerated. I understood why she said that the farewell meal would put the welcoming banquet to shame. The amount of exquisite food and its lavishness was simply over the top. There was a full suckling pig, roasted with an apple in its mouth. It was surrounded by tropical imported fruit. Six ducks à l'orange, lobster thermidor, beef Wellington, an immense fountain of shrimp in garlic sauce, a fricassee, lamb with mint, cilantro, and mushrooms, plantain bananas with Grand Marnier. All around us Camila and Trabuto poured very expensive French champagne continually. I raised my glass of the bubbling beverage to toast them.

"*Salud, amor, y pesetas*[6], and a lot of time to enjoy them. Let's cheer and give our most sincere thanks to Chandee for this most beautiful gift and effort. She has one of the most beautiful qualities any human being can have and the most terrific treasures any human being can offer: love and friendship. To you, and to all here present today, I wish health for the rest of your life."

They raised their glasses in toast. In unison, they replied, "*Amor, salud, y muchas pesetas*[7]. Hurrah, hurrah, Chandee!"

We ate until we were ready to burst. Chandee gave Camila and Trabuto instructions, who started to wrap the leftovers: some for us to take on our trip, some for themselves, and some for Padre Rodrigo. Chandee added, "But nothing at all left in the refrigerator. We have no idea how many months this house will be closed up."

They thanked Chandee. Padre Rodrigo joked, "You want to make me fatter than I am?" He patted his paunch with both hands.

Everyone laughed, and Chandee said, "Father you need a few more pounds to be promoted to bishop!"

"No, no, no, my daughter. No more pounds for me, and I don't want to be a bishop. The last one I saw isn't walking any more—he's rolling like the wheels on a car!"

We all laughed at the Father's joke. Mayari casually saluted me, grabbed his AK and slung it over his shoulder. "I'm done. I'm going to go cover the exit."

"OK. We'll see each other in a little while on board the plane." I excused myself and went out to the sitting room. I opened the briefcase full of money. I took a wrapped bundle of $10,000. I went into the kitchen through the

---

[6] Health, love, and money

[7] Love, health, and lots of money

dining room. With the exception of Mayari, everyone was still there, finishing their champagne and dessert while Camila and Trabuto finished packing our food for the trip in a couple of coolers filled with dry ice.

"Father," I said, "I want to ask you a little favor."

He smiled. "Of course, what do you need my son? I'm here to serve you. You guys have become my favorite servants of God."

"The Ford Bronco—if you have no other objection, when you take Camila and Trabuto home, please leave it with them. I know many people in this town probably need a car like that, but I don't see anyone so far in the short time we've spent here that deserve it better than they do."

He nodded. "I agree wholeheartedly, and I can assure you this is not a favor; it's an absolute pleasure. These are very, very good people, some of my favorite people."

Camila could not control a couple of tears as she held a hand to her face in disbelief. Trabuto came over and enthusiastically pumped my hand before giving me a hug. "Thank you," he said, "Thank you, Doctor."

Camila recovered and came over to hug me in gratitude. I said, "Wait a minute, there's something more I want to share with you." I put the bundle of money on the edge of the table and unwrapped it. Without counting it out, I split it into two stacks as equally as I could, measuring the levels against each other. I handed one stack to Camila. "Please, when you need bolivars, don't exchange it yourself. Have Padre Rodrigo do it for you; in this country, you could get into trouble for having dollars unless you can justify where you got them."

"OK, OK," she said. "I understand. The government is very meticulous with that. Thank you very much."

As she took the money, she handed it to her husband. She hugged me again. "God bless you, my son." She turned to everyone else and said to Chandee, "God bless you on your trip. Thank you, everyone."

"Thank *you*," we replied, "for your attention."

I handed the other stack to Rodrigo. "Will you please give this to the people that you know for a fact are the neediest in town?"

He nodded. "I will do what you ask. Thank you, my son. I wish and I pray that God multiplies this for you."

"God already did that, Father. Thank you anyway. Believe me—just asking God for peace and tranquility for everyone with me. When you go back to the church tonight, please light a couple of candles to Jesus Christ so that He protects on our trip and keeps us out of danger. I want to get back to California in one piece."

"Yes, I will do that for you."

Chandee smiled, showing her beautiful teeth. She stood up. "Thanks to you, as well, for your generosity, and allowing us the time, even though you thought it was putting us at risk to enjoy this beautiful meal that so much time and work went into preparing. And thanks especially to Camila and Trabuto for their hard work and for giving you this surprise on your birthday. I don't want to stop it for that cowardly, unhappy captain. But I'm sorry for holding you here later than you wanted to be today."

"No, no—don't feel that way. I'm the one feeling guilty. I had no idea what you had in mind. I almost spoiled this beautiful dinner and that magnificent surprise. Thank God that you convinced me, and I thank you for that. I had the happiest birthday I've ever had in my life."

Chandee interrupted the flow of gratitude. "I believe we've delayed enough." She was no longer smiling and was a little nervous. "We should cut this short and get out of here as soon as possible."

"Everything is already packed," Camila said. "The coolers are ready to take to the plane, and the rest we take with us."

Chandee hugged them and the priest. "I'll walk you to the door. I will maintain contact with you guys so that we keep communications open. You can keep me in the loop as to whatever happens here after we leave. Padre Rodrigo will take you guys home."

Rodrigo smiled and shook his head. "No." He turned to Camila and Trabuto as everyone looked at him curiously. "They will be taking me back to the church. Remember? The Bronco belongs to them." He took the keys out of his pocket and handed them to Camila.

We smiled at his intentional joke to Chandee. Chandee hugged him and said, "Well, Father, to you I say the same: keep communications open, so that they don't take us by surprise."

We got up from our chairs. We waved farewell to those who had been aiding us so well and loyally. They were now our friends, as well. After they left, I asked Yaneba, "Is something worrying you?"

She grimaced unhappily. "Maybe the same that worried you."

I smiled and replied as she took another sip of champagne. "You don't look very much in a rush. If you have my same worries, you know how to hide them very well."

She smiled at that. "Yes—I also learned that from you."

"You guys always drop my own words in my face. Well, well—let's not abuse our luck. I'm going to take the briefcase to the plane and make sure it's secured there. Please tell somebody to help you to bring those coolers of food to the plane as soon as you finish your champagne. Not the bottle, just whatever is left in your glass."

They acknowledged my directions, and I left the dining room, briefcase in hand and the loyal Rocco at my heels. I went out the front door of the cabin. I met Chandee on her way back from saying goodbye to our friends. I could see from the door the gates closing once more and the rear lights of the Bronco driving away. Chandee asked, "Is everyone already on the plane?"

I smiled. "You just left the dining room. Why are you so nervous?"

"I'll tell you later on the plane. Let me rush our friends. We have to leave here as soon as possible."

I raised an eyebrow. I didn't understand what had changed so abruptly for Chandee to go from calm to agitated. I assumed at that moment that Padre Rodrigo had told her something on the way out that he had not shared with me.

I continued walking. As I crossed the landing field, I went to the plane and snapped the handcuffs on one of the legs of the seat I would be occupying and shoved the briefcase under my seat.

As I walked back, I could hear isolated shots. First, individual shots, like from a rifle. Then possibly shots from the AK-47 of Mayari, defending our friends.

CHAPTER 5: MY TERRORIST LOSES HIS HEAD

I found out a little while later that Mayari had responded to the shooting. I practically jumped down the steps of the plane and ran the distance of the landing field to the patio with both pistols in hand. I went directly to where Mayari would be located. I could see a military truck blocking half of the bridge nearly on our side of it. Two soldiers were either wounded or dead hanging from the bridge's rails. A couple of soldiers had survived and were shooting, using the truck for cover. They were trapped there. The gate was closed; there was no way forward for them and going back would expose them to Mayari's fire. He was not letting them move. Every time one of them poked a head up, he let loose with a volley.

I approached him slowly, taking care not to let my shadow from the decorative floodlights along the trees and flower beds betray either my presence or movement. Very carefully, I moved closer to his position. I finally reached him. I signaled to him with a birdcall to identify myself. He replied with an owl's call. I came up to his side.

Figure 16 Soldiers approaching the bridge

"The soldiers came in that truck early. They shot towards the cabin's front window indiscriminately. When Chandee sent demands to the captain to surrender, he had orders to detain everyone here. They tried to ram the gate open with that truck. They hadn't counted on me being here. I got those two behind the truck in the leg, another two are dead, as well as the driver. The other two tried to jump into creek, where they probably broke their legs. Is anyone in the cabin hurt?"

"I don't know. I was in the plane when this whole thing started. I was just stowing the briefcase in a safe place. How much ammunition do you have?"

He opened his bulletproof vest to reveal two bandoliers of ammunition. "Very well. You have enough there to hold all night, and we won't need that. Maintain your position. I'll check on those in the cabin and get them to the plane. When everything is secure, I'll be back for you."

"Very well."

"OK. I'll see you in a while." I touched Rocco's head and gave him the signal to go. Rocco had already been trained for this type of situation, and he followed me in a crouch, dragging his belly in the dirt. Every now and then he would growl. I would pat him and say, "Good dog. Keep down and keep quiet."

I went around the cabin to the back, behind that small hill. I noticed that all the lights in the cabin were off. I felt better at that. I felt in my pants pocket for the key to Chavez's special door. I unlocked the top lock, then the bottom. Then, using my foot, I slowly opened the door. I saw no one inside. "Rocco, go. Check."

Rocco loped inside. I kept both pistols out and ready to fire. After a few seconds, I could hear Yaneba's voice.

"Guys, it's OK. It's Rocco. Julio Antonio must be very close behind him."

I had by this point moved up behind her. "I'm right here."

Yaneba spun around. She used her flashlight to light first her face, then mine. "You scared the *hell* out of me!"

Elizabeth and Chopin were close by, weapons at the ready. "Where is Chandee?"

Yaneba shone her light to a table in the corner of the kitchen. Chandee was seated there, sipping from a glass of champagne, a bottle by her side. She raised her right hand and said in a low voice, "Yaneba, could you please get that stupid flashlight out of my face?"

As she pulled it down, I could see a slight mark on her arm. "Are you OK?"

"Oh, it's superficial. A bullet grazed my skin. That filthy Captain Augusto tried to get me in the sitting room, but he shot and missed again. He came in that military truck, but it's stuck there now. He had a megaphone, yelling that he had a green light from President Chavez, and that we were to either surrender or be taken out by force. When I sent him to hell, he sent his soldiers to try and break the gate down. But they didn't count on the foresight of the Lightning, much less the good aim of Mayari. In a matter of a few seconds, he not only killed some of the soldiers, but he disabled the truck itself and shot out its tires."

I smiled. "OK. Elizabeth, go with Yaneba and Chopin. Wait for us on the plane. Chopin, start the engines right now, and have that plane ready to leave at any minute. Leave through the same door I came in, don't look back, and don't stop for anything until you are seated and fastened in onboard the plane. OK?"

Everyone nodded.

"You, Chandee—go and look for a white pillowcase and a broom."

She hesitated slightly but went into the garage to get what I had asked for. When she came back, I said, "Remember, stay away from any window. They could see you through the glass outside."

Chopin, and Yaneba had just stopped in the door.

"Are you sure you don't need any help?" Elizabeth asked.

"You'll help me by getting out of here."

"What are you going to do?"

"I'm giving that son of a bitch captain a lesson he'll never forget—if he lives through it. Go. We have no time to waste. He might be requesting reinforcements from his general headquarters, which might not be far away." "OK, OK." She left, followed by Chopin. Chandee asked me Elizabeth's same question.

"What do you have going on in that head now?"

"Rage—very much rage. But controlled. The only thing I want you to do is for you to go tell something to Captain H.P[8]. You won't let him see you so that you don't get in any danger. This guy clearly has something against you. Be sure to scream it at him."

She took a notepad from her pants pocket. "What do you want me to say?"

"Tell him that your boss is going to send him an emissary to negotiate with him. We'll stop firing while the negotiation lasts. We have millions of dollars, which will open his eyes. But he has to come onto the bridge before the gate. We won't open the gate; we'll talk through it. He must come unarmed. If he doesn't accept our conditions, we will burn the cabin and burn the money. This is not a point of negotiation. I don't think his dictator boss will be very happy to hear that his precious cabin has been burned."

---

[8] *Hijo de puta*, "son of a whore"

Chandee had been writing everything down. "I don't have to scream to him. I think I have a megaphone in the garage for the landing field equipment."

"Go. Don't waste any time. Those reinforcements could show up at any moment, which will make what I'm going to do more difficult."

She found the megaphone and turned off the floodlights. Pitch blackness descended. She came back with the bright orange bullhorn in her hand.

"You don't have anything else?" I asked her sardonically. "You may as well walk out there with a flashlight."

"I'll cover it with one of the kitchen towels."

She turned the megaphone on, and it made an electronic squeal. Rocco howled in protest. I lowered the volume of the speaker and handed it to Chandee. "Test it."

"One, two, three. Testing. Testing." She raised the volume until she was satisfied with the level. "Don't worry—I turned off the light sensor, so I can hide by one of the wooden pillars on the front porch. No one will see me—I'll be a ghost, like you."

"OK, Ms. Ghost. Go do your job. When you finish your negotiation and he agrees, I will go and talk to him. Put that horn down. Leave at once and wait for me on the plane. If he doesn't, well, I have something else for him. Do you understand?"

"Yes. Clearly." She smiled mischievously. Perhaps she was having fun imagining what I was going to do with that guy.

"Remember, these people are like bacteria that produce different symptoms: fever, vomit, and diarrhea. That is my diagnosis."

She went out onto the porch and hid behind one of the thick wooden columns. She repeated what I'd told her to say through the megaphone. She waited for a few minutes. The young captain took the bait.

"Very well," he called. "I accept and will meet whomever you send to the gate."

I knew that an offer of millions would work with someone like him. I could not help but smile as I rubbed my hands in immense satisfaction. "OK, Chandee. Retreat, and please take Rocco with you."

Chandee tried to take Rocco by the collar, but he resisted.

"Rocco, go with her," I commanded. He went with her, but then stopped. "Rocco! Go!"

She took him again by the collar again, and he obediently left with her.

I went over to Mayari's position. I had no problem, since the only light around was that cast by the truck's headlights. I gave him his instructions. I walked to the gate at the entry of the driveway. I could see the young captain slowly walking up, a white flag in his hand. I held up the broom, with the case from the pillow tied to it. Mine was higher. We both scanned our surroundings, looking for traps.

As soon as he was close to the truck, the two soldiers tried to join him. I yelled, "Get back behind that truck! Or else I will turn around and go back where I came from."

The captain made a sign, and they ducked back around the truck. "Stay where you are!" he commanded. "We'll rejoin when I've finished my business with this individual."

I stopped a few steps from the gate, and we were looking eye-to-eye through the wrought iron of the gate. We could see each other in the glow of the headlights, and I could see the shot-out tires.

Captain Augusto was a skinny youth, tanned slightly from the sun, wearing a moustache which reminded me of Hitler's. He looked at me with spite, a slight cut running across his face. He glanced at his cheap wristwatch. He said in a despotic manner, "You are the messenger? Tell your boss that he has perhaps ten or fifteen minutes. If you don't surrender, my reinforcements will be here, and we'll get you all by your asses, including that filthy Asian woman. We'll stick our feet up all your asses as you walk out of here."

I replied, "That makes you a filthy pig."

He was not used to someone confronting him, and he reached for his empty holster. "Watch out, watch out," I warned calmly. "Even the smallest gesture you make toward a weapon you might be hiding.... My best man has an AK-47 pointing at your head at this very moment."

He realized at that point that I was not a simple messenger.

"You see the holes in those tires? Imagine what it would do to your head."

Augusto swallowed nervously. He had no reply to that. I continued, "You told me that the Asian with us is a filthy woman. But according to her, you want to eat her. What does that make you? It makes you a filthy pig."

He gulped and tried to give me a mocking expression, but his demeanor changed from one of arrogance into one of fear and panic. He realized the vulnerable position he had placed himself in. He looked at me silently. He started to sweat profusely, all over his face. He was like a thermometer; he was very hot but encountered a block of ice opposite him.

"Do you believe in God?" I asked. He shrugged uncertainly. "You are a communist. An atheist. Is that not true?"

He swallowed, but this time found his voice. "Yes, I'm Marxist Leninist."

"Are all communists like you, trying to extort women to go to bed with them?" This was the decisive moment in our conversation. He understood that, by now, for certain that I wasn't just a messenger. "Why did you try to kill Chandee and her friends? Because she didn't let you blackmail her, or on orders from your master?"

He cleared his throat nervously. He tried to speak, but words failed him. He started tugging on his left ear. Finally, he replied, "The President doesn't want to know anything more about her. He says he considers it very, very dangerous for his government."

"*Claro, claro.* And of course, you haven't contributed with anything if your master, your President, is thinking that way. Isn't that true?" He started to reply but thought better of it. He looked indecisively into my eyes. I could see his nervousness was growing, especially with this last question. He could see now that I wasn't there to negotiate at all, but to dispense justice for his horrible conduct with Chandee. He started looking around, as if for an exit—typical behavior for a coward. He remained silent, filled with panic.

Finally, he yelled, "It makes no difference what you do to me now! You'll never get out of here alive, because my reinforcements will be here any minute. This is the only, I repeat, the only way out of this place!" He smiled. "Unless you guys have a plane on the patio." He laughed.

I smiled in response. "Oh—you must be a fortune teller."

He looked at me in confusion, then, seeing my own tranquil appearance and satisfied smile, he nodded in disbelief.

This time, with a more tense smile, I continued, "Yes." I held up the remote control. "Yes, you are exactly right." He realized that we must, indeed, have a way of escaping—he couldn't know that the control was actually for a detonator.

It might not have been right, but it gave me tremendous satisfaction, possibly on the border of mental insanity, to see the expression of this conniving murder's surprise as he understood that justice on this earth had finally seized him by the neck, and that I wasn't going to let him breath any longer. He had no other options left. I turned around and started to walk away. Over my shoulder, I yelled, "Burn on earth, you demon!"

He stayed by the gate, howling like a caged beast, his agony and desperation echoing as he realized that he was going to die that night. He turned and tried to run. I hooted to Mayari, who broke his position to come down and protect my back. I pressed the button on the control, and the bridge exploded in flames, illuminating the dark night and all its surroundings.

Another truck arrived, the reinforcements on the scene at last. They started to shoot at us, but Captain Augusto and his men had already been sent to face their judgment. We ran to get cover behind the hill by the landing field, the other truck cut off from crossing the bridge. Once we were out of the line of fire, we stopped and gave each other a high five. We walked, smiling, to the plane. Its engines were already running, waiting for takeoff. Chandee walked down the steps, waving both arms at us in joy at observing our approach.

We got into the plane. Chandee gave me a very strong hug and kissed me on each cheek. We greeted everyone, and I stored my weapons in the pouches along the wall beneath the window. We fastened our seatbelts. The hydraulic system raised the ladder, and once the vertical takeoff and been achieved, we streaked off in silent flight. It seemed like we floated through the white clouds.

Elizabeth was seated next to me. I asked, "How is our patient?"

"Sleeping like a repentant devil."

I grinned in response and leaned my seat back. Fully content, I focused on enjoying the interior design of this advanced aeronautic technology and the most exquisite detail I had ever seen in any plane.

I don't know exactly how much time had passed. All the stress I had endured the previous days combined with the comfortable temperature the air conditioner provided and the comfort of the seat caused me to drop off. What awoke me were the unceasing squeal of emergency sirens.

We were right behind the pilot's seats, Chopin and Elizabeth once more seated up there. Chopin yelled desperately, "Mayday, Mayday, we're going down! Give them these coordinates!" He relayed the coordinates of the coming forced landing on the Yucatan Peninsula to Elizabeth.

"What happened, brother?!" I yelled up.

"Electrical storm! Both engines are fried!"

"Oh, my God!" I glanced at each of my friends' faces. I crossed myself and said quietly, "My worst nightmare—

please, Jesus, protect us." I put both hands behind my neck, tucked my head down between my knees, prepared for the worst, and prayed to God, hoping for the best.

Though the crash in the helicopter had seemed to be in slow motion, this one seemed to go in double speed. The impact was hard, sharp, with a frightening, moaning, shrieking noise in my ear. Everything went absolutely black.

Figure 17 Wreckage of the prototype

I had no idea how much time passed. The first thing I heard was running water, almost like a waterfall, and the voices of my friends as if from a distance, even though I could clearly hear every word. I was initially very happy, since everyone was safe. I could even hear Rocco's barking, and so knew he also was safe. I thought that it was a miracle that everyone had survived. It shook me with wonder and consternation. Even though I could hear what they were saying, I could not comprehend it. I could hear Chandee, Yaneba, and Elizabeth sniffling as they spoke with Mayari and Chopin.

Gradually I began to make sense out of the words. "We've lost not only a great teacher but a great friend," Chandee was saying. "This is a great tragedy for us. Who is going to be our leader now?"

I realized what was going on as I listened to their despairing confused conversation. I tried to open my eyes, but I could not. I wanted to scream to them that I was all right, but everything continued dark, and I was unable to speak. I thought I was in a nightmare. I tried to move my arms and legs, but they wouldn't respond. I continued to listen to their conversation, which was all I could do at the moment.

"It's not just the tragedy of the loss of our friend, but also this plane," said Chopin. "It's something that I've never seen in my life and probably will never see again."

I wanted to smile at that, to hear him mourning the plane as much as me.

Mayari asked, "Who has the duty of breaking the news to his family?"

My adrenaline surged, and I realized something very serious was wrong with me. I could not move at all, and a cold feeling swept my body, starting at my head and right on down to my feet. It occurred to me that all I was feeling presently could be a part of the dying process. After all the times I had cheated her and made fun of her, now at last she was winning, as she always did. She must be laughing at me right now, and probably kept me in that limbo state of semi-consciousness to hear my friends lamenting me before bringing me the news that I no longer belonged in the world of the living.

Yaneba said, "What an irony that the terrorist ended up decapitated. Like the Bible says, 'Whoever lives by the sword will die by it.' Maybe that was God sending him a little message, since that's what they've been doing to so many people all over the world."

Mayari said, "Ah, please! Don't believe that—if I hadn't ducked, I would have lost my head, too!"

Yaneba replied, "And who do you think might have made you bend forward so quickly, you moron?"

Mayari answered, "Hm, now that you mention it, I did feel a hand pushing me forward. I knew it couldn't be my best buddy in the world, because he was up front, not behind me like he had been when he took off. By the way, what are we going to do with this terrorist's body before the rescue team shows up?"

Yaneba was emotional as always and said curtly, "Burn it! He never meant anything to us, and he deserves nothing better. We'll have more space in the chopper for the body of our friend, Julio Antonio."

For a second time, the cold sensation swept through my body, again from head to toe. I wanted to scream out that I was alive and ask what was wrong with them. But nothing came out of my lips. I questioned my nightmare state once more. It was possible that my day had come, and that I was dying. Perhaps one hears everything but cannot see or communicate. It was a horrible thing, and I imagined what the people burned in the Nazi ovens must have gone through.

The third wave of coldness swept me, but this time it continued in my face. I could hear the barking of Rocco and I felt a strange sensation, much like the first crash with the chopper.

I suddenly heard Yaneba, Elizabeth, and Chandee yelling at Rocco. "No, Rocco—leave him in peace!"

I felt like I was in an aircraft with turbulence, getting bumpier and bumpier. I felt a splash; then, suddenly, I could not breathe. In this commotion, I managed to open my eyes. I was lying in a pond full of water, which flowed from a small river. I looked up towards the bank of the river and saw a waterfall, which fed the pond we were in. The three women were yelling at Rocco and beginning to take their pants off in order to jump into the water to retrieve my body. I moved and saw Rocco holding my head above the water by the collar of my shirt. When I moved, he let me go. I felt like I was awakening from a deep sleep, and yet I started to breathe deeply and coughed up some water. I patted his head in a loving gesture of gratitude.

"Thank you, Rocco," I said. He licked my face enthusiastically, overjoyed to see me conscious once more.

I started to swim towards the women, who were now looking at me in complete awe. To them, it must look like

I had been resurrected. By then, Chopin and Mayari had joined them, both in complete shock.

Chopin took a step back. "How is this possible? You've been dead for over two hours!"

I could not believe what they told me. Each of them stepped back. The only one dancing around me for joy was Rocco, who could not contain his happiness. Yaneba grabbed her medallion, kissed it, and got on her knees to pray. "Thank you, Lord, for bringing him back to us." They crossed themselves, while I remained in confusion, still trying to piece everything together.

Chandee came over to me and squeezed my shoulder. "What is wrong with you?" I asked her.

"I just want to make sure you're flesh and blood, and not a ghost." She shook her head. "I have no doubt at all that God has something special planned for you on this Earth. It has to be so important that no one else can do it, and that's why you're still alive."

Yaneba came over, tears in her eyes, and looked into my face. "We thought you were dead! You weren't breathing, and you had no pulse at all." She touched Rocco's head and smiled. "The only one that Death could not fool was Rocco."

He wagged his tail at the mention of his name.

"I covered your body with a blanket almost ten times. Every time I turned and left, he would remove the blanket and uncover you. I came back, and scolded him for being a bad dog, and he continued to do it. I finally gave up on it; it was clear that he didn't want you covered. One of the last times I sat and watched to see what he did. He pulled the blanket completely off your feet and licked your face. He went to the pond, drank some water, and jumped into it, after swimming around for a bit, he would come back close to you, and shook himself out, spraying you with water. He must have been trying to wake you up, because you were soaking wet each time he did it."

I put my hand to my forehead. "Oh, my God! In my semiconscious state, I could feel that cold sensation several times, but I could not open my eyes, even though I could hear you guys speaking the whole time."

Her eyes opened wide. "*The whole time?*"

"Yes. I heard everything." I looked at my dog lovingly. I touched his head. "There's no doubt in my mind that animals have the same feelings we have, but at a much higher level, more developed than we can ever dream. That is the reason I love this dog so much." I got down on my knees and petted him. He jumped into my arms, and we rolled around on the ground as I showed him my love as a reward. I hadn't done that since I was a kid with the dog I had back then.

Yaneba had waited patiently until I finished with Rocco. I stood up, and she opened her arms with a pouting expression. "I don't deserve a big hug like that and a roll in the grass?"

I gave her a big hug. "You deserve both a big hug and a big kiss." I planted one on her cheek.

Elizabeth came up behind her. "Welcome back to the land of the living."

I shook my head with a smile. "Thank you, sweetheart, thank you."

Next was Chandee, her voice cracking with emotion, "I know for a fact that you cannot fail on me." I looked at her in surprise.

"Fail on you? What is that?"

"You are a man with only one word, and you invited me to go to California and be your guest. How could you break your promise in this absurd way?"

I laughed and gave her a big hug and kiss on the cheek. Chopin was next in line. "Man! When I saw you on the floor unconscious, checked you several times, put my ear on your chest, and saw that you weren't breathing and had no pulse, kicked you in the face without a response—"

I interrupted him, "Oh, really? I'm going to get back to you on that later, OK?"

He playfully slapped my chest with the back of his hand. "You broke my heart, man!" His eyes were moist with tears, betraying the depth of his emotion.

"Yeah," I said to play around with him some more, "but more so that beautiful plane!"

"What?!"

"Yeah, I could hear everything."

He looked to the others for support, and said, "How can you say that, brother? I said nothing!"

"Yeah, brother—like you call me all the time. I heard you cry for me, but you cried more for the plane."

He turned to the others, who nodded. "No, no—that's not fair!"

Yaneba said, "Yes, Chopin—it's true."

Chopin said indignantly, "No, this is a falsehood, and a defamation of character!"

We could not hold it any longer and burst out laughing at his serious outrage. "Oh! You guys!"

Mayari slapped him on the back. "Got you!"

He turned and walked toward the wreckage. When he came back, we were still laughing. We didn't notice that he held something behind his back. When he got close to the women, who were sobbing with laughter, he pulled out the head of the terrorist. They screamed and ran off, Chopin ran after them, thrusting the head before him. Instinctively, they ran in three different directions. Yaneba was the first to recover from her surprise.

"You want me to kill him again?"

Chopin raised the head up. "OK. Go for it."

"Hold your hand up higher. I don't want to hit you, and if there's any life left in him, I will give him the coup de grace." She cocked the pistol in preparation of firing.

I yelled, "No! What are you doing? Are you crazy?" I stood between them, both hands held high. I went over to Chopin. It was clear I was no longer joking, and everyone was taken by surprise. Yaneba lowered her pistol as she watched me snatch the head from Chopin, clearly unhappy. "A joke is a joke, guys—but this is not a joke. It's part of our work. Elizabeth, please go and see if the coolers

Camila sent with us are broken. If they are intact, bring them over. With the dry ice. I will explain to you the importance of preserving not only this head, but also his hands."

I turned to Chandee. "Please, look for the first aid kit in Elizabeth's luggage. All the surgical instruments are in those. We have to cut Abdul's hands off and ice them with his head to preserve his fingerprints." Chandee grimaced in disgust. "We need this in order to validate all the information I obtained from this man. Maybe the next information our technicians in our labs can obtain from his brain, if we can preserve it in good condition—at least until we get to Corona del Mar in Orange County."

They looked at me in confusion.

"I'll explain later, but we have the resources and very sophisticated technologies in our scientific facilities. We can take this to a different level, with ways that have already been tested and proven. We've used it before with the team of neurologists and scientists in our research labs. It might be difficult for some people to believe, but maintaining this brain in good condition, we can bring it to life, connect it to specialized computers, and the scientists can download all the memories in that brain like you would from a computer. Maybe it sounds like science fiction, but I have with my own eyes seen it done. I'm sorry to have been so rude, but when you started to use it for target practice, I thought we would be wasting all the information he had given to me but also had not yet given us. Our people will not only be able to corroborate what he told me but they could bring it to another level by finding what he kept from me."

Elizabeth yelled from the wreckage, "Both coolers are intact! Which do you want, the small one or the big one?"

"Bring both, please."

Mayari went to help Elizabeth, the smaller one on top of the larger. After we had emptied the little one of the cheeses and cold cuts, I smiled. "Chandee, I think Camila put food in here for the trip—I think she gave us food for a month!"

"I told her to clear the refrigerator. Apparently, that's exactly what she did!"

I continued with my work. I wrapped the head in the plastic bag and packed it in the smaller cooler with dry ice. I took more dry ice from the larger cooler to cover the head entirely. I took the surgical kit and when over to Abdul's body. I cut off his hands and went back to my friends to deposit them in the other cooler. I looked at my friends, who were watching my every move. "Well, let's hope that this slows down the process of decomposition. This is the best I can do under the circumstances and with the resources we currently have."

I got up from where I had been kneeling. I felt acute pain in my chest on the right side. I put my hand on my chest and balanced myself against Yaneba.

Full of worry, she asked, "Are you OK? What happened to you?"

I motioned to her to give me a minute. I was in such severe pain that I could not even speak. I held my ribs with my right arm over the pectoral area. Chandee had returned. She saw my condition.

"What happened to you?" she asked.

I made the same signal, the pain not yet having subsided. They could see I was perspiring heavily and my complexion was pale. Gradually, the pain became bearable, but it did not completely disappear. My hand over my ribs provided some relief. Helped by the pair of them, I took my shirt and T-shirt off. I could see a massive hematoma over the right side of my ribs which extended almost the entire way to my abdomen. I shook my head, touching the painful, tender area around the bruise. "I might have several fractured ribs."

I asked Chandee for a roll of very thick gauze from the kit, as well as a tube of antibiotic and one of anesthetic cream. I rubbed it over the affected area and wrapped it up. I could almost immediately feel the soothing of the cream, and the pain grew less. "I'm sorry, in all this commotion, I forgot to ask if you guys were all right."

By this time, Chopin and Mayari had come over, asking what is going on with me. "I probably have fractured ribs, which would explain my difficulties in breathing. "It looks like the only one hurt here is me, since none of you are even limping."

They smiled. Chopin replied, "I not only have several scratches all over my body, but I have intense muscle pain."

I handed him the anesthetic cream. "You should try this."

"OK, thank you, brother."

"I think we're all made of rubber, protected by God. Every time someone gets hurt, we bounce right back." I pointed at the bandage wrapped around my torso. "I cannot complain; it could be a lot worse."

I started to put my clothes back on, aided by Elizabeth, Chandee, and Yaneba. Chandee nodded. "Yes, yes—you more than anybody, after seeing you practically dead for nearly two hours. It could certainly be proof—and if you need it, look at that." She pointed at the cooler at our feet.

Chopin put a hand gently on my shoulder. "Our ride is already on the way. I gave them our exact position when we went down. They replied that I should look for a clean area where a chopper could land so they can pick us up. I also activated the beacon on the plane, as well as my personal GPS beacon." He took something out of his pocket, which looked similar to a TV remove. A green light flashed on it. "Doesn't matter how far away we move, they'll be able to find us."

I saw that the first motor of our plane had taken a hit. I reported "This is between the Yucatan Peninsula and the coast of Florida. I don't think we'll have to wait too many hours. The rescue team will show up in the Mexican skies quite soon. Good job, Chopin. Thank you for your good work." I patted him affectionally on the shoulder.

He smiled greatly. "I only do my work as best as I can, trying to make out of the chicken shit a chicken salad, brother. You deserve nothing less."

I smiled reassuringly. "There is no doubt in my mind that you did precisely that." I turned to the others. "Take only what you need and leave everything else behind. We need to move fast so that the choppers can find the right location without blowing their cover. The most important thing is the food—we cannot leave that behind. The absolute most important thing is to burn this wreckage. We cannot allow *anyone* to find even so much as a gauge from this plane. Every bit of metal must be melted down, every instrument must be burnt and smashed beyond all ability to reconstruct. Our extraction could be here in a few hours, but our expectations, however optimistic we can be, it could be a few days or a few weeks we get to spend in this jungle before they can rescue us. We have to thank God yet again for the plenty of food we have. It will probably be a lifesaver in these jungles." I raised my head and sniffed. "I can smell sea air. We must not be too far from the coast. Let's start to walk towards the ocean. With luck, we might find a suitable place for the chopper to land."

Chopin and Mayari took the coolers, tying the smaller one with the head and hands on the top, the larger one with the food between them. They walked behind us. Chopin went over to the wreckage. After a few moments, he said, "I found the beacon! We'll bring it with us."

We began our walk towards the coast. After a while, we could hear the singing of seagulls mixed with the other birds, telling us we were getting close to the coast. My right leg began to bother me.

I stopped for a few seconds and lifted my pants to see if I could see anything. It had started to swell. Chandee came up behind me. "Is anything wrong?"

"Yes, yes—looks like I hit my leg in the crash. In the rush of adrenaline in the rest of it, I never noticed. I'm starting to get some muscle spasms." I went over to a tree and used my knife to cut a thick branch away to fashion of rough cane to support me and avoid putting too much weight on it. The rest of the group caught up and voiced concern. "Let's go," I told them. "We want to make it to the ocean right away."

Chandee said, "Maybe the wound on your right knee opened up. I think it's worth it to stop and check that out."

I shook my head. "That's the first thing I checked, and the wound is in perfect condition. Almost healed, in fact. I assume it's muscular spasms, probably from some impact. I'll manage. Let's get to the coast. I assure you the first thing I will do is to find the exact origin of that pain."

Chandee shook her head in resignation. "OK. We're close, anyway. I can hear the seagulls."

Figure 18 The extraction point at the lagoon

Half an hour later, we saw the beautiful view of a very small cove between two massive rocks and waterfall which issued from them. The water was crystal clear, and in the sun, it looked transparent and blue. The fall fed into a small lake. It was very inviting to refresh oneself in. We stood there, fascinated by that small tropical paradise in the middle of the jungle. Because it was so far from civilization, it appeared to be virginal in this crazy world.

We climbed down the small hill with our packs on our shoulders, Mayari and Chopin still lugging the coolers between them. We sat down on some rocks surrounding the pond. It looked like Nature had specifically prepared this place for us to rest and revitalize our souls. Chandee, Elizabeth, and Yaneba removed all their clothes save for their underclothes and jumped into the pond. I sat on one of the rocks. After I took my boot and pants off, remaining in my shorts and T-shirt, I examined my leg. As I thought, the wound under my knee was nearly completely closed. But on my right foot, a massive hematoma surrounded the ankle. I breathed in relief as I moved my ankle. I gingerly touched the area around it and knew that it was not broken.

Chandee approached behind me. I hadn't even realized it. "Do you have a fracture?"

"No, no—maybe a little sprain."

She smiled. "I used to like you, I like you, and I will always like you, because you're an optimist."

"That is part of my character but thank you for noticing. Optimism will help you even heal your injuries quickly." I pointed at my head. "Healing starts here."

She smiled and nodded her head in agreement. "Yes, you're completely right. Are you hungry?"

"Yes," I replied, touching my belly.

"All right," she answered with a big smile. "Let's go and have a high-class picnic with Chavez's expensive champagne in this beautiful place. We have several bottles of it."

"That is why it's so heavy! You crazy women! But that champagne sounds like music to my ears. There's no better pain killer in the whole world, especially in combination with such delicious, exquisite food."

"Well—stay here, don't move. We'll prepare everything and bring it to you."

I smiled. "OK, OK. Thank you, love."

Chandee left to prepare. Elizabeth and Yaneba brought me the creams, and after applying them to my ankle, I wrapped it with the gauze. I put my sock and boot back on, and they helped me get dressed the rest of the way. I picked up my cane, and with dignified class, I walked to where the food was set out. I was very hungry, and the memory of that wonderful food we had eaten the night we'd left the cabin not only opened my appetite, it also opened my hopefulness.

After several hours, while we had been eating like kings and queens (and finishing four bottles of champagne), we lay in the shade of a vast mango tree. Some of the fruits were already ripe on the ground, so we had them for dessert. We were laughing and joking, and suddenly we could hear the rotors of a chopper in the air.

Chopin and Mayari ran to the beach. The sun was going down, so they shot flares into the air. The helicopter landed slowly on the beautiful sand of the beach. A little while later, we were resting on the comfortable seats of the helicopter, making our way to Florida.

As we flew above the puffy white clouds over the ocean, I was deep in thought about the ironies of life. This mysterious web of destiny encircled our lives, bringing our ancestry into the present in a very strange way. At the same time, it was taking us by the hand as if we were blind, guiding us back in time to whenever our ancestors lived and died. I thought about the tremendous coincidence, if it could be called so, that the repentant terrorist Abdul Hussein, bin Laden's right hand, would come to live and raise his family in the same coastal town of La Guaira, the capital of the Venezuelan state of Vargas, in which my great-great-great grandfather had lived and died in the 19th century, himself a victim of the same evil forces that we were fighting today in the 21st century. His name was Don

Francisco del Marmol, who was the governor of that prosperous Venezuelan town in 1818.

My mind was completely lost in abstraction as I watched the clouds pass by out the window, and it was in that frame of mind that I followed that web and transported myself to that coastal town in 1818.

CHAPTER 6: THE FIRST GENERATION

As I gazed out of the plane's window, I began to daydream, thinking of the history of my family and incorporating myself into it. Like a rainbow of light coming out of a woman's belly, multiple fetuses were holding hands and floating in the air. The last one was attached to the mother by the umbilical cord. They made a circle in the air moving slowly over my head, stretching the umbilical cord to the max. The one in front reached for my hand and pulled the others behind him. As he grabbed my hand, the last fetus' umbilical cord detached from the mother.

Immediately then the fetuses circled faster and faster and I felt I was sucked into the circle, moving a very high speed. We seemed to float out of the plane somehow, and I felt I was out in the sky and the plane was moving away from me in a different direction. Then the circle stretched out into a straight line. We moved like a comet back in time. I saw we were crossing through different eras and the cars were getting older and the dresses changed and then there were no more cars, just horses and wagons. I felt like they were carrying me. I was the last one in the line. Every time we crossed an era or decade, one of the fetuses dropped off, and it was as if they were staying in that time. They all looked identical, as if they had all multiplied from one.

Slowly they disappeared one by one, and slowly the speed reduced, and we reached the early 19th century. Suddenly I found myself alone. They had all disappeared. I began to turn slowly in circles again and I descended to a colonial house with enormous round columns. I could see a large, beautiful room with long curtains and a huge bed in the center. There were many people around and a man who was dressed in a military uniform. To my surprise, he looked exactly like me. With a big smile on his face, he held me in his arms and said he was very proud that I had red hair like his father and blue eyes like his mother. He said, "We shall call him Raymundo del Marmol in honor of his grandfather."

Everyone smiled and laughed and raised their glasses and said, "*En hora buena*[9]"

One chubby black lady, who was very kind looking with a lovely face, took me out of his arms and took me to the bed beside a lady who was resting there. She said, "OK, enough celebration and noise. We should let little Raymundo have his first meal with his mom and we should all get out of here and let her rest, which she needs very much."

The nice lady helped the white lady get her breast exposed and between the two of them placed me where I could feel the warm milk in my mouth. I fell asleep, warm and happy. March 14, 1803. This was the birth of Raymundo del Marmol, Margarita Island, Venezuela.

Figure 19 La Guaira, Venezuela

---

[9] In good time

Fifteen Years Later, 1818

Don Francisco del Marmol, the father of Raymundo, was the governor and representative of the Spanish crown in La Guaira in Venezuela. He watched his son, now fifteen years old and already in the military, practicing sword fighting with another young man. Several families were in the patio, guests of the Governor that waited to have lunch with him. It was a party. The servants brought food to the tables while the slaves put flowers on the tables and helped with the service. Don Francisco's wife came close to him. They both looked proudly at their son and then kissed.

The guests began to eat. There was roast chicken, corn, rice, black beans, fried bananas, and plates of tropical fruits. A small band played the music of the time. Everyone looked happy. The families had brought their children, and they were all running around the patio. The Governor, Francisco del Marmol, raised his glass and they all drank wine, laughed, and made toasts to Spain, to each other, and to the royal army. Beautiful peacocks walked in the gardens right on the beach. The waves came in and out, dancing in the sun. The breeze blew in from the ocean on this warm summer day and the beautiful green tropical trees moved with it as if they were dancing in harmony, celebrating the wonderful peace that all were enjoying.

Figure 20 Beach near the del Marmol hacienda

A few kilometers from there on the beach and not too far away from the colonial house two large rowboats with about twenty men in each docked on the beach. They joined another group of men with weapons who had been waiting for them. These men gave the others weapons, too. When everyone was armed, they began to whisper to each other, exchanging plans. The men who were waiting for the men from the boats looked like loyal soldiers to the Crown. The others looked more like rebels and civilians. Evidently they were in a conspiracy of some kind against the Spanish crown. They took the boats out of the water and hid them in the bushes away from the ocean so they could not be seen. Then they covered them up with branches. When they finished, they all got together to confirm their plans. Then they divided into two groups. One walked toward the del Marmol hacienda while the other went into the bushes. In this way they could attack the hacienda from both angles, front and back.

Back at the hacienda everyone was laughing and enjoying themselves, totally unaware of what was coming. In the patio the children were still playing and running around. The small group of soldiers which were guarding the hacienda and protecting the governor were also totally unaware of what was coming. There had never been any problem before, so they were completely at ease. The tranquility which had existed for so many years was about to end. The beautiful music the band played on the patio echoed over the ocean and could be heard far away. The pleasant black nanny was sitting around the children. She was much older now, of course, and had been with the family for many years. All the children were fond of her, and not only the visitors' children but the black children were all playing together. She had been telling the children tales. One of the tales was about a sultan who went around protecting the poor and the good people as he flew through the sky on a magic carpet. That is the reason the bad men could never get to him. He was able to fly away on his carpet and drop rocks on the bandits who then ran for their lives and left the good people alone. The children laughed at the story.

Figure 21 Spanish Colonial Army uniforms of that time

Raymundo walked close to the tree where the children and the black lady were and laughed with them. He had heard the same tale for many years before from her. He looked up and saw a ripe mango close to his shoulder. He raised his arm to get the mango and then began to clean it with the knife from his uniform. His little brother,

Francisco Jr., about seven years old, watched him doing this and got up from the group and extended his hand for a piece of the fruit. Raymundo ruffled his hair affectionately as if to say *you little devil* and cut a slice of the mango and gave it to him. Francisco Jr. smiled, and with very proper manners, bowed to him, thanked him, and then returned to his friends.

Raymundo cut another piece of the mango and looked towards the ocean. He saw a group of men with weapons running towards the patio. He did not understand what was happening, and before he could react, he heard the first shot. In slow motion, Raymundo turned around and saw the beautiful black nanny looking at him in surprise. She had been shot between the neck and the chest and a stream of blood was pouring out of her like a faucet. She touched herself, looked at her bloody hand, and realized what had happened. Then she fell forward onto her knees. She was still holding herself where the bullet had entered and was trying to control the flow of blood.

Time stood still for a few seconds and then he heard many more shots and saw people collapsing around him. A few shots hit the mango tree where he was standing. Then he reacted and ran close to the nanny. With tears in his eyes he asked her, "What happened?" as he tried to help her.

She looked at him as her life faded, and said, "Please, the children, the children, *patroncito*[10], please save them. *Por Dios, ellos son criaturas innocentes*[11]. Save them."

The good black slave died in Raymundo's arms. He looked at her lifeless body and tears rolled down his face. He was in shock as to what was happening. He was filled with anger and frustration. His mind recalled how when he was a little boy and fell down, she came to help him and with a big smile had wiped the scratches on his little knees, comforting him by saying "It's okay. Everything will be alright." Now he wished he could say to her, "It's okay.

---

[10] My dear boss

[11] For the love of God, they are innocent creatures

Everything will be alright." But he could not because he knew she was dead. He wiped his tears with the sleeve of his uniform jacket and the screaming of the children brought him back to reality. Slowly, lovingly, he let the good black nanny down on the grass and closed her eyes.

He stood up abruptly and pulled his sword from its sheath as the two rebel soldiers approached the children. With a strong swing he nearly severed the head from the neck of one of the soldiers. The other one tried to reload his musket but before he could do that Raymundo pushed his sword through the soldier's chest and pierced his heart. The man screamed in acute pain and fell to his knees. Raymundo pulled his sword out and the man fell dead on his face in the grass.

Raymundo heard more gunshots and felt the bullets whistling close to his head. He turned around and saw a group of rebel soldiers running towards him. They were still a distance away but coming fast. He realized he could not confront them as their numbers were far superior. He grabbed his little brother's hand and said to him and the other children, "Run to the forest! Save yourselves! These bad men have come to kill us all."

The children ran in all different directions screaming. As Raymundo ran with his brother, he heard more gunfire and two of the children that were running with them collapsed. He thought for a minute he should stop to help them but then he realized the soldiers were getting very close and he had to save his little brother. Practically dragging his little brother, he ran as fast as he could into the forest. The rebel soldiers separated, trying to catch the little children who were running for their lives.

After they had been running in the forest for a little while non-stop, little Francisco tripped and fell on the ground, causing Raymundo to fall as well. Both of them rolled on the ground. Raymundo recovered his footing and tried to help his little brother. Just then he saw one of the soldiers not too far away, crossing between the trees. He dropped down again and pulled his brother down next to him. "Shh!" he whispered. "Be quiet!" He pointed to the soldier.

The soldier came closer and closer, looking around the bushes but did not see them. They both stayed quiet and still in their hiding place. The soldier came very close to where they were hiding. He used his musket to move the bushes aside in order to look for them but he did not find them. When the soldier was only a few feet away from them he was ready to give up. He raised his musket from the bushes and turned away to leave. Just then, Francisco moved and stepped on a branch, making a small noise. The soldier heard the snap of the branch and turned around. He still didn't see anything. He was not sure what had heard but he began to search the bushes again with his musket.

He parted one of the bushes with his musket and saw both brothers' faces looking up at him. Like lightning, Raymundo jumped up and drove his sword up into the neck of the soldier. It penetrated from the front all the way through the back. As the sword went through his neck, he leaned back and fired his musket into the air. The shot went up into the trees and caused many birds to squawk and fly away. Raymundo pulled his sword out of the soldier's neck and was ready to stab again when he saw the man had dropped to his knees, holding his neck and desperately trying to breathe. He had dropped his musket and was dying. He knew his life was flying away out of the wound in his neck and he looked at Raymundo helplessly.

Francisco came out of his hiding place and walked over to Raymundo. He looked at the dying soldier with compassion and then looked at his brother, who still had his blood-covered sword in his hand. Raymundo was frozen in shock as he watched the man die. He was only fifteen years old, and in only a few hours he had killed three men.

Finally, the soldier collapsed completely, his last breath of air rattling out as he died. Francisco held his brother's hand and, hearing the voices of oncoming soldiers attracted by the shot, shook it to bring Raymundo back to the present. Raymundo stirred and, realizing the danger, began to run again, dragging his brother along with him. They found a little cave in one of the hills and squeezed into it. Raymundo covered the entrance with branches. They were coated with blood and dust and feared for their lives. The two brothers stayed in the cave and hid for many hours.

Every once in a while, they heard the screaming of women and children who had been caught in the forest by the rebel soldiers, begging for their lives. Then they heard isolated shots as the people were executed. The day waned and finally the sun went down. They heard no more voices or shots. It began to get dark, and Raymundo decided to leave their hiding place. Very carefully he began to walk towards the house to find out what had happened to his family.

The rebel soldiers had tied everyone up on the patio. Among all the guests and slaves, he saw his parents and his two sisters. They were tied in a long line behind a wagon where they had placed the rebel soldiers who were wounded. Everything they had stolen from the house—food, jewelry, anything of value—was already placed in the wagon as well, since they were preparing to burn the house.

As the caravan began to move out of the patio, the soldiers set fire to the house and stables—everything on the property. As they took the road to La Guaira, the two brothers followed at a safe distance in order to find out the destiny of their family. As they walked behind the caravan on the dusty road, Raymundo thought of how many times they had played there in peace and harmony with his friends; now, in just a few hours out of the blue, how things had changed to dramatically.

Raymundo and his little brother followed them in anguish, fearing the worst as they looked at the killers who had burned their birthplace to the ground with their torches, the place Raymundo's father had built with so much love and dedication. As the representative of the Spanish crown, no one had ever had any complaints about his father. Everyone loved him because he treated everybody with respect and dignity. Raymundo wondered why they were doing this not only to his father but also to his mother, who even the slaves adored because of her generosity and the way she treated everyone with love, respect, and equality. And why include his two sisters? What did they have to do with this? Tears rolled down his cheeks as he thought about his family.

He wiped his tears with the sleeve of his uniform jacket as he did not want his little brother to see him crying. He tightened his jaw in frustrated pain and shook his head as he thought to himself. He saw one of the rebels push his mother to make her walk faster. His mother tripped and fell onto the dusty road. He saw his sisters try to help her and his father filled with indignation over this. Another soldier kicked his father with his foot to make him get back in line. He kicked him so hard that he lost his balance and he, too, fell to the ground. All the soldiers laughed like it was amusing to see a man who had both hands tied behind his back and who could not defend himself still trying to defend his family. They displayed a complete lack of decency and respect.

Raymundo dropped his brother's hand and drew his sword. He took a few steps toward the caravan with the intention to stop the abuse of his family. He was so incensed that for a moment he forgot he was alone, only one against many. But his little brother was watching him and realized what he was going to do. Francisco stopped him by grabbing his hand. With a very sad face, he shook his head and said, "No, no—they will kill you, my brother." Raymundo turned and looked at his little brother, who continued, his voice rising, "What will I do if they kill you? I don't want to be alone."

Raymundo understood and reassured him, saying, "Shh, calm down. We don't want them to hear us." He lovingly caressed his brother's cheek. "Okay, don't worry. I understand."

Francisco nodded and remained silent. They continued behind the caravan towards La Guaira. When they arrived, they saw that the rebels had built a cage in the middle of the plaza to house the prisoners. They had used wooden poles with sharp points on top to prevent any escape. They began to put all the captives into the cage. Some of the people who were already in there were begging for food and water. The rebels ignored their pleas and told them to shut up or they would be killed before anyone else.

Every once in a while, they pulled out one of the prisoners, tied him or her to a wooden pole, and a firing squad shot that person dead. They did this throughout the night. Nearly every half hour they shot another prisoner. The brothers watched all night in fear, thinking that any minute their parents or one of their sisters would be next. They were on a low hill where they had a perfect view of the plaza where all of this was happening. It was dark and they were in the bushes where they were secure.

Raymundo looked down and saw his mother, his father, and his two sisters. They were close together in the cage comforting each other. Maria, one of his sisters, was seventeen years old, and was on the right of his mother, her arm around the mother's neck. Teresa, his other sister, nineteen years old, was on the other side, trying to calm their father, who was pacing up and down like a caged lion. Even though they were still very young, they maintained their dignity in front of the enemy. Others were begging for their lives and to be released, but his sisters were trying to assure their parents that all would be well.

Raymundo became aware that the night was nearly over, and that day would soon dawn. He said to his little brother, "Let's get out of here before they find us. We have to go and find a safe place where we can spend the day, feed ourselves, and rest." They went to a different part of town, far from where the rebels were. They walked for a little while until they were on the other side of town and found a little bucolic house with chickens and goats outside.

They walked onto the patio and the dogs started to bark at them. A black woman, about thirty-five years of age, wearing a white turban, and carrying a half-full bucket of milk in her hand, approached them from the other side of the yard where a cow was grazing. When she saw them, she put the bucket of milk on the ground and ran towards them with tears in her eyes. She said, "Oh, my God! That you, Lord. You are alive! Are you okay?"

Francisco said, "No, we're not. They have my father and mother and sisters in the cage. They killed Mama Supra and many other people. But Raymundo killed three of them!" he added proudly.

The lady, Tomasita, was an old friend of the family. She looked at Raymundo's bloody face and clothes, realizing what he had gone through. She hugged him. "Oh, my boy—I'm sorry that you had to go through that." She kissed his face lovingly. "Come on. Let's go inside. You need to wash yourselves, eat, and rest."

Francisco said, "Oh, yes, I am so hungry. I did not have any food all day yesterday and no breakfast today."

She smiled. "Don't worry. I am going to fry some eggs and give you a big jug of chocolate milk." Raymundo picked up the bucket of milk and they went into the little house. She took Raymundo to a small kitchen where there was a sink, gave him a clay bowl of water, some soap, and a towel. "Go ahead and clean up, my son." She grabbed another towel, wet it, and began to wash little Francisco's face. "We need to take off those dirty clothes. I am going to wash them for you."

Francisco protested, "I cannot take my clothes off—I have no more to put on."

She smiled. "Don't worry, my little boy. I will give you something to wrap yourself in and you can get some rest. When you wake up your clothes will be already washed, clean, and sparkling."

She noticed the dark circles under their eyes. They had not slept and had had no food or water for about thirty-six hours. She felt so sorry for them. Her son, Andre, who was sixteen years old but tall and muscular, came into the house with a basket of eggs. He greeted both the brothers and put the basket in the kitchen. Her ten-year-old daughter Tomasa came in with her brother. She began to prepare breakfast and said, "Mama, how many eggs shall I cook? Do you want me to warm up the chicken and beans from last night?"

Her mama said, "Yes, honey. They have not eaten since day before yesterday, and I know they are hungry. For them this will be lunch, dinner, and breakfast all in one!"

Francisco looked at the good lady while she was serving the food and asked with a sad expression, "Do you think they will kill my mother, father, and sisters?"

Tomasita tried to comfort him. "No, I don't think they will dare harm your family because your papa is the governor, and they know that. If they do anything to your family, they will be in big trouble with the Spanish Crown." She was not fully convinced herself of what she was saying.

Francisco was also not entirely convinced. "Do you believe what you are saying? They killed at least twenty people last night. They are killing everybody."

She put her hand on his head and said, "Let's pray to the Lord that it doesn't happen."

Tomasa came over to Francisco in silence and put her arm around his shoulder. She said very lovingly, "Don't worry, Francisco. They are going to be okay."

Raymundo was sitting at the table and said, "I am not going to let that happen. I am going to free them even if it costs me my own life." He spoke with such conviction that the good black lady felt chills.

She said, "Go ahead my son. Eat in peace. We are all going to help you free your family."

Andre stood up and looked under his bed. He pulled out a rolled-up blanket, place it on the bed, and unrolled it to reveal two muskets and a couple of hands full of ammunition. He said, "Don't worry. We have something here to defend ourselves with and to free your family."

His mother looked astonished. "Where did you get those?"

"The rebels gave them to me a few days ago. They told me there was going to be a revolution and that I was supposed to be a part of that. However, I changed my mind."

"But why *two* muskets? They should only have given one to you."

"The other is for my friend, Bernavete."

"Bernavete is involved in that, too?"

He looked at her and said, "Mother, everybody is involved. They told us we were going to be free from colonialist Spain and we were going to have the respect we deserved like any white man."

She stepped over to him and slapped him. "Stupid! The same white man who is telling you that is the same white man who will enslave you again! They don't send their own sons to do that. They are using you! But why did you change your mind? Why didn't you go with them?"

"Because they told me they were going to take Don Francisco prisoner. He is a good man. I didn't want to be a part of that. They will kill every Spanish representative in the country. I know you love the del Marmol family and I love you, Mom. I didn't want to be a part of anything where I could not look you in the eye afterwards because it broke your heart."

Tears welled in her eyes as she hugged him. "I'm sorry I slapped you, my son. You are a good boy. I love you, too. We are all in danger, then. When they realize you are not with them they will come and hunt you down because they will believe you are their enemy."

Raymundo wondered to himself as he listened, realizing that this had been going on for a long time, and yet his father and the authorities had no idea.

Andre looked at Raymundo as if he were reading his mind. "Don't worry. We are going to free your family from those people. We will not let them harm them. I know where your father's fishing boat is, and I will get my friend Bernavete to help me put it in the water. After we free your family, we can all take off in the boat to another country. There we will be able to get help from the Spanish authorities."

Raymundo smiled. "Thank you very much. You go and prepare the boat and see that there is enough food. I will check on my family."

Francisco said, "My brother, I will go with you to help you."

"No—you stay here until I get back. You can help us later."

Tomasita said, "My boy Raymundo—we will all help you, but you should rest now. You are very tired, and you will be able to think more clearly after you rest. I think you should stay here all day, and when the night comes, with your mind clear, we will think of a way to free your family. It is too dangerous to walk into town during the day. Anybody could recognize you and it could cost you your life. Think about it. If you are dead, you cannot be of any help to them."

Raymundo thought about what she had just said and realized the truth in her words. "Yes, you are right. You guys prepare the boat and have it ready to go. I will stay here with my brother and rest. Tonight, we will all sail to freedom."

Tomasita said, "Tomasa, you stay here with them. If anyone comes around, wake them up so that they can escape to the forest. Pretend to be playing in the front yard until I come back."

"Yes, mama." With a smile on her lips, she walked out onto the patio.

Tomasita and Andre said goodbye to the brothers, assuring them that they would return as soon as possible. Tomasita added, "Don't worry, it will be a while because the boat is quite a way from here, and we have to get it ready, stock all the food, and store all necessary items for the trip on board. We will probably not be back until night. Don't get anxious. We'll be back as soon as possible."

Raymundo walked them to the door. After they left, he turned to Francisco and said, "Let's go to bed. We need to rest." He was too late; Francisco had already fallen asleep at the table before he had even finished eating his food.

Raymundo walked over and shook him by the shoulder to wake him. "Come on. I will help you to bed. You cannot sleep here like this. You will have a terrible pain in your neck when you wake up."

Francisco was still half asleep and resisted. "Please, leave me alone. I'm too tired. I don't want to go anywhere."

Raymundo took him by the arm with compassion and pulled him up. He put the boy's arm around his shoulder and half carried him to bed. "You don't have to walk. Just hang on to me."

Francisco smiled and said nothing as he let Raymundo help him to bed. Raymundo took him to one of the small beds in one of the rooms and covered him with a sheet. He took off Francisco's shoes and then took off his own shoes. He lay down close to his brother, exhausted. He looked up at the roof of the house. It was made of palm branches and the walls were of palm trunks which had been cut in half. The floor was compacted dirt—no, cement. The whole house was very rustic, and he realized how differently these people lived compared to his family. In that moment he felt very bad and terribly sorry for the way these people had to live.

Everything had happened so fast that his head was whirling around like a tornado. At that moment he thought how great it was that Tomasita, who was a personal assistant to his mother, had not been in the house on the day all this had happened. That sparked some darker thoughts. Why was Tomasita not there that day? She was always there. She never missed a day, and that day had been a special one because of the party his father was throwing for important friends. His doubts increased, and he became suspicious. He began to wonder if she had known ahead of time what was going to happen. Had she only been putting on a show when she slapped her son in front of them and chastised him for being a part of the rebellion? Maybe she had not gone with her son after all to prepare the boat for their escape. Is it possible she had gone to tell the rebels where they were and that they would get captured while they slept?

He sat up abruptly in the bed. He thought they should get out of there just in case, in order to be safe. Through the window he could see little Tomasa swinging in a rustic swing made out of two long ropes and a piece of wood for a seat. It was hanging from a huge tree on the patio. Raymundo began to sweat. He got out of the bed and left the room. He went into the kitchen, grabbed the clay container, and filled it with water. He wrapped some of the food including a couple of pieces of bread that Francisco had left on the table in a rag. He took one of the muskets Andre had shown him and draped the strap of it over his shoulder. Then he picked up his still-sleeping brother, held him against his chest, and walked out of the back door of the house.

Francisco protested sleepily. Raymundo said, "Shh. Our enemies could be close. We have to get out of here!"

The little boy opened his eyes when he heard this. "Oh, no!"

Raymundo said, "Don't worry about it. I am going to take you to a secure place."

The back door that they used was the one that was normally used by the people who lived there to go to the outhouse, which was about fifty feet from the house. Raymundo went straight to the outhouse with difficulty due to his arms full, carrying his brother, musket, water, and food. He was thinking they could hide in there. The door was hanging by a couple of pieces of goat skin, and it looked as if it would fall down any minute.

When Raymundo opened the door, he covered his nose immediately. The smell was overwhelming. Even half asleep, Francisco noticed it and said, "Oh, yuck!"

Realizing it would be better to confront the rebels than to stay there, Raymundo stepped back a couple of feet, allowing the door to close by itself of its own weight. He looked to his right and saw a small barn, perhaps a hen house. It was almost in ruins. Half of the roof was gone. He walked towards it. When he got close, he pushed what looked like was the door and went in.

From inside he could still see Tomasa swinging on the patio. He could also see the front and back of the house. He went under the boxes where the hens would lay their eggs and put his little brother down there to hide him. When his brother laid him down on the dry grass, Francisco in his half-awake state got comfortable and immediately fell sound asleep.

Raymundo sat down and put the rest of his load on the floor. He tried to make himself comfortable. He realized this was a safe place to rest, as he could see everything, but no one could see him. With that feeling of safety he laid back, thinking he did not want to walk all the way to the forest just now. He was very tired; besides, he knew if he saw anything critical happening it was not too far to run to the forest, where they would be safe. He had never felt as comfortable as he did in that dry grass. Looking up through the cracks in the little boxes, watching the hens laying and hatching their eggs, he felt safe. He fell into a deep sleep.

Meanwhile, on the other side of La Guaira, the man who was in charge of the rebels was in his small wooden military hut. He was of mixed race and was holding a document in his hand. He was dark-skinned, tall, and very muscular with straight hair. He ordered two of his men to take the Governor and two of his assistants out of the cage and have them begin to dig their own graves. He told his men to give them each a shovel and said, "By order of the Chief of the Revolution, Simon Boliyar, if the Spanish authorities do not release our prisoners by tonight, we will kill the Governor, his family, and everyone else. After we kill them, we are going to burn them. That way, they will not even be able to find the bodies and they will know without a doubt that we are at war." He screamed at his men as if he really was mad at the world. "Do it now! What the hell are you waiting for? Go and do what I tell you to do!"

I

Figure 22 Simon Bolivar, c. 1818

The two men rushed to get out of there. They had seen too many heads rolling and men hanging for minor offenses in the past few days of the revolution. The chief stood up from the rustic table where he was sitting and looked out the window to check on his men to make sure they were complying with his orders.

The men took the elder Francisco del Marmol and his two top assistants and pushed them violently, forcing them to walk a short distance from the cage, where they began to dig. The chief smiled from his window and muttered to himself, "Piece of shit Spaniard. Your position as Governor will not save your skin. You are not a big guy anymore. You are in my hands now."

Some of his men nearby wondered what he was saying but did not dare to ask him. Everyone was afraid of him. They wanted to keep their heads attached to their necks and so maintained their silence. The chief got a large cigar out of the pocket of his shirt. Two men rushed to offer him a light. After he lit the cigar and inhaled deeply, he exhaled the smoke in satisfaction as he watched his soldiers kick and abuse Francisco and his assistants, compelling them to do the job quickly.

He walked out of his cottage, closely followed by five of his soldiers. He went to where the Governor was digging. He stopped a few steps from them and asked sarcastically, "*Señor Gobernador*[12] Don Francisco del Marmol, how do you like our hospitality? If you do not feel comfortable or satisfied with your treatment, let me know. Don't hesitate to call me."

Francisco looked up to see who was speaking and where he was. His eyes met those of the chief; he recognized him immediately. He maintained his calm but spoke with indignation. "Porfirio! It had to be somebody like you behind all the atrocities committed in the past few hours. Only someone like you, so immoral and indecent, could have done this. Even as enemies in war, we don't treat each other so wickedly. I believe you are not only a disgrace to your revolution—or whatever you're representing—but you have also dishonored yourself."

Porfirio smiled cynically. "What are you going to do? Send me to jail for several years again?"

Francisco replied, "No. You are not going to jail this time, like you did for raping that little girl. This time mark my words, you are going to pay with your life. Killing these innocent people, including women and children who have not done a thing to anyone is only excusable to a sick mind like yours."

One of the soldiers close to Don Francisco struck him on the neck with the butt of his musket. Francisco fell onto the ground and the soldier began to kick him viciously on his shoulder, chest, back, and anywhere else he could. As he did so, he exclaimed, "You Spanish are all full of shit. You with your fancy words. You think you own the world and that you can control everybody. Your power is

---

12 Mister Governor

finished—now the Venezuelans will be free, and *we* will be the ones in control! You shut up, or we will send you to hell!" He then pointed the muzzle of his musket at Don Francisco's head.

Porfirio raised his hand. "Enough! This is not yet the moment. We might need this piece of shit until tonight to save the lives of our patriots that the Spanish have imprisoned."

The soldier obeyed Porfirio's command. Don Francisco started to get up, and said, "My superiors will never release those murderers that you call patriots. I will die with dignity and decency. You, however—what kind of legacy will you leave behind? You will die soon, and people will remember you only as murderers of innocent people and the rapists of young girls."

Porfirio raised his eyebrows, not liking what he heard. "If it was in my hands, I would have sent you to hell from the very beginning, the moment my men arrested you. Maybe I will still have that pleasure tonight if your government does not comply with our demands. It will be a great personal satisfaction to send you to hell where all Spaniards belong."

He turned around, very upset, and inhaled deeply from his cigar. He walked away furiously; Don Francisco had revealed in front of the men under his command the real reason he had been in jail—not for political reasons, but because he was a pedophile.

Like any revolution, people who had ill intent mingled freely with those whose motivations were purer. There were many opportunists, criminals, and those pursuing vendettas. There were also people who were resentful towards their social environment, their own limitations, and the unjust political rules they were subjected to. They were unable to receive a proper education, which limited them financially as well as socially. These people took part in the revolution.

However, there were also great patriots, men with dignity and decency. They were the ones who were looking for the liberation of their own country, looking to end the oppression of Spanish colonialists and to create a better system with equality for all, to make a better nation to live in. These men did not get involved in the revolution out of personal desires, whether for gain or revenge. These men were the only real patriots, who rebelled out of love for their nation.

The colonialists were only looking to suck the resources of the little nations in their power in order to get rich themselves. They cared not about their own people, let alone those in other nations. They imposed very high taxes and unjust laws which not only affected the natives but their own Spanish descendants who decided to live in those nations, looking for better opportunities and qualities of life.

Porfirio went back to his cottage, ranting and raving at his men. He told one of his assistants, "Double the guard around the governor. If he tries to escape, kill him immediately. I don't want any excuses."

The man looked at him fearfully. "Don't worry, my chief. If he tries to escape, he will die." He stepped out the door and repeated the order to the other soldiers guarding the men digging their common grave. There were still about ten prisoners left in the cage, who exchanged terrified looks, sensing that their own ends were near. Some of the soldiers formed up at once to create a doubled guard around Francisco.

Many hours passed, and the sun began to set. Tomasita returned to the little house with Andre and another young black man, about 18 years of age. When they came into the house, little Tomasa was very happy as she ran to her mother. "Mama! Mama! They left, they left!"

"What?!" Tomasita exclaimed.

"Yes, mama, they are gone. They left a long time ago. I came into the house for a drink of water and noticed they were already gone. I looked for them all over the place and I could not find them."

Tomasita stopped to think for a moment. "Where can they be?" She began to look around. As she walked, she asked Tomasa if she had checked even the hen house.

"Yes, mama, I looked everywhere. Maybe they went into the forest."

Tomasita thought about that for a moment. "Hmm. Bernavete, put that sack with the two muskets under the bed where the other two are."

When Bernavete came back, he said, "There was only one musket there." Everyone went into the bedroom to verify what Bernavete had reported. Tomasita grew worried when she saw that one of the guns was indeed missing.

"Oh, my God—I hope those kids don't do anything crazy. OK, you guys go and look in the mango tree field, while I check behind the outhouse. Come back in half an hour if you do not find them. I will meet you here. Don't take too long."

They divided to search as she directed. When she reached the outhouse, Tomasita pushed the door open to check that no one was there. She put her hand to her nose immediately and murmured, "Oh God, this is not an outhouse anymore! It's a slaughterhouse. We'll have to dig another clean hole."

She continued to look around on the left side of the outhouse. She noticed the tall grass was smashed down a bit, leading towards the chicken coop. It looked trampled, as if someone had walked there. She followed the tracks; even though it could have been an animal seeking to kill the chickens, she decided to investigate. When she got to the hen house, she noticed that the door was not completely closed, as if someone had walked inside in a rush and neglected to close it all the way. She followed the trail inside the coop and saw that it went out the back. She followed it to the back of the structure and saw footsteps in the grass under the boxes. She knelt down. At first, she didn't see anything, but on second glance saw the two brothers sound asleep under the boxes.

She grabbed Raymundo's foot and shook it to wake him up. She said softly, "Niño Raymundo, wake up, wake up. It will be dark soon."

Raymundo started up, fully awake. He groped around for his musket, and then noticed Tomasita. "Oh, oh! What happened, what happened?"

Tomasita smiled and tried to calm him down. "Nothing. Everything is OK, everything is fine. We've got two more muskets from Bernavete, and now maybe we can figure out how to free your family."

Raymundo looked at her smiling face and felt ashamed of himself for not trusting her. Still doubting slightly, he asked, "Why didn't you go to work yesterday? You missed the party. You never miss work—were you OK?"

Tomasita did not understand why he was questioning her about that at this moment. Finally, she said, "I lost my baby in a miscarriage. Your mom told me to stay home."

That hit Raymundo like a knife in his chest. He got out from under the hen boxes. "Please, forgive me."

"Forgive you for what?" she asked as she picked feathers out of his hair and clothes. "Why did you guys come in here to sleep? Did you hear a noise or something?"

Raymundo met her eyes and then bowed his head in shame. "I thought maybe you were going to hurt us. I thought you might go to the rebels." Tears streamed down his cheeks. "I am sorry. I was afraid that at any time rebels would show up at the door, and I decided to bring my little brother over here where I felt more secure and would be able to sleep."

She hugged him with motherly affection. "I would never hurt you or your brother, or anyone in your family. But thank you very much for being honest with me and thank God that you are okay. I feared the worst. I thought you had taken that musket to go and fight the rebels to try and free your family. I feared for your life."

Raymundo smiled a little bit. "For that I will need all you guys and all the help we can get. I have a plan. It might sound crazy, but it might just work. I will explain it to you in a little while when we get back to the house."

Little Francisco was stretching out under the boxes. Tomasita hugged him as well and began to pick the chicken feathers out of his hair and clothes. She smiled and said, "You crazy kids. You could have been sleeping comfortably in the house."

Francisco asked, "Yes, Raymundo—why did you bring me here?"

Raymundo answered, "I was afraid the rebels might have followed our tracks when we went into the house, so I felt we would be safer here."

Tomasita and Raymundo looked at each other and smiled, knowing that was not his real reason. The trio walked to the house, where Raymundo explained his plan to everyone over the next two hours.

At the end of all the planning, Andre asked, "Do you think the rebels are stupid enough to fall for this?"

Bernavete said, "Just figure it out for yourself. They gave me two muskets before. One was for me and one for you. They apparently did not remember because now they gave you two muskets: one for you and one for me! Tell me, don't you think they are stupid enough to fall for this?"

Andres nodded his head. "You have a point. As crazy as Raymundo's plan sounds, it might work, thanks to their stupidity."

Raymundo smiled. "Yes—they've already given us four muskets. This gives us the advantage of knowing they are either very stupid, or very disorganized. Either works in our favor."

Everyone laughed. Tomasita said, "Okay, let's eat before we leave. We can take all the food we can with us, since we may not be able to come back to the house after we do what we're planning. Andre, release the animals. Whatever animal is tied up or in the corral, let them go. That way, they will be free to survive. We should all eat as much as we can. If we die, at least we will die with our bellies full."

Tomasa and little Francisco looked at each other. "Who is going to die?" he asked.

"Nobody!" Tomasita said.

Raymundo shook his head. "Don't say 'nobody'—a lot of rebels will probably die!"

They ate and prepared all the things they were going to take with them. They put the things they were going to take with them in sacks. They took everything to a hiding place on the road to Guaira, covering the sacks with branches. They continued their walk into town, going to the same place Raymundo and his brother had hidden the day before. From there they had a clear view of the cage with the prisoners. They knelt down in the bushes, trying not to make any noise. They were so close they could hear the voices of the prisoners asking for water, bandages, or something to stop the bleeding of those relatives who had been shot. The soldiers ignored their pleas, knowing the prisoners were about to die shortly anyway.

Raymundo tried to locate his family. He could only spot his sisters and his mother. He kept looking for his father, starting to stand up as he forgot how close they were to the rebels. He whispered, "Tomasita, Father is not in that cage. I think they have killed him already."

Tomasita put her finger to her lips and placed her right hand on his shoulder. "Lower your voice" she whispered back. "They can hear you. We are too close—in the night, your voice travels further." She pushed him down with her right hand, while with her left she pointed to an area a little way from the cage. There were three men digging a ditch was already so deep you could only see their heads when they stood up to throw the shovelfuls of dirt out of the ditch in the dim light of the torches.

When Raymundo saw this, he felt better, as his heart started to beat again in the hope that one of the men was his father. As he tried to discern whether one of them was Don Francisco, he saw a large, tall man smoking a cigar come close to the ditch. He was surrounded by several guards. He was giving orders to the soldiers guarding the ditch. In a few seconds, they pulled the men out of the ditch, tied their hands behind them, and lined them up in front of the ditch. They took away the men's shovels. A few other soldiers brought some wood and started a fire inside the ditch. Then the soldiers began to form up as a firing squad in groups of three. Each group lined up one behind another.

Raymundo could now see the men more clearly and spotted his father as the man in the middle. He also could tell the men on either side of his father were his assistants. He was elated to see that his father was still alive, but that was cut short when he saw the tall man with the moustache signal to some of the guards to step back to execute the prisoners.

The prisoner on Don Francisco's left shouted, "*Viva España, Viva Venezuela!*[13] Death to the rapists, cowards, and murderers!"

The prisoner on the other side yelled, "Porfirio! You don't know what decency is! At least bring us a priest before you kill us."

Porfirio smiled cynically and ordered his men to begin shooting.

The first group of three shot their muskets, and one prisoner fell to the ground. They missed a fatal mark, as that prisoner managed to get back up a few moments later. They moved aside to reload, and the next group fired. This time the other assistant fell to the ground, and he, too, got back up a few moments later.

The third group fired at Don Francisco. He fell to his knees, but also managed to stand once more. He yelled, "Porfirio, you are a cowardly murderer. You will pay for every single one of the decent lives you have ended today!"

The soldiers continued to reload and shoot the prisoners. Their marksmanship was so bad that they still hadn't killed the prisoners after several shots. Porfirio finally yelled, "Don't waste any more ammunition! Push them into the hole!"

No one moved. These men who had been shot so many times still managed to stand, even though they were

---

[13] Long live Spain, long live Venezuela!

bleeding profusely all over from so many wounds. It seemed as if they were protected by a divine being. Some of the rebels began to feel remorse at what they had been doing. They knew these prisoners were honorable men who had never hurt anyone.

Porfirio grew enraged at the blatant disobedience. He walked up to the prisoners. As he kicked them into the fire one by one, he yelled "Burn in hell!" at each instance. The screams of the men being burned alive pierced the night. Like an echo, their screams resounded for miles, heard in the most remote locations. This horrible event that night, done by the hand of Porfirio, came to be one of the darkest and most shameful things that happened in the history of this revolution.

Raymundo and the others watched in horror at the massacre from their hiding place at the top of the hill. Raymundo could not control himself any longer and stood up as he pointed his musket at Porfirio. Before he could fire, Tomasita jumped in front of him and said, "No! They will kill us all! Remember your plan, remember your sisters and mother are still alive down there in the cage. If we don't do something about it now, not only will we be dead, but they will die as well!"

Raymundo, tears running down his face, realized what she had said was true. He threw down his musket, frustrated beyond speech. He paced back and forth for a few minutes. He dried his tears. "Okay. Let's not waste any more time—let's do this!"

As Raymundo got ready to move out, he turned and saw Francisco crumpled down, sobbing quietly. He went over to him and put his arms around him. "Don't cry, my brother. Before the night ends the man who killed our father will be dead. I promise you; I will kill him myself."

Francisco, still sobbing, raised his head and said tearfully, "That is not going to bring Papa back. He is gone forever, and I will never be able to hug him again." The little boy continued to cry.

"You are right, little brother. Your words show what a savvy boy you are. But the man who committed this atrocity and inflicted such horrible pain on us must pay for his crime. We have to make sure that he can never do this to anyone else."

Little Francisco tried to wipe away his tears and compose himself. Acting like a little man, he said in resignation, "Whatever you say, my brother. You are my older brother and now my papa, because Papa said that if anything ever happened to him you would step into his place, and I was to obey whatever you say."

Raymundo couldn't control himself any longer. Tears rolled down his cheeks once more. He hugged his brother to him tightly. "Don't worry, my brother. I will protect you and take you to safety when all this is over."

He continued the fierce embrace a few seconds longer. He released Francisco and asked, "Are you going to be okay?"

Francisco tried to smile. "Yes. You go now. You have things to do."

Raymundo turned to the others. "Everyone do your part. The plan is in action."

Tomasita crossed herself. "God be with you, my son." She took her daughter's hand. "Do you remember what you have to do?"

Tomasa smiled. "Yes, Mama."

Tomasita kissed the forehead of the little girl. "Go with him now then."

Raymundo took Tomasa's hand, and they began to walk down the dusty road toward the military camp. When they were near the cottage, Raymundo saw a group of rebel soldiers standing outside it. He gave Tomasa a rolled-up document before disappearing into the night, sneaking into the barn where they kept the horses.

Tomasa continued walking towards the soldiers. When she was close enough to them so they could see her in the light of the torches, she began to yell, "*Viva Venezuela libre. Que mueran los Españoles opresores!*[14]"

---

[14] Long live Venezuela and death to the Spanish oppressors!

The rebels began to laugh. "Good, good! What are you doing here at this hour, little girl? Where are your parents?"

She began to cry very loudly like a prima donna as she yelled, "They killed them! The bad Spanish soldiers killed my father, my mother, and my brother!"

One of the soldiers asked, "When? Where?"

"They are there—by Don Francisco's hacienda!" She pointed in the direction where the mansion was and continued sniffing and crying.

"How many ships do they have?"

"Many! Many! A lot!" As she spoke, she was waving her arms in the air with the paper in her hand.

One of the other soldiers said, "Come over here—what is that you have in your hand?"

"I don't know," she replied. "They told me to give it to the rebels. You are the rebels, aren't you? They said if you harm anybody from the governor's family you will all have your heads cut off." She moved her hand across her neck as she made a croaking sound.

One soldier exclaimed, "Too late for that—they are already dead!"

Another said, "God, I told you we should not kill the governor!"

A third swallowed nervously. "God have mercy on our souls. We should not have killed those men."

A soldier had taken the document from Tomasa's hand, opened it, and read it aloud. "'Anyone involved in this conspiracy against the Spanish Crown will be dead before the sun rises tomorrow morning.'"

Other soldiers came over to see what was happening. One of them asked, "What is going on?"

One of first group answered, "The Spanish troops are disembarking at Don Francisco's hacienda, not too far from here. They killed the family of this little girl."

Another of the newcomers asked, "Why did they kill her family?"

Tomasa cried throughout this entire interchange and piped up, "They confused them with the rebels because my brother had a musket."

"Who is your brother?" the soldier asked.

"Andre."

One of the soldiers said, "Andre. Oh, yes! He was supposed to be with us yesterday with his friend Bernavete."

Tomasa said, "They killed him, too. They cut his head off."

The soldier felt his neck nervously. "How many ships? Five, six?" To emphasize his point, he held up five and six fingers, respectively.

Tomasa shook her head and held up both hands with all her fingers outstretched, gesturing dramatically as if to indicate at least ten or twenty. "I don't know—many!"

One of soldiers said, "I think it's time to retreat. We need to talk to the chief."

Another said, "We don't have enough ammunition. We will all be killed. We'll end up being hung or decapitated."

They were talking louder and louder, attracting the other soldiers guarding the cage, horses, and supplies, who joined the group. They all started to ask questions and began to panic when they heard that the Spanish troops were nearby, coming to the rescue of the governor. In their panic, they began to exaggerate more and more what had been told them by the little girl. They grew very agitated as their voices grew louder. They began to anticipate that the Spaniards were going to be there at any minute.

They were all looking at the cottage, waiting for Porfirio to come out and tell them when they could leave. They were growing incredibly anxious. Meanwhile, on the other side of the cage, Raymundo was cutting the ropes on the roof of the cage and began to get the people out and into the forest. He held his finger to his lips to indicate the need for silence.

He hugged his mother and sisters, and then helped the wounded who needed assistance to walk. There were a couple of people lying on the floor. When he checked them, he discovered they were already dead from their wounds, having bled to death. He brought them all to a safe place in the forest some distance from where the rebels were. "Don't move until I return. There will be a great deal of shooting in a short while."

Raymundo went back towards the cottage, observing the restless, agitated rebels, all eager to leave. He managed to crawl into the small shed where the ammunition was stored, taking advantage of the fact that the guards had abandoned their posts. The soldiers continued throwing nervous glances down the road that led to the hacienda, expecting at any minute to see Spanish troops marching towards them.

Finally, Porfirio showed up at the door with the document in his hand. He yelled, "Stupid, cowards! Imbeciles! Calm down! How do you know this document is valid? Maybe there are a few people trying to trick us! Don't you know that the enemy always tries these kinds of tricks? Where is the little girl who brought this paper? Bring her to me!"

The man who had brought it to him said, "She was crying a few minutes ago right over there." He pointed behind the group of panicky soldiers. They turned to look for the girl, but she had vanished without a trace. Instead, by the light of the torches, they saw the door of the cage open and all of the prisoners gone.

The soldiers' fear increased, since they now no longer had anything to bargain with to get their own prisoners released. Additionally, their chief had killed the Governor and his men; if the Spaniards were indeed coming, their lives were over.

Suddenly, there was a vast explosion as the ammunition shelter blew up. Bullets flew all around the area. The soldiers were petrified in fear. Some dropped their muskets and ran. Others were hit by the bullets, many getting killed in the deadly hail. The man next to Porfirio fell down dead, a bullet in his forehead.

Porfirio dove for cover behind a barrel. Bullets whizzed by him, and he realized they came from the top of the hill. The soldiers who were not already wounded began to run in the opposite direction of the road from where the

Spanish army was expected. Suddenly, they heard what sounded like marching troops coming towards them from the direction they had thought safe. It seemed as though they had been caught in the middle of two Spanish forces. They were in shock, and then they saw the horses that Raymundo had stampeded by firing his musket in the opposite side of town near the stables.

The soldiers panicked and began to run in all directions. They dropped their muskets and ran like madmen, attempting to save themselves.

Porfirio yelled from his hiding place, "Stop! Don't run! Offer some resistance, don't be cowards!" Seeing they were ignoring him, he muttered to himself, "What pieces of shit these soldiers I have are." However, every time he tried to get out of his hiding place, Tomasita, Andre, Bernavete, and Francisco shot at him. The plan was to keep him there until Raymundo was able to apprehend him. The stables and several small houses near the military compound began to burn as Raymundo began to set them on fire.

After half an hour, it grew quiet. There were no more shots; only the insects in the night could be heard. Porfirio finally decided to stand up and try to get out of there. Just then, he saw two Spanish boots next to him. He looked up and his fear disappeared when he saw it was only a teenaged Spanish cadet, Raymundo. Porfirio himself was around six feet four and muscular.

He smiled cynically as he asked, "Are you here to seek revenge over the death of your father? Or are you coming to die as well? Do you want me to burn your ass, too?"

Raymundo answered, "No, I am not here for revenge. I came for justice and maybe to put you into the same fire you dropped my father in while he was alive. Just as it says in the Bible: 'an eye for an eye and a tooth for a tooth.'"

Porfirio drew his sword. "Do you think, you little shit, that you can do that to me? I am going to cut you into pieces!" He began to swipe his sword in an attempt to decapitate Raymundo, but the youth defended himself with his own sword, parrying the swipe. They began to fight, clear over to the cage.

Porfirio swung once, getting past Raymundo's guard and causing a small cut just below his left shoulder, which began to bleed. Porfirio gained confidence from this, feeling superior to Raymundo's skills. He lunged even harder, backing Raymundo up against the ditch and its still-burning fire.

Raymundo parried a swing from Porfirio so hard that the young man nearly lost his balance. Porfirio swung his sword furiously, trying to thrust directly into Raymundo's chest. Raymundo tried to avoid the thrust, bending his knees and steadying himself with his left hand behind him on the ground. With his right, he kept his sword at the ready. Porfirio lunged once more, this time missing, his sword digging into the ground on Raymundo's left. Porfirio's body was left open, and Raymundo swung upwards, cutting from the groin into Porfirio's belly, the sword running all the way through his body.

Raymundo jumped up, his sword still in Porfirio's body. He pulled the sword out, lunged again at Porfirio, and drove his sword into the larger man's chest. Porfirio abandoned his own sword and grabbed the blade in his chest. He stepped back, trying to pull the weapon out, but fell into the fire with an agonized scream. As he fell, the sword slowly slid out of his chest in Raymundo's hand.

Raymundo watched for a few seconds and then turned to see the smiling face of Tomasita next to him, holding little Tomasa by the hand. His little brother Francisco was also there, with Andre and Bernavete, all of them smiling.

Andre said, "My God! I did not believe for a minute, even though I went along with it, that your plan had even a chance to work. But God must have been with us! Let's not abuse our luck. Let's go get the prisoners and get out of here before the rebels realize what we did to them."

They walked to the place where Raymundo had left his mother, sisters, and the other prisoners. His family hugged him; his mother, though mourning her husband, was glad the rest of the family was all right and overjoyed to see

Raymundo and little Francisco. Everyone cheered him like he was a hero.

Raymundo was very modest and protested that the real heroes were Tomasita and her family. He patted her on the shoulder, saying, "If you really want to name some heroes, it would be Tomasa and little Francisco. Tomasa, because of her brilliant performance in convincing the rebels that the Spanish were coming to get them, and little Francisco because of his courage after seeing those murderers kill Father and still able to pull himself together to pull the trigger against them."

They slowly walked with the prisoners to the place where they had left the food. Raymundo took a few of the prisoners with him to the house of Tomasita to get more food, if possible, because of the greater number of people to feed. They caught a few chickens, collected some eggs, and then all went to the boat.

They boarded the ship and sailed out of Venezuela towards an uncertain future. A week later, even though they had tried to conserve their food, they were extremely thirsty and hungry. Fortunately, they encountered a Spanish galleon en route from Spain to Cuba, saving their lives. Raymundo del Marmol and his family, along with Tomasita and hers, and the rest of the refugees were transported to Cuba, where they stayed and never returned to La Guaira, Venezuela.

CHAPTER 7: BIN LADEN'S MOST TRUSTED

We returned in our private plane to Orange County, California, via Miami. I got in touch with Abdul's contact in Newport Beach. After a brief conversation with Brenton Cooper, we arranged to meet at his house in the suburbs called Old Newport later that day. We proceeded to have physical exams performed by trusted doctors we who had been assigned to our team. We received many tests, including blood tests and X-rays, since we had just returned from the tropics. The results from the X-rays showed that my ankle had a small fracture which had produced the swelling. I also had several fractured ribs. The good news was that the wound in my knee was nearly completely healed. The fact that I knew that none of my friends had any major injuries or health issues after the Venezuelan ordeal gave me a great deal of joy and satisfaction. The news from the vet who examined Rocco also made me feel great when they told me he was in excellent health, as if he had come from a picnic. Rocco had worried me lately because I'd noticed some blood in his urine. Evidently, however, it was merely the result of a piece of bone he must have eaten.

After I left everyone in one of our Corona del Mar safe houses, I put the cooler with Abdul's head and hands in the back seat of the BMW along with the briefcase containing one million five hundred thousand dollars and drove to my meeting with Cooper with Rocco taking up the front passenger's seat. It was around 6:30 in the afternoon, and the sun had begun to set. From the high hills of Corona del Mar, I was able to observe the ships coming and going down in the marina, both large and small craft, which created a beautiful panoramic view at those late hours.

For the past hours, I had been worried and a little confused. The voice of Cooper sounded very familiar to me. I had been thinking about his own words during our telephone conversation; he hadn't been surprised by it. In fact, it seemed like he had been expecting my call. The strangest thing was what he told me when I asked him if we had by any chance ever met before. His answer was that we had never before met, but that we both had the same friends and enemies in the past, and they were the same as the ones Abdul Hussein had. It was that part which completely puzzled me. How could terrorists have the same kind of friends and enemies that I had?

Another thing which raised my level of suspicion was that Cooper was so friendly and joyous with me—the bearer of supposedly bad news. The fact that he had even invited such a messenger to his own home was strange, especially when he asked how Abdul was doing. I had let him know that I had bad news about Hussein but wasn't going to give him more details over the phone. He betrayed no curiosity at all about what else there might be. Our conversation had continued very normally, even mundanely.

It seemed to me like he had previous knowledge as to what had happened already. That created a tremendous mountain of suspicion in my mind. His comments took me by surprise, something which rarely happened to me, especially given my experience as a spy and an intelligence advisor.

I wondered who this unusual individual really was. When I tried to check him out, I could find no record or information; everything about him was vague, foggy. I had to be honest with myself and admit that I found him a challenge. It raised my curiosity, and I wondered continually about him.

However, he had invited me to his own house—what was he going to do? Shoot or poison me? I knew that I would have to be very careful with him. He might be another ghost, like I was. The most curious part of the whole thing to me was what his association between him and that high-profile terrorist really was.

It also caught my attention when I told O'Brien that I would be having a meeting with Brenton to complete the circle around Abdul and see what else I could get from this man, taking of course all necessary precautions. O'Brien replied that I would have nothing to worry about with Cooper. He offered no further explanation than that. There was nothing unusual in that in itself; our conversation had taken place over the phone, and our routine there was to never give out much in the way of details using that communications medium. Whatever information O'Brien had about Cooper, for whatever reason, he didn't want to share with me or be too explicit due to the circumstances of our method of communication. His words indicated that I would have nothing to worry about. However, being a cautious man, I took every precaution my sense of survival dictated—without, as O'Brien accused me of, worrying too much.

Figure 23 Old Newport, Brenton's neighborhood

Still thinking about all these things, I arrived at Brenton's address. I parked my car in front of his house. A five-or-six-year-old girl with blond, wavy hair, and blue eyes was playing with a Rottweiler dog in front of the house. The front yard was enclosed by a white picket fence about three feet tall. The little girl enjoyed rolling around in the grass with her dog, trying to take a large, multi-colored ball out of his mouth. Once she got it, she would throw it once more to the other side of the garden.

Beneath the shade of a large tree on a swinging porch bench a couple happily watched their beautiful girl playing with their dog. The lady also had blond, wavy hair with large blue eyes. She would occasionally yell at her daughter to throw the ball even farther. The man who sat next to her was perhaps in his late thirties or early forties. His head was completely shaved, and he wore white shorts, a black summer sweater, white socks, and black sandals.

As soon as he saw me get out of the BMW, he stood up and left the lady behind. With a big smile on his face, he walked towards me. I could tell he was walking with some difficulty; his pace was very slow. He walked over to the fence, looking curiously at me to determine if I was the visitor he was expecting. As I watched him get up and walk over, I told Rocco, "Stay here and be a good boy, OK?"

Rocco wagged his nub of a tail and licked my hand obediently. He continued looking through the window, anxious to join the girl and the other dog. I left all the windows open a crack for Rocco so that he would have plenty of ventilation, even though the evening ocean air was quite cool.

I raised my hand in greeting. The man waved back at me, his smile growing even larger with the confirmation that I was who he was waiting for.

As I came over to him, I could see with greater clarity his face. I had no doubt that I knew this man, but I could not yet place where and when I had known him before. He opened the gate for me, and I walked in. "Welcome to the humble but happy Cooper residence," he said, pointing to a small tile sign bordered by flowers hanging on the gate of the fence which read the same.

I smiled. "Thank you for your gentle, happy greeting."

Brenton looked at my car and noticed my dog watching us eagerly through the window. "Is your dog aggressive?"

"No. Rocco is very well trained. He is only aggressive on my command. Otherwise, he is very, very loving and gentle, especially with kids and other dogs."

He smiled again. "Why don't you bring him with you? I believe he'll be a lot happier to get to know my female Rottweiler. Her name is Dark Chocolate. My little girl's name Sunset."

I smiled. "That is a beautiful name, I like that—she looks more like sunshine than a sunset. Sure—if you don't mind, I didn't want to impose." I pushed the remote control for the BMW to lower the windows. "OK, Rocco—come on! Come to get to know your new friends." I didn't need to invite him twice. He eagerly jumped through the window and ran over to my side.

We all entered the garden. The dogs came over to get to know us. I said to the dog, "Hello, girl." I petted her. "This is my friend, Rocco—be nice to him, OK? I know how you women are!" I got onto my knees. "Hello, Sunset. My name is Julio Antonio. *Mucho gusto*."

Sunset smiled. "Nice to meet you. Is Rocco a boy?"

"Yes, honey—he's a boy." I got up and came face to face with Brenton's wife, who had walked over to us.

She held out her right hand and said with a smile, "I am Massile Cooper, Brenton's wife."

"Nice to meet you."

"It's a great pleasure to meet you."

"The pleasure is all mine," I said. I took her hand and kissed it.

"Oh, my! You are quite the gentleman!"

I was captivated by the physical beauty of that woman. Brenton understood my admiration for her attractiveness.

He said proudly, "Massile was a finalist in the Miss Universe Pageant."

I nodded. "I don't doubt it at all. Your wife is a very beautiful woman."

He grinned. "Thank you."

Because I was so close to him, I noticed something strange about him—his teeth were very uneven. It looked like a genetic defect. That detail was all I needed to remember exactly where and when I had met him. I kept silent, but my guard increased. I remembered him from the days of the Zipper operation and my arrest by the Secret Service.

Massile asked, "Would you like something to drink?"

"No, thank you," I said. "You are very kind, but don't bother, please. My visit will be very short, and I don't want to take you away from your family too much. Especially on this beautiful start of the weekend."

She smiled and came quite close to me, displaying her beautiful teeth. "For me it's not a bother at all. I'll leave you guys alone so you can have privacy in your conversation and business. Excuse me." She walked into the house.

It looked as if Sunset and Dark Chocolate had known Rocco all their lives. The girl had acquired a new member in her game of baseball. Rocco was more agile and strong and chased the ball rapidly, bringing it back to Sunset. Both dogs would then try to get the ball from each other. Sunset burst out laughing as her dog tried unsuccessfully to get the ball from Rocco.

Brenton closed the gate. He leaned towards me and put a hand on my shoulder. "It looks like Rocco has made a quick friendship."

"Like I said before, he is a very lovely and gentle dog—unless I command him to be otherwise."

"I see, I see. Exactly as you said before, you've trained him very well. Let's go and sit down at the table beneath the tree. We have a lot to talk about."

We walked over to a small umbrella table next to the bench swing. We sat down on the comfortable cushioned chairs. The cushions didn't just cover the seat, but also the back and arms. He stretched himself out, making himself comfortable. "Before anything, I need to apologize to you twice. The first is for lying to you and not telling you that we've known each other from before." He pinched his nose in embarrassment.

I smiled and nodded. "I know." I raised my right arm high. "Don't worry about it."

This time, he was the one who smiled. "You already recognized me? Isn't that true?"

"Yes, as soon as you smiled, I immediately remembered you in the bathroom mirror in the dungeons of the Santa Ana federal courthouse. When you guys in the Secret Service dropped a full pot of boiling water for coffee in my groin. But let me say also that you were one of the most decent in that whole bunch because you're the one who took me to the restroom and removed my handcuffs so that I could put cold water on my injured parts." I looked him straight into his eyes for a few seconds. I could clearly see his remorse and shame for the incident I had described.

His voice broke as he replied. "That was the motive behind my other apology. It's on behalf of the Secret Service. That is not what the organization stands for. What those guys did to you is a disgrace to the Secret Service. They were the rotten apples."

I continued to hold his eyes with mine. "Well, it's been a long time since all of that happened. The Secret Service chief in Washington, D.C. already apologized to me several times for that disgraceful incident. You had nothing to do with it, so you have nothing to apologize for." I stroked my chin. "You guys are lucky that I'm not a vengeful person or resentful. Can you think for a minute what would have happened if you had done that to a professional hit man—or just a trigger-happy man? Poor babies—I don't think any of you would be alive today. Even you."

Brenton nodded and the shame deepened in his eyes. He gulped. "I have to tell you the truth—I would not blame them." He rubbed his forehead. It was clear he was trying to forget the past unsuccessfully.

Massile reappeared with a large jar of lemonade and four glasses. As she came over, she said with her beautiful smile, "Who can say no to a glass of homemade lemonade in the summertime?"

We smiled back at her. She put the jar on the table and filled on glass, which she handed to me. I took the glass as she served the second one to Brenton. The third glass she kept for herself and raised it high. "*Salud.*"

Brenton and I raised our glasses and said, "*Salud.*" We clinked glasses and took drinks. The lemonade was delicious, and I expressed that to her. She poured a fourth glass and called Sunset over.

"Do you want a lemonade, honey?"

"Yes, Mommy!" the little girl called and ran over to get her glass. She downed it in several gulps and then ran back to play with the dogs.

I breathed in a little more relief when I watched them take long drinks themselves and observed the little girl down hers. Massile said, "OK, I'll leave you guys alone." She left, leaving behind the jar on the table.

Brenton poured himself some more and offered me a refill. I stopped him with a wave of my hand. "Not now—maybe more later." I held up my still-full glass. I had only taken a tiny sip to avoid being impolite. I was unused to drinking anything that I had not seen opened myself or had prepared for myself.

We were alone again, and I said, "You have to forgive me. We've been talking about everything except for the reason I'm here: Abdul Hussein and the money that I'm supposed to get to you to distribute you his family in La Guairá, Venezuela. With all the respect you deserve, I want to know now, before we proceed any further, what role the Secret Service is playing in all of this. Or if you're doing this separate from them—for patriotism. To my modest knowledge, the Secret Service has no jurisdiction with international terrorists. Please correct me if I am in error. I would be delighted if you would get me out into the light on this." I remained silent after that, carefully observing his reactions with a small smile on my lips. I stroked my chin once more. Sunset had drunk a full glass of lemonade and was playing with the dogs. So far, she hadn't collapsed. I decided to take a few more sips.

Brenton had also been observing me and smiled. There was a little sarcasm in his voice when he spoke. "The Cuban Lightning. There is no doubt in my mind that you have earned your reputation. That's probably the reason you're still alive after fifty-six attempts on your life and your compatriots in Cuba say you are *vivito y coleando*[15]. Like a fish we take out of water who continues to move his tail to return to the water."

He picked up his lemonade with his left hand and raised his right on high. "I want you to do me a favor. Please relax. I know this is very hard for you after the way you've lived your life. But I think it's very possible that we can learn a little from each other. I have a great admiration and profound respect for you as a man. Even though you've never had reason to offer me your friendship, you're on my list of people I have absolute trust in. I know your ethics and I know the rare caliber of individual that you are. If I didn't feel that way, I never would have given to you my personal address for this meeting. Here I have my most precious and valuable treasure: my family."

I smiled. "I really appreciate your compliments. And your vote of confidence. For that, I thank you very much."

Brenton smiled once more. He pointed at my nearly full glass of lemonade. "You can drink that and the whole jar if you want. That is why Massile and I drank it and gave it to our little girl in front of your eyes. That way, you know you are with family and don't have to worry about anything. That is the kind of conversation I want to have with you today. That's why I asked if you would please relax—not put your guard down, just relax. Leave your worries for somebody else. You have nothing to worry about with me."

---

15 Alive and moving

I took the glass on the table with a smile on my face, twirling it around and examining the lip of it. "I think you're asking a little too much. If you were in my shoes, I don't believe you would be capable of doing what you're asking of me." I paused and rubbed my eyebrows. "Don't take this wrong. You are a great individual and have a beautiful family. You've been very nice, polite, and accommodating with me. But you cannot forget how and where we met and how—the Secret Service has given me the worst memories of my life, only comparable to those with the Cuban communists. Even worse is your direct association with the right arm of the most wanted terrorist of this century." I frowned in incredulity.

Brenton replied, raising both hands in the air in a gesture of surrender. "Listen to me, and later you can verify with O'Brien."

"Hm," was all I said. I looked at him expressionlessly. Inside, however, I wondered who this guy was. I was a little surprised to hear him mention O'Brien but gave no indication.

He observed me closely and smiled. "I think we should start from the beginning. Later we can continue with Abdul Hussein.

"First of all, I work with counterintelligence, with international and domestic affairs in coordination with O'Brien and other departments within the intelligence community. I've been in this position for many years under different administrations and different presidents. I know a lot about the personal lives of those presidents because I was on the team close to them, off and on. That's why I was called from Texas when your arrest happened in 1989. The Secret Service of Los Angeles did not have sufficient personnel available for your arrest.

"Your case was classified as high profile because all the evidence indicated that the governor of California, or possibly even President Reagan, was directly involved in the illegal printing of the currency. Or maybe both. And possibly other high-ranked politicians.

"When they communicated this, I immediately passed that information to O'Brien. Unfortunately, the news came too late for anyone to do anything to prevent you from knowing about it, and you were arrested."

He paused. "I'm telling you all this so that you have a better idea of who you're dealing with and who I am. Now you have the knowledge of why I was with the team with the Secret Service; not because I'm actually with them, but because I was called for that particular case. I'm not telling you this to try to win brownie points, but all the beatings and indignities you suffered after your arrest turned you into a hero in the eyes of everyone—including the members of the Secret Service. Because of your defiant attitude and your complete silence and integrity, even the ones who beat you up wound up admiring you.

"Now, let's go to the second subject: my friend Abdul Hussein. He's a great freedom fighter, loyal, and a patriot." He said that with emphasis and emotion in his voice. "I hope God has him up in Heaven. O'Brien already told me what took place. I can assure you that we lost one of the most valuable warriors in our organization. He never was a terrorist. He was always one of the most intelligent clandestine agents and double spies we ever had in our organization in our fight against international terrorism. We're not only fighting terrorists internationally; we're also fighting against the corruption in our own government that's growing daily thanks to the penetration of the communists and ambitions of the corrupt politicians who will sell out their country for a handful of dollars. If they have to blow up their own families inside a building to obtain power, they'll do it."

He paused again, observing me for a few seconds in silence. I could see he was reading my reactions. I maintained my calm and met his look directly as we each studied each other's gestures and movements.

I recalled O'Brien's words when he told me I was meeting with Brenton—that I had nothing to worry about with him. I thought that all he had been telling me was perfectly logical. Unfortunately, until I could verify any of it with O'Brien, I had to be very careful and push his buttons to see what I could get anything out of him without offering him any information. I had to concentrate on what I had come there for—to get the information and documents of all of bin Laden's safe houses and what we needed to dismantle al-Qaeda and kill his leaders.

I asked, "Well, if all you're telling me is true, you don't have the documents Abdul told me that you would deliver to me."

He shook his head silently.

I continued, "Then that makes Abdul, with all my respect, nothing more than a liar and not the valuable warrior you called him. You have to forgive me, but this is the reality that I have right in front of my eyes."

Brenton looked at me once more. I could see his ears and face reddening like a ripe tomato. He rubbed both hands on his face in frustration at his failure to convince me as to who he actually was. After a few seconds he regained control of himself. He tried to find the best words to convince me that what he was saying was the truth. By the same token, he realized that what I was saying made sense.

"Well—let me start again. Please, hear me out calmly and analyze what I'm saying. Abdul was not a liar. He believed that I had those documents in my possession. But what he didn't know was that after we separated and before I left Venezuela, I found myself in a predicament because I had information from my contact that I would be arrested very soon. I had to change the plans myself, improvise, go back to his house in La Guairá, and hide all the documents in a safe place where I could find them later on and protect them from falling into the hands of the Venezuelan intelligence. Thank God for that—if I hadn't improvised and done what I did, when I was arrested trying to leave at the airport, not only would we have lost all that information, but I probably would also have been executed for being a spy. According to the authorities, I had been arrested for engaging in clandestine activities on behalf of the United States of America. Abdul returned to Cuba without knowing what had happened to me. He assumed I had taken those documents with me and returned here to Newport Beach."

He stopped and took a deep breath. "I was arrested and tortured for several weeks in Caracas. A few days ago, the State Department managed to bribe some high intelligence authorities there for my release. O'Brien didn't know and assumed that Abdul still had all that information in his possession. That's the reason they sent you guys to retrieve it. Abdul lost contact with me and my whereabouts. Evidently, he got really worried, thinking the worst—that I was dead or in prison. He decided not to talk to anyone. Knowing your reputation, he contacted O'Brien and told him he would only speak with you. If he didn't see your face, he wasn't going to release anything to anyone. He assumed we were betrayed from the inside and that I might be dead. That is exactly what we had agreed before separating in Caracas. I would do the same as he did if that was the case."

I leaned back in my chair. "I'm sorry. I followed my instincts, and I might have been a little unfair with you."

Brenton tried to smile, but it was clearly forced. I thought he still was a little upset with my previous attitude. I felt a little guilty for all the distrust I had with him, but unfortunately that is my natural survival instinct. My training, thanks to that distrust in others, is what has kept me alive all these years.

Like a flash of lightning in the sky, my mind was now illuminated with reason and logic. I now understood clearly that I might have been a little harsh with him and overprotective of myself. When I had called him on the phone, I never told him that Abdul had given me his personal address—I had only told him that I had been given the cellular phone number Abdul had when he communicated with Brenton. The reason for that was nothing more than prudence and politeness—I had no notion of showing up at his house unannounced in the first place. Additionally, I never gave out my personal address, and it might be shocking to him to learn that Abdul had been so careless to give Brenton's out.

When I had spoken with Brenton over the phone, I was in fact surprised when he gave me his address. However, it now made sense that, if he knew O'Brien, he would know already who I was, and so would feel comfortable doing that. With this new clarity and understanding, I now considered the reason that Abdul had given me the address was because he wanted me to corroborate if Brenton was arrested and alive.

However, as I untangled this web, I still had to verify certain details with O'Brien. That was the nature of our business: trust but verify. Everything was coordinating perfectly, and I understood that nothing in life was as expected, and he presented something else to our eyes. It's absolutely vital in life to take your time and analyze everything before you decide, especially when this can bring serious consequences to us in our future. Either one of these two individuals could come to be what I had been expecting; to my surprise, what I believed had been my enemies in the end came to be if not my friends at least my best allies in the cause. It looked like every one of us worked at defending the same principles.

Brenton started to take his sandals and socks off. This caught me by surprise. Observing him, as he took first one and then the other, he looked at me kind of seriously but silent. It didn't even cross my mind what his purpose was in removing his sandals in the midst of our conversation. I could see he had bandages on his toes. As he unwrapped them, I saw that all the nails were missing—only blood where they should have been on both feet. I could imagine the pain he must be enduring when those nails had been removed. When he saw my consternation, he said resentfully, "This was part of my torture with which I had been victimized by the intelligence officers in Venezuela. I wanted to show you what those sons of bitches did to me and the vultures who serve Chavez in his intelligence."

Massile, as they had scheduled, showed up once more with a pan with a solution of some kind in it. After she unrolled a small rubber mat, she put the container down on it. She took Brenton's feet and placed them in the solution. With great care, she took a towel and began to clean his feet gently as he poured more of the solution on top of his feet.

I asked him, "This happened recently?"

Brenton replied, "Yes. Only three days ago."

I shook my head in distress as I watched what had been done to his feet. "This is disgusting. I know this is done to make people talk, but I've never seen it so close."

Massile smiled and crossed herself. "Let's give thanks to the Lord that he's still alive. I have understood, as Brenton told me, that Abdul didn't have the same luck."

I squeezed my chin and shook my head silently.

Brenton said, "Did you know what these degenerates did for the three days after they did this? They made me put both feet in a vat of ninety-five proof alcohol for the entire three days. I could not control myself and urinated in my pants like a baby." Brenton shook his head. "If I had even one of them in my hands right now, I think I would cut him into pieces." There were tears in his eyes. "It's not the horrible pain I went through—I could handle that. The worst humiliation of my life was giving those vultures the pleasure of seeing me piss my pants." He tapped his forehead with his left index finger several times. "Right here. Right here. I have the laughter of these cowardly bullies. That humiliation doesn't let me sleep anymore."

I had a knot in my throat at his narrative. Massile had finished cleaning his feet and applied a cream. She then put on fresh bandages and put fresh socks on. I couldn't stand it anymore. I stood up, walked over to him, and squeezed his shoulder. "Remember what Massile said—thank God that you're still alive. Tomorrow is a new day, and you can enjoy it with your beautiful girl and your wife. Try to forget the humiliation they put you through. Take strength from all these experiences so you can destroy those bullies. Don't let them get away with the double satisfaction that they actually succeeded in making you so ashamed of yourself that you cannot sleep. Be brave, destroy their purpose."

Brenton looked at me, this time with a small but genuine smile. "Thank you. You're one hundred percent right."

Massile was ready to leave. She stopped by my side and squeezed my shoulder. Without saying a word, she smiled and nodded her thanks to me with an expression of pleasure. She went back into the house.

When we were alone, I said, "Well, Brenton, with all the information you shared with me today, I have no alternative but to go back to the land of my ancestors, to La Guairá, Venezuela." I went back to my chair and sat down. I raised my cane up. "As soon as I recuperate from these small injuries, I will return to retrieve that package that you unfortunately had to leave behind. Please, all I want is the details of where you left that package. That precious information should be in the hands of our people, so that we will destroy the heads of this organization around the world. At the same time, I will bring to Abdul's family, like he asked me to, the money I was supposed to bring you today to send them. I will deliver it personally so that I will be at peace with my conscience. Now that I know what sort of person you are, I don't want to put you at any further risk. I'm sure you don't want to go back to Venezuela anytime in the near future."

He looked at me with tears in his eyes. "Thank you. I will give you a map with all the details so that you can retrieve that package. With all my respect, though, I don't think you should go alone. I could perhaps be of help. Abdul's family have known me for many years, and I left the package hidden on their property."

I raised my hand. "No, no, no—repeating your words, with all my respect, you are the last person I want to be seen in Venezuela. Especially after your recent arrest and torture. Besides, I always have a fabulous team by my side and at my back. I'm accustomed to working alone; that allows me to improvise without putting anyone's life at risk. When the circumstances require it."

Brenton nodded. "Yes, yes—as you say. I know how you work. You don't like to leave any witnesses or evidence of anything you do anywhere."

"That's right. I'll give you a small piece of advice: do exactly the same as I do. I don't want to blame anyone for your bad fortune, but your grand friend and contact, Abdul Hussein, may be without realizing it commit an indiscretion. That indiscretion can make you play with your life. That is the reason I move from one place to another I do it quickly without advising anyone. That way, they cannot follow my trail. Most importantly, don't leave witnesses. The indiscretion of others many times even our friends can be part of the flaws of the human being and most of the time occur in an innocent way. But in our job, we end up paying a high price, sometimes with our lives, as you paid a horrible consequence. Why take this absurd and unnecessary risk?"

Brenton smiled, this time with some irony in his face. He pointed to his feet and nodded his head. "Yes, yes. You have all the reason in the world. In my case, very painful consequences."

I could not avoid looking at the good time this little girl, Rocco, and Dark Chocolate were having in the front yard. "I don't think I've ever seen Rocco enjoy so much the company of anyone, even when he was chasing the flamingoes by the river in Venezuela. I saw him enjoying so much the company of your little girl and dog."

Brenton smiled. "I was thinking the same. As I've been talking to you and watching her, I've never seen her laugh so much. Anytime you want to or need to leave Rocco anywhere, this is your house. Don't hesitate. You can leave him here with trust in us for the time you think is necessary. It will be a pleasure not only for us but for Sunset, too."

I smiled and nodded. "Thank you. Thank you very much. I might take you up on your offer when I have the need."

"When you need it, remember, we are here for you. Not just for your dog, but you, too. You're both welcome in our home."

I smiled and thanked him again. "You know something? As you told me before, I never offered you my friendship; now I have the opportunity."

Brenton smiled. He looked very happy with my words. He stretched himself in the chair and extended his right hand to me. We shook hands and I said, "Thank you very much, my friend."

He replied with a genuine smile, "Thank you for your confidence and for your trust."

"Thanks to you for your great honor and offering me your beautiful home and family. I guarantee you that nobody—*nobody*—without exception, will learn from me where you live unless you tell me to do so. Any conversation we've had here today is completely confidential between us."

Brenton grinned and nodded. "I know, I know."

"Well, now I only have one thing left, not really pleasant. Something I have to show you before I take it to the labs. That is the head of your friend, Abdul. I need you to verify for me that it's him, that he was who he said he was."

Brenton shook his head in surprise a little unhappily. After a few seconds he asked, "You mean to tell me that you have the head of Abdul with you?"

I nodded without saying a word. Brenton instantly looked at my BMW. He pointed. "In your car?"

I nodded again. Brenton shook his head and grimaced in distaste and revulsion at the thought. He took a deep breath and said, his eyes misty with emotion, "Please, don't ever tell this to Massile. OK?"

I shook my head. "Of course. Believe me, this is as unpleasant to me as it is to you. I spent a few days with him, and I developed a very good impression of him. I believe I earned his respect as he earned mine. But remember, no matter how unpleasant, this is the business we chose to be involved in, and we have to be responsible about it and do what we have to do."

Brenton changed his expression completely. Before, it was white; now it looked transparent. His eyes were bloodshot. He took a very deep breath and rocked back and forth a bit before getting up determinedly. "OK, let's get this over with."

I took my cane out of my chair and we walked towards the small gate. As we crossed the garden, Rocco stopped playing and ran over to me. I patted his head. "No, no, Rocco—we're not leaving yet. Go back and play." He understood and bounded back over joyfully to play with his new friends.

A seconds later we opened the gate and walked out to the street. I opened the rear passenger door. "Get in," I told him.

After he got in, I closed the door, and I walked around to the other side. I entered through the other rear door. The cooler sat between us, and I opened it. I pulled out the transparent plastic bag which held Abdul's head. He could not control his emotions and two tears involuntarily ran down his cheeks. He hurriedly wiped his tears with the sleeve of his sweater. He shook his head. I asked him, "Are you OK?"

He nodded silently. "Is that him?"

"Yes, it is."

I took the plastic bag which held his hands out so that I could smooth the ice and properly re-stow the head.

"What is that?" he asked.

I lifted the bag so that he could more clearly see what it contained. "These are Abdul's hands. We brought them to verify his fingerprints."

This, for whatever reason, was more than Brenton could handle. He put his left hand over his mouth as if to contain an urge to vomit. His hand moved down to hold his stomach. Desperately he clutched for the door handle with his right hand. As soon as he found it, he moved quickly out of the car in a rush. I remained inside the car, meticulously positioning everything so that I could close the cooler. From my seat I could clearly hear the retching sound of his vomiting.

I took some Kleenex, got out of the car, and offered him the tissues. "Are you OK?"

Brenton was leaning forward, vomiting into the grass median. "No, but thank you for the Kleenex." He took the tissues desperately and nodded reassuringly to me as he wiped his mouth.

I pressed the trunk function on my remote and went over to the trunk and pulled out a bottle of lime-flavored Perrier water. I opened it and handed it to him. "Take it a little at time, sip by sip, and you'll feel better."

He looked at me and without thinking twice began to chug the bottle, downing in two gulps. After he finished, he said, "Thank you very much. How do you carry this in your car?"

"I'm always prepared for every occasion, my friend."

He smiled. "I swear to you this mineral water tastes better than the lemonade my wife made for us."

"Oh, oh!" I said jokingly. "Don't worry about it, I'm a clam. I won't ever tell Massile what you just said, or you'll be condemned by her to sleep on the sofa for several nights."

He chuckled. "How the hell have you managed, after all you've been through, not just recently but all your life, to maintain that great sense of humor?"

I smiled again. "Thanks be to God for that great sense of humor. On the contrary, I don't believe I would even be born without it."

He looked at me in surprise.

I shook my head. "My nanny Majito, who was the one who received me when I was born into this crazy world, told me that my head and body were twice as big as the opening through which I was born. Evidently our Lord wanted to play a not-really-funny joke on me, or perhaps He wanted to test my sense of humor and my tenacity at the same time. By the same token, this almost cost my poor mother her life. I was determined to get out, and the small inconvenience of my size was not going to stop me. According to Majito, I might have come out of there swimming like a fish, proud of making it, because instead of crying, she said I had the most beautiful smile she had ever seen on a baby. Very hard to believe, eh, like everything that has happened to me all my life."

Brenton smiled again, laughing. It looked like he had recuperated pretty well. "I don't know if the story you just told me is true or not, but one thing I can guarantee—your story managed to wipe out of my mind the horrible nightmare I endured inside your BMW. I don't know if it was intentional or not, but you did a great job."

"No, the story is true! Well, if it's not, you have to blame Majito, since she's the one who told me. But if you feel better now, that is the most important thing. The bad moments in life we should push to go faster through so that they don't leave any secondary effects in our personality."

"There's no doubt that, besides your other good qualities, you are a very smart man."

I looked at him seriously this time. "Do you need any cash?"

He was caught off guard. "What?"

"Too many compliments—I was expecting you to ask me for money now."

He shook his head, and I maintained my serious face for a few seconds before smiling.

When he noticed my smile, he said, "You are really something, you know?"

"I know."

Brenton reached into the pocket of his sweater and pulled out a long, skinny wallet. He pulled a document out and handed it to me. "Here's the map to find that package in Venezuela." He put an arm around my shoulder. "You know—really—you are something!"

"I know," I repeated, and we both laughed as we started to walk back to the garden.

He opened the gate, and we walked back to sit down under the umbrella. He asked, "What are you thinking of doing with Abdul's head and hands?"

I held a finger to my lips. "Shh. People will think we sell body parts for a living. You just told me that you never wanted Massile to know about this." I was genuinely serious this time. "After our scientists finish with what they're supposed to do, I will try my best to return them to his family so that they can give them a proper Christian burial. From what Abdul told me, his wife is a Christian. She should decide what is best for them."

"Hania."

"What?"

"Hania is the name of Abdul's wife."

"Oh—OK. A beautiful name. Hania. Very beautiful name for a woman. What nationality is she?"

"Pakistani." He grimaced. "You think my wife is beautiful? Wait until you see this woman. I asked myself many times how the hell Abdul managed to get such a beautiful woman. By the way, I want to apologize to you. I don't know what happened to me inside your car, but I couldn't control my emotions, first to see his head and then his hands. Everything went blank in my mind, thinking that when you held that plastic bag in front of my face, that it could be my head and hands. My stomach turned inside out at that thought."

"You don't have to apologize. It's perfectly normal, especially when it's a personal friend. Somebody as close to you as Abdul used to be."

"Not only a friend—we've been working together for many years. I left him behind only a couple of weeks ago. I guess my reaction had to do with the tortures I just suffered. Losing Abdul is a huge tragedy for the intelligence community. 'Geronimo' visited his house many times with his own family. It was the perfect opportunity to not only get rid of him but put his whole family in jail. We made a proposal to the President several times to catch him in there and extradite him from

Venezuela to here or get him clandestinely. But for one reason or another, the President never gave us the green light. He feared creating a diplomatic incident and wanted to catch him in international air space. We lost many opportunities to bring him down."

I rubbed my forehead in exasperation. "I don't know who, but it must be one of the many bureaucrats in the intelligence community that picked the name 'Geronimo' for bin Laden as a codename. Bin Laden is a sadistic individual—how could anybody come up with that name? I think it's offensive to the Indian nations and the native North Americans. Geronimo was a brave warrior and patriot who fought to defend not only his country but his people against the invasion of the settlers. Correct me if I'm wrong—you know more about the history of this country than I do. The establishment came to take his land, his wealth, killed his family—and what did he do? He fought a fair fight and lost."

Brenton nodded. "I know a lot about the history of my country, and I'm glad you said that. It was grossly unfair what we did to them. All that land belonged to them by birth. What code would you give to bin Laden?"

I smiled. "The one most suitable: The Polygamist. He has five wives."

Brenton smiled. "You *really* are something else, but I agree with you. From now on, let's not call him 'Geronimo' anymore. Let's call him 'the Polygamist.' I like that a lot more. To hell with those bureaucrats in the intelligence community! Let's leave Geronimo's memory in peace."

We stood up and high fived. Massile came out of the house at that moment. As she walked towards us, she grinned. "I like that! That is a very good signal that we've gained not only a friend but also a new member to our family." She looked me in the eyes. "Can I add another plate tonight for dinner with us on this beautiful summer night?"

I grinned back and waved negatively. "No, no—I was supposed to be out of here an hour ago. Thank you, Massile, you are a great hostess and wife. Brenton, you are very lucky. But I have a cooler in my BMW that's full of head —" Brenton looked at me with a panicked expression "—cheese imported from Venezuela." He breathed an audible sigh of relief. "My friends are waiting for me to deliver it to them. Even though it's on dry ice, I don't want to take the risk of it decomposing. In reality, I was only going to stop for a little while." I looked at one of my watches. "My God, I've been here two hours!"

Brenton grinned, still obviously relieved. "Time flies."

"Yes, my friend. But if you give me a rain check, I promise you the next time I'm in town, we will have dinner together."

Massile smiled. "Yes, I'd like that. You have a rain check, anytime you want. This is your family and house now."

"I really, really appreciate that." I took her hand and kissed it.

Brenton stepped forward and gave me a bear hug. "Don't forget, whenever you come back to visit us, I want you to bring Rocco with you."

I smiled and nodded. "Yes, I know. Rocco conquered you both. I will bring him with me next time. He is very likeable, like me." They both laughed. "Rocco! Let's go!"

Rocco ran over to me, leaving his two new friends behind. We walked out of the garden toward my car. I put the passenger's side window down a little so that Rocco could say goodbye. He looked at Dark Chocolate and Sunset like a little boy who didn't want to leave them behind.

As I drove off towards the lab to deliver my package, I thought about the strange circles which take us through life. After all, I might have to go back, as I had told Brenton, to my ancestral home of La Guaira, Venezuela. If it was the last thing I did in my life, it would be to bring the money to Abdul's family and restore his body so that he could have a Christian burial.

I knew I had faced death many times in my life and would likely have to face it once more. I had a strange feeling in my stomach lately that I might meet my Maker very soon. This particular trip back into the lion's den where, this time, the lion would be waiting for me, would likely be the worst encounter I would ever have in my life with Death.

But as my great-grandfather never looked on Death with fear, I was not about to allow that grim specter to intimidate me and prevent me from doing what my honor and integrity demanded of me. I knew it had to be done soon and as I recovered from my minor injuries I would have to return to those ancestral lands, completing the circle I had already started. God had protected me as one of His warriors and the spirit of my ancestors had been with me to help me finish this new adventure, even if I had to face and defeat Death once more.

Abdul had left for Cuba on heaven knew what mission, separating him from Brenton Cooper and resulting in Cooper's arrest. My journey might take me to my direct genetic trail, after all, and my country of origin, Cuba. Perhaps there I would disentangle the details to reveal who bin Laden really was and who were his key powerful friends in different governments around the world who had been supporting his network of terrorist enterprises for so long.

CHAPTER 8: THE SECOND TRAIL

Thirty Years 1840's, Santiago de Cuba, Spanish Colonial Era

Figure 24 Santiago de Cuba, Spanish Colonial Era c. 1840

Donato del Marmol, my great-great-grandfather, was a Major General during the Ten Years' War in the Cuban battle to attain independence from the Spanish Crown. He was one of the first men to burn his hacienda and free his slaves, heading into the jungle to fight for Cuba's freedom.

When Donato was around ten years old, he traveled with his family to Spain on a business trip of his father's. They returned home on a wooden sailing vessel with his father Raymundo, his mother Clotilde, and his eight-year-old sister Maria. Donato was playing catch with Maria on the main deck of the ship. They could see the land and trees as the ship neared the coast. Their play was interrupted momentarily as they looked over the rail at the sound of sirens. A small boat was approaching the ship. It was a Spanish Royal Navy pinnace coming out to inspect their ship because it was far from the harbor in a part of the coast frequented by smugglers.

Their curiosity satisfied, they resumed their play. Maria threw the ball, but it escaped Donato's attempt to catch it and rolled down the stairs. He ran behind the ball, trying to stop it. Maria followed, and they ran down the stairs for several decks until they were deep in the hold of the ship, only one deck above the bilge. From the stairs they could see men with dark beards, most of whom were missing teeth. They looked like pirates to the children.

They also noticed that there were black slaves in chains in that part of the hold. The slaves were shackled hand and feet, with chains that continued up to their necks. The men hit the slaves to force them into a hole in the deck. Some cried out for mercy, while the younger slaves tried hopelessly to defend themselves. Those who attempted to defend themselves were struck even harder, some knocked unconscious and pushed into the hole anyway. Donato and Maria watched, paralyzed with fright, but remained unnoticed in one of the breaks in the stairway.

Figure 25 Spanish slave ship

One of the men yelled, "Hurry up! Hurry up! The Spanish Armada will be here any minute to inspect the ship. If they find these slaves aboard, they will throw us in jail!"

The hole in the deck the men were being shoved through opened directly to the ocean. Most of the slaves were begging not to be dropped into the water. One of them pleaded, "*Señor, señor, quita cadena. Quita cadena negrito.*[16]"

The men, instead of showing mercy, reacted more violently, pushing them around and one by one shoving them through the hole. The children tried to grab the ball, which had stuck in the railing of the stairs. They looked at each other fearfully, knowing they should not be witnessing what was happening. They also knew that if they were seen by the men they would be in big trouble. As they tried to release the ball from the handrail, it moved, and there was a wrenching sound as the top of the rail snapped off and clattered down onto the deck. It fell directly in front of the man who appeared to be in charge.

He looked up and yelled, "*Quien demonios anda por aqui?*[17]" He quickly climbed up the stairs, catching the children before they could get away. He looked at them and said, "Stupid kids! You put your noses where they shouldn't be!"

They looked at him in horror. He had missing teeth and a long beard, and the smell of tobacco and rum lay heavy on his breath. He looked at them as if enjoying their fear. "I am going to cut your tongues out. That will teach you not to stick your noses where you are not supposed to be."

Donato was infuriated. Even though he was terrified, he reacted violently. He kicked the man in the knee as hard as he could. This took the man by surprise, and he screamed in pain. He let go of them, and though they tried to run, he caught them again. This time he was rougher, clearly not about to underestimate them again. "I'm going to teach you a lesson, you nosy kids!"

---

[16] Sir take the chains off. Please remove the chains, mercy, have mercy on the black men.

[17] Who the hell is there?

Like music to their ears, their father's voice called them from the upper decks just then as he descended into the hold. "Donato! Maria! Where are you?"

Raymundo came down the stairs and saw the ugly man holding his children, one on each side of him. He himself was very well dressed and held his hat in his hand. He looked angrily at the man and demanded in a very authoritative voice, "What is going on? What did they do?"

Donato yelled, "Papa, papa—our ball fell down here, and we just came down to get it. We did nothing wrong!"

The ugly man looked at Raymundo with an expression of extreme stupidity. He released the children and said, "They did nothing wrong. They came down here and I did not think it was safe for them. I was going to bring them back up on deck." He smiled, showing his ugly teeth.

The children ran under their father's arms, and he hugged them protectively. Before he turned around to go back upstairs, he saw the men down below as they dropped the last two slaves through the hole. Their despairing screams were clearly heard, and he looked at the man, shaking his head in disgust. The man tried to appear as if nothing was going on, his stupid expression of exaggerated innocence betraying his falsehood.

Raymundo ushered the children back up on deck in silence. As they ascended, Maria and Donato tried to tell him what they had seen. Donato said, "Papa, we both saw those men dropping slaves into the ocean."

Raymundo put his fingers to his lips. "It's better if we don't talk about it. I know what they are doing is not right, but there is nothing we can do about it now."

Slavery was a matter of international debate at the time. Officially, no new slaves could be captured and brought to the slave markets in those countries which still followed the practice, but smugglers still continued to ply the vile trade. A man's worth in slave-owning areas was still determined by how many slaves he had on his plantation, as the size of his labor force determined the size of his crop. Some slave owners were humane, at least. Others, however, treated their slaves like animals, beating, even killing them for the smallest failure or infraction. When conditions were continuously terrible, it often caused a slave rebellion, during which the slaves killed the master only to run off into the jungle and become outlaws, running for their lives forever or until they were caught and killed.

As a result, the price for slaves had gone up so fewer people could afford to have them. Others acquired slaves through illicit means, as the cost was much less than "legitimate" slaves, requiring no paperwork from the government. Smuggling slaves was punished with jail time by the Spanish. Consequently, when a smuggling ship was about to get caught, the smugglers would throw the slaves overboard in shackles to prevent them from floating.

The Spanish authorities boarded the ship to ensure everything was in order. Their duty done, they bid farewell to the captain and lowered themselves back down the companion ladder into their small pinnace. Donato watched the soldiers curiously and looked out over the ocean, wondering if any of the slaves had survived. He shielded his eyes from the sun with his hand as he searched for them and noticed one of the slaves was holding onto a dangling rope hanging from the opposite side of the ship from the soldiers. He was delighted to see one of the slaves was still alive. Raymundo was not paying any attention to his boy, who threw his ball into the water near the slave, who let go of the rope to grab on to the ball. He used it as a flotation device and began drifting toward the shore.

Santiago de Cuba was still some distance, but it was in view from the deck. All along the shore one could see sugar cane refineries, smoke coming from the factories' chimneys. Donato waved covertly at the slave, who returned the gesture. Donato smiled with satisfaction.

A few days later, Donato was playing on the beach with another boy named Jacinto Castro, one of his neighbors. The boys were pretending to be pirates, using wooden sticks for swords. As they ran around, they found a cave suitable for being a pirate's hideout and went inside to continue playing. They heard voices and hid behind a rock, knowing they shouldn't be in such a dangerous place. They thought for a second it could be their friends, but they soon realized the voices were too mature. They were those of men who sounded angry.

One demanded, "How could you do something so stupid?"

Donato quickly recognized the next voice—the ugly man with the rotten teeth from the ship. "I'm sorry, sir. We got caught. We weren't expecting that they were going to search the ship so far from the harbor. The captain had already arranged it with the authorities. We had no choice but to drop them into the ocean. We didn't want to get caught and go to jail."

"Why the devil did you have to drop them into the sea? You guys don't know how much money this represented for me!"

The men were walking and now drew close to where the kids were hiding. Jacinto had been already hiding as best he could, since he had recognized the angry man's voice as that of his father, Ramon. The boys looked at each other in fright, but remained silent, knowing how much trouble they would be in if they were caught.

Ramon said, "You tell the captain I'm not giving him any more money until I get my slaves in my hacienda. If he doesn't do that, tell him I am going to cut off his head and sink his ship. Nobody makes a fool of me. I don't care how he does it—I already paid for half, and he's not going to get any more until I get my slaves!"

The men walked out of the cave, the ugly man trying to convince Castro that the paid-for slaves would get delivered, all that was needed was some money to cover food and water for another voyage. Eventually, they walked far enough away that Donato and Jacinto could no longer hear them. They came out of the cave once they thought it was safe and headed down to the beach.

Jancinto was three years older than Donato and knew that dealing in contraband was a major felony. In those days, it was considered to be about as low an occupation as drug dealing is today.

He turned to Donato and said, "Please don't tell anybody what we heard in that cave. I don't want anyone to know that my father is a *contravandista de negros.*[18]"

"Don't worry, I won't say anything to anyone. You are my friend. I saw them drop all the slaves on the ship into the water. They were chained. The men were hitting and abusing them and then drowning them. Those men that work for your father are really bad men, and God will punish them one day. But I saved one of the slaves!"

"You saved one? How?"

Donato smiled proudly. "One of the slaves was hanging onto the rope on the side of the ship, so I threw him my ball. He used it to float to the shore. I am pretty sure he's alive. For some reason God did not want that one to die, and I was able to save him. I was his angel."

Jacinto grew angry. "The big ball with the red and white stripes? That beautiful ball your father gave you as a present?"

"Yes," Donato replied innocently, though still feeling proud of himself.

Jacinto scowled. "Are you stupid? Why did you throw away that ball on that stupid nigger? That was a beautiful ball! Your father gave it to you, and now you'll never get it back!"

Donato became angry in his turn at the insult. "I'm not stupid—you're the stupid one! It was *my* ball and I'll do whatever I want with it. I wish I had more balls to save more lives. Who cares about a stupid ball? It was a human being drowning, for God's sake! Don't you read the Bible?"

Jacinto pushed Donato so violently that the younger boy fell onto the sand. He screamed, "You are stupid, stupid, *stupid*! Three times stupid! You wasted that beautiful ball on a stupid nigger!"

---

[18] A dealer in contraband Negroes.

It was obvious that Jacinto was accustomed to his father killing slaves for the slightest thing and so viewed them as little more than animals—things that could be killed without remorse. Donato was frustrated because he was smaller and felt humiliated. Being younger didn't help his standing any, either. He became so angry that his face grew red from the mounting blood pressure. He stood up and jumped on Jacinto's back. He bit his ear and then yelled, "I am not stupid! I am not stupid! This Negro is worth a lot more than your father! Your father is a filthy slave trader!"

Jacinto got even angrier. "You promised to say nothing—you promised!"

He punched Donato in the face, which sent the smaller boy back down onto the ground. Jacinto leapt on top of him and continued to punch him in the face. Donato's nose began to bleed, and still Jacinto didn't stop. Donato looked around in the middle of all these blows and saw a piece of wood. He grabbed it. It must have been in the water for a long time because of the growth of barnacles which gave it a sharp, jagged edge. He lifted it and struck Jacinto in the face as hard as he could. Several cuts opened on the larger boy's face. Jacinto screamed in pain and let go of Donato. He put his hands to his face; when he pulled them away and saw the blood, he began to cry.

"What have you done?" he sobbed. He turned and ran down the beach towards his house, wailing loudly the entire way.

Donato stood up, his hair full of sand, his nose bleeding. He yelled after Jacinto, "Yes, you slave dealer! That's what you get! Like father, like son! You are bad people! Next time, I'll hit you in your crotch!" He waved the stick in the air with one hand, while with his other he held his bleeding nose. "God is going to punish you all!"

He dropped the stick and went to the water's edge to wash his face and clean his bloody nose. He saw his blackened eye reflected in the pool of water and thought, "Oh, no! Mother is going to kill me!"

Donato knew that she did not approve of fighting. He was going to be in trouble. He walked home, attempting to walk around the back of the house to conceal his injuries. Clotilde, however, saw him trying to go up the stairs to his room.

"Where have you been?" she demanded. "Come here right now."

"I have to go do something in my room," he answered lamely, trying to forestall the inevitable.

"Stop it! Come here right now!"

Guiltily, he turned and walked over to her. She took one look at his eye and the smears of blood and exclaimed, "Oh, my God! What happened to you?"

Donato put his head down, trying to hide his black eye. However, his mother grabbed his chin and raised his head up. As she saw the state of his eye, she called out, "Tomasa! Tomasa!"

A heavy-set black woman came running from the kitchen into the room. "Yes, Mistress—what is it?" She took one look at Donato and covered her mouth. "What happened to your eye, little Donato?"

Donato didn't answer. Clotilde said, "That is exactly what I want to know. What happened?"

Donato looked at the two of them in silence. Tomasa tried to protect the boy by trying to deflect the attention of his mother. "The most important thing right now is to put some aloe vera cream on his eye to stop the swelling."

They took him into the kitchen and made him sit down in one of the chairs. Tomasa began to put the cream on his eye, and then tied a cloth around his head to protect it.

Donato said, "Please don't tell Father." He was worried about getting into even more trouble if his father knew as well.

Clotilde tried to remain very calm. "Don't worry. I am not going to tell him anything."

Donato looked at her with his uncovered eye. "You probably will not believe it, but I was playing on the beach with Jacinto Castro and some other friends, and I fell and hit my head on a rock."

"You're right," his mother said. "I don't believe you. Were you fighting with one of the kids?"

He looked away, unable to meet her eye. "Mom, no, no—I wasn't fighting."

His mother didn't want to give him a bad time, given his injury, so she said, "I hope you don't have any internal damage to that eye. If so, you're going to have only one eye."

Donato's sister came running into the kitchen. She took one look at the scene and exclaimed, "What happened to your eye?"

Donato said nothing, looking up at the ceiling to avoid answering any more questions.

Maria laughed then. "You look like a real pirate now with only one eye! Were you fighting with your friends and they popped it out?"

This was a little too close to the truth for Donato. He looked at her with his uncovered eye as if he could kill her. He started to stand up to go to his room.

Clotilde said, "Go and rest. Don't come out until I call you for dinner."

The next day his eye was still swollen, but a little better. With rainbow brilliance, the coloration started to form as green, yellow, and black. He went down to the kitchen and asked Tomasa, "Can you make a patch for me to cover my injured eye? Just a little patch to disguise it."

Clotilde was close by and came over to look at it. She nodded. "Go ahead and do it for him."

Tomasa took him to her room. After putting more cream on his eye, she made a black patch for him. She said, "You have to hurry and get dressed. In a little while we are all going to leave for the city of Bayamo. Your father is supposed to be picking up some horses from Spain, and we also need groceries and a few other things."

Figure 26 Paso Fino horse

Donato jumped up. "Hooray, we're going to the city! We'll probably visit my cousin Francisco Jr., and I'll get to see my uncle Francisco, too! I'll go and get dressed at once."

He passed Maria on his way to his room. She started to laugh when she saw his black eye patch and began to tease him. "Now you really look like a pirate! Save yourselves, the pirates are here!" She began to laugh and giggle.

Donato smiled sarcastically and stuck out his tongue. "I'm a pirate and you're not! I'm a pirate and you're not!"

Maria stopped giggling and looked sad. "I want a patch, too, Tomasa."

Tomasa looked at her, smiling all the while. "OK, my little girl." She pulled Maria close and put her arms around her affectionately. "Okay, I will make one for you, too."

Maria smiled in satisfaction. "Thank you, Mama Tomasa."

Outside, Raymundo was preparing the coach for their trip. It was drawn by two fine white horses. Donato and Maria, each with a patch over their eyes, were already in the coach, along with Tomasa and Clotilde. Tomasa was trying to keep order in the coach while the children played.

Figure 27 Style of carriage at that time

As they left the hacienda, a group of slaves and servants of the house waved goodbye to them. They left the Valle del Cristo where they lived. The smoke of their sugar refinery rose into the sky behind them. Hours later, they arrived at the house of Francisco del Marmol, Raymundo's younger brother. They were received warmly by the whole family, giving Raymundo and his family lemonade and a list of groceries they wanted as well.

Francisco, Jr. was also around ten years of age, the same age as Donato. He convinced his parents to let him go along on the trip. They continued on their trip to Bayamo, arriving two days later. Tomasa and Clotilde went shopping for groceries, various fabrics, and shoes. Raymundo was looking over his horses that had arrived from Spain—an Andalusian stallion and mare. The kids began to yell when they saw a man with a bear on a chain walking in the street, followed by another man on stilts. Then they saw a small band of musicians following these two, playing circus music.

Donato yelled, "The circus! The circus is in town! El Circo Bandini!"

Donato, Maria, and Francisco Jr. begged Raymundo to let them go. He smiled and said, "Okay, okay. If you kids are good all day long today, we will all go to the circus tonight."

The kids jumped up and down with joy. Tomasa smiled to see them so happy. She said, "Okay, calm down or there will be no circus tonight." That got them to calm down immediately and straighten themselves up.

Some men finished loading the cloth, grain, lamp oil, and other supplies into the wagon. When they were finished the family went back to the hotel. Around eight p.m. that night, all of them were ready to go to the circus. They dressed well and went down to the coach. Tomasa was already there waiting for them. The children were very excited. When they arrived at the circus, Raymundo bought tickets for everyone, and they went inside the big tent.

A marvelous time was had at the circus. A few hours later, as they were leaving, they walked through the sideshow area where there were displays, cotton candy, and games. They all got cotton candy, including Tomasa, and came to a shooting game tent in which customers were to shoot at wooden ducks moving in a row in water. Raymundo paid to shoot and hit a duck. He won a small pink rabbit, which he gave to Maria. Then he shot and hit another duck, winning a small toy rifle this time. When he offered it to Donato, however, the young boy stepped back and shook his head no.

"Don't you want it?" his father asked.

Donato had a sad expression on his face as he shook his head again. "Give it to Cousin Francisco."

Raymundo smiled at his son's generosity. Francisco said, "Thank you, Cousin Donato."

Raymundo said, "Okay, I'll get another one for you." He shot a more difficult target, winning this time a small air gun. The operator was not very happy that Raymundo kept winning prizes, but his military background made Raymundo an excellent shot. He held out the gun to Donato, who stepped back, shaking his head once again. "I don't want a gun."

Raymundo was confused. "What's wrong?"

Francisco was also looking at his cousin in confusion. Tomasa leaned over to Donato. "Why don't you take it? That's a good present your father won for you."

Donato began to tear up in anger and crossed his arms. "No! I don't want to die in a fire like my grandfather." He looked at his father, expecting the worst. Raymundo looked at Clotilde.

She was also confused. "I don't know. I never told him anything."

Raymundo grew annoyed. He held the gun out to Donato again. "Hold it. I told you to hold it!"

Donato hesitated. He was angry, but he took the gun out of respect for his father. He walked a short distance away from him. Raymundo was satisfied with the obedience, but still confused by his son's attitude. "Okay, let's go. It's getting late. We should go back to the hotel now, since we have to leave early tomorrow morning."

Donato walked by the games unhappily. They passed a midget in front of one of the tents standing on several boxes. He yelled into a megaphone, "Come see the bearded lady—it's sensational! You have never seen anything like this!"

The other two kids looked at each other in delight, but Donato was still upset. Maria said, "Oh, Mama, before we leave, can we go see the lady with a beard? I have never seen a lady with a beard!"

Clotilde looked at Raymundo for approval, but he still had a long face. She leaned over to him and whispered in his ear, "I think you should talk to him. He really doesn't look very happy. You need to find out what is going on."

Maria kept pleading to see the bearded lady. Clotilde turned to her. "Ask your father. He wants us to go back to the hotel."

Maria turned to her father. "Please, Papa—just one more, please, the lady with the beard."

Raymundo looked at Donato, noticing that his son looked angry. He decided this would be a good opportunity to talk to him alone. "Okay, you guys can go.

Donato, do you want to go with them?" As he spoke, he pulled some coins out of his pocket to give to Clotilde.

"No, that's okay. I'll stay here."

Raymundo nodded, as this is exactly what he wanted. "Okay, you can stay here with me, and I'll show you how that air gun works." The others got in line to enter the bearded lady's tent. Raymundo put his hand on Donato's shoulder. "Let's go and sit down on that bench over there."

They walked over in silence to a wooden bench beneath a tree. After they sat down, Raymundo took the air gun out of Donato's hands and put it in his own lap. From where they were sitting, they could see Clotilde, Tomasa, Maria, and Francisco Jr. all in line, happily waiting for their turn to enter the tent. Raymundo spoke to Donato in a carefully modulated voice, calm and friendly.

"This is a beautiful night, such a full moon. Now, can you please explain to me why you said your grandfather was burned alive?"

Donato raised his head and looked his father straight in the face, trying to discern if he was still angry. "Are you mad at me?"

Raymundo smiled. "Why would I be mad at you? You haven't done anything wrong. I was only upset a while ago because I tried to give you a gift and you rejected it. That made me feel kind of bad. And when I asked you what was wrong, you remained silent. If there is any problem, you should communicate with me so we can resolve it."

Donato realized his father was in a better mood, and so he asked, "If I tell you what is wrong, will you promise me that you will not get mad at me?"

"I see, I see. What did you do that would make you think I would be mad at you?"

Donato said, "If you don't promise me that you won't be mad at me, I'm not going to tell you. You have to promise you won't be mad."

Raymundo smiled. "Okay, okay. Go ahead. I promise I won't get mad."

Donato took his father's hands and looked at them. "Don't cross your fingers. If you cross your fingers you're cheating. Then you're not really promising anything."

Raymundo chuckled. "I'm not crossing my fingers."

"Promise me, no matter what I did, you won't get mad."

"I promise you that no matter what you did, I won't get mad. Are you going to tell me now?"

"What happened was I ran out of paper, so I looked through your stuff in the attic. I looked in the chest where you keep your military uniform and stuff from when you were in the army and where you keep the memory of my grandfather. I looked through it searching for paper for my homework...."

Raymundo interrupted him in an angry voice. "How many times do I have to tell you not to snoop through that stuff? There are dangerous things like knives and swords. You could get hurt."

Donato raised his hand and shook his finger at his father. "Ha! You promised you wouldn't get mad. A promise is a promise!"

Raymundo got himself under control. "Okay, okay. Continue. I am not mad anymore."

"I found in the box a declaration that you and my uncle Francisco wrote to the King of Spain. It said you wanted to get out of the army after you had served for so many years in Cuba because of the suffering you had endured in the past when your father, Don Francisco del Marmol, was burned alive in La Guairá, Venezuela. It said you wanted to retire to a peaceful, quiet, and civil life with your brother Francisco in order to raise your families away from the horrors of war. You and my uncle wrote that document to the King and Queen to get out of the army. Even though you continued to serve in the Spanish army of Cuba, and my uncle Francisco followed in your steps and the steps of your father, you guys would never forget the horror of seeing your father burned alive. That is why you got an honorable discharge. That must have hurt a lot, Dad. I don't think I could stand to see that happen to you."

Donato said this as if it were memorized. A tear rolled down his face. Raymundo could not control his emotions and felt a knot constrict his throat. His eyes also filled with tears. He looked up at the circus lights so that his son would not be able to see the tears running down his face. At the same time, he stroked Donato's hair.

Donato asked, "Is it really true, Papa? He really was burned alive on the orders of the rebel Simon Bolivar?"

"I don't know if Bolivar ordered this atrocity or if it was just a cowardly act of one of his men in his revolution." He put his left arm on his forehead as if he was trying to brush away a bad dream. "Yes, my son, with no reason or excuse, because they were only military enemies. That is not a reason to kill a man in such a dishonorable way. Just because you win a battle doesn't mean you should humiliate the losers. You should be very proud of your grandfather. He always treated his enemies with respect and dignity. He did not deserve what was done to him." There was a sad resentment in his voice. "His enemies, however, did not have the same principals or decency that he had. They not only tortured and shot him, they dropped him to die in that most horrible way, being burned alive."

He could not control his emotions anymore, and hugged Donato while crying. Donato cried as well while they embraced. Raymundo composed himself a little before speaking again. "It's hard to believe how some people behave. Even your own countrymen when we should be brothers and sisters and protect each other. I remember my father stood up for principals. He used to tell me you have to defend Venezuela because this is the land of your birth. What irony! The country he told me to defend is the same one that killed him, and I had to abandon it to save my life and my family. He taught me to defend my principals and my country. But it doesn't always work like that. I concluded that I should always defend my principals and my family first, and then my country. Not necessarily the country you were born in but the country you love with all your heart. You are too young, and I didn't want you to know these things until you were older. I didn't want you to be resentful. The reality is we del Marmols mature very young. It is our destiny to mature at a young age, just as it was your destiny to find those documents. We all have short childhoods. But we are in Cuba now and should not be scared."

"Papa," Donato said, "I am not a little boy anymore. I am a man now."

Raymundo smiled. "Yes, I see, I see. You have become a big man and I didn't even notice. That is the reason I am going to talk to you now like the man you are, and I am going to ask you a question. I want you to tell me the truth."

"Yes, Papa?"

"What really happened yesterday to your eye?" Before Donato could answer, Raymundo put his hand over his son's mouth quickly. "Remember, you are already a man, and we are talking man to man. You are going to tell me the truth. Not the version you gave your mother yesterday."

Donato swallowed. "Okay. I was in a fight yesterday."

"Who were you fighting with?"

"Jacinto Castro, Ramon's son."

"I'm pretty sure you didn't want to fight him. You are not a fighter. What were you fighting about?"

"Because he pushed me to the ground and called me stupid. I had no other choice, I had to defend myself."

"Why did he push you to the ground?"

"He started the whole thing." Donato then recounted how he had saved the black slave's life with his ball. "I'm sorry about the ball, Papa. I know it was a present from you," he said.

Raymundo looked surprised. "You did that? You threw your favorite ball in the water to save his life?"

Donato thought he might be in trouble again. "Remember, Papa, you said you would not get mad if I told you the truth."

Raymundo smiled. "No, why would I get mad? I am very proud of you, my son. Why was this any business of Jacinto Castro? Why did he call you stupid?"

"I don't know. He just asked me why I threw my ball into the ocean to save the life, as he put it, of a stupid nigger."

Raymundo shook his head. "Why doesn't that surprise me? Like father like son."

"He is crazy. He pushed me on the ground, then got on top of me and punched me several times in my face. Look what he did to my eye." He raised his eyepatch so his father could see his badly bruised eye. Donato was getting angry at the memory of what happened. "But I found a piece of wood and almost smacked his face into two pieces." He looked a little satisfied and smiled. "He then ran away like squawking like a hen."

Raymundo looked at his son and smiled slightly. He ran his hand through the boy's hair. "That is the reason I told you that you cannot be afraid of weapons. They are not for attacking anyone. They should only be used for your own defense. We have a duty to defend our friends and family, and when people like Jacinto try to hurt you, you have to do something about it. You have to defend yourself. For example, what if someone tried to rape your sister or your mother? That is what weapons are for. If you have nothing to protect yourself with, they will abuse you and get away with it."

Donato did not answer. He was thinking and listening to what his father was saying.

"I know the memory of your grandpa burning alive scares you," Raymundo said.

"No, I'm not scared. I'm not scared, Papa."

Raymundo put his hand over Donato's mouth. "It is okay to be afraid. But we cannot let our fears control us. We have to control them." He took the small air gun from his lap. "You see, you have to respect this weapon, and you have to learn to use it. The time could come when you have to use it to protect yourself and your loved ones. Do you understand?"

Donato looked at his father and nodded. "Yes, I understand." He took the gun out of his father's hands. "I want you to teach me, Papa. I don't want anyone to do any harm to my sister, my mother, or to you. I promise you that even if I pee in my pants, I will control my fear and will not fear weapons anymore."

Raymundo looked at his son proudly. "I believe you, my son. You are a del Marmol, and I have no doubts that should the moment come, you will protect your family and your dignity." He patted Donato on the head.

Just then the family came out of the tent laughing and walked towards the bench. Donato spoke before they were close enough to hear him. "Can you do me a favor, Papa?"

"Yes, my son—what is it?"

"Don't tell Mama and the others that I'm afraid."

"My son, remember this is a conversation between men. It is no one else's business."

Donato smiled. "It's not a big deal—I just don't want them to know that I was afraid of the weapon because of what happened to Grandpa. Don't tell Francisco, either."

"Don't worry about it." He mimed putting a lock on his lips. "This is between you and me. Man to man, remember?"

"Thank you, Papa. Thank you very much."

Clotilde approached them with a smile on her face as she observed the good mood both of them were in. "I see you guys have made up already."

Raymundo answered, "Of course. We did more than just make up. We had a great conversation and clarified a lot of things." He patted his son on the shoulder. "We have a great warrior here."

They walked through the circus to meet the coach to return to the hotel.

Early the next morning, they began the return journey to their home and the sugar refinery. The coach was loaded with merchandise. When they arrived at the hacienda of

Francisco Sr., they took a break and unloaded some of the supplies they had been requested to obtain. Donato, Maria, and Tomasa decided to spend a few days there. As the rest of the party got ready to leave, Francisco said, "Don't worry. We will be coming to your hacienda in a couple of days, and I will bring them home then."

Raymundo said to Donato and Maria from his seat in the coach, "Behave yourselves, or Tomasa will tell me."

The children nodded and promised to behave. Then they began to play in the large garden.

The coach left, the two Andalusians tied behind it. Raymundo said to Clotilde, "What gorgeous horses they sent me from Spain. I am going to love breeding them. I will have the best horses in this area!"

Clotilde smiled. "I notice you seem kind of worried. You haven't been acting like yourself. What's wrong, my love?" She took his hands compassionately.

"I cannot hide anything from you. I don't want to scare you, but I think the political situation we have on the island is not going to produce anything good."

"Why do you say that? Have you seen or heard something that concerns you?"

Raymundo looked at her and rubbed his forehead in worry. "The same things that are happening here now I saw happen before in my childhood, in my native country of Venezuela."

"What do you see, my love? To me, everything seems fine."

"There is too much injustice, too many abuses. The Spanish governor has denied freedom to the people and is abusing his power. That will eventually create rebellion, and revolution always brings out the worst in people."

Clotilde nodded in agreement. "My three brothers are going to be deported to Spain next week."

"You see? That is exactly what I am talking about." He put his arm around her and kissed her cheek. "That is why I'm so worried. Your brothers are taking it very casually, but some others would not. They would rebel, and that could cause great problems for the future of Cuba and our sons. I have been trying not to create any problems for the Spanish governor so that I don't put our family at risk. Nor do I want our family to end up in the same situation as my father."

She smiled as she hugged and kissed him. "Thank you. You are a very considerate and good man. That is why I married you."

They kissed passionately. He squeezed her face between his hands. "Don't worry, my lady. I will do the best I can not to create any confrontation. I just hope they don't continue to abuse their power and create the spark that could ignite a revolution. I am really sorry about your brothers, but I told them that they could not insist and proclaim that the constitution of 1812 was still in effect today. The Spanish governor would not allow that, and it would just create a great confrontation. We are all descended from the Spanish, and we have all inherited their hard heads. We should know better than anybody that they are not going to allow any political changes unless it is by force, which would cost a lot of bloodshed before they would give up their power and corruption."

"And that would not be good for anyone, because everyone would be losing husbands, sons, and brothers."

Raymundo looked depressed. "Unfortunately, my love, whatever side we choose to be on, we would still be losers: we would lose our loved ones. I hope God makes it possible for them to change their ways, to become more humane to the Cuban people. A war is not good for anyone. I ran away from Venezuela to avoid the violence, and it has followed me all the way to this beautiful land of Cuba, where I thought I would find happiness." He looked out the window of the coach at the scenery passing by.

Clotilde embraced him and tried to cheer him up. "Well, love, we should not be so sad. We are not at war yet, and we have happiness and a nice family. We are going to enjoy this happiness for as long as peace endures."

They looked at each other, smiled, and kissed again.

Meanwhile, back near the hacienda of Francisco Sr., three men, one black and two white, were running into the jungle. They looked like rebels. They were being followed by ten Spanish soldiers who were hot on their trail. One of the white men had a reddish beard and was wounded in the shoulder. A rag was wrapped around his wound. Their clothes looked as if they had been in the jungle for a while. One of the Spanish soldiers took aim and shot the other white man in the back, close to his shoulder. The man fell down for a minute but managed to get back up and continued running. Their faces were cut and bloody as they ran for their lives.

At the hacienda itself, the kids were playing in the front yard. Francisco Sr. said, "How would you like to go fishing in the pond?"

Everyone enthusiastically embraced that idea, and Francisco Jr. ran into the house, followed by the other two. He yelled, "Mama, Mama, we all want to go fishing in the pond. Will you let us go, please?"

She looked at them. They were so happy at the idea that she could not say no. "Okay, but you have to be careful on the way to the pond. Between the high cliff and the strong currents in the river, it can be very dangerous if you fall down. Don't go too close to the river."

Francisco Jr. said, "I know, Mama. You've told me a thousand times. Don't worry, we aren't going to go near the river."

Tomasa was in the next room. She had a turban on her head because she was just coming out of the shower. She heard the conversation and rushed to add, "My lady, I will go with them and watch over them."

Mama smiled. "It is not necessary for you to go. Finish what you were doing, don't worry."

Tomasa insisted. "But, my lady, they are too little. Somebody should go with them."

"They are not that little anymore. You are being overly protective. They have to learn to do these things by themselves. That is the only way they will grow up. My little

Francisco is very obedient. He knows not to go near the river. The pond is very safe. Go ahead and finish your hair."

Another slave with a smoking iron showed up at the door, waiting for Tomasa. She was not happy, but she did not want to show disrespect by continuing to insist, so she said, "Okay, my lady. If you think they will be okay." She went back into the next room.

All the kids yelled happily as they would be by themselves and be able to have more fun without supervision. They got their fishing equipment and walked out the house in the direction of the pond. A little while later they arrived at their spot. There were trees all around, mango trees, coconut palms, and a huge flame tree, looking like a weeping willow but with fiery red flowers.

After some time had passed, they had caught several fish. They decided to go swimming in the pond. They took off their clothes, climbed into the trees, and jumped off into the water repeatedly. They played in the water, and after a bit Maria asked, "How far is the river from here, Francisco?"

"It's not too far away, but we cannot go near. My mother will get very mad if we do that."

Donato said, "I would like to see it. I don't want to go in it."

"No, I promised my Mama. I won't break my promise."

Maria made a long face. "That is fine. You can stay here with the fish and wait for us. Donato and I will go and see the river for a little while. That way you don't have to break your promise."

Donato said, "What a good idea, Maria. We can go and see the river, and our cousin won't get into any trouble for breaking his promise."

Francisco Jr. looked at them in silence, not liking the idea at all. He felt it could be dangerous. Finally, he said, "You are going to get me in trouble, and you'll get into trouble, too. That cliff above the river is dangerous. Sometimes pieces of it fall and if you are walking there you could fall from the cliff into the current. Then you'll get swept away and nobody can save you. Last year one of the cows that belonged to my papa fell down the cliff to be taken away by the current."

Donato said, "Well, go and tell your mother that we are coming along behind you. We are cleaning the fish and be there in a little while. That way you will not be guilty of what we are doing. We can go quickly, take a peek at the river, and come back right away. No one will get in trouble."

Francisco Jr. was growing angry. "No, I am not going to lie to my mom. I will tell her that you went to the river."

Maria yelled, "Then you are a gossip and a *chismoso, chismoso*![19]"

Donato interfered at that point. "Maria, stop. Don't call our cousin a snitch."

Maria lost her frown and smiled. "Well, tell your mother that we are still in the pond, and then you will not be a snitch but a loyal cousin."

Francisco finally gave up. "Okay, okay."

By this time, they were coming out of the water. Maria went to him. "Thank you. I knew we could count on you. You are a loyal cousin."

Francisco pointed to the trail. "Follow that trail, but don't get too close to the cliff and don't take too long. That way you guys won't get into trouble with my mom."

Donato said, "Thank you, Francisco. We owe you one."

Francisco picked up his catch and fishing gear and walked away, heading back to the hacienda. Donato and Maria followed the trail to the river. When Francisco got home, his mother asked him, "Where is everyone else?"

He answered, "Oh, they're coming back soon. They were still at the pond when I left."

Tomasa was in the kitchen close by and overheard the conversation and did not like what she had heard. She knew the only fish here weren't just those in the pond. She

---

[19] Snitch

took the fish out of Francisco's hand and said, "I will take care of that. Let's go and wash your hands."

She walked with him to the kitchen and asked, "How do I get to the pond?"

He looked at her suspiciously. "Why do you want to go to the pond?"

She replied in a commanding voice, "Because I am going to go and get them! You should not leave your cousins alone. They aren't from around here and don't know their way."

He felt a little guilty. "Yeah, they know. It's not too far away. I told them how to come back."

"Okay. How do I get there?"

He knew he had no choice but to tell her. "Follow the trail behind the barn and it will take you straight to the pond."

"Okay, thank you." She turned around and approached Francisco's mother. "My lady, I am going to go and get the kids. Please let me go. I am very, very worried. They do not know the surroundings around here very well."

Francisco's mother could not say no to Tomasa. She saw how worried the nanny was and admired how much she cared for the kids. She smiled. "Okay, go ahead. Go and get them and bring them back here if that will ease your mind."

Tomasa took off her apron at once and wrapped it up in her hand. "Thank you. Thank you, my lady." Francisco accompanied her out of the house and took her behind the barn to show her the trail. She left quickly and headed for the pond.

Shortly after Tomasa left the dogs in the front yard started barking. The three fugitive men from the jungle were approaching the house and came onto the patio. The slaves were scared because the two white men were bleeding profusely. One of the white men yelled out, "Help! Help, please!"

The slaves were afraid to approach them, seeing that all three were armed. Francisco Jr. was still on the patio and saw them. He ran into the house. "Mama! Mama! There are wounded men on the patio!"

Francisco Sr. heard the commotion. He put on his boots and asked his son, "What's going on? What's happening?"

Francisco Jr. ran over to him. "Papa, there are three men in the front yard. Two of them are bleeding."

Francisco Sr. walked down off the porch and approached the men. "What do you want? Can I help you?"

The men put down their guns. The black man replied, "We are *mambises*, rebels who are fighting for the freedom of Cuba. Most of my friends from the group are dead, but we were lucky and managed to escape from the ambush the Spanish soldiers set for us. My master and his brother are badly wounded. They have lost so much blood they can barely stand. We're closely followed by some Spanish soldiers, and we need refuge. I beg you, in the name of God, even if you don't sympathize with our political ideas, spare our lives. If they catch us, they will cut off our heads without mercy."

Francisco Sr. thought for a moment. He did not want to be a part of this, but his good nature compelled him to help those in need. He turned to his slaves. "Quickly! Get these men into the barn and get them some food and water!"

The white man with the red beard raised his hand. "Thank you very much! God bless you, good man." Then he collapsed, unconscious.

One of the taller, stronger slaves came over to help them. He picked up the unconscious man as if he weighed no more than a feather. He put the man over his shoulder and walked towards the barn. The other slaves ran over to help the other two men.

The black man looked at Francisco Sr. "God bless you, good master. You are a kind man."

Francisco did not answer him. He looked on them compassionately, but he knew what he was doing could very well create a big problem for him and his family. He continued rapping out orders to his slaves. "Quickly, clean up this blood!"

Some of the slaves started to sweep dirt to cover the blood while others brought water to clean the blood from the steps of the porch of the house. Meanwhile, the bearded man began to slip off the shoulder of the big slave, who nearly dropped him just outside the barn. A skinny slave rushed over to help carry him into the barn. The rag covering the wound fell unnoticed to the ground, landing under the horse trough.

The Spanish soldiers who had been pursuing these men came into view. The porch was empty by this time. Some of the soldiers went over to the water pump next to the horse trough to refresh themselves. They did not, however, notice the bloody rag.

One of the higher-ranking soldiers yelled to one of the slaves, "Where is your master?" The slave ignored him, so he repeated his demand. "Where is your master, you imbecile?"

The slave was petrified in fear and said nothing. Francisco Sr. was watching through the window. He was tall and more strongly built than his brother Raymundo and had a commanding presence. He had changed regular pants for his old army uniform trousers, as he knew this would impress the soldiers. He added a decorated pistol on one side of his belt and hitched his sword on the other. Then he walked outside and down the porch stairs.

In a commanding voice he called out, "What can I do for you, Sergeant?"

The sergeant looked at him. He knew the gold stripes on those uniform trousers meant this was an officer he was addressing. "You are an officer for the Crown?"

Francisco Sr. replied, "I am a Lieutenant Colonel for the Royal Army. Retired."

The man saluted him smartly. "We are looking for a group of insurrectionist rebels that escaped yesterday from a battle. We have been tracking them for over a day and lost their trail close to your hacienda. Have you seen anybody?"

Francisco stroked his chin in thought. "No. I haven't seen anybody today." He looked at the soldiers who were serving pumping water into the trough. He smiled and said, "I see your men are thirsty."

The sergeant was a little embarrassed as he realized they had not asked permission and apologized. "I am sorry, sir. My men are indeed thirsty. Is it okay for them to drink your water?"

"Of course. They are already drinking it, and that is not a problem. Go ahead and let them drink all they want. Good luck to you and your men, Sergeant, in finding those rebels." He saluted the sergeant and turned to go back into the house.

The sergeant returned the salute. "Thank you, sir. We appreciate your hospitality. We will be on our way in a little while."

The slaves in the barn did not realize how close the soldiers were. They opened the barn door to leave and return to their duties. When they saw the soldiers, they attempted to turn around and close the door, but they were only a few feet from the group, practically face to face. The skinny slave was wearing a white shirt and pants, both of which were covered in blood. s

"Hey, slave!" said the sergeant. "Where are you going? Come over here!"

The slave was paralyzed with fear. Francisco Sr. was not yet in the house. He turned at hearing the sergeant's yell. "I told you to come over here, negro! Come over here or I will cut off your head! Are you deaf or what?"

The slave looked to Francisco for guidance.

Francisco could not see all the blood at that distance. Trying to please the sergeant and avoid confrontation, he said, "Go ahead, do what the sergeant tells you." He was expecting the worst, and so subtly reached down to undo the leather peace bond on his holster.

The slave began to walk slowly towards the sergeant, who took a couple of steps towards him. He grabbed the hand of the slave to look at the blood. "What is this? This is fresh blood. What have you been doing?"

The slave looked at him in fear but replied instantly, "I have been killing a pig."

"All that blood on your clothes came from killing a pig?"

The slave tried to cover up and played a desperate last card. "Yes, ask my master." He looked up at Francisco. "Master, I explained to the sergeant that the blood on my clothes is from the pig you told me to kill!"

Francisco immediately understood the situation. He walked down the steps. "Yes. Are you done?"

One of the soldiers noticed the rag under the trough. He picked it up and waved it around. "Sergeant, look at this. This is fresh blood, too! This is from the pig, too? Did your pig have a wounded shoulder? This slave is lying, Sergeant, I think these people are hiding the rebels."

The sergeant grabbed the skinny slave, nearly strangling him, and put his sword to the slave's throat. "Where the hell are the rebels?"

The skinny slave remained silent, his eyes wide with terror. He shook his head to indicate his ignorance. The sergeant struck him in the face with the hilt of his sword, knocking the slave to the ground. He raised his sword to strike, yelling, "You tell me where the rebels are or I'll cut off your head right now, nigger!"

The slave crossed himself and looked toward the sky. He closed his eyes, expecting to die at that moment. The sergeant swung his sword to decapitate the slave, but before the stroke fell a shot rang out. The other slave by the barn door had shot the sergeant in the right arm. The sergeant fell to his knees, grasping his wounded arm in pain.

The slave who was about to be killed jumped on the sergeant and began to strangle him. One of the soldiers closest to this drew his sword and stabbed the slave through the chest. The two other slaves were charged by the soldiers and were killed.

Everything happened quickly. Francisco Sr. reacted immediately and drew his revolver, shooting the soldiers. He killed two and wounded three more. He was down to one last shot, so he tried to turn around to go into the house for more ammunition. The other soldiers were shooting at him, and a bullet went through his left leg, causing him to collapse before he could get to the door.

His wife ran out of the house in an attempt to help him. She grabbed him and helped him to get inside the house but was shot in the back as she did so.

Francisco Sr. ordered the slaves to barricade the doors and windows with furniture. He opened a cabinet in the living room where he had several rifles, revolvers, and boxes of ammunition. He told the slaves to arm themselves and fight for their lives. Two female slaves ran in from the kitchen and tried to stop Clotilde's bleeding, but the bullet had punctured a lung. She was coughing up blood. Francisco Sr. held one hand, and Francisco Jr. came to her other side to take her other hand.

Francisco Jr. sobbed, "Mom, please don't die." He squeezed her hand.

She turned to her husband and gasped weakly, "Please, save our son. That is all I ask of you." Her eyes closed and she slumped in their arms as she died.

Francisco Sr. stroked her hair and slowly laid her down to rest. During this, the slaves and soldiers were exchanging gunfire and the house had turned into a war zone. He grimly gave his son one of the rifles, and they went over to a window to open fire.

One of the soldiers outside was patching up the sergeant's shoulder. Two other soldiers entered the barn and started beating the rebels, hitting them with the butts of their guns until they killed them. They shot the slave who was lying on the floor of the barn in the head. Meanwhile, some other soldiers were on the ground taking cover, while two others wheeled in a barrel of gunpowder.

They spread the gunpowder around the house and left a trail all the way back to the barn, leaving the barrel near the house.

Maria and Donato were behind the bushes on a little hill watching these events unfold. Donato saw a soldier was about to light the fuse. He raised his air gun, pointed it at the soldier and shot him in the rear.

The soldier yelped in pain and grabbed his butt. Another soldier asked him, "What happened?"

"I don't know—something bit me in the ass!" He pulled down his trousers and asked the other one to look to see what it was. There was a tiny cut there, bleeding very slightly.

The second soldier laughed. "For God's sake, man—you don't have anything. There is a tiny little cut there. Just finish the job." Donato took aim again and shot the other solider in the neck. He yelped and exclaimed, "*Que carajo*![20]" He put his hand to his neck and noticed it, too, was bleeding.

The soldier who had been hit first took his turn to laugh. "Oh, it's nothing, eh?"

The second soldier yelled, "Sergeant, there are more rebels hiding in the forest. They're shooting at us!"

Due to the distraction, they did not notice that the torch had been dropped close enough to the powder, which was now lit. The flame streaked towards the barrel. Ignoring that, the soldiers began to shoot into the bushes. Donato and Maria ducked down to avoid the bombardment of bullets. Tomasa came from behind them and pushed them both to the ground by their necks. There was a tremendous blast as the gunpowder exploded. Some of the soldiers had been standing up to fire in the bushes, and they were hit by splinters of wood and other flying debris as they were knocked to the ground by the blast.

A female slave engulfed in flames came running out of the house in an attempt to save herself but was shot dead by one of the soldiers. Some took refuge behind the water

---

[20] What the hell!

trough. The house was completely consumed in flames and started to collapse. No one could survive this fire. Twilight was showing in the midst of the smoke and fire.

One of the soldiers yelled, "Sergeant, we might be surrounded by rebels. Should we retreat?"

"No, hold your positions. I don't hear anymore gunfire."

Tomasa grabbed the two kids and ran into the forest. After they had run for a while, they felt they were a safe distance from the soldiers. They began walking towards the river. They knew that if they followed the river, they would eventually arrive at their own hacienda. It was by now completely dark. Tomasa, Maria, and Donato held hands as they walked through the forest. Maria let go of Tomasa's hand when she heard the sound of the river's current. She ran close to the cliffside and looked down.

"Oh, my goodness, it's beautiful!" she exclaimed. The moon was out, and the reflection was shining down on the foaming waters of the river.

"Little Maria," Tomasa yelled, "don't go too near the edge of the cliff!"

Donato added, "Remember what our cousin said: the dirt on the edge of the cliff is very unstable, dangerously so. You could fall and be killed!"

Just then, they saw a silhouette come out of the bushes. It was a soldier. He grabbed Maria, who began kicking in her attempt to get away. She yelled, "Let me go! Let me go! You are a crazy man—let me go! I haven't done anything!"

Donato and Tomasa started to run towards the soldier. He was holding Maria with his left arm and held his drawn sword in his right. "What are you doing in the forest at this hour?" he demanded. "You are with the rebels!"

Tomasa was filled with terror and said nothing while shaking her head no.

"You are rebels! I'm going to cut off your head, you damn nigger!" He had evidently been sent to check the surrounding area. "Are these the children of those traitor who were hiding the rebels?"

Tomasa found her voice. "No, sir. They are not Francisco del Marmol's children. They are the children of his brother, Raymundo."

"Oh, so these are relatives of the traitor. They are most likely traitors, too!"

Tomasa covered her mouth, realizing too late that she should not have told him the identity of the children. She tried to fix it. "But, sir, Raymundo is very loyal to the Crown—he is no rebel."

The soldier paid her no attention. He let go of Maria and grabbed Tomasa by the neck.

"Please, sir, we have nothing to do with this. Please don't harm us."

The soldier hit her in the face with the hilt of his sword and then kneed her in the stomach. She bent over in pain, dropping to her knees.

Donato ran over. "Tomasa! Tomasa, are you okay?"

Tomasa was on the ground, clutching her stomach as she tried to conceal her pain from Donato. "I'm okay, I'm okay."

The soldier came over and yelled, "Get up!" He threatened her with his sword. "Move, dammit! Or do you want me to cut the heads off of the children?"

Donato grew enraged with the soldier for what he had done to Tomasa. He raised his air gun and shot the soldier in the eye. The soldier screamed in pain and dropped his sword to clutch at his eye with both hands.

Maria picked a branch off the ground and hit the soldier in his right knee. He screamed in pain, cursing them, "Dammit, dammit, you little bastards! What have you done to me?" He fell to the ground screaming in agony. He rolled over and aimed his gun at Donato, who was closest to him. Donato was terrified as he stared right down the barrel of the weapon.

A black hand holding a large branch came out of the bushes and struck the soldier on the side of his neck with such force that the man dropped his gun and started to roll. His motion carried him over the edge of the cliff, dropping him into the water. A young slave emerged from the bushes, his smile showing his perfect white teeth. "That soldier is not going to kill any more black men," he said.

Tomasa got up and came over to the man. "Thank you."

Donato looked at the slave, who smiled at him in recognition. "You're the kid from the ship. You saved a black man's life."

Donato touched his forehead for a second as he looked at the man, trying to remember. Then a big smile split his face as he recognized who was standing before him. "Oh, my God! You are the slave I threw my ball to!" He ran over to him and hugged him joyfully. He now had proof that his action had in fact saved a life.

The black man felt the youth's genuine joy and happiness at seeing him alive. He smiled and nodded. He raised his left hand and said, "Wait a minute." He disappeared into the bushes and returned in a few seconds with a sack. He put it down on the ground and opened it. After he removed a few of his things he pulled out the red and white ball, which he gave to Donato.

Donato grinned from ear to ear, ecstatic with joy. "Thank you, thank you!" he exclaimed. "You saved it for me."

The slave replied, "I was saving the ball until I found you in order to give it back to you. Thank *you*—you saved my life."

Donato turned to Maria. "Maria, Maria! This is the ball—I got it back! And Jacinto said I was stupid and would never get it back!" He turned back to the slave. "Tell me, my good man, what is your name?"

"My name is Antonio Maceo Grajales."

"I am Donato del Marmol Tamayo. Do you have a place to live?"

Antonio shook his head. "No, I don't, little Donato."

"OK, you can come with us and live with us on one condition: stop calling me 'little'! I am Donato del Marmol."

Antonio smiled. "Okay, I can do that." He held out his hand. "Thank you, Donato."

Tomasa smiled, full of pride in the boy. She told Antonio, "You are lucky, because the del Marmols are a great family, and we get three meals a day. The only thing is you cannot be lazy, okay?"

Antonio smiled at her. "Oh, no, I am not lazy. I am a hard worker." With that, the four of them began walking towards the hacienda.

CHAPTER 9: CATCH AND RELEASE

After we left the Coopers' residence, I drove directly to the lab to drop off the cooler. When I arrived, I left specific instructions that when they finished the job I didn't want them to destroy either the hands or the head. They were to preserve them as best they could so that I could return them to his family.

Figure 28 Entrance to Lido Island

I then drove to Lido Island. When we got home, I fed Rocco and fed myself a cold plate of seafood. I took a small container of tartar sauce and some breadsticks from the Crab Cooker restaurant. I poured a glass of wine and played the CD of my latest album on the house's sound system. I began to eat in peace as I listened to my song, "Insanity: I Love It!"

I smiled because of the reality behind the words I wrote for that song. It really did describe the insanity that has been my life. Little did I know that after what I had lived in the past—all the crazy commotion—what lay in the immediate future, I was completely unprepared for. If what I had been living was insanity, the next song I would have to compose would be about madness, for that is what was waiting for me. Even though I had been well trained and had extensive experience, not even I could ever have dreamed what would happen next.

Once I finished my dinner and a couple of glasses of wine, I called the Corona del Mar safe house where I had left my friends. Chandee knew my code and answered the phone. "Private residence occult and restricted from the ghost of the Cuban Lightning team."

I smiled. "Where the hell did you get all this lingering? *Chinita cubanita*! You must be very happy."

She laughed. "*Mas feliz que una lombriz.*[21]"

"You are in a great humor today."

"Who would be in a bad humor in this beautiful palace with this spectacular view of the ocean? Only someone insane!"

"Well—maybe I am a little bit, but I love that you're happy in one of our modest refuge houses."

"Have you already had dinner?"

"Yes."

"Are we waiting for you tonight?"

"Yes. Tell everyone that I should be there in about half an hour. We'll all take you for a walk on the beach and show you some small details that you must know if you're going to hang around with us for a while. They are strategically important for you to survive in these surroundings. The place is not just beautiful, but very convenient. It is also safe and secure."

"Alright, alright—I'm ready for the Lightning tour."

---

21 I'm happier than a little worm in the dirt.

"Very well. We'll see each other in a little while."

"*Arrivederci*!"

"OK, *bambina*."

We hung up. I had scarcely set down the receiver when the phone rang. I picked up, wondering if Chandee had forgotten something, so I said jokingly, "What's up, *chinita cubanita*? You cannot live without me even for one second?"

A voice completely different said, "Daddy, it's me."

"Oh, I'm sorry, Birko," I told my daughter. "What's up? How are you?" I could hear that she was very stressed and agitated.

She ignored what I said and went straight to her point. She said angrily, "I cannot keep living here with my mother. Please, Daddy, let me come right now and live with you. I promise you that I will be loyal to you and will never tell Mom what I see or hear in your house."

I smiled, knowing that she wasn't mature enough to understand my work. No matter how much I tried to work with her, she continually repeated to her mother everything she saw and heard. It could compromise me, since I didn't trust her mother in the slightest, but I also couldn't have her around for her own security. Until she was old enough, I had decided to keep her at a distance.

As we spoke, she got more upset, crying and screaming. "Mom just called the police on me. I've had it! I cannot live here any longer! My mother is a compulsive liar, borderline schizophrenic personality, a wacko! I cannot live here anymore, please Dad!"

"Birko, you have to control yourself. Stop crying and stop screaming. I cannot even understand what you are trying to tell me. This is not the first time you've had a conflict with your mother. I don't see any reason we cannot resolve this problem, but you have to calm down."

I knew that this was difficult for her because Loren was not an easy person to live with. She was also, as I had discovered when I lived with her, a complete mercenary.

I asked her once more, "Please, can you explain to me calmly what happened? Don't exaggerate anything that happened, so I can analyze it to the best of my ability and help you resolve the problem with your mother. But you have to try and calm yourself down."

I could hear her breathing hard as she tried to calm down and regain control. After a few seconds, Birko said, "Daddy, my mother is trying to get you in trouble. The other night three men were in our home. They've been coming for months, all dressed in black. They looked like FBI or Secret Service. I hid myself this time inside the library closet close to the living room where they were having a meeting. They were talking about accumulating evidence against you."

I interrupted her. "Against me?"

"Yes, Daddy. They were talking about you. I heard them repeatedly mention your name."

"Why me? I'm not in any trouble."

"Because she's a royal you-know-what. She's very upset with you because you won't take her back. She's missing the glamorous life she had by your side. Now she has to work like everybody else in a job eight to five."

I nodded. What she was saying was certainly true. "What else?"

"I heard them offer her lots of money, which she took. They gave her some documents." She paused and breathed deeply again. "She put the money and documents in her dresser in the master bedroom. This is strange, since she has a safe in the living room. She keeps the dresser drawer locked."

She went silent for a few seconds, as if trying to not cry, pulling herself together. "This morning, when she left for work, I got a knife from the kitchen and tried to open the drawer. The knife broke, and I couldn't open it. When she got home this afternoon, she realized what had happened. She called me all kinds of names: little traitor, disloyal, all kinds of insults. I denied everything. Then she called the police. Can you imagine that, Daddy? She called the police on her daughter."

"I believe it, honey. That is the way your mother is."

"The policemen told me that if I didn't tell the truth, they were going to take me to jail. I knew she told them to say that, since I'm a minor and in my own house—they couldn't arrest me for anything. I denied and denied, like you taught me, but they insisted that I was the only in the house to have done this. I told them that I wasn't the only one here, my mother and her boyfriend also lived here, and I was gone all afternoon. I need to talk to you immediately, as soon as possible. I've got a couple of things I want to tell you and don't want to talk about them over the phone."

"Where do you want to meet me?"

"I'll be at China Cove where we always get together in Corona del Mar in fifteen minutes."

I thought about that for a few seconds before answering. I decided it would be a good idea to meet with her and try to calm her down and resolve her problem. If she wanted that document, it was clear she wanted to protect me. She might be exaggerating a little bit, but her motives were good. I needed to see her in person to know exactly what was going on.

"I will see you there at the same location in an hour. Don't rush—even an hour and a half is fine."

In between sniffs, she said, "OK, Daddy."

We hung up, and I dialed the safe house in Corona del Mar. Chandee answered the phone. "Hey, you cannot live without me and have to call me right back?" she teased, still in a good mood.

"Yes, you're right. But this time, you're passing a message to Yaneba."

"Oh, really?"

"Yes, honey, please. Tell Yaneba that I just called you and told you to let her know that she has to activate Plan 303 immediately."

"I assume she knows."

"Yes. She has been expecting this."

"OK. I will do that at once. See you in a little while, then."

I stood there for a few seconds, trying to digest what was going on between Loren and those men. The description worried me. But Birko had the same vivid imagination as her mother. I decided not to let this distract me more than necessary, at least until I could speak with my daughter in person. Then I could get to the heart of the whole story and how much truth was in what she had related.

I called my loyal Rocco to my side. "OK, Rocco—let's walk off our meals on the beach." I picked up his collar and he bounded after me, ecstatic that we were going out.

Figure 29 Corona del Mar, in the neighborhood of the safehouse

We went into the garage, jumped into the BMW, and I drove to China Cove. When I arrived, I parked, opened the trunk, and took out two small canvas folding chairs. Followed by Rocco, I walked along the desolate and semi-private beach until we were a few feet from the water's edge. I noticed there were two jet skis, one beached on either side of the small cove, their mooring ropes leading into the sand where there could be a mooring ring. It looked like they were owned by the local residents. I opened both chairs and let Rocco off his leash. He trotted around, marking his territory. I took my cane and drew a semicircle line in the sand connecting the ends of the mooring ropes of the two jet skis. I had to make sure I stayed inside that line, but I made sure the chairs were close to it so that I was sitting near it. By now, it was nearly midnight, perhaps 11:30. There wasn't a single soul anywhere on the beach. A few houses still had lights on, but it looked like nearly everyone had gone to bed.

Figure 30 China Cove, site of the attempted kidnapping

I was sitting by the oceanography labs and could hear music coming from one of the nearby houses. I had downloaded my songs onto an iPod and listened to "The Lightning: Hombre Solo" while I waited. As I listened to my most recent release, I watched the boats coming in and out of the channel, which offered a pleasant, relaxing view.

I looked once more at one of my watches and saw that it was now 11:40. I thought that this day had passed with the speed of light in an extraordinary way, thanks to the beautiful company of the Cooper family. I smiled as I thought of the many beautiful memories of my own girl from when she was that age. At the same time, the velocity and intensity with which they had passed, dragging with them the most beautiful moments, even of love in our lives, only leaving us very deep memories which proves to us that nothing in life is permanent. Life itself is temporary and evaporates as we open and close our eyes.

Distracted by my thoughts and memories of Birko, I had not realized that the dark silhouette had been added to the empty scenery of that dark, deserted beach. I had in the past great moments many years before there with my best friends. Maybe now some of those past friends had gotten to know the details of where I lived, disappeared from my life, and some could even become accomplices to my enemies. Thinking of all of these things, I realized that we should reconsider moving our headquarters to someplace else.

I thought I saw some movement behind me. I looked to my left, but it was only the reflection of boats' lights over the waves. A few more minutes passed. I checked my watch, and it was almost midnight. I started to wonder why Birko was taking so long. Something in my instincts made me feel uncomfortable. I turned abruptly when I heard Rocco's unusual growling. He had seen, smelled, or heard the presence of a stranger he didn't like. I thought perhaps Birko had shown up or was about to at any minute. I could see someone approaching us wearing a black jogging suit and hoodie. In that dark night I could not distinguish his or her face, but I saw the shadow was coming directly towards me. I stood up.

"Birko—is that you?"

A feminine voice answered, "No. Birko cannot make it. It's me—Loren. Payback is hell, sweetheart!"

"Are you going crazy?" I looked to my side as I heard Rocco yelp in pain. I saw he was swaying groggily and then fell into the sand. I felt a strange stinging sensation in my neck and back, as if stung by two bees. My vision grew blurry, and my legs began to feel numb and weak, losing the strength to support myself. I had nothing to hold myself up and began to sway unsteadily. I turned around to see who the other person was. There were four silhouettes with scuba suits coming out of the water towards me. I could not do anything and tried to raise my arm to use some of my concealed weapons, but my body was so weak that I could only half raise it. The individuals approaching me had strange-looking pistols, like something out of a science fiction show. I could not hold myself up any longer, and like Rocco I finally fell onto my knees in the sand. I managed to reach over and touch Rocco's head. He groggily started to pant. I could see one of the frogmen hand Loren a waterproof briefcase.

He said, "You can count it—it's all there. Exactly what you asked for: one and a half million in unmarked hundred-dollar bills."

When I heard that, I tried to smile. There was an irony in that, because I still had the suitcase with the exact same amount in the back seat of my car. That amount was also in unmarked $100 bills. Apparently, that was Loren's price for my head.

She opened the briefcase and, like a mercenary, made sure she wasn't getting cheated. The men said goodbye to her and said, "Say hello to your friends in the FBI."

That was a surprise. What is the connection between the Loren, the FBI, and these individuals? They were obviously involved in criminal activities and had drugged both me and my dog in a plan to kidnap me.

Two new silhouettes emerged from the water, both dressed in black. Each of them jumped on one of the jet skis. One knee was on one side of the line the other was over it, and so I let myself roll over to the other side of that line. I started to drag myself along the sand, trying to put some distance between myself and the line. My body was virtually numbed, but I wanted to be completely clear of that half-moon. I seized Rocco's rear paws to drag him clear as well, perhaps five or six inches away from the chairs.

One of the men with Loren yelled, "Hey! Where do you think you're going?"

Another laughed. "The fish wants to go back to the water."

They started to approach me. I stayed motionless. I could hear both engines of the jet skis start simultaneously.

The remaining two who had arrived with Loren started to walk in my direction. When they got inside the semicircle, the two jet skis ran out in different directions into the water. The ropes sprang up out of the sand, revealing that each was attached to the edge of a large net. The edges of the net sprang up, the tension on the rope drawing it closed like a laundry bag, snaring the four men near me. They dropped everything they held, and even their wallets fell out of their pocked onto the sand. The rope was so taught that it looked like a violin string.

Loren watched everything going on. At first, she walked away rapidly, but now she tried to run in her attempt to escape from the place. However, she found her escape route blocked by Yaneba, who held a 9mm pistol with a silencer to her head. Terrified, she stopped.

Yaneba motioned back. "Go on—back that way."

She grabbed the briefcase from Loren, who started to wrestle with her. Yaneba did not waste the opportunity and began to slap her face back and forth. She then kneed Loren in her privates, and Loren doubled over in pain. "You'd better keep your mouth shut," she warned, "unless you want to pay a visit to your dentist. Now get moving, traitor."

Loren just received her first lesson to never mess around with Yaneba. One either obeyed her or pay a high price for disobedience. She brought Loren over to stand by me. Both silhouettes from the jet skis came over to me. They were Chandee and Mayari. Chandee asked, "Are you OK?"

"I'm a little groggy, but I'm fine. I have a high resistance to tranquilizers. Evidently they injected me with some kind of anesthetic."

Chopin and Yaneba put the four men in handcuffs while Elizabeth kept them covered. To our surprise, two of our enemies proved to be women. One of them was Arabic, the other was Venezuelan. Yaneba walked over to me.

"What do we do with them?"

"You know the drill. Take them to the dungeons in the safe house. But before you take them anywhere, make sure they are blindfolded."

"What do you want me to do with Loren? Take her to the desert?"

"No. Separate every one of them, and you will be in charge of questioning Loren. I want to know who in the FBI have their hands in the caca. The sooner we find this out the more secure we will all be." I looked at Mayari. "Will you please help me put Rocco in the car? He's kind of groggy." Rocco was showing signs of coming to but was still quite helpless.

Chandee started to help Mayari with Rocco, but he waved her off. "No, no, I've got him. You help Julio Antonio." Even though Rocco was a large, heavy dog, he picked him up.

I stood up but nearly lost my balance. I clung to Chandee's shoulder to keep myself upright. "Are you going to drive like this?" Chandee asked me. "You can't even walk straight. Please, let me drive you home. Or do you want to keep playing Russian roulette? If you don't want to do it for yourself, do it for Rocco. He might not make it to his destination alive. I know you don't care about life anymore."

I looked her straight in the eyes and saw she was serious. I could not help but shake my head. "OK, *chinita cubanite.* You have to wait until I'm drugged to take advantage of me? OK, you win, get in the driver's seat."

She smiled. "OK, let's do it for Rocco."

Mayari put Rocco in the back seat of the BMW, and Chandee got in behind the wheel. Before we left, Yaneba came over to the passenger window while Elizabeth and Chopin put the other four in the van. "Our enemies are already safely secured in the van. We have all five birds in the cage without firing a single bullet." She patted me on the shoulder. "I have to congratulate you—your plan was genius. Now go back to your cave and rest. Remember you're not in very good physical condition yet. I will see what information I can get for you by later this morning. I'm not going to wait, I'm going to start on them tonight, right now. Mayari, you will be helping me, just as we arranged previously."

"Please, Yaneba. Marinate them—don't cook them," I said. She smiled. "Otherwise, there won't be much for me to get out of them. Remember, good cop, bad cop. I want you to put fear in them, so that when I come back in the morning, it will be easier to obtain the information I'm looking for." Both Mayari and Yaneba smiled. "Remember, Mayari, I'm holding you responsible. Marinate them, not cook them."

Yaneba joked, "Not even rare?"

I shook my head and tapped Chandee on the shoulder. "OK, go." I rolled the window up as we left. "That woman drives me crazy."

"Yeah, me, too," Chandee agreed.

Chandee, Rocco, and I were going to handle the rest of Plan 303. We had called it this from the beginning when we received information that Loren had been negotiating with terrorist elements, the prize being my capture. Chandee drove slowly, since she had never been to the place on Lido Island. I gave her directions as we went. We went along Pacific Coast Highway towards Lido. She looked at the exotic car dealerships along the PCH and the Balboa Bay Club as we drove past them.

She said, "This area is not only beautiful, but you can also appreciate the wealth and exclusivity of this city. It's a beautiful place to live. You have a refined taste for the good and beautiful things in life. I also know that you love to enjoy the most exquisite things life can offer. That's why I cannot understand the huge contradiction in your life."

I smiled. "Just one?"

She returned the smile. "Well, as far as I know, there's only one, but it's huge."

I chuckled. "That is nothing new. Nothing with me is little."

She looked at me suggestively. "I know. I'm a personal witness to what you just said."

I shook my head. "No, no, no—I'm not referring to what you're thinking about. Don't have a dirty mind."

She grinned. "Who, me? A dirty mind? Ha! Who is the one that nothing with you is small?"

"That is not what I meant," I protested. "Forget about it, *chinita cubanite*. I surrender, I don't want to argue with you. When we get home, will you at least tell me what my gigantic contradiction is? I won't be able to sleep until you do."

She was serious now as she took a deep breath. "I ask myself, if you love life and the beautiful things it has to offer, why do you take such unnecessary risks, which can take your life in one second? What if those terrorists, instead of shooting you with sedative darts, had decided to use bullets? Instead of driving you back home right now, I would be arranging your funeral."

She said all this in one breath. She stopped and took another breath. She shook her head. "At first, I didn't know what was going on. Elizabeth explained to me that this is all your idea. At first, I believed the idea came from our crazy compatriot Yaneba, but Elizabeth clarified it. She told me that everything has been planned by you from the very beginning when you received the information relative to Loren."

I remained silent, listening and observing her.

Chandee asked again, "How did you come up with idea to be the bait yourself? Why not one of us? I don't think you realize how important the role you play in everything we do."

I took her hand from the wheel and brought it close to my lips and kissed it. "Thank you."

She looked at me, and I could see tears in her eyes this time. "Thank you, from all my heart. It's beautiful to see you actually worried about my life. Believe me, the same way I love you, all you guys, and life, I love my life, too. I intend to be around you guys for a long time. I took all my precautions before I made my move and waited. I didn't even know if she was moving tonight, but I had a hunch, which is why I activated the plan. Believe me, there's no way in hell those guys would succeed, because China Cove is extremely strategic. We even have a submarine there every once in a while for when we need to depart in a rush. I took every precaution I could think of, not only to protect my life, but to make sure that none of you guys gets hurt. It's difficult for you to understand because you haven't been with us for a while. When we get home, I will debrief you intensively in the details. That way, you will understand the tremendous value that this operation today will have not only today but also yesterday, tomorrow, and for many years in the future."

Chandee looked at me and shook her head, unconvinced. She breathed deeply again. We had arrived at Lido, and I hit the remote control. In the back, Rocco was trying to stand on his own but was still groggy. I asked Chandee to help me carry him into the living room where he had his large basket with a comfortable cushion where he usually took his afternoon naps. I got on my knees and caressed his head.

"Rest, Rocco. Stay there. In the morning, you'll be like brand new, especially after all this sedation. You'll have energy like a lion."

Chandee smiled. "Yes, let's thank God that Rocco is OK. You actually are unscathed, too. Just sedated. I have no doubt you have a very, very big guardian angel, and it's none less than Jesus Christ. You wouldn't be in the land of the living anymore if you had a lesser one. Remember, you've been playing with Death for too long. Don't get used to it; one day you will lose that game."

I smiled. "Let's hope that day is maybe forty or fifty years from now. Something I can tell you is that you're right. I have the most powerful guardian angel anyone can wish to have, and it is Jesus Christ."

"Amen to that." She crossed herself, as did I.

"I'm going to open a bottle of champagne to celebrate the success of everyone on this beautiful summer night. No one got hurt, and we got all the fish in the tank. Let's also celebrate that you're here with us and celebrate life itself—that beautiful divine gift we should appreciate and enjoy every second on this earth."

She grinned broadly. She caressed my face with the back of her hand affectionately. "I like that idea very much." She pointed at the Jacuzzi. "Do you feel in good enough condition to enjoy your hot tub?" The ships crossing by in the channel could be clearly seen from the living room, and the steam from the hot tub was visible curling up. The terrace was surrounded by beautiful landscaping.

I nodded. "I'm in perfect condition, physically. If you think my idea with the champagne is good, I think your idea with the hot tub is even better. After all this excitement, there's nothing better than a deep bath and relaxation. The champagne will be the tranquilizer. Whoever invented the Jacuzzi invented it to celebrate—let's use it then as part of our celebration."

I took a couple of glasses from the bar and opened a bottle. I looked at her mischievously. "I don't know and can't evaluate what potential effect this will have when we take into consideration my broken ribs and other minor injuries I have."

Chandee took the bottle and glasses from me. "For precisely that reason, I don't want you to make any effort at all. Don't raise a finger. Let me do all the work, OK?"

I smiled in acceptance. "OK, Chandee. Let's go out onto the terrace."

She followed me and I rolled the bamboo Venetian blinds so we could get some privacy. We could still see out, but the darkness shrouded us entirely from outside view. Chandee put the bottle and glasses on the small bar by the Jacuzzi. She poured two glasses, handed one to me, and raised hers to me. "*Salud, amor, y pesetas.* And a lot of time to enjoy them all."

"Thanks to all three of you."

She smiled and we both took deep sips of the chilled beverage. She came over and kissed each side of my cheeks right by my mouth. Then she kissed me tenderly on the lips. She put her glass on the bar and started to remove my clothes. I started to help her, but she said, "No, no—remember, I'm doing all the work."

"OK."

"You've been working all day long. Save your energy."

"What do you have in mind, *chinita cubanite*, that I might need all those energies later on?" I smiled and relaxed, allowing her to take all my clothes off. Then she poured refills, took her own clothes off, and slipped into the Jacuzzi.

We looked at each other and began to kiss passionately. She looked for a comfortable position to slowly seat herself on my lap. Slowly she lowered herself down and put her arms around my neck. She murmured in my ear, "Love, you don't know and can't image how long or how many times I have dreamed of this moment. Now I will enjoy it for all that time. Thank you for helping me to convert this dream into a reality."

I smiled. "Thanks to you for offering to bring me home tonight. You are the best compensation for my spirit for the whole stretch of the rest of the week."

She smiled with pleasure. We made love for a long time. After we finished the bottle of champagne, we continued making love until we were exhausted. We got out of the Jacuzzi, dried each other off, put on our bathrobes, and wrapped ourselves in blankets. We got into the huge hammock I had tied between two columns on the terrace, still naked. We stayed there until the lights of the crossing ships, satisfied, and fell deeply asleep, holding on to each other.

Around 4:00 a.m., I woke up. I could feel from the movement of the hammock that Chandee had jumped out and was getting dressed. "Where are you going?"

"Returning to the safe house."

"Why so early?" I looked at one of the watches on my wrists. It was 4:10.

"I don't want any emotional problems with our friend, Yaneba."

"Yaneba and I haven't been together for many years."

"Yes, that is possible, and you and I believe it. But in Yaneba's heart, you are still the fire that turns her on and off. You may not understand, but many times, even when you finish a relationship with a woman, this doesn't mean that love is completely gone out of from her heart." I was going to say something, but Chandee put her hand to my lips to stop me. "You don't have to explain anything to me. I know you're not with her, you're not a man to be with two women at once. But still you never approached me out of respect to her. That is the kind of gentleman you are. But I want peace on our team for the time I'm here with you guys. OK? I don't want any problems or hard feelings."

"Very well. Whatever your heart desires, sweetheart. You sure you don't want me to take you back home?"

"No, no. I can go myself. Relax, sleep. You'll have your hands full later, and everyone in Corona del Mar will be waiting for us later. Which car should I take?"

"Whatever car you like the best. There's three in the garage, fully gassed, keys in the ignition."

She smiled. "Whatever I want?"

"Whatever you want. You don't intend to take it to Venezuela?"

She smiled and kissed me on the lips. "Thank you very much or another unforgettable night." With a mischievous expression on her face, she added, "I hope we will repeat it."

I returned her smile. "*Claro, chica.* Of that, don't have any doubts. I enjoyed it immensely, and it brought back beautiful memories."

She turned and went inside the house. I turned in my hammock, wondering if I should leave the hammock and go to the master bedroom or stay there. I was too comfortable, so I stayed, right next to my buddy Rocco. Great memories flooded my mind, the beautiful experience after so many years of the juvenile love Chandee and I shared, reborn again and took so much strain in a few hours. It filled my heart with hope and happiness as I remember the Rio Cristal in Havana back in Cuba. Once again, I thought of the circle of life and destiny, which had both of us in this world of espionage.

We might have found each other, without many options, since the intensity of life at such a young age, surrounded by constant danger of losing our lives at any minute without knowing if we would make it to the next day alive, and see the sunshine in the day. In that macabre game of espionage, a game of Russian roulette played not only by those who lived in Cuba, but those who lived in all totalitarian countries around the world, and especially by such young spies—desperate, looking to find just one person in whom he or she could trust. But also looking for that person you could love before you came to that final day in which you could lose your life.

CHAPTER 10: THE THIRD TRAIL

1870's, Bayamo, Colonial Cuba

Figure 31 Major-General Donato del Marmol y Tamayo

The mansion belonging to Donato del Marmol was just outside the town of Bayamo. It was white with beautiful gardens of roses, gardenias, and other tropical flowers. The hacienda had a high gate at the entrance, and inside the grounds were barns and stables with twenty-five stalls for the beautiful Paso Fino horses. A large white Paso Fino was running back and forth in its corral in the front stable. The horse was lively and displayed lots of spirit.

On the other side of the stables were farmyard buildings with ducks, chickens, turkeys, peacocks, and guinea hens. In front of the hacienda stood a large fountain decorated with all kinds of beautiful tilework. The peacocks strutted near the fountain. In the garden beside the hacienda goats and sheep grazed in a small pasture.

One could see in the distance a large area of low barns and pens for pigs. The large barracks that served as the slaves' quarters were close to the hacienda. Many women with their turbans around their heads were walking around the area while others were preparing food for the men when they came back from working in the cane fields.

A man was ringing a bell near the slave quarters. The man was dressed very well in beige pants, a beige and white Panama hat, and high, light brown boots nearly up to his knees. Around his waist he wore a leather gun belt with bullets in sleeves. In the holster was an expensive revolver with the design of an anchor carved into the ivory handle.

Figure 32 Cruel masters frequently hunted their slaves like animals

The slaves heard the bell and came running. Some were tying the drawstrings of their pants while others pulled on their shoes as they came. The man started to yell at his slaves impatiently. "Come on! The day is going to be over before you get here!"

He carried a short riding crop which he tapped against his boots while he waited for the slaves. Several wagons pulled by massive zebu bulls came slowly into the yard. The wagons pulled up in front of the slave quarters, and slaves began to get into them. Once the wagons were full, they pulled away to drive towards the cane fields. The man watched the process from the patio of his hacienda, tapping his boots impatiently with his crop as he waited.

When the last of the slaves had left their quarters, two of them brought a white Paso Fino to him. One of the slaves, the biggest and strongest, was Antonio. He wore a small military vest and cap. He led the horse by its bridle and then leaned down to help his master up into the saddle.

Two young boys came running around a corner of the hacienda. One was Donato Jr., age fifteen, and the other was Julio Antonio, age twelve. Donato Sr. was the master of this place, and the two boys ran up to him.

Donato Jr. asked, "Father, may we come with you? We want to ride with you into the cane fields."

Julio Antonio also asked, "Father, please let us go with you."

Donato Sr. looked down from his horse, thinking about it for a moment. Then he nodded. "Well…all right. But hurry—I don't want to wait for you too long." Two slaves brought the boys' horses over to them and helped them mount. Donato Sr. saw what was going on and laughed. "Oh, I see." The boys were smiling with satisfaction, waiting for their father to lead the way. "Let's go," he said as he started to ride towards the fields.

A few kilometers from the hacienda smoke rose from the del Marmol sugar refinery where the sugar cane was processed by the slaves, where they fed the raw cane into the pressing rollers to extract the juices. Donato rode in the direction of the refinery, his two sons following.

After they left, the slaves started talking amongst themselves. One said, "The master doesn't look like he's in a very good mood. It's a good thing his sons are riding with him. Maybe that will change his mood for the better."

Another said, "I don't know what kind of fly bit him today. We should not get involved in those things. It's the master's business how he feels."

As they rode across the fields, Donato and his sons heard yelling voice, barking dogs, and gunfire. Donato reined his horse in, holding up his hand for the boys to stop, then listened. They could hear cursing and more yelling in the distance.

An angry voice was shouting, "You son of a bitch, I'm going to cut you into pieces when I get ahold of you!"

Donato turned his horse toward the sound of the commotion and rode off in that direction, followed by his two boys. He almost ran over a black man running for his life. The slave was out of breath and his clothes torn to shreds.

The slave looked at Donato, pleading with his eyes. Donato pulled his revolver out and pointed it at the slave. The slave's eyes grew wide, but Donato motioned with the gun towards the thick sugar cane. He motioned his sons to be quiet. The slave, too frightened to understand, stood paralyzed with terror.

Donato waved his pistol toward the cane again and whispered loudly, "Go! Before they find you! Hide over there quickly!"

Finally comprehending, the slave took off like a rabbit, diving into the cane and hiding himself. Donato Jr. rode over and positioned his horse in front of the bush to help hide the slave.

A few moments later, the bearded man, riding an Arabian horse with a white spot on its forehead galloped up in front of them. The horse was high strung and nervous, and the rider wheeled the horse around, finally coming to a stop in front of Donato. He was accompanied by six fierce-looking slaves carrying machetes. The large man was well-dressed, though his clothes were dirty and not very well kempt.

With a sarcastic smiled he nodded to Donato. He knew he should not be on this property, so he said, "Hola, Donato. I'm just chasing one of my slaves. He escaped from my hacienda this morning, the son of a bitch."

Donato looked at him and raised his eyebrows as he looked straight into the man's green eyes. "Jacinto Castro! How many times do I have to tell you, these people are human beings? If you treat them well, you won't have to chase them like wild animals. I've also repeatedly told you not to come onto my property for any reason or excuse. I know that you have chased your slaves onto my property many times before, and I am not happy about that."

Jacinto looked frustrated and angry at this reply but composed himself. "Does this mean that you are not going to let me go and get that son of a bitch slave?"

"And do what? Kill him like you always do?"

"Does that mean you're going to let him get away? Are you going to protect him, Donato, like you always do with the niggers?" Donato continued staring relentlessly into Jacinto's eyes and said nothing. "Everybody in town and everywhere knows you are a nigger protector. Probably you are in love with one of your female slaves." Jacinto laughed at his own insulting joke.

Julio Antonio glared and tapped his brother's boot with his leg, but Donato Jr. was older, and trusted their father's judgement. He waved Julio Antonio away and tried to calm his younger brother down with a gesture of his hand for patience.

Donato Sr. raised his eyebrow again but showed no other expression nor did he bother to reply to the low insult. "I have not seen anybody here on my hacienda, especially not one of your slaves. Now I am going to tell you one more time: don't come on my property ever again. This is the last warning that I will give you, Jacinto. You are right about one thing: I would rather be known as a protector of the blacks than to be known as you are, a killer, cattle thief, and fence mover. You Castros are all outlaws and bandits, and I don't ever want to see you here again." Donato drew his revolved and trained it on Jacinto. "Get off of my property—right *now*!"

During this exchange, Donato's slaves had begun to gather around them, attracted by the shots and yelling. At first, five or six slaves came to see what was happening, but now there was about thirty who stood with Donato and his sons. Most of them had machetes, but some of them had revolvers and muskets. All of them looked at Jacinto with anger and loathing. Antonio, in particular, looked at Castro with disdain.

Castro noticed all the slaves surrounding him. Seeing Antonio dressed in pieces of a soldier's uniform, he saluted the slave mockingly and asked Donato sarcastically, "Is he a soldier in the Royal Army?"

"It's not your business, but those are gifts from me to him."

Jacinto glared without saying anything. He saw he was outnumbered and slid his machete into his waistband to indicate he was not about to fight. Frustrated in his homicidal goal, he turned to Donato and said, "Raise crows and they will peck your eyes out!" He spun his horse around, waved to his slaves to follow him, and galloped away.

Donato watched Castro's departure angrily. He kept his Paso Fino tightly reined in and said to Antonio, "Take some of the other men with you and make sure that killer gets all the way off of my property." Antonio nodded and waved to some of the slaves to follow him. They walked off in the direction Castro had gone. Donato turned to a skinny slave named Jose. "Do you see that slave over there behind the bushes? Take him up to the hacienda and make sure he is fed and those wounds are treated properly."

Jose walked over to the man who had just emerged from the bushes. He was still in shock from his traumatic experience. He crossed himself and ran over to Donato's horse, kissing one of Donato's boots. "Thank you, master, for saving my life. Thank God you were here at the moment you were."

"What did you do for that man to beat you so badly and chase you out here?"

"My master accused me of looking at my lady mistress with bad intentions, but I swear to God that is not true. My lady mistress always comes in when I am taking a shower and tries to get me to sleep with her. I would never do such a thing—I have a wife and children."

Donato looked at the man sympathetically. The black man had tears running down his bloodied face. Donato closed his eyes and shook his head. "I know. I believe you. This has happened in the past several years at least every two or three months. Jacinto's wife, Lina, has a very bad reputation when it comes to seducing young slaves to satisfy her own sexual desires. Evidently, Jacinto can't. You are very lucky we came along when we did, or you would be rolling along in pieces behind a horse in a sugar cane sack by now."

The slave looked towards Heaven and crossed himself again. "Will you be my master from now on? I don't want to be a *simarron.*[22]"

"Yes, I will be your master. Be a good man, and maybe eventually I will be able to buy your family from Jacinto through a third person. I know he would never sell them to me." He turned to his sons. "You two, ride back to the hacienda. I want to make sure there isn't any trouble with Jacinto Castro. If Jose needs your help, give it to him. Keep an eye on the fields around our home. If there is any trouble, come and get me. And be careful—now go!"

The two boys smiled, waved, and rode off as if they were in a horse race. Donato turned his horse towards the sugar refinery.

The slave was helped along by some of the others. He walked with a limp through the fields. "What is your name?" Jose asked him.

---

[22] A runaway slave with no home, living in the forest with no means of support and no family

"Dionicio."

Jose smiled broadly, showing his perfect white teeth. "You have been lucky twice today!"

"Yes, I know I have been very lucky, but why do you say twice?"

"Because Donato del Marmol is the best master in all of Cuba. At the hacienda we all get three good meals a day."

"I have been extremely lucky today, then. I think all my gods have been with me: Yemaya, Elegua, and Chango have definitely been with me."

"Yes, there is no question," Jose agreed. "You have been saved from your teeth to your tongue." The two slaves smiled and continued on their walk to the hacienda.

A Sugar Plantation.

Figure 33 Sugar cane plantations with sugar mills

Close to the refinery, Antonio sat on top of his horse, lecturing the other slaves on how to cut the sugar cane. "No, no, no! You are cutting it too high. It must be cut low, or next year the cane will not be very productive." He waved to one of the slaves. "Come over and hold my horse." He got down and took a machete from one of the slaves. "Here, watch me. Like this! See? Like this, and this, and this."

Twelve slaves stood around and watched as Antonio grabbed the cane and cut it down with the blade of the machete. Antonio hacked away at the cane. In the midst of one of his swings he saw something shining in the distance. He stood up to get a better look, putting his hand to his forehead to shield his eyes from the sun.

He saw Jacinto Castro approaching with some Spanish soldiers, an officer leading them. He looked again to make certain and said to himself, "Oh, no!" He turned to the other slaves. "Run! Jacinto Castro is coming with some soldiers! Run as fast as you can!"

The slaves all looked at him in confusion. He mounted his horse and they all ran in different directions. At this distance, Castro could see the slaves running and was able to identify Antonio as he mounted his horse. He yelled at the sergeant leading the soldiers, "Look, Sergeant! See that slave wearing your uniform?"

The sergeant looked through his telescope and saw Antonio in an army hat and jacket trying to escape on his horse and the other slaves running off. He did not hesitate and snapped to his men, "Fire! Fire at those insurrectionists!"

Castro yelled, "That man with the hat! He's trying to escape on a horse. He is one of those men who killed your soldiers today."

The sergeant became enraged. If he had any doubts before when he had arrived at the Castro plantation with his inquiries into a slave rebellion, he had none now. He yelled, "Fire at that man! Shoot to kill!"

Most of the soldiers fired their rifles at Antonio. One of the bullets hit him in the shoulder. His hat came off, and he almost fell off his horse. He recovered from the shot and galloped away.

The soldiers surrounded the running slaves, shooting until nearly every one of them was dead.

Jacinto Castro rode into the chaotic scene and spotted Antonio's hat. He got down off his horse, picked it up, and then gave it to the sergeant. "This is the proof, Sergeant." The sergeant looked at the cap wordlessly. He examined it and nodded as he looked at Castro with appreciation.

A few of the slaves escaped the massacre and ran towards the refinery through the cane fields. About twenty slaves were working inside the refinery. Machinery was crushing the cane as the slaves fed the long cane stalks into the rollers. Other slaves were tending to the large pots with a huge fire burning underneath, cooking the syrup.

Donato del Marmol was working at his desk. Alicia, his secretary, poured him a cup of café con leche.

A black hand reached for a rope dangling down and pulled on it. A steam whistle blew loud and long. Donato looked up curiously and asked Alicia, "Who is sounding the whistle? And why at this time?"

Alicia looked her own question back at him. "I don't know."

Donato got up and walked curiously to investigate what was happening. When he reached the whistle, he found Antonio on the floor, bleeding from his wound. He reached down to help him. "Get help. Call everyone, quick. Blow the whistle again." He raised Antonio's head. "What happened, Antonio? Who did this to you?"

"Crown soldiers. They killed most of the slaves who were with me. They are coming this way. Jacinto Castro is with them."

Donato was shocked. "Jacinto Castro? But why?"

The other slaves picked up Antonio and carried him to the office, laying him on a small sofa. Alicia cried as she touched Antonio's face. She got a cloth and worked to try and stop the bleeding from his shoulder wound.

Donato walked over to the window and saw the soldiers arriving, Castro riding his black Arabian. They were at the front of the refinery, Jacinto guiding the soldiers and pointing to the building as he waved his arms. Donato turned away from the window and to the other slaves. "Bring Antonio into the other room behind the office, and then clean this blood off the floor. Hurry up!"

The slaves jumped and started cleaning the floor with a bucket of water and some rags. Others carried Antonio into the next room. The small uniform jacket was lying on the floor near the sofa. One of the slaves noticed the jacket, picked it up, and put into the bucket of water, concealing it under the rags.

The soldiers were coming closer. Their boots sounded on the stairs loudly as they clumped up them. Suddenly the door flew open and soldiers rushed into the office. The slaves looked up in surprise. As the door flew open, it knocked over a small oil lamp behind it. The lamp fell, broke, and spilled oil all over the floor.

The sergeant burst into the room. "Where is the rebel?" Some more soldiers stood behind him, while Castro stood by the door.

Donato angrily looked at Jacinto with a look which could kill. He stood up behind his desk. "What is the meaning of all this? What is going on, exactly? Why did you come into my office like this?"

The sergeant was surprised by this reaction. "We have been informed that you are hiding rebels in here. Where is the man we shot and followed all the way here?"

Donato looked again in fury at Castro, and then turned his anger towards the sergeant. He pointed at Jacinto. "I see. This man must have been filling your head with lies. Sergeant, I come from a military family devoted to Spain. My father is retired from the Royal Army, having served Spain all his life. My reputation will speak for me. You had better speak with your commander, Count Valmaseda. Is he not still Commander-in-Chief of all Royal Army forces in Cuba? He has invited me, with my family, to a party welcoming his daughter's return from Spain. Why are you listening to this cow thief? This fence mover and bandit? Why do you listen to his lies and then run into *my* office like I am a criminal?"

The sergeant could see Donato was beside himself in rage. He was confused and afraid and looked around at all his men. He began to act humbly. "Well, uhh, possibly there has been some terrible mistake and erroneous information was given to me."

The sergeant pointed to one of his soldiers, ordering him to pick up the lamp and clean up the mess. The soldier complied and tried to fix the lamp, but it was too broken. Jacinto Castro began to act nervous. One of the slaves who had been cleaning up the room tried at that moment to leave. But Jacinto noticed something in the water. He put his foot out and tripped the slave, who fell to the floor. The bucket spilled the water, the rags, and the uniform jacket all over the floor.

Jacinto bent down and picked up the jacket, raising it into the air. "Oh? Wrong information, eh? Lies, huh? Well, Sergeant, look at this—this is the same jacket worn by the man we shot in the field a little while ago."

The sergeant took the jacket in his hand and examined it, noticing the bullet hole in the shoulder. "Donato del Marmol, you are under arrest for crimes against the Spanish Crown."

Donato kept himself very controlled and unruffled. "Sergeant, don't allow yourself to get involved with this man. He is a well-known thief. His words are all lies. That jacket belonged to my grandfather, and I gave it to my slave because he is very trustworthy and a good worker. I have known him since I was a child. He is neither a criminal nor rebel. He is a good man."

The sergeant stepped forward. "You are under arrest for hiding a rebel who is running from the law. Where is he?"

Donato said nothing. He stepped back and tried to draw his revolver to defend himself, but before he could, the soldiers stepped in and pointed their rifles at his head. He had no choice but to surrender. Castro smiled in satisfaction.

The sergeant asked again, "Where is the rebel we are looking for?"

Alicia was nearby and spoke up. "Sergeant, everything my master is telling you is true. He is a very respectable and honorable man. Everybody around here loves him. This man," she pointed at Castro, "is a cow thief, a bandit, and a murderer. He kills people just for the pleasure of it and he…."

Castro stepped over and hit her in the mouth so hard she was knocked down and rolled across the floor, blood dripping from her mouth. He jumped over and picked her up by her neck. "Where is the rebel slave? Tell me now or I will kill you!"

Alicia glared at Jacinto. She twisted her head and spit in his face. Jacinto drew back his hand and hit her again. She was knocked almost unconscious. Jacinto drew back to strike her again, but before he could, the side door opened violently, catching everyone by surprise. Antonio jumped into the room. He grabbed Jacinto and hit him in the face four times. Antonio was a big man. Even though he had lost a lot of blood, his punches were still strong. He broke Jacinto's nose, split his lips, and knocked out some of his teeth.

Even with only one arm to swing, Antonio kept hitting Jacinto, snarling, "You broke the mouth of my wife, I will break your mouth in return!" Jacinto fell to the floor.

One of the soldiers ran in and struck Antonio with the butt of his rifle. Then he spun the weapon around and pointed the barrel in his face. The soldiers pulled Donato and Antonio out of the office and walked down the stairs. Jacinto Castro followed behind with the help of one of the soldiers. He used a white handkerchief to clean his face and wipe the blood from his mouth and nose.

As they came down the stairs of the refinery, everyone heard the steam whistle blow three times and then stop.

Then it blew three more times and stopped. Alicia was pulling on the cord, clearly sending some kind of signal.

As the soldiers came outside, they found themselves confronted by almost three hundred slaves assembled in front of the refinery, waiting and angry. The sergeant glanced worriedly at Donato. The slaves were armed with machetes, pistols, and muskets. Jose had a musket in his hands as he came forward.

Jose pointed at Donato and said, "This man is innocent." Then he glared and pointed at Castro. "But behind you is the worst thief and murderer in this area. He is not worth this trouble." He spat on the ground. "All those men who died out in the cane field were murdered. Someone is going to pay for that. You better release my master and Antonio if you want to leave this place with your heads on your shoulders!"

The soldiers looked around at all the slaves and became nervous. They could see that the slaves were not going to let them get away. Fear started to show on some of their faces.

Donato was growing concerned, seeing that this was the kind of trouble he had been trying to avoid for himself and his family for a long time. He raised his hand and said, "No, Jose! Don't let our people be the ones to make any problems. I don't want to see anybody else shot or killed over the lies of Jacinto Castro. I will talk to Count Valmaseda as soon as possible and describe everything that happened here today. These two will pay for what they have done."

Jose was not happy, but he respected and believed that Donato could save the situation. He waved and gestured for all the slaves to get back and let the soldiers pass. They made a small opening, but otherwise stood their ground. The sergeant and Castro started to walk toward that opening, the soldiers following, with Donato and Antonio in the middle. The soldiers were scared as they passed through the small path the slaves allowed them as they saw the angry faces on both sides. It looked like at any moment they might attack and eat the soldiers.

When they were almost through the human pathway, one of the younger soldiers, in his fear, tried to push Donato to make him walk faster. However, he pushed too hard, and Donato tripped and fell. Antonio turned and saw what had happened. Even with his wounded arm he bent down to help Donato up.

The soldier's fear turned to irritation, and he struck Antonio with the butt of his rifle, right on the wound. Antonio screamed and blood began to flow again. The pain drove him to the ground next to Donato. At that, the slaves could no longer control their anger. They began to yell and began to attack the soldiers, swinging their machetes, smashing them with wooden sticks.

The soldiers turned back and began to defend themselves. They shot and killed several of the slaves, which only infuriated the mob even further. A shout of "Kill them, kill them!" arose, and those slaves with firearms opened fire, while those with machetes began decapitating soldiers.

The sergeant and Castro were almost through the crowd. At the commotion, the two of them turned to see what was happening. They saw the killing going on and did not wait any longer to run. The sergeant looked at his remaining men and yelled, "Run! Save yourselves!" The few remaining soldiers sprinted to their horses. A few soldiers in the middle of the conflict tried to hold the slaves off, but one by one they were killed. The sergeant reached his horse, jumped on, and yelled at the top of his lungs, "Retreat! Run for your lives!"

Once on their horses, the few soldiers who were with the sergeant and Castro rode like the wind to get away. By now the slaves had killed all but a few of the soldiers. The ones that were left were surrounded and knew they were going to die.

Donato and Antonio were still on the ground. Donato tried to help Antonio by holding the bandage on his arm tightly in an effort to stop the bleeding. They were outside the area where the soldiers were fighting the slaves.

Finally, Donato was able to get to his feet. He was frantic to stop the slaughter and raised his arms to get the attention of the slaves. "Stop! Stop at once! No more killing! Stop, I say!"

The mob stopped and fell back. They made a little opening for Donato to make his way through to the center. He looked at the few remaining soldiers, bloody and terrified, but still fighting. He raised his hands again to yell at the soldiers. "Stop! Surrender now, or you will die! You have no choice; you cannot win! Look, your sergeant has run away. He is gone!" He pointed in the direction of the sergeant, now in the distance in his flight with the few men who managed to get to their horses. "Don't be idiots! Don't die for the lies of that criminal Castro. Surrender now and I promise your lives will be spared."

The three remaining soldiers put down their weapons, and the slaves disarmed them. Jose began to scream, "Hang them! Hang them from the flame tree!"

Another slave said, "Yes, hang them from that tree over there!"

A group of slaves grabbed the soldiers and prepared to put a rope around their necks. The soldiers looked at Donato in desperation. Donato cried, "No! Bring their horses and let them go. We have already won! They have surrendered. Now let them go—this will be a lesson for them for the rest of their lives. We don't have to kill them."

The slaves reluctantly brought the horses over for the three soldiers and stood by as the terrified men mounted up. The soldiers walked their horses a few feet and glanced back, not believing they were actually being let go. They continued walking at a slow pace in disbelief until they were a safe distance away. Then they spurred their horses up to a gallop and rode off like mad.

Donato looked sadly around at all the dead soldiers on the ground. He buried his face in his hands and looked up to the sky, seeking an answer from God. He turned to face the slaves. "Do you realize we just declared war against all the armed forces of Spain in Cuba? After this killing there is no way to turn around. It's too late."

He clasped his hands behind his back and paced around, deep in thought. He looked up at his slaves with an expression of pain and resignation.

Jose came over to him. "My master, whatever you want to do, we are with you."

"Well, my good and loyal Jose, we are at war. We have no other choice now." He put his hand on Jose's shoulder. "Thank you. Go now to the hacienda and tell my wife to pack everything needed to survive for a long time. Include weapons and some slaves for an escort. I want her to take the children and go to her family's hacienda. I don't want anything to happen to Guadalupe or the children. We should expect retaliation from the Crown."

Jose bowed his head in acquiescence. He walked to his horse and rode off quickly towards the hacienda. Donato turned to the other slaves. "Go on up to the hacienda and pack your things. I will be there in a short time, and then I will tell you what we are going to do." The slaves looked at each other in confusion. "Go! Go now! I will be there in a short time."

The slaves began to walk toward the hacienda while Donato and Antonio went inside the refinery. They walked up the metal staircase to Donato's office where they found Alicia, who was sitting on the small sofa, crying. Donato tried to comfort her. "Don't worry. Everything will be all right. Thank you for trying to defend me."

She saw that Antonio's shoulder was bleeding again and she proceeded to change the bandage to try and stop the bleeding. She still had blood on her mouth and face. As she worked, Antonio tried to clean it up by licking his finger and wiping away the blood. He said, "You're a good woman, Alicia."

Donato smiled. "Yes, she is a great woman."

Alicia looked up at Donato. "What is going to happen now?" Her concern and fear were evident.

"Well, Alicia, pray to God that whatever happened here today will be for the best of all Cubans tomorrow, and our children will live in a free and independent country. For now, however, you must get out of here and take Antonio to the hacienda. I will see you there in a little while."

They both looked at him in surprise, wondering what Donato had planned. Out of respect, however, they kept their questions to themselves and did as he said.

Donato went over to his desk and started looking through some documents. After a short time, he walked out on the balcony of the refinery to the railing. He gripped it with both hands while he thought about his situation. He looked out at the sugar cane and around at the refinery, then up to the sky. He closed his eyes and pounded the rail with both fists.

He opened his eyes and walked back inside. He went down to the steam engine inside the refinery. He closed all of the valves. He looked up and saw a few slaves still there. "Get out of here now! Run up to the hacienda. This place is going to blow up."

The slaves saw what he was doing and glanced uncertainly at each other. Was the master going crazy? There was no time to ponder the question—they ran out of the refinery immediately.

The needles measuring the steam pressure in the gauges indicated the increasing pressure, creeping up towards the red zones. Donato watched the gauges rise and then ran out of the refinery, over to his Paso Fino. He mounted the horse and galloped away.

Soon after there was a massive explosion that blew the large chimney clean off the roof, reducing it to rubble in the process and sending pieces flying in all directions. Then an even larger blast occurred, and the refinery itself blew up as the main boiler exploded. Large pieces of metal and stone flew in all directions as the refinery collapsed in on itself.

I

Figure 34 Burning the plantation

Donato turned to look at the explosion and saw that the place was utterly decimated. Sadness and guilt nearly consumed him as he watched the total destruction of what his ancestors had sacrificed for so many years to build. He felt bitter that the political situation had forced him to destroy all that work in just a minute. He spurred his horse toward the hacienda, passing by Antonio, Alicia, and some of the slaves, all who were looking at him in disbelief. Behind them, the refinery burned wildly, the smoke curling high up into the sky.

He found the rest of the slaves waiting in the front courtyard of the hacienda. Guadalupe was waiting in a large wagon loaded with supplies in the front of the house. Donato rode into the courtyard and over to his wife. She got up and hugged him, his sons surrounded him, but nobody asked any questions. They all knew what had happened and that they must leave.

Guadalupe brushed some dirt off his shoulder, a remnant from when he had lost his balance after being shoved by the soldier. "How did you get so dirty?"

He smiled at her gently. "I wish that was the only thing we had to worry about, and I wish this had never happened. I will explain it to you later. The important thing now is you have to leave. It isn't going to be safe here after the soldiers come back."

Donato Jr. and Julio Antonio both stood their ground, not wanting to leave their father. Donato Jr. said, "No, father! We will stay with you and fight—we won't go!"

Donato put his arms around the boys and hugged them tightly. "No, no, my sons. You make me very proud of you, but you cannot stay here. I want you to take good care of your mother and sister. Now go on, up into the wagon."

Obediently, reluctantly, the two boys got into the wagon with their mother. Those remaining behind bid a tearful farewell to the wagon and those slaves going along as an escort. Donato turned and climbed up on top of some boxes to face the slaves, raising his hand for quiet. "Today is an extraordinary day for every one of us. We will never forget it as long as we live. Today we are going to be free. It may be God that is determining my decision about what to do next."

The slaves all looked at him in confusion and wonder. "All of you," he continued, "have been my slaves for many years. For that, I give you my sincere thanks. But, I too, have been a slave—a slave to the Crown for all my life. I cannot expect any gratitude from them. All I can expect from the Crown now is death and sorrow. Nothing else. But, like you, I have had a dream of being free. Today we are going to make that dream a reality. From now on, *you* are going to be free. I give you your own freedom, just as I give myself freedom as I will no longer be under Crown's colonial control. Not anymore."

Screams and weeping broke out among the slaves. "Today we are going to burn all my property. Anyone who wants to fight with me is welcome."

Silence descended as the slaves looked at him in horror and shock. "We are going to fight for freedom and against all injustice, all the abuse, for a better Cuba. If you don't want to fight with us, we will respect you and you are still free to go wherever you want. Choose whatever you want to be. But don't let your dreams of freedom fly away. Remember, the decision you make today is very important and will affect you for the rest of your lives. Real freedom always has a high price. Sorrow is what I see as I watch my hacienda and refinery burning. When I see all the people I loved killed by the soldiers, I grieve. But we have to go through these twisting roads of sorrow and grief to obtain freedom."

Some of the slaves looked sad, and a few started chanting, "Freedom! Freedom! Freedom!"

A small group of slaves who did not want to become involved started walking silently towards the gate, pulling their wagons loaded with their belongings. Some of those remaining reached down to pick up rocks, yelling "Traitors!"

Donato saw this and yelled, "No! Let them go. It is their choice to live as they wish. They are free now, just as you are."

The former slaves dropped their rocks out of respect for Donato. "Good," he said approvingly. "Now, I name Antonio my First Lieutenant in our new rebel forces. Jose I name as Sergeant Major of the battalion. Freedom or death!"

The battle cry was picked up at the top of their lungs. "Freedom or death! Freedom or death!"

Donato stepped down, followed by Antonio and Jose. They took some torches and began to set fire to the house.

Donato instructed others to release the animals and help them set everything on fire. He said, "When the Crown's forces arrive, all I want them to find is ashes!"

The cane fields erupted in flames. Combined with the flames from the already burning refinery and the homestead's fires, the flames and smoke could be seen from several miles away.

The wagon with Guadalupe and her family rolled along toward the hacienda belonging to her parents, Canoa de Cedeno. One of the slaves who had been scouting ahead came back to the wagon. "Put out the torches. There are a lot of soldiers coming this way," he reported.

Donato Jr. took charge as his father had told him to do. "Take the wagon over there to those bushes and cut all the branches you need to cover it up completely," he said. "Everybody hide and keep silent."

Guadalupe heard this and poked her head outside. "What are you doing?"

"I'm going to try and distract them away from here so you can go on."

"No, no, my son. It is too dangerous! The soldiers will catch and kill you!"

"Don't worry, Mother. God is on our side. He will protect me."

Guadalupe looked at him and smiled. She sighed and crossed herself. She nodded. "God bless you, my son."

Donato Jr. walked over to the slave in charge of the group and whispered in his ear. "If I don't come back in an hour, don't wait any longer. Continue the trip without me. Take my mother, brother, and little sister to my family's hacienda."

The slave looked at him and gave him the sign of the cross. "God be with you. Be careful."

The youth mounted his horse and rode away. He didn't go far before he spotted the patrol. There were perhaps twenty soldiers, checking all the bushes on both sides of the road and carrying torches held high over their heads for better light. He watched the soldiers for a moment. Suddenly he heard a noise coming from behind him. He turned his horse around and tried to hide. Someone was riding a horse like mad and coming up the road towards him. The rider reined in and stopped about twenty feet away.

A voice whispered loudly in the night, "Donato, Donato—where are you?" He was surprised to hear someone calling him by name. The whisper came again. "Donato, where are you?"

This time Donato recognized the voice of Julio Antonio. He whispered to him angrily, "What are you doing here? I told you to stay with Mother and our sister!"

Julio Antonio answered with a slightly mischievous smile, "I came to help you. I know you will be needing it."

Donato bent over on his horse and tried to smack his little brother, nearly falling out of his own saddle. "I told you to stay with them! You could get yourself killed here!"

"Calm down, my brother. In a little while you will be thanking me for coming to help you."

The soldiers were still checking both sides of the road. One of them fired a shot at something. Donato and Julio Antonio both looked into the night toward the gunfire. The soldiers came nearer. In order to protect their family and decoy them in another direction, they rode towards the group. They fired their weapons into the air, turned their horses and galloped away. The soldiers, hearing the shots, began to chase them. The darkness was a great benefit to the brothers.

As they galloped along, Julio Antonio yelled, "Take this road! This is the way I came to find you before you got to the soldiers. I came to save your behind, big brother!"

Donato smiled and shook his head. "Okay, military genius."

Julio Antonio saluted him. "I learned from my father."

They turned off the road as Julio Antonio had indicated. They could hear the soldiers still pursuing behind them. Julio Antonio yelled, "When we get past the last row of trees, get way down in your saddle!"

"What?!"

"I said get down—I have a special surprise for those soldiers. They're getting close. I'll tell you when. Be ready—do you hear me?"

Unsure what his brother was planning, Donato went along with it. "Yes!"

The basic plan was already working, as the soldiers remained in close pursuit. After they had ridden for a while, the soldiers were much nearer.

Julio Antonio glanced over at his brother. "Now! Get down!"

The two boys ducked down and leaned over the necks of their horses, lower than their horses' heads. The two leading soldiers saw them duck down but continued riding upright. They found out the hard way that, as they passed two trees, a thick rope had been stretched across the road, high enough for a horse to pass under, but not an upright rider. As the soldiers hit the rope they gasped and were yanked out of their saddles and flung back hard to the ground.

After they rode past the trap, the boys slowed their horses down and looked back. Julio Antonio asked, "Do you think they're dead?"

"Maybe, or close to it," Donato answered. "You know, you really are a military genius."

Julio Antonio smiled. "See what happens when you chase me? Wait here for me. I'm going to go get the weapons from those two soldiers before the others get here." He gave his musket to his brother.

"I don't think that's a good idea. The others are already too close."

"We might need those guns." Without waiting for further argument, he rode off towards the two downed soldiers.

Donato remained under cover, watching anxiously. The next thing he saw was Julio Antonio being escorted by several soldiers, two of whom were wounded. His brother was tied up. "Oh, no!" he said quietly to himself. He thought to mount a surprise attack to rescue his brother, but then more soldiers appeared, led by a captain. He was steaming mad and yelled, "Damned insurrectionists! Damned Cuban rebels! You Cuban idiots! You Cubans are all insane!"

Julio Antonio was still defiant and full of fight, kicking at the soldiers and mocking them as they pushed him. He got mad and jumped on top of a soldiers, clawing and biting him. Two more soldiers came into the fight to separate the two when Julio Antonio took a bite out of another soldier's ear. That soldier screamed and clutched at the wounded ear, blood running down the side of his head. Another soldier gave the man a handkerchief as he writhed in pain. One of the soldiers raised his rifle and took aim at the boy.

The captain yelled, "No! Don't shoot! I want him alive so he can be decapitated!"

The soldier ignored the captain and fired a shot. The bullet hit Julio Antonio in the shoulder, and he fell to the ground, screaming in pain.

The captain jumped over to the soldier, snatched the rifle away from him, and slapped him three times in the face. "Casimiro, you stupid idiot! I said no, *don't* shoot! And you did it, anyway, disobeying my orders." He turned to the other men. "Arrest him. Put him in isolation."

"Yes, Captain Valdes," one of them said. Four soldiers arrested Casimiro and led him away. Julio Antonio smiled his defiance at Casimiro as he went by. Casimiro kicked out at Julio Antonio as he was brought past and hit the boy in the leg.

One of the soldiers picked up Julio Antonio to prepare him for execution. Peering at him, he took pity on him and said, "Captain, this is only a little boy."

"Freedom or death!" Julio Antonio shouted.

This infuriated Captain Valdes. "Execute him! I don't care how old he is!"

As he was hustled by the captain, Julio Antonio managed to get loose from their hands and kneed Valdes in the groin as hard as he could. He yelled once more, "Freedom or death!" The captain doubled over and fell.

One soldier began to tie a blindfold around Julio Antonio's eyes, but the boy yelled, "No blindfold! Never! You're going to kill a del Marmol! You're going to kill a man!"

Donato watched helplessly from his place of concealment, tears streaming down his cheeks.

Julio Antonio held his head high. A soldier held a sword, ready for the execution. Once again, the soldiers crowded around with torches held high for better light. The captain was still in great pain, clutching at his genitals with his right hand. A drum rolled a death beat, and the soldier raised his sword to swing.

Valdes yelled, "Kill him!"

Before the blow landed, Julio Antonio yelled his last defiance. "Freedom or death! Long live a free Cuba!"

As the soldier swung, the blade hit one of the torches, and burning embers came flying down all over the place. Some came down on top of Julio Antonio. The drum beat its last ruffle. The sword swished down, the blade flashing in the red torchlight. Blood spurted from Julio Antonio's neck as his head was separated from his body, splashing the soldier in the face.

Weeping silently, Donato carefully crept back away. He was reminded of the stories told him about his great-grandfather, the Crown's governor of Venezuela. It was now long past the hour he had given, so he carefully made his way back to the road and nudged his horse into a cautious canter. Once he was far enough away from that dreadful scene, he galloped until he caught up with the wagon, reuniting with Guadalupe, his sister, and the others as they headed for the family hacienda.

CHAPTER 11: THE LIGHTNING, SURVIVING LOCO

Several hours later, I woke up and saw the sun was high in the sky. I had to be honest with myself and admit that I still felt a little tired from the events of the previous night. My body was still stressed with its recuperation, and the tremendous exercise from last night. It wasn't just the encounter on the beach; and though it gave me a great deal of pleasure, my exertions with Chandee were not precisely what my body really wanted as part of its recovery. I smiled, thinking as I touched my sore ribs that Chandee had provided me a more powerful anesthetic than my enemies had administered in their attempt to neutralize me. Perhaps the combination of the two gave me the sensation of being badly beat up. I looked at the watch on my left hand and saw that I had overslept that morning. It was already past 10:00 a.m.

I jumped out of the hammock and took a shower. This was unusual for me at that time of day, because I preferred baths in the morning. But I was late; I took some fruit, eggs, and yogurt for a light breakfast. I wasn't particularly hungry but wanted something cool to soothe my insides.

Rocco ran around like a madman free in the jungle. He looked like a soldier waiting for the order to enter combat. Instead of calming him down, the tranquilizers he had been given had re-energized him. He had eaten all the food in his bowl. That was unusual for him, as whenever I refilled his bowl in the morning was that there usually was still food in the bottom. It could also have been the result of my sleeping in so unusually late. He sniffed his bowl slightly, apparently already full. He followed me and jumped into the Jaguar.

"Oh," I said with a smile, "you're picking the car for us today, eh?" He growled urgently. "OK, let's put the top down. It's a beautiful day today."

I had arranged a meeting last night with O'Brien at the C'est Si Bon café in Newport Beach. I drove down the Pacific Coast Highway and arrived on Riverside Drive and the small bakery. We sat down facing the parking lot near the door at the bar. We each ordered a Black Forest ham sandwich, the house specialty. As we waited for it to arrive, O'Brien pulled a folder out of his briefcase and handed it to me.

Figure 35 Riverside Drive, Newport Beach

Figure 36 C'est Si Bon

"According to the fingerprints Yaneba got to us early this morning, this is what we found out about the birds you have in the cage. Be careful with them. They are extremely dangerous, especially Carlitos el Jakalito. This guy is supposed to be the son of Carlos Ramirez Sanches, the Jackal of Venezuela."

Sanches was serving a life sentence in France and was a notorious terrorist and a friend and confidante to Che.

Figure 37 Carlos the Jackal

"Also, one of his students is from the People's Friendship University of Russia," O'Brien continued.

Also known as RUDN, the Moscow university, established in 1960, provides "higher education" for third world students. It became an integral part of the Soviet offensive in non-aligned countries. In very simple words, it was an advanced school for international terrorist expansion from the Soviet Empire in that decade.

The waitress, a beautiful blonde with blue eyes and a beautiful smile, brought our sandwiches and asked, "Anything else?"

"Yes," I replied. "When we are finished, could you please bring us a couple of fruit tarts for dessert?"

"Do you want them mixed, or one variety?"

"Mixed, please."

O'Brien added, "The same for me."

She nodded. "Yes, I like it that way myself. I'll bring them as soon as you finish your sandwiches."

"Thank you very much," I said, "you are an excellent, pleasant person to deal with."

O'Brien smiled. He looked at me and shook his head. "Your taste and appetite make me ask myself sometimes how you're not fat."

I smiled. "First of all, I'm very picky and careful. Second, you must be kidding! With all the physical activity I have in my life, day and night, how am I ever going to get fat?"

As I spoke, my physical activity with Chandee came to mind, and I smiled and chuckled.

O'Brien shook his head. "Remember what you taught me that they say in your country. Whoever laughs by himself is remembering some mischievous thing he got away with."

I nodded. "Yes, my friend. I am remembering my midnight exercise from last night."

He smiled with an awed expression and pointed to my ribs and cane. "Even with those injuries, you're not taking a rest?"

"That is precisely part of the recuperation plan."

He grinned and shook his head as he ate. He took his late bite, and our waitress arrived with fresh fruit tartlets, taking the empty plates away. She returned and asked, "Anything else?"

"Yes," I answered. "Could you please wrap up two pounds of Black Forest ham to go? You want anything, O'Brien?"

"No, no," he said. "I'm never home. It would just spoil."

"Anything else at all?"

"No. After the ham, bring me the bill and two policemen. I'm an expert in the martial arts, and one policeman won't be enough." She smiled at the joke.

O'Brien shook his head. With a mischievous smile he asked, "Didn't you get enough last night?"

"Come on, come on, don't become at your young age a grumpy old man. Where is your sense of humor?"

"You have enough for both of us." He started to dig into the tartlet.

"Hold on, old man—you're missing the best."

"What's that?"

"The Grand Marnier, you don't know what that is like with this!" I reached into my bag and pulled out a small bottle and began to baptize our tartlets in the name of the Father, the Son, and the Holy Ghost. When I finished my ritual, I did the same to my dessert. O'Brien smiled as he watched.

"Mr. Lightning, will you allow me to start on my dessert now, or are you going to use your lightning to make a flambé now?"

I smiled. "You can begin, my friend. Be my guest, please." O'Brien started to dig in with great satisfaction.

His face broke into a surprised expression as he took his first bite. He held his plate out towards me. "Would you please put a little more liqueur on this please? You cannot deny your Irish friend."

I poured some more. "Let me know."

I had almost emptied the bottle when he stopped me with his left hand. Grand Marnier dripped from the corner of his lips as he sampled it. "Who taught you all these exquisite things you indulge yourself with?"

"I never told you? My mother taught me to treat everything you do in life as if it were going to be your last dessert."

O'Brien nodded. "Well, whatever that means, I have to give my most sincere thanks to your Mima for teaching you those exquisite pleasures so that I can enjoy them in my old age. Thanks to you again for sharing them with me."

I smiled. "It's that good, my friend?"

"Good? No, it's *damn* good!"

"Do me a favor—don't keep calling yourself an old man. You're starting to make me feel old."

"OK, OK—now please let me finish my dessert."

The waitress returned with my ham and the bill. He tried to fight me for the bill, and I said, "No, no—this is on me. You've been doing too much for me lately." I left a generous tip for our lovely waitress.

O'Brien smiled. "I know blondes are your weakness, and blue eyes. She's a deadly combination for you."

He walked with me to my car. He patted Rocco in greeting, who was hanging half outside the window of the passenger seat. I opened the package of ham, took a few slices out and gave them to him. He hardly even chewed as he gobbled up the slices, his tail wagging furiously.

O'Brien asked, "Did you like your birthday present?"

I smiled. "Oooh, what a present! It was the most expensive present I've ever had in my life. Even though every member of my team is still mourning because it lasted shorter than a package of M&Ms on a schoolyard."

He smiled. "The most important thing is that none of you lost your lives. Everything else is replaceable." He stroked his cheek with the back of his fingers on his left hand. He smiled mischievously. "If you think that was the most expensive gift you've ever received, I can only imagine your expression when you see what we've prepared for you and your next trip."

He grew serious. "I want you to keep in mind that these prototypes are the absolute highest classified in terms of confidentiality. It's a thousand times better they get destroyed than land in our enemy's hands. Under no circumstance can we ever let that happen."

I nodded. "Yes, I agree. That is why whenever my guys tell me it's destroyed in pieces, I told them to burn it to the ground so even the scraps are completely melted down."

He put his arm around my shoulders. "Thank you. And thank you for everything you've done for this country and the responsibility you show in everything you do."

"Thank you for placing your trust in me and my team, that we can always do the work and obtain the best results we're looking for with great satisfaction."

"Let's remember that you're not getting a paycheck for it."

"That is why you guys send me all these very expensive gifts?"

He shook his head. "No, no—please! These are only the necessary tools for you to do your work as best you can."

We both smiled and embraced. His face was serious again. "I know you always look at life on the bright side, and I love your sense of humor. But tread carefully. They've already sent one team, and they failed. They will certainly send another—you know the drill—and they will be more effective because they'll better trained. Be prepared—this will be inevitable."

"Don't worry about it. I'll be waiting for them with my eyes open. More birds in the cage."

He smiled. We said goodbye, and I pulled out of the parking lot. I put the folder he had given me in the back seat of the Jaguar. As I drove off, I had to stop at a red light to get onto the PCH. I noticed an Audi with four men inside following me. I didn't want to be paranoid and waited for the light to change. I looked into my rearview mirror and watched the dark Audi stay behind me. I changed lanes twice, and they were inept enough to change lanes with me. I figured they were unprofessional, stupid, or desperate to catch me. I got into the right lane and saw the entrance to the Balboa Bay Club. I turned in there to confirm my suspicions.

Figure 38 The Balboa Bay Resort

They followed me in, and I drove to the main entrance for the valet parking. I casually pulled my car over towards the right, near the bushes. The Audi, however, went to the self-parking. They were close to us, but I could see all four men remain inside, watching. I waited patiently as the two cars ahead of me got checked in and then pulled up for my turn. I kept them under observation behind me using my special sunglasses with the rear mirrors. No one was leaving the car. I could see from the exhaust coming out of the tailpipe that the engine was still running. They were by now processing the car in front of me. A beautiful woman with long red hair and a body like she was on "Baywatch" got out of her Bentley convertible. When she got out, both parking attendants' mouths dropped. Even my pursuers were a little crazed. One of them put his head out of the car, to be reprimanded by one of the others of his team.

I used this spontaneous, God-sent opportunity to get out of my car, taking my cane with me. Not wasting a single second, I called Rocco to me and went back to the trunk. I pulled my canvas fishing bag which contained my emergency utility equipment out of the trunk. It was a long green and black canvas bag with a long zipper. I did not leave my key in the car. There was plenty of room for traffic behind me to go around. Very stealthily, I made my way casually around the parking lot towards the rear entrance.

The four men wore dark sunglasses. They followed me slowly in the black Audi through the parking lot. I entered the large doors of the rear entrance. Since they could no longer see me inside the building, I double-timed myself along the long corridor until I reached the men's room. I went inside. Once inside, I looked for the utility closet. I opened the door and called Rocco over to me. I pointed into the closet, and he obediently jumped inside the closet and looked at my curiously.

"Stay there." He sat down among the mops and brooms, looking at me expectantly. "*Marañon.*[23]" He growled softly in response, baring his teeth. I smiled and patted his head. "Wait right here and be quiet." I closed the door but left it open just a crack. Rocco obediently remained inside, still growling. "Shh."

I put my canvas bag down, resting against a sink. I went over to the urinals and put my cane on top of my right shoulder, tip pointed towards the floor. I opened my

---

23 Cashew.

zipper and began to relieve myself. As I finished urinating, two very tall, muscular men that looked like gorillas in dark-colored suits and ties that were inappropriate for the time of day, temperature, and summer beach wear came in. They clearly did not belong there and had no idea how anyone in that area of California dressed. I watched them behind me using my sunglasses. One stayed by the door while the other came over my way. I had no idea what he was going to do, but another man who looked quite wealthy entered. The man approaching me hesitated.

The rich man started to wash his hands. The man approaching me continued and took up another urinal slot, pretending to relieve himself while the other man remained by the door. I kept my eyes on all three men. The rich man at least looked like he belonged there, but I had to be sure.

I finished, went over to the sinks to wash, shifting my cane to my right arm, hooking it over my elbow. The old man greeted me.

"Hello," I answered. "Beautiful day today, isn't it?"

"Yes," he said. He looked at my white jacket admiringly. "Lovely jacket—where did you buy it?"

"Nowhere. It's tailor made."

"That's the only way to get it. I love your crest—is that your family crest?"

"Yes, it is."

"It's also quite lovely!"

"Thank you."

He finished washing his hands and walked out.

This is what the man at the urinal had been waiting for. As soon as the old man left, the man at the urinal turned and reached into his jacket. He started to untangle what looked like a wire—it could have been a garrote. I pretended to clean my nails with a toothpick, so that it wasn't obvious I was seeing that, even though he could clearly be seen in the large bathroom mirror. Of course, I was able to keep him under direct observation through my sunglasses.

I watched him come over to me with his hands high, the wire taut to loop around my neck. I waited until the last second, still pretending to clean my nails. As he started to lunge toward me, I leaned down on top of my cane, tucking my head down almost into the sink.

Figure 39 The head of my weaponized cane

Using the cane as a pivot point, I continued to use that momentum to swing in a half circle, coming up now behind the man. Continuing in one single motion, I raised my cane in both hands, and swung it furiously at the back of the man's head. The impact sent him completely off balance over the sink, his head cracking the mirror as his forehead collided hard with it. He screamed as he hit the mirror.

The man by the door, as soon as he saw what was happening, pulled a large pistol with a silencer attached out of his jacket. Before he could shoot, I pulled the man next to me over and in front of me, using him as a shield. The gun fired twice, both bullets striking my shield in the chest. As he fired, I yelled, "*Marañon*!"

The utility door crashed open as Rocco flashed out as quick as lightning. He charged the man with the gun, jumping and grabbing him by the groin. The man lost his balance, and as he fell lost his grip on the pistol. It skittered across the marble floor and under the urinals. The man in my hands was dead. I put the body inside of one of the stalls and closed the door. I picked the pistol up and put it in my waistband. I waited for a few moments, allowing Rocco to have a little fun as the man screamed murder.

"Release him," I commanded Rocco. Rocco obeyed. The man started to pick himself up off the floor. I put my cane up toward his neck and activated the blade. His eyes widened as he saw the size of the blade. I told him, "Don't move, if you want to live for a few more minutes." I stung him with my poison ring.

After a few moments, the man started to convulse, his mouth frothing. I heard voices outside, obviously investigating where the screams had been coming from. I quickly leaned down and gave him the antidote to the poison. I knew he would be out of commission for two to three hours at that point. I opened the door and saw people approaching. Some were coming out of the women's bathroom.

I said, "Hurry up! There's a man down here with convulsions. I think he needs medical attention." I squeezed out of the bathroom, my canvas bag over my left shoulder and my cane in my right hand, followed by Rocco. I walked briskly but kept myself looking natural.

The Audi was still parked outside in the lot. I could see the surprise in the eyes of the two remaining men inside the vehicle as I walked out the door. They got out and started approaching me. One reached into his jacket. At the same time, I reached inside my jacket, and both men froze. They started to angle towards the door, while I walked away from it, passing within a few feet of each other. Rocco growled at them as they came close, but I calmed him. I kept my eye on them, my hand still on the pistol inside my jacket. They did nothing, so I continued to my car. When I got to the front parking attendant, I apologized to the two men.

"I'm sorry, I forgot to leave my keys." I gave them each twenty dollars.

One smiled broadly. "Don't worry about it, sir. It happens all the time when people are in a rush." They helped me put the bag in the trunk.

I started the Jaguar, watching my pursuers carefully through both the rearview mirror and my sunglasses. I watched carefully for the Audi. I turned right onto the Pacific Coast Highway and headed towards Corona del Mar. I was unconvinced that someone else was not on my tail, so I did not go directly to the safe house. I drove to Balboa Island so that I could cross on the ferry. It was a large circle to do it that way, but it meant that I could be certain I was not being followed. I patted Rocco's head, opened the bag of ham, and gave him more slices.

"You are a good dog, my friend. Let's go and see our friends who have been waiting for us in Corona del Mar."

My enemies had disappeared from the map. I looked everywhere. Neither the black Audi nor any other car was following me any longer. Everything was strangely quiet. Apparently, these guys had had enough with the loss of one of their buddies and the shutdown of the other for several hours. They likely decided to postpone their plans, or they were consulting with their superiors as to what the next step should be. I could see that the coast was clear.

Once I arrived in Corona del Mar, I circled several times the large neighborhood block which contained our safe house. It was the cage in which we currently held our would-be kidnappers. I checked one more time the surroundings and saw no one was around. I pushed the remote control to open the garage. I pulled in quickly and closed the garage door. I took the package of ham, my cane, and the folder O'Brien had entrusted to me. I tucked the last under my arm and, followed by Rocco, I opened the door connecting the garage to the kitchen.

Chandee came up to me as I walked in, having seen me on the security cameras. She gave me a hug. "How are you feeling today? How are your small injuries doing?"

"Thank you. Better, thanks to your night massages."

She whispered in my ear. "Thanks for your great effort. It was very well received, and for that I thank you very much."

I smiled. We separated. "You're welcome, my love. To me, it's come to be a really great pleasure."

She smiled and petted Rocco's head. I showed her the folder as I walked to the bar in the kitchen. I started to go through it as we both sat down on the bar stools. I went through the pictures of our enemies one at a time. As I did, Elizabeth came up behind me and joined us with a big smile.

She asked, "How are your injuries doing?"

"A lot better, with Chandee's help." I winked at Chandee.

Elizabeth asked a little mockingly, "What did you do to him, Chandee? Remember, he's a wounded man."

"No, no—she actually gave me a great massage and some Chinese acupuncture. Believe me, to be honest with you, I woke up today a little sore. I guess as days pass, the pain will increase before it starts to decrease with the healing. Where is everyone else?"

"Yaneba and Mayari took off very early this morning. They took Loren on a little tour of the desert. Chopin is downstairs in the basement. He's seasoning your guests. I think all four of them are ready and waiting for the chef. We'll move back and let you cook them over a slow fire."

I smiled. I pointed at the picture of Carlitos, which was the first one in the folder. "This is the leader of the team:

Carlitos, alias, the Jackalito. This gentleman is the son of Carlos Ramirez Sanches, the Marxist hit man and student of Che Guevara. He is rotting in a French prison for his notorious assassinations around the world. He was sentenced in a French court to life imprisonment. Looks like the toothpick came from the same stick. Carlitos has decided to follow in his father's footsteps."

I looked Elizabeth in the eyes, tapping my index finger on his picture for emphasis. "El Jackalito. This is the one we must concentrate all our efforts on. After we break him, the rest will be very easy. Or at least simpler."

Elizabeth and Chandee nodded. Elizabeth asked, "When did you want to start with the guests we have downstairs?"

"Right now."

"OK, let's go."

"Hold on." I held the folder out to her. "You can see inside this folder and show the others, the names, physical constitution, skills, and criminal careers—every single detail you will need to find out that they are extremely professional and skilled terrorists with international backgrounds. According to O'Brien, we not only hit the jackpot in apprehending these guys at the same time, but he also warned me we had to walk with extreme caution around them. The two women, the green-eyed Arabian," I pointed at the picture of Alya, "and the Venezuelan," I pointed at Valeria's picture, "are even more dangerous than Jackalito himself. Even though he is supposedly the team leader, and we have no doubts about that, the only one that is a question mark," I pointed at the remaining picture, "is this guy Omar. He's rated in the intelligence community as armed and extremely dangerous. We only know that he is the personal security chief to the Shah of Iran, Mohammad Reza Pahlavi. This man disappeared off the international radar when the Soviets invaded Afghanistan. We have no concrete evidence, but we have suspicions that Omar Hamari is one of the most important men in the chain of the international financial backing of the most dangerous terrorist organization, al-Qaeda, with his leader, Osama bin Laden."

I paused. "Any questions?" Chandee and Elizabeth shook their heads. "Well, if you have no questions, let's get to work."

We left the kitchen and walked to the elevator. "Wait for me for a few seconds so I can put Rocco in the living room, where he'll be more comfortable. He's used to napping there when he's here. OK, let's go, Rocco." I opened the door to the living room, and he trotted over to his comfortable rug before the fireplace and lay down.

We entered the small elevator to the basement. Before I pressed the button, I said to them, "I want you to remember who we're dealing with here. These are the most dangerous terrorists in the world today. Under no circumstance, even if this building catches on fire, never let them out of the handcuffs or open their leg shackles. Number two, these are not men and women. They are demons dressed as sheep. They've been trained to kill mass groups of innocent victims without caring for their race or religion. The only way to deal with them is to treat them in the same sadistic way, even if this makes a knot in our stomachs. Remember always who we are dealing with, but never morally descend to their level. OK?"

They both nodded their acknowledgement. I pressed the button to take us to the basement. When the elevator doors opened, the first thing we heard were the screams of Carlitos. Through the excruciating pain he was suffering, he yelled obscenities in Spanish at Chopin. The entire basement had been thoroughly soundproofed, so there was no concern of anyone hearing him.

Figure 40 The Marinating Room

Chopin said, "You can scream all you want. No one can hear you. I don't care what insults you throw at me; I will continue my work until you tell me what you know and what I want to know. Until then, I'll keep working even if you die here with all your partners in crime, one at a time. The only possibility you have of getting out of here alive is to provide to us the best information you can. That's your decision. Will you talk, or die?"

The subject was strapped to a rack-like device. He was manacled hand and foot between two metal poles. The chains wrapped around the poles to a winch in front of Chopin with a large, spoked wheel. He turned it one notch, pulling the man's limbs even further apart, stretching him. The winch was toothed, so the latch locked in place as the tension was increased, one notch at a time. Carlitos screamed again in the agony of feeling torn slowly apart. He continued screaming obscenities desperately to Chopin.

Every click in the wheel was like bubble gum stretched out of one's mouth, so thin that it eventually breaks. The difference here was that it was a human body getting stretched; hence the name we had given the machine, "The Stretching Workout Machine." Very few people passed the test of not talking after being put inside this equipment. The stretching was bad enough, but the stretched limbs also were the victim's only support of weight, and so the pain continued even when the tension was not being increased. The purpose of this machine was more not to damage the subject as it was to terrify not just him but also those who had to watch. The principal object here was to scare the daylights out of the individual until we got the information we were looking for or, in the best scenarios, to recruit them to provide us additional information in the future, working as spies behind enemy lines. Of course, that was the most difficult of the targets, especially when the subject held the terrorist ideology of jihad. Such individuals were already virtual psychopaths, ready to die for what they believed. It provided better results when we were dealing with mercenaries or simple individuals with no strong convictions.

We could never completely trust anyone after they were exposed to this kind of treatment, of course. But at least for a time they provided us important information. Once the fear of this treatment wore off, and they resumed their earlier allegiances, we could quietly dispose of them later.

As I got out of the elevator, I yelled to Chopin, "Stop, stop! What are you doing? Who told you to do this?"

Chopin, knowing the drill, acted his part. He faked surprise as he replied, "OK, Dr. del Marmol—I was only doing what Yaneba ordered me to do: extract necessary information from these terrorists, no matter what the price, even if it takes their lives."

"No, no," putting some irritation in my voice. "You've been around me for a while. You know I don't agree with these methods. Torture is unnecessary. Besides, the information we get through it isn't reliable."

Chopin kept his act up and faked his own irritation. He spoke with respect, but let unhappiness show in his voice. "What do you want me to do with him in order to make him talk then? You want me to offer him something cold to drink?"

I smiled slightly. "That's not a bad idea, Chopin. But first put a chair under his butt, release him from the stretching machine, and let the man sit down and rest. We'll talk to him in a civilized way."

Chopin looked at me after he put a chair under the man and began to release the tension of the machine. As he did, the body sagged until he was able to almost sit down. Carlitos smiled. He breathed happily and yelled, "Thank you, Dr. del Marmol. It's good to meet somebody civilized. I had a rough twenty-four hours, and felt I was no longer with human beings but with prehistoric animals."

Chopin heard that and suddenly released the wheel two more notches. The man gasped as he fell abruptly on the chair and nearly fell. He smiled cynically. "Oops. Sorry—the wheel slipped in my hands."

"I'm very sorry," I said to Carlitos, "that I cannot say the same for you. I have a very clear memory of one of you, when I was half-drugged with your crazy cocktail last night on the beach, who came by my side while I was defenseless in the sand, kicking me with his boot. I don't know if he wanted to corroborate that I was unconscious or if whoever did it is a prehistoric animal, too."

Carlitos got very serious, recalling that it was he who had kicked me. He knew as well as I that I could recognize his voice when he spoke to Loren. He remained silent in the face of that remark. He gulped in silent shame and lowered his head after he glanced at Chopin and saw how the black man clearly despised him.

At that moment, the elevator bell dinged, and the door opened. Yaneba shoved Loren out of it with great force. Loren fell onto her knees and rolled across the marble floor, leaving behind her a trail of blood from multiple puncture wounds on her arms. Her hands were handcuffed, and she sobbed as she yelled insults and obscenities at Yaneba the like of which I had never heard before. Yaneba came over to her and pulled her 9mm out.

"You had better take that back quickly if you don't want to die right now," Yaneba said. "My mother is not a whore, and my father is not a prick, bitch. You should respect their memories. You're not even worth their shit."

Loren got up and spit in Yaneba's face. "Your mother is a whore, and you're a little whore, too."

Before anyone could stop her, Yaneba cocked the pistol and shot Loren point blank in the back of the head. Loren fell forward onto the floor in a large pool of blood. We were frozen at that horrific scene, completely silent. The two women, Alya and Valeria, were tied near Carlitos, and they could not help but urinate as fear made them lose control of their bladders. Carlitos and Omar looked at each other in fear and confusion, clearly wondering if they would be next.

Yaneba grabbed Loren's head by the hair. "I told you, bitch: my mother is not a whore, and my father is not a prick." She dropped the head and let it fall back onto the floor.

I shook my head disapprovingly at Yaneba. She raised her pistol up and shook it. "Don't worry—I have all the information we need already. The names and who in the FBI have been corroborating in the attempt to kidnap you."

As if nothing had happened, she turned to Mayari and Chopin. "Will you guys please take her body out? You know what you have to do with her. Elizabeth, Chandee, would you please bring some buckets and mops from the utility closet to clean up this mess? I need to talk to Dr. del Marmol immediately. We must determine quickly whatever we're going to do with the rest of these terrorists. We only have a few hours, as it's very possible that some of us must leave the country tonight. Something unexpected of supreme priority at the last minute." Yaneba spoke, scarcely taking a breath and in a very loud voice, displaying her emotional distress. She must have wanted to impress the rest of the terrorists there psychologically and make clear what she had in mind.

At that moment, I replied, "Let's go upstairs, Yaneba. We have to talk in private." As Mayari and Chopin took Loren's body wrapped in a sheet into the elevator, Elizabeth and Chandee rushed to get the large bucket of water and cleaning solution and began to clean the blood spread over the marble.

Yaneba and I looked at each other as we waited for the elevator to return. The bell dinged again, and we got into the elevator. Carlitos yelled to me, "Dr. del Marmol—please, before you leave today, I would like the opportunity to speak with you in private! I have important things to discuss with you, if it's possible."

I nodded. I pointed to Yaneba. "Sure, as soon as I finish my conversation with her, I'll come back, and you and I can talk."

"Thank you," he replied, his chain clinking as his right hand saluted me.

Yaneba pushed the button and the doors closed. I took a deep breath and looked straight into her eyes. "Please, tell me that Loren is OK and that all this was an improvised plan at the last minute that you put into effect to completely terrorize the terrorists." She did not reply immediately, just looking at me in deadly seriousness. After a few seconds of agony for me, she smiled and shook her head.

"It was true about the information from thc FBI. Loren spilled her guts as soon as we took her to the desert, stripped her, and tied her to a cactus with a five-gallon can of gasoline next to her. Even as I started to baptize her with the gas as you do a fruit tart with the Grand Marnier, she started to beg for her life like I've never seen anyone do before. She would do anything I wanted to in order to save her neck. She agreed to wear the blood pack and squib to make it look like I executed her."

I took a deep sigh of relief. The last thing I wanted to see was my daughter orphaned. I was so happy that I couldn't control myself. I hugged Yaneba and kissed her on the cheek. "You were an Academy Award winner—that was the most ingenious performance I've ever seen!"

She smiled mischievously and nodded her head cockily. "Thank you—but with that kiss you'll start a fire. If you don't have the time or intention to suffocate it, you'd better not kiss me again."

She was daring me, so I grabbed her and kissed her again. "OK, Wildfire—what are you going to do?"

She shook her head. "You see? You're very predictable! Yes, I'm a wildfire, Mr. Lightning. That's what you leave behind after a torrential storm."

I smiled and caressed her cheek with my fingers. "Never will I leave you behind, Wildfire. I hold you very close to my heart."

She smiled. "Thank you. I like that."

"Where is Loren now?"

"She's a little cleaned up and will be en route to her home in a few minutes. Chopin and Mayari are taking her to the car she left by the Marine Research Lab's parking lot. I assure you that she'll have to take a couple of showers to remove all the red dye. I believe strongly that you'll never have to worry about her anymore. I've never seen in my life anyone with so much fear of dying as I saw in Loren today so early this morning. For a moment, I thought she might die of a heart attack before I could finish my work. Once, I thought she even farted, but she defecated in her pants."

I could not hold it in any longer and laughed. "You are a little devil." I patted her on the shoulder. "Thank you. Whoever doesn't know you as I know how sweet natured you are in your heart, full of love for everyone, you can come across at times as being ruthless and a crazy woman, a very scary person."

She smiled and pointed to her chest. She then started to remove the blanks from her pistol. "What are you doing?"

"Replacing the blanks with real bullets. I don't want to have egg on my face in my next encounter!" She put held the muzzle of the pistol against her cheek. "You think I'm crazy enough?"

"Don't go cuckoo on me or pull that trigger—you might have a real bullet in there, not a blank!"

"I'm a little crazy, but not enough to kill myself, don't worry. If you don't mind, I'm going to go and take a long, long shower. Tell everyone not to bother me. That Academy Award performance took my last energy. I've been up since four a.m."

She put her pistol away in her waistband and gave me a bear hug. She murmured in my ear, "Thank you for your beautiful words." She kissed me and added, "If Chopin and Mayari's seasoning wasn't enough, I think I completed the marinade. Go and get them, Lightning."

I smiled. "OK, Wildfire. Go and take your shower and cool off." I pushed the button. As the doors closed, we shook our heads at each other. Just before they closed, I added, "You are something."

When I got down there, Chandee and Elizabeth had nearly finished cleaning up the supposed blood from the marble floors. I said to them in a normal voice, "Thank you for your help, girls. I might have to leave the city tonight with Chopin and Mayari. You guys will stay here with Yaneba. She'll oversee the prisoners. I'm trusting you guys to give them good treatment, but whatever she says, goes." I turned so the prisoners couldn't see my face and subtly winked at Chandee. "I hope on my return that I'll find all of our prisoners in one piece as when I left."

They both nodded. Carlitos, a short distance away, tried to catch my attention, clearly getting more anxious to reveal whatever it was he had to say. I pulled up a chair near to him.

"OK, Carlitos," I said. "What did you want to tell me? I wanted to give you a warning and let you know that my time is extremely limited as I have to leave on a trip for a while very soon."

"Yes, I heard you say that."

"You understand that I have to put a few things in order before I leave the country?"

He asked in great worry and fear, "Who will be in charge of us while you're gone?"

"Yaneba."

He gulped nervously and furrowed his eyebrows pleadingly.

"Also, Chandee and Elizabeth will stay with you guys."

"What are you planning to do with us?"

"It all depends on you. If you produce what I need, not only can you save your skin but also all the others with you on your team." I added that last in a loud voice so they could hear me.

"How do you know I'm in charge of the team?"

I held my right hand high. "Elizabeth—please bring me the folder with the information about Carlitos, Omar, Alya, and Valeria." All four looked at me in surprise, completely unable to figure out how I got all that information in such a short time. Elizabeth brought the folder over to me and put it in my hands. I opened it and showed Carlito his picture. He smiled then, and I showed him the pictures of the others.

"Well, there's no doubt in my mind that you know as much about us as we know about you," he said. "This makes it clear that we don't have much to hide."

"Yes. The tremendous difference is that all of you guys are in chains and are our prisoners."

He tried to impress me, playing his last card. He smiled to hide the fear that I could still read in his eyes. "Yes, yes—but for how long? The man behind our organization, which is the most powerful terrorist organization in the world today, has paid us $2 million—one million as a down payment, and the rest when we bring your body in good condition to him. He's not going to keep his arms crossed over his chest for much longer. He might next time catch you by surprise. And maybe the roles will be reversed, and just maybe I won't be *your* prisoner, you'll be *mine*, and I'll be your interrogator."

I smiled confidently. I stroked my chin with my right as I held the folder in my left. I shook it slightly. Carlitos raised his eyebrows, and his eyes widened a little more than he might wish. It was an involuntary signal that he was completely panicked. "Too many maybes, my friend. I told you my time was limited, and you're starting your conversation wasting that precious time. You're trying the impossible. Until today, many have tried before to intimidate me, and they have never achieved it. That won't work with me, my friend. To me, life is like a good, expensive perfume. No matter how exquisite it can be, whatever you do, it eventually must disappear. Then why worry about something that you cannot remedy? Eventually, it must happen, death comes to us all."

I got up from my chair from where I had been sitting face-to-face with him. "I believe that when you have to talk to me, it will be better that you tell it to Yaneba after I leave tonight. I'm pretty sure that you will probably fail with her as well, and you will have a very sad, hard lesson if you try those same techniques on her. You had better think about your situation right now." I pointed at the other. "Whatever you do, it won't be just your life—it will be theirs, as well. Better think quickly."

I saw Carlitos turn as pale as a cadaver in the morgue, even to the light blue, transparent coloration. I could also see Aya and Valeria's expressions had similar peculiar fear that I could see in Carlitos. Something caught my attention—the brunette, green-eyed Omar did not look either impressed or scared. He seemed completely unaffected by my words; to thc contrary, a small smile escaped his lips that he tried to control. It turned more into asmirk. That gave him away to me as someone who was not an associate or part of the group. He was perhaps a supervisor behind that group on behalf of the man who had paid the money for my kidnapping, sent along to make sure that the job had been done the way their employer wished it done.

I changed tactics at that point. "We're done with this conversation. You're dealing with Yaneba from now on."

Carlitos tried to hold me there. "I have very important information that your boss in the CIA might be interested in obtaining. It cannot be found anywhere else."

As I looked at Omar, I could see them glance at each other as if consulting with each other about the next step to follow. I smiled. "It looks like you have very little information about me, my friend. Your handler or whoever is behind this gave you a very, very short debriefing. If they had taken the time to inform you properly, you would know I have no bosses. I don't work for the CIA. I work *with* them and other multiple agencies around the world in the intelligence community. Let me make this clear to you: I'm a freedom fighter, as you are a terrorist. Let's not get confused, Carlitos."

He raised both hands as best he could with his restraints. "OK, OK. But you have to have someone above you for you to give some accounts to or consult with or deliver information."

I smiled fully this time. I nodded. "Yes, yes—and my 'boss' is very demanding. His name is Jesus Christ."

Carlitos shook his head, this time with a small smile. He raised his right hand. "You mean to tell me that you have no one to supervise you?"

I looked at him. "Hard to believe it, eh? I'll show you an example right now. Elizabeth!" Elizabeth came over. "Take his chains off."

She said, "We're not supposed to do that."

"Who told you not to do that?"

"You did."

"Now I'm telling you that we can, and you go ahead and release this man from his chains."

She didn't argue and walked over with the key and released him. Carlitos looked at me in shock, not expecting this.

"Elizabeth, when you're finished, take him back to the control room." She took him into the office which looked like a music recording studio with a thick glass partition at the end of the basement. "Offer him something to drink," I called after her. I looked at my watch on my right arm. "I will give you an extension on your time, Carlitos. Fifteen more minutes, a lot more than I had planned. Use it productively or your time will be ended. At that point, I won't care what you can tell me. After that time is up, you are done."

The elevator bell sounded again. Chopin and Mayari stepped out. They looked at what Elizabeth was doing and were utterly surprised. Carlitos remained mute at my decision that took him to the isolated office at the end of the basement. The other prisoners looked at us as we walked.

I said to Chopin and Mayari, "Is everything in order?"

Chopin replied, "Yes, sir. Fresh food for the sharks."

I nodded. I gave him a thumbs up with my left hand. I followed Elizabeth closely with the folder in my right hand. After she turned the lights in the control room, she proceeded to tie him to a pipe in the wall using the manacles on his hands. I stopped her with a raised arm and with a shake of my head. I said to Carlitos, "Sit down. Do you want something cold to drink?"

He smiled and shook his head. "You're not really joking, are you? Well, in keeping with your joke, how about a Negra Modelo?"

"Well, you're in luck, my friend. That is my favorite of all the dark beers I've tried around the world." I signaled to Elizabeth. "Bring a beer to the gentleman. Do you want it in a bottle or in a glass with ice?"

He could not believe what he was hearing. "No, no—it's fine. A bottle."

"I don't want you to complain in the future to a human rights commission protecting terrorists that you didn't get decent treatment from me."

He was so confused by the courtesies I was offering to him, especially when he saw Elizabeth pull a beer out of the minibar and hand it to him, "You really are something!"

"I know."

Elizabeth contributed to the whole playacting by asking sarcastically, "Would you like a napkin, sir?"

He looked like he might be feeling uncomfortable with all the luxury following all the waterboarding and other psychological deprivations and harassments. He took a long sip from the bottle and wiped his mouth with his shirt sleeve. "I really cannot figure this out. You're either extremely intelligent or you know something I don't know. How you did you catch the signal that I couldn't speak in front of Omar?" He was growing more relaxed. "If I had dared to say anything no matter how small, and this guy reported it to my handler, I know even if I got away from the psychopath Yaneba's hands, I would not keep my head on my shoulder for very long. That's why I'm dying to know how you figured it out."

"Unfortunately, my friend, that is classified. You're not precisely trustworthy. Maybe, one day, if you build my trust, I'll give you an answer for that."

He took a deep breath. "My friend, what I'm about to do could not only cost me my life, but it could also cost the lives of all my family and friends. If Omar has any idea of what's going on here right now and what I'm going to say to you, my head will last on my shoulders as long as a rabbit lasts in the mouth of a lion."

I raised my right arm. "You have five minutes left out of your fifteen. You had better finish your beer; it must be your last wish in life. And you must answer very truthfully my next three questions, and don't even leave a hair out. We already have the information from Loren before she died as to who in the FBI worked with you in the plan of kidnapping me. Now I only need to know from you: who is the one paying for all of this? Who is behind the execution of the plan? What is the purpose for all of this? Why, precisely, me, and not one of the high-ranking bureaucrats in the intelligence community?"

Carlitos shifted uncomfortably in his seat. My question, he knew, had to be responded to or he would completely waste the most vital time of his life. He only had a few minutes, so that is perhaps why he replied, "Dr. del Marmol, you've put me between a sword and the wall. If I reply to these questions, I will lose my head. If I don't, you'll abandon me to the hungry lioness."

I stroked my chin and looked straight into his eyes. "All you have to think about is one single thing before you decide what you want to do: you are in our hands, not in theirs at this moment. I personally believe that you have the great opportunity with us, not only to change your life totally and get out of the darkness you've been in all your life and leave behind all the weird violence, killing of innocent people, that have been victimized by your hands and bombs in shopping malls—I cannot even figure out how you can live with yourself. Maybe you can totally change that route."

I raised my right hand high. I spoke in a very friendly tone. "But if you don't tell me all the truth, and I find out only one hair of treason and lies in what you confess to me here today, I guarantee you only one thing: you will pass from being my enemy ideologically, you will become my personal enemy. I don't take that lightly. Very few times my personal enemies live for more than a few days; like the ones responsible for the death of my son, they never live long enough to tell the story to anyone." I looked again at my watch on my left hand. "You only have two minutes. You're running out of time. I want you to know, when I stand up from this chair, there will be no word left in you capable of detaining me. You will be on your own and your time will be ended. That beer you just drank? It will be the final wish in your life."

He drained the bottle quickly. He took a deep breath. "What guarantees can you offer me that you will respect what you just told me today?"

I shook my head. "Guarantees? None. Only I will tell you what I said before: you have my word of honor that nothing will happen to you or anyone with you if you comply and don't betray my trust."

This time Carlitos took another deep breath and grew a little emotional. "Aya and Valeria, I'll put my hand in the fire for them and want to protect them. But Omar—he is the representative of the man who wanted me to kidnap you and bring to his face. He either wants to have the satisfaction of killing you, converting you, or Heaven knows what. You can do whatever the hell you want with him. I would even appreciate if he never came back from this. The man, the handler, the financier, of this whole operation, is the most wanted man in the world—Osama bin Laden."

CHAPTER 12: THE LIGHTNING AND THE POLYGAMIST

Three weeks after my injuries had healed, I continued to walk with a cane as a preventive measure It had become my best ally as a personal defense weapon, while also giving the wrong impression to my enemies that I was at a disadvantage from an apparent handicap. I concluded it would be a great way to take any new attempt on my life by surprise. I was in the safehouse on Lido Island, discussing with Chandee and Chopin how I intended to proceed to Venezuela with the purpose of bringing to Abdul's family the enormous amount of money he had left them. His family deserved it more than anyone after losing his life doing such great work for our cause. Every day that I had postponed this trip, which was a personal commitment I had made with myself, took a toll on my conscience. That is why I decided to make the trip on the weekend. Normally, the tourist season would allow me to arrive in that beautiful tropical country without attracting attention, in spite of the dramatic political changes that were occurring at this time. The communists were transforming the beautiful Venezuela into another totalitarian regime like Cuba, becoming another communist Marxist satellite. They will continue to expand, like Hitler, never stopping until they destroy the world and then eventually themselves, leaving only ruins and ashes to the next generations.

The phone rang. I picked up the dining room phone. "Hello?"

Brenton's voice said, "This is Brenton, Dr. del Marmol. Brenton Cooper. Do you remember me?"

"Of course," I said. "It's a great pleasure to hear from you. How is your family? How is your daughter, Sunset? And most important, how is Chocolate? We'll leave your wife for later."

Benton chuckled, but I noticed his voice was stressed and nervous. "I need to talk to you immediately, if possible. It's a matter of extreme importance. Where can we meet if you're OK with that?"

"Yes. If it's OK with you, we can meet in the Balboa Bay Club in half an hour."

"Yes, that's great. So you know for an advance, this is in reference, to the polygamist. You remember, don't you, the last conversation we had at my residence?"

I smiled. "Of course. I have an elephant's memory. Just keep that a secret because I want those who I consider indiscrete to think that I don't remember anything."

He laughed slightly. "Absolutely. I do the same thing. Don't worry about it. I don't repeat anything of a conversation I have with third parties, unless they happen to be my enemies. Of course, you are far from qualifying for that category."

"OK. Thank you. I will meet you in the lobby of the club in a short while."

I hung up and said goodbye to Chandee and Chopin. Rocco followed me to the garage where we both got into the Jaguar. We drove from the house on Lido Island towards my appointment. As I drove, I thought how extreme a surprise as well as and a source of great curiosity this phone call was. I had not seen Brenton or had any contact with him after the first visit to his house in Newport Beach.

A few minutes later I arrived at the Balboa Bay Club and left the Jaguar in the valet parking. I came in with Rocco by my side to the lobby, but I saw no one that even looked like Brenton anywhere. There was a family with several kids at the front desk waiting to check in to the club. A very old Amish man dressed their customary attire, all in black with a black hat, reading a magazine in the lobby while he sat in an armchair. I thought that this individual was waiting for his turn to check in. When he saw me wandering around the lobby for a few seconds, he closed the magazine and stood up. I didn't give it too much importance; he looked like he was in his '80s, and I decided to continue through the lobby to the hallway leading to the bathroom.

As I approached the restrooms along the club's long corridor, I felt a prickling along my neck and turned around to see to my surprise the old Amish man walking towards me rapidly, as if he were trying to catch up to me. For a man of that advanced age, he walked awfully fast. I entered the restroom already on guard and wondering. Instead of continuing to the urinal, I ducked behind the door as I entered and flattened against the wall. I said, "Rocco, sit." He trotted over and sat down by the sinks. "Stay." He sat facing the door obediently.

A few seconds later, the Amish man entered the restroom and with the energy of a much younger man looked around. He saw Rocco and reached out, wiggling his fingers to call my friend. I had pulled my pistol and screwed the silencer onto the muzzle. He looked Rocco for a few seconds in the eyes and then said, "Hello, boy. What's up, Rocco?" That surprised me, but I was even more surprised when Rocco's stubby tail wagged, cocked his head to one side, and then got up to trot over, where the Amish man scratched at his head. It was apparent Rocco knew him.

I stepped forward and asked, "Are you looking for someone, my friend?"

The old man started and spun around. He saw my silenced pistol pointing at him. "Yes, yes, Dr. del Marmol. I'm Brenton Cooper."

"What?"

He pulled his beard down and removed the hat. I looked at his face in surprise. "You're unrecognizable. I'm good, but you're even better at disguising yourself!"

"I'm sorry. I believe I'm being followed. My wife, Massile, managed to get me out of the house in the back seat of her sister's car, who brought me here. I didn't want to take any chance and bring you my burdens."

I shook my head. "With that disguise, I think even Rocco had a hard time recognizing you. Fortunately, dogs have a great olfactory gift we don't have and smelled the pH of your skin the moment you opened that door. They can do that miles away. Now I understand why he didn't bark at you when you opened the door and allowed you to pat him on the head."

He looked a little nervous. "Do you have any place here where we can speak in privacy out of everyone else's sight without interruption?"

I nodded. "Sure." I picked up a pencil and wrote on a piece of paper the name of my yacht. "When I leave the restroom, follow me. After you locate the yacht, wait for ten minutes. Don't approach until I can use my binoculars to scan our surroundings to make sure you haven't been followed. When you see the signal light on the mast come on and off several times, proceed. If you don't, wait until I come back to you. OK? If you see me leave the yacht, come here to the restroom again. I'll give you another location where we can meet. Do you understand?"

"Yes. I'll do exactly as you tell me."

I left the restroom, Rocco at my side, and headed to the yacht *Guantanamo Bay*. Several minutes later on board the yacht, I went up to the top deck with my binoculars and scoured the area. I saw nothing suspicious or out of the normal, so I signaled to Brenton to come aboard.

When he got on board, I offered him something to drink. He said, "A glass of wine would be great to calm my nerves."

"A glass of wine is always welcome to my stomach." I got a bottle of Malbec Mendoza, Argentina. It had a fruity flavor and medium body that I liked, with soft tannins and a smooth finish. I put it on a tray with some salami, mortadella, cold cuts, cheese, and some Mini-multigrain

Bites from Trader Joe's, my favorite brand of cracker. We walked across the deck to the stern of the yacht and sat down to watch the different vessels coming in and out of the bay along the channel.

Brenton held his glass up. "This is not a domestic wine. Am I right?"

"It's a present from an Argentinian friend who recently returned from Mendoza. He brought me this case of wine."

"Not bad at all."

"If you like it, remind me before you leave and you can take a bottle home to enjoy with your wife."

"Thank you. You're always so generous." For the first time, he gave me a little smile. A little more relaxed from his two sips of wine, or perhaps it was the environment, he added, "I don't think I should get close to my family for a while until I find a solution to the problem that I've created for myself. I want to kick my butt. I've been too honest with the rest of my colleagues and externalized my personal feelings with the wrong people."

"You should not ever repent of your honesty, but communicating to the wrong person? Of that you should repent. These occasions can cost you your life, and in the past has given me a lot of headaches. It's not just your life, but also the lives of your family. Now you have the stressful and horrible remorse that you opened your mouth. That is why I learned to bite my tongue and only communicate my intimate feelings to my pillow. A great majority of people are question marks."

He raised his glass and turned profoundly serious. "You're right. We must be careful who we give our confidence to. But we have to find someone we can trust. If we don't, we can strangle like a fish out of water because we have no pressure valve."

"Yes, of course. Trust in someone, but very, very carefully and little by little, like how you go into water of unknown depth or without knowing how level of the terrain beneath the surface is. This way you don't fall into deep well with no exit and end up drowning from your own weight and lack of precaution."

Brenton nodded his head, his face filled with anxiety and frustration. "You're 100% right. That is the way I feel right now at this moment."

I patted him on the shoulder, trying to give him some support. "Remember, the problems of the present are absolute necessities that sometimes are fruitful in providing the experience necessary to resolve problems in the future. What is impossible now to resolve tomorrow resolves the simplest things we don't even see. That's why we should never aggravate ourselves. The only problem that has no solution at all in life is only what we call *la pelona*[24]. From that lady, there is no solution."

He looked at me seriously and nodded. He took a deeper sip of his wine. "I think I'm going to need your advice. I believe strongly you can help me get out of this well I've fallen into. But I want at the same time as I tell you this to avoid bringing my problems to you. That's not my intention at all. Can I ask you for something?"

"Yes, go ahead."

"But I don't want you to feel obligated in any way. If you don't want to hear more than what I'm saying, please stop me. Just bring one of your hands up, and I'll stop; I will understand. I'm not going to load you with something you don't feel comfortable with."

I looked at him and smiled. I nodded. "OK, I think that's very fair."

Brenton leaned back in his comfortable canvas cushioned chair and took a sip of wine. "Last week I had an important call from Washington, D.C. from someone special, who offered me the reins of an extremely classified operation that will take place in a short time. This individual is my old supervisor when I was working for the Secret Service, Mr. Walker. He told me that he wanted me to partake in this operation not only as the leader but also

---

[24] Lady Death

to supervise all the details that will transpire throughout the operation. At first, it was intensely interesting, because he relayed to me that they were all connected to the polygamist. Do you remember that?"

"Absolutely. Is the polygamist still at large? Is this a catch and release? Or a catch to kill?"

"That is the tricky part. It's not either one. This is the point where I started to lose interest. He left out the details that the country they had selected to relocate the polygamist with his family would be Venezuela, which they had arranged with the communist government in exchange for an enormous amount of money. It would be a diving board to jump off to go to a different country where they intended to make him disappear from the public eye. They cut a deal with the polygamist and bribed him with assurances for his safety and well-being not only for him but also his family for the rest of his life. All he has to do is what they ask of him: drop everything and go into hiding."

"What is this for?"

"Politics. The only way this President will get himself re-elected is by making a big catch like this in the eyes of the public."

"What if this guy ends up in the wrong hands, they conduct DNA tests, and find out the truth? It could blow up in everyone's face. Everything has been planned very well, beyond your imagination. It will be the greatest fraud and joke in history. It will be worse than when Russia, Cuba, and the USA declared the October Crisis over and made the world believe the intercontinental missiles and nuclear weapons were removed from the island—."

I held up my hand to interrupt him. "Stop there. I know exactly where you're coming from. They made everyone believe that everything is OK, and the missiles left Cuba, everything will be happy ever after, and kumbaya." I leaned back and took a sip of wine. I was amused at what I heard; it had not taken me by surprise. I already knew in the past decade how the political leaders manipulated and picked their puppets in intelligence.

Unfortunately, they used such political maneuvers to get exactly what they wanted, motivated by personal interest and political ambition, by altering or creating their own history until they achieved their purpose. If the agenda was productive to these hypocrites, they never cared about the common good of the people who put them in power. Now that they had a taste of it, they would do whatever to not lose it.

I looked at Brenton and shook my head sadly. "My friend Brenton Cooper, in what kind of a well of excrement have you fallen into that you don't even know how to get out, and at what level of the government are the people involved in this fraud? If that's not confidential, of course."

"Everything is confidential and classified. More than that, this doesn't even exist, nor will it exist in the future. The level goes from the President, the Secretary of State, and the National Security Council, also at the highest levels of the CIA and the puppets now in charge of this prestigious entity. These leaders are taking all precautions by not using anyone in the intelligence community. They're using a group of contractors and pèople they absolutely trust: ex-military, Marines, or Secret Service, all retired or no longer active, to eliminate any liabilities or fall-out consequences for these politicians. It wouldn't surprise me if everyone who partakes in the operation will be eliminated at the end of it." He shook his head. "I don't want to be involved in this kind of fraud, immorality, and indecency. After I listened to Mr. Walker, I was nauseous. Imagine what it would be like if I had taken part of this. I don't think I would be able to look in my wife or little girl's eyes again for the rest of my life."

"Of course. I assume that you haven't externalized these feelings with anyone, especially those who offered you this job. Not even to your old friend who offered it to you."

He looked guilty and nodded. He said sadly, "Unfortunately, that is my problem. I made the worst mistake by trusting my old friend Mr. Walker. I not only told him I didn't want to be part of the mission anymore, but I also made the greater mistake of telling him he shouldn't be a part of something so immoral and deceptive to the American people. This tasteless joke of a mission represents a profound deception and slap in the faces not only to the victims of the 9/11 attack but also those of the families of the victims. The polygamist was at least 75% involved in it for many years."

When I heard that I stood up abruptly. "Are you sure you understood what they were telling you?"

I slapped my forehead with my left hand in disgust. I nearly tipped the entire tray off the table with my elbow in my abrupt motion. Brenton quickly moved forward to rescue the tray from falling onto the deck and spilling its contents. As we both moved, two whispering sounds of silenced shots zipped by. One broke the crystalline glass Brenton held, while the other shot hit the back of my canvas cushion. Several feathers flew up in the air.

I looked up immediately and saw the glint of a telescopic rifle reflecting the sun on a luxury yacht passing by us from the top deck of the four-level yacht. I yelled, "Assassin! Sniper! Don't get off the deck!"

As I dove to the deck, I pulled two pistols out, handing the silenced one to Brenton. I put the silencer onto the other pistol. Protected by the transom, I said, "Don't shoot unless you've got a target, or you have to defend yourself from a boarder. Let's pretend we're both dead. Evidently, your friend Walker has sentenced you to death after he communicated to you the President's plans for the polygamist. Without knowing it, you've sentenced me to death as well since you came to me and revealed them. You'll probably sentence to death everyone you get in touch with from now on. They cannot allow any chance of someone discovering the plans and intentions and revealing them to the public or the press." He looked at me in panic. I removed my clothes as I spoke. He looked at my action uncomprehendingly.

"I'm sorry, truly. This wasn't my intention at all."

"I know. Don't worry about it. All you have to do now is keep yourself alive, for yourself, for Massile, for your little girl Sunset, and for me. Your secret can become a great resource and powerful weapon against our enemies and corrupt politicians. That is why they sent that assassin to eliminate us today. That's why I'm asking you not to move from here until I come back. This could cost you your life. We don't know if they sent more than one assassin to do this job."

He looked at me and nodded. "OK. What are you thinking of doing?"

"I don't know yet. I will keep you informed, but right now I don't want you to worry about anything, and I don't want myself to worry about you. So, please—don't move. Stay on the deck. If you even have to pee, do so right here."

He nodded again. The transom I was shielding my body with had a compartment with diving gear stored inside. I had by now finished removing my clothes and put on my mask and snorkel. I pulled a belt with my Commando knife and a CO2 shark pistol from its place beneath the seat. I handed him my other gun. "You might need this. I won't need it where I'm going. Keep your head below the rails. We don't know how many of them are looking at us through the telescopic lens. If they don't see any movement here, anyone watching will be confused and come to the conclusion that we're both dead. That's what I want them to think. Now, please—follow my instructions to the letter."

I descended to the water from the side of the boat opposite to the direction in which the yacht was cruising. Brenton gave me a salute and said, "Good luck, my friend."

I nodded wordlessly and slid into the water. I had noticed the name of that yacht as it passed by, and I only needed to locate it. The speed in the harbor channel was minimal. They could not exceed that without catching the attention of the authorities if they created too great a wake. This enabled me to catch up to them in a short time.

I swam around to the stern of my ship. I put my mask and snorkel up on my head and climbed aboard my dinghy. I started the engine and left at the indicated speed of the harbor alternating with brief spurts of speeding: cruise at 10 knots, then a sudden burst of 25 or 30 knots, then back to 10 for a bit. I cut the distance without catching any harbor authority attention. I looked ahead and saw the yacht I was searching for right before me. They were heading out for open sea, perhaps with the intention of leaving the harbor in case anyone saw what had happened and called the authorities; or, if we had been killed, someone reported finding two bodies to the harbor police, and they wanted to avoid being questioned. They would be far from Newport Beach and Corona del Mar.

After I caught up with them, I moved up alongside their dinghy, lashed the two dinghies together, and cut my engine. I looked up at the four levels that towered above me. I climbed to the stern of the yacht *Maritius Code Circle* by the rope that attached the dinghy to the mother ship. When I got on board, no one was around. Apparently, all the crew's concentration was on the second deck, where I could hear music and the laughter of men and women, like a celebration or party was going on in the middle of the whole thing.

I stopped for a moment to watch these men and women. They were almost completely naked, wearing transparent tunics. Around their necks they wore silken black and white scarves. The tunics were tied around the waist by a three-inch black leather belt with an ostentatious large golden buckle. It might have been plated, but in the center of each buckle was a half-moon design in stones with two horns, like a horned jackal, surrounded by stars. Everything was in black save for the stars, which were blood red.

They danced to the music, a strange rhythm between Middle Eastern with Caribbean bongos. The women ululated shrilly, and an Asian gong reverberated in my chest strongly. It was a little too much for my ears; I found the whole noise irritating. However, the participants did not seem to mind as they danced to that strange music. When the gong sounded, the women convulsed as if in ecstasy along with a few men. The women touched their breasts with both hands, rolling down their stomachs and then to their private parts as if they had been choreographed. They raised the index fingers of their left hands and sucked on them as if seeking for moisture. The gong rang, and they reached back down towards their groin, as if the dance were a form of masturbation. They wore carnival style masks, but very expensive black and white Asian porcelain masks from China decorated with precious stones of blue, red, and black.

I had seen many of these Satanic cults all over the world, but never had I seen one like this, with such a high level of wealth and education apparent. Rarest of all, I had never seen this in Middle Eastern culture where the majority of the inhabitants have deep religious roots. It seemed very strange, this tremendous contrast. Such worship was completely contrary to the religious principles of the majority of educated Middle Easterners, which is what had caused me to halt in surprise. When I boarded this vessel, I thought I would find a group of semi-savage terrorists with long hair and disgusting untrimmed beards. Instead, I found a group of men and women with very refined carriage, trimmed beards, and excellent haircuts. Those that had long hair had it neatly braided, some wearing tiaras, turbans, and head necklaces. Some wore golden chains with different symbols and emblems. It looked like an afterhours party from the Academy Awards show.

The vast room in which they danced was breathtaking, décor very much to my taste. All they needed that I didn't see around were bottles of Grand Marnier. Floor to ceiling curtains in red, white, and black were flanked by gigantic idols of naked men and women, probably replicas meant to look like stone. Marble lions and large medallions rested against the columns like ruins; broken arches, one piece resting against the other, all gave the impression of an ancient temple ruin. The artistic skill of the designer was astonishing to me as both an artist and a composer. These decorations grabbed me. It was like a submerged temple, even with fish designs along the walls. You felt like you were on the bottom of the ocean exploring the ruins of Atlantis. Nets hung along some columns and marine vegetation was included. I had no doubts in my mind that of the participants of this Satanic group, many of them might be famous artists.

They had lost their purpose in life and had no idea of the atrocity they were committing by being involved in these kinds of rituals. They had probably given large amounts of money to those who conquered them by manipulating their feelings and claiming their souls, bringing them into darkness and recruiting them as mercenaries and terrorists through the oldest tricks since time began—politics, sex, and religion. They no longer sought creativity, seeking instead destruction. They lacked the talent and divine grace that is only given from God to those with good hearts and great spirits that is ultimately the divine grace of creativity. I shook my head in disgust to see those beautiful women, two of them now bringing lambs and placed them on wide tables in the middle of the room. The music stopped, only the bongos and timpani continued with a sinister rhythm of death. The triangles eerily mixed in with the percussion. When they stopped, the men brought down small swords and decapitated the lambs. They picked the carcasses up by the rear legs and allowed the blood to run into a glass bowl in the middle of the table, which had small cups hanging around the edges on hooks like a Christmas eggnog or punch bowl. Two large ladles sat inside on each side of the bowl. Several black cats with green and blue eyes entered the room as men and women came together and served themselves a cup of blood from the bowl.

The other two men took their time to slowly skin the lambs and hung the skins over some music stands. They removed the viscera and cut those into small pieces and put them on transparent small plates on the floor for the cats, who began to devour the treats. They began to butcher the carcasses into small pieces, placing them on small plates around the table for the guests. After they sprinkled the meat with salts and oils, the guests started to come and serve themselves, taking white linen napkins over one wrist. They ate the raw meat, wiping their mouths on the napkins, leaving smears of fresh blood on the white cloth. Like any social gathering, they served appetizers and took a break for food. The music began playing again as the musicians returned to their places. I shook my head and wondered at the palate of these supposedly refined people to be able to eat meat raw like that.

Barefoot, I climbed the exterior circular metal stairs that climbed up all four levels used by the yacht's crew. Deck by deck, I continued my ascent, passing the deck with the party with a live band, champagne flowing, and went all the way to the topmost deck. Unlike most top decks, which were open, this was covered by a canvas awning. I saw a man kneeling by what appeared to be a box of grenades. He held a rifle with a telescopic lens that he was tearing down and cleaning before wrapping it in a thin blue and white blanket with red lines. I was ready to get out of my hiding place to confront him, but I heard someone coming up the other set of stairs.

"Omar!" a man called. "I've brought you something to drink and some food. I know you like Heineken beer."

I shifted my position so I would not be seen, concealing myself under a pile of tarp-covered boxes of dynamite and C4. I wondered how it was possible that these individuals would have all these munitions and explosives in the middle of the harbor on a luxury yacht in the heart of Newport Beach and Corona del Mar. I had no doubts left in my mind that these criminals were very well-connected to the highest levels of our government to be able to get away with this.

The other man handed Omar a tray of food and a bottle of Heineken. As Omar turned to accept the tray and lifted the bottle to drink, I could see by his green eyes in the sun, his manners and air of royalty that Omar was no one less than the personal assistant and trusted right arm of the polygamist, Osama bin Laden. After we had finished interrogating him and let him go free, he obviously gave a debriefing to his boss that was not very favorable to me, and now a kidnapping mission had become a dead or alive mission, the proof of which I could see from the holes in my favorite chairs on my yacht.

I had no doubts now in my mind that certain elements in the government and intelligence were in direct contact with these terrorists. I decided that, not just for the safety of me and my team, but for that of society at large, I could not give them a second chance. I had already told Carlitos that there would be no other opportunity for kidnapping or murder. I thought of the strange deceptions existing between these individual terrorists and the people that we all considered worthy of our trust and decent enough to occupy high positions in our government. In the end, however, we always had bad in between good and good in between bad. Like seeds you plant in the soil, some good and create life, others simply became trash. I thought at that moment that Omar, bin Laden, and all these unscrupulous terrorists were like the seeds when they germinate, the fruit they produced was the fruit of evil and destruction by the hands of Satan over the Earth.

I pulled the CO2 pistol as I left my hiding place. "Hey, Omar—we see each other again, and it looks like in similar circumstances." He heard my voice and spun to face me. He tried to pull his weapon. I said, "Uh, uh, uh. Unless you want to fly into the sky in pieces and serve as a lunch for your brothers the sharks." I took his pistol from him and made him get down on his knees on top of a small wooden prayer bench. He looked at me in hatred and frustration. I could feel the negative energy trying to penetrate my heart, but in vain.

He smiled. "I guarantee you that the next time we see each other it will be different. You're not going to have the same luck. You can have it twice, but not three times in a row, and no one lives forever. You've run out of luck.

Next time I'll cut your head off and put it as a trophy in my harem."

"Until that time, if you're alive, because I let you go once. As you see, I've got three, you've got two. I want to ask you a single question before I blow you to pieces. Did they send you to kill Brenton Cooper, or me?"

He shook his head. "No, the initial target was Brenton for interrupting our plans. But his friend Walker thought he might take us to you, and then we would have the jackpot with you. You're never in the same place for long, and you're a difficult target to track. I assure you that your luck has burned up. Today, you just escaped by a hair."

I smiled. "And who told you there will be a next time? Maybe you're right and my luck has run out. But like everything in this life, but I can assure you that yours has run its final course today. Maybe your boss, bin Laden, will follow you to Hell where you both will be very welcomed, not by virgins but by donkeys with horns. I guarantee you that from now on you will be screaming in pain for the rest of eternity. By any chance do you have any Vaseline in your backpack?"

Omar looked at me in confusion at first and then looked at me in disgust once he understood what I was saying. "You Americans are all perverts and disgusting."

"Yes. The difference we joke about it, but you're actually doing it."

At that moment, the man who had brought the food and drink to Omar appeared on the stairs with what appeared to be a jar of ice and two bottles of beer. He saw me pointing my pistol at Omar. He dropped the bucket on the deck and reached for his pistol.

I said, "Don't move, or I'll blow you into pieces." He either ignored me or thought I was bluffing. As he cocked his pistol, I fired. The CO2 cartridge went right into his chest.

Using the confusion, Omar threw the bottle at my head. I ducked, and it shattered on the metal handrail of the stairs. Seeing he didn't hit me, he picked up the metal tray and hit me in the chest with it. I staggered back a few steps as he pulled a massive Arabian curved knife from his leg. He ran towards me, and I fired the CO2 pistol once more. The cartridge went into his stomach. Both Omar and his friend inflated like balloons, exploding in bloody rags a few seconds later. Body parts flew all over the deck. Because of the loud music two decks below, nobody noticed or heard anything. I began to descend the stairs I had just used, trying not to be seen. I got to the rope I had climbed and went back down to the dinghy.

As I was about to start the engine of my dinghy, I heard gunshots. The bullets whizzed over my head and the water splashed as the bullets hit. I pulled out a flare gun and shot the flare into the air—right over the yacht. The incendiary landed on the canvas, which erupted into flames. They stopped firing at me as the winds whipped the flames into an inferno.

We were about fifteen miles from the coast. I started the engine and got out of there at top speed. When that thing blew up, the debris would fly like deadly projectiles for several miles from the explosion. I wanted to get a great distance between me and that yacht as soon as possible. I thought I might have been caught in my own trap for a bit when I heard the first explosion behind me. I craned my neck to look back and saw everyone jumping from the yacht into the ocean, abandoning the vessel. Several other explosions, more powerful, roared out. I increased my engine to maximum. The largest load had not gone up yet, and my concern grew by the minute. I had no desire to be one more victim of it when it came.

As I piloted, I continually looked back on instinct, watching the yacht go up in flames. I didn't think I was far enough, and that enormous yacht was going to explode at any minute. I crossed myself and said quietly as I shook my head, "God, if only those stupid men hadn't shot at me, they would still be at their party and on their way to wherever they're going. But terrorists in the beginning, terrorists in the end. What can we expect from them? They forced me to do that. Unfortunately, those who play with fire end up burning themselves." I heard the explosion happen in a chain sequence. Pieces of debris fell from the sky. "Well," I said to myself, "if these terrorists get out of this alive, they have a long way to swim back to the harbor. Maybe you did this, God, to give them a final chance in their lives and give them a little taste of their tart medicine."

Pieces of fiberglass started to fall on my dinghy. I stopped the engine, donned my mask and snorkel, and got into the water. I swam to the stern of the dinghy and took the rope. I dove down until I needed air, went up to breathe through the snorkel, and then dove back down as pieces of debris entered the water. When everything finally calmed down, I surfaced and pushed my mask and snorkel up onto my head once more. I looked around, and to my surprise the massive luxury yacht had disappeared, leaving only some smoke and debris floating in the water. Seagulls flying among the debris looking for food marked where it had last been. I saw several people in the distance swimming with life vests.

I crossed myself and said compassionately and sadly, "Lord, those You think are redeemable, please don't abandon them. Save their lives. But those who have innocent blood on their hands, please don't interfere and let them drown. Let them fly to the Inferno, from where they should never have left. They will there find their true destiny. Amen. We ought to obey God rather than men; when the commands of men, even of those in government or religious authority conflict with the commands of God; we must obey *God, not men. Amen.*"

I crossed myself three more times and gave the blessing in Spanish, English, and Italian, thanking God once more for still being alive. When I tried to get back into the dinghy, I saw that some of the debris had punctured it, and water was slowly accumulating inside. I looked up at the sky and asked, "Don't take me for being ungrateful, Lord, but why do you make it so difficult for me all the time?" I shook my head. "You never make it easy, that's for sure, and now you've sent me another obstacle to continue my work. You certainly want to keep me active!" I took the rope and started to tow it behind me into the harbor. I pulled on my fins and began the long swim back with the rope tied to the belt around my waist, bringing my wounded dinghy back to her mother.

From this distance, the coast looked near, but the reality was that it took me several hours to arrive at the harbor's mouth. The fenders along the sides of the dinghy helped keep it afloat, enabling me to bring the dinghy back to my yacht for repair later on. I tied the dinghy off and got out of the water. I found Brenton on the deck in the exact same position I had left him hours ago. He was very happy to see me alive.

I said, "You are a very good soldier, since you did what few could do: follow orders to the letter. I assure you that if any other sniper exists on standby, you have completely thrown them off and convinced them that we are both dead. That is a great thing since it serves a purpose. They will report back to the brains behind all this that we are out of commission. The one I'm completely convinced now is behind all this is your supposed friend from your old job with the Secret Service, Walker. I corroborated that from the horse's mouth with the sniper before he was blown to Kingdom Come." I pointed with my right finger at the hole in the back of my favorite canvas chair. I poked my finger into the hole. I shook my head in thought. "The first name of Walker is David?"

Brenton nodded. "Yes, you're right. How did you know that? I never mentioned his first name."

"To be honest, I'm not sure. I had a flash of memory of this individual when you were involved in the counterfeit case. You guys were following me all the time, which I thought a joke. It lacked professionalism and was extremely careless; it lacked discretion on the part of the Secret Service. Even a five-year-old kid would know he was being followed. On one occasion when two men were following me in a Costa Mesa neighborhood, I pulled in front of a house to throw them off at night. I pretended to walk up the driveway to go into the house. Instead, I went around the bushes in the front yard of the house, crossed the garden, and waited until they parked. Since it was night, I managed to cross the street, get behind their car carefully, and appeared right by the passenger door of the sedan. Both men were looking through binoculars trying to locate me at that house. I stuck my hand inside the open window and took them by surprise by ripping the passenger man's binoculars out of his hands. The man gave an extremely high-pitched scream of fright at my unexpected action like a ghost from the darkness. He instantly put his hand on his weapon inside his jacket, and I saw his Secret Service badge with his name uncovered, and the name on it was David Walker. At the same moment the dome light in the car lit up as the driver, not knowing what was going on, opened his door and got out with his pistol in his hand. He yelled to me to raise my hands up, his eyes bulging out of their sockets. He then asked me what I was doing there, and I replied, still holding David's binoculars in my hands, that I wanted to know the same thing. I asked who they were, if they were following me or if they were Peeping Toms, looking for undressed young girls. I spoke loudly, and lights started coming on in the houses. I demanded to know why they were pointing their pistols at me. I started to walk towards my supposed house, even though I didn't know who actually lived there, and I yelled at the neighbors who opened their doors to call the police, indicating that I thought these men were sexual perverts. The couple who opened the door and turned the porch lights on released their dog, who ran out and started to bark at the driver's door. It was a Doberman pincher, and they got back in their car and sped off, their tires squealing on the pavement. I still had David's binoculars and saw that it had a gold plate with black lettering with his name on it. That's how you tripped my memory. I still have those binoculars on my St. Martin's residence in the Caribbean! When you mentioned Walker so many times, I had that flash back."

Brenton looked at me in surprise. "This is unbelievable. How do you remember all these details so many years later so clearly?" He shook his head and smiled. "Nothing you told me sounds even remotely strange. The assistant to Mr. Walker in those days used to be a retarded, ignorant Secret Service agent name Esquivel. That Mexican American was a good-for-nothing piece of trash, and probably pointed his pistol at you. He was like that even with his colleagues, and that's why we called him Billy the Kid. He was written up several times for threatening his colleagues and partners with his pistol, with or without reason. We all made a joke out of him because of his inferiority complex. He felt that showing his pistol was intimidating and made him feel superior and in control of any situation, especially to those who didn't know him."

"Now, refreshing my memory a little more, this Esquivel was the one who poured the boiling water from the coffee maker on my testicles, as you know."

"Yes, I remember."

"But what I hadn't yet put two and two together in my mind is why this person had such a personal and particular vendetta against me. Now that I've put it together, I see the connection and the reason. My humiliation of him before his boss after he threatened me with the pistol and acting like a chicken with his head cut off by speeding off that way, leaving his boss' binoculars in my hand, now I understand his personal animosity against me. It's possible, this is an assumption, that Mr. Walker recriminated him and made fun of him for a while before my arrest."

"It's an assumption, but it's very possible. Mr. Walker *loves* to make fun of people. I can assure you that this guy Esquivel, even without any motive to hate or mistreat anyone is a sourpuss. He doesn't really need a motive to be nasty with anyone. Since the day he was born he has been a nasty guy."

I nodded. "Yes, you're right. Unfortunately, some human beings have very little of being human and have more in their DNA of the savage beast. Speaking of beasts,

I will try to resolve your problem now. Even though you didn't want to bring it to me, it has come to be my problem as well." I helped him up off the deck. "I believe that I will take a little trip to Washington, D.C. to finally close the circle of what happened here today and what has been bothering you. I don't think it will take me long, but I believe the most prudent thing is for you to stay here on my yacht, don't move until I come back. It's for your own security as well as your family's. Then we can take that trip to South America so that I can be at peace with my conscience over what I owe Abdul's family. Maybe you can consider it a small vacation, because during my trip I intend to contact the wife of your friend Abdul. I have no relation to her at all, have only seen a picture; but you know her very well as well as their sons. That will be of great help. But I want you to think about it very carefully. Like you told me, I tell you now with your problem: I don't want you to feel obligated in any way. Come only if you want to. It will be very convenient, your company will be pleasant, and I'll visit my relatives in my paternal ancestral land of La Guaira. Maybe there I'll find a way to put behind me what has been bothering me for a while and something I promised myself. I believe this is the most decent, human thing to do for someone who deserves it, who sacrificed for our freedom in the time he walked with us on this world."

Brenton nodded. "Let me tell you that for me it will not just be a pleasure to travel with you but also a great honor. To know that you entrust in me the confidence to be your backup in case something goes wrong."

I grinned. "What could possibly go wrong in Venezuela?"

Brenton raised his pants leg and pointed at his feet. "Yes, yes. Especially in Venezuela. I have a vivid and memorable experience from those *sicarios*[25]."

---

25 Assassins

I turned serious. "I was only joking, but that this why I told you to think about it, even though this is not a dangerous mission or complicated like in the past. This is a most personal thing I need to do. When we travel to a communist country we have to be prepared. You know how you can come in, but you cannot predict if you will be able to get out because you cannot predict how the whole thing will turn out. Some aren't lucky like you and lose their lives in the process during a single trip. This is something normal people, especially the young, don't understand when in curiosity they decide to visit a country like Cuba, Venezuela, North Korea, or China. In their political ignorance and curiosity, they end up with a one-way ticket to Hell. Some don't even have the opportunity to repent of it, especially if they get falsely and arbitrarily accused of being CIA agents and get sentenced to execution by firing squad."

Brenton looked at me seriously and caressed his chin with his left hand. He touched his leg with his right hand. "Yes. You're right on the money. I've been very lucky and have only lost my toenails. It could be a lot worse. But if there's anything I can tell you is that high in the learning process a very sour but good lesson is that you never, under any circumstance, show them fear. When they see that you are not frightened of them, then you terrify them and you're on the top of the game. All it is mental and psychological intimidation, the fear they try to put into your head." He added sarcastically, "You can't even imagine the personal satisfaction I will have to have before me in a different situation one of those guys with their hands tied and full of anger. I will give anything to be able to look at least one or two of the ones who tortured me face to face in the future."

I understood his psychological state and tremendous anger. I gave him a little pat on the left shoulder. "I want you to remember, Brenton, that God works in mysterious ways. Maybe He, before you die, will give you the opportunity to find that in this world, which is turning every day. Like the wheel of fortune, today you're on the top and tomorrow on the bottom and then vice versa. Maybe you'll find them on the bottom while you're on the top, but you have to remember that vengeance is a very negative feeling; like vinegar and oil it doesn't mix with good, Christian feelings. My advice to you is to leave it in the hands of God and time. Time is the factor that determines everything in life. Don't think of revenge. Maybe the Supreme Architect wills surprise you one of these days. You might end up one day with the power to take those who tortured you, assuming they're still alive. They could repent from the evil they did to you, or they could be sent to Hell for their crimes. But do so with no revenge in your heart; only leave it to Divine Justice."

Brenton nodded with a small smile. "Yes, you're right. Every time I think about this, I get completely enraged even with myself at how I allowed it all to happen. Of course, this is not good for me because it fills my heart with hatred and a thirst for revenge." He looked at me more calmly and with a different reflection of peace in his face. "Thank you, Dr. del Marmol. Your words made me see things more clearly and rationally. I have no doubts in my mind that not only your words but also being by your side makes me and my character create a better person every day, growing closer to God and the principles we all defend. We should never stray far from those principles." He stood up and opened his arms to invite me to hug him. I stood up and we gave each other a bear hug. I felt his sincere gratitude.

I said, "Please don't leave here unless it's an extreme emergency. I'll give my team instructions to bring anything you need here and to keep you in communication with your family. Follow the protocols that we use so your enemies can't track you down here and come close to harm you. Until I return from DC, where I might have to give a spiritual baptism to your supposed friend David Walker in the Potomac River."

Brenton smiled. "I don't think that would be too much fun for him at this time of year."

"Well, I can assure you I'm not looking to give him any pleasure, nor cultivating a new friendship. According to what I've seen so far in your supposed friend, the way he treats you as a friend I would prefer to be on his list of enemies."

Brenton nodded. "Please, be careful. This individual is a man of many faces. You know how dangerous this can become to us."

I nodded. "Don't worry about it. I'll be back in a few days. This problem, yours and now mine, will be resolved once and for all."

CHAPTER 13: MOSSAD, ISRAEL'S INTELLIGENCE, AT ITS BEST

We said our goodbyes and I left the yacht to go to the lobby of the Club, followed by my loyal friend Rocco. When I got there, I went to the house phone and dialed to call Chopin. I told him to get ready to travel to Washington D.C. that night. He assured me he would make all the arrangements, and I thanked him before hanging up. I picked up the receiver again and dialed the number of Dr. Zayas-Bazan in Boston, Massachusetts. I found it practical and convenient to ask for his help since he was relatively nearby to realize my plans. I gave him in code some of the preliminary elements of what I was planning to do without specifics. He suggested we meet in the Jewish café close to the State Department in D.C. where we had already had several meetings before. We called this location #33.

The café was famous for their classy pastrami and rice sandwiches. Many State Department employees went there for their lunch breaks. I didn't want to distract my team from the other important things they were handling at this time and tying up the final details left over from the last operation. I didn't think this plan would take very much time to implement, and I didn't think it was a high-risk operation. At least, that is what I thought: an in and out extraction or a turn around. I decided that Chopin and Chandee would be more than sufficient help. I knew from experience that nothing seldom goes as planned. If the unexpected happened, I would at least have backup. If for any reason we had to deviate and change the initial plan, we would have an emergency plan on standby.

I communicated the details of the plans we were to develop with Dr. Zayas-Bazan's help to my friends. I thought we could enact it successfully without major problems through using the element of surprise. We left Orange County by the John Wayne Airport of Southern California. Our travel time was seven hours and some minutes, which gave us plenty of time to discuss the specifics. Chandee went over the details which had transpired over the last twenty-four hours during the visit with Brenton on my yacht. As we landed in DC, the sun was getting hot. A beautiful day was about to begin.

Chandee went to get the car she had rented. It was a very curious vehicle, a turquoise blue Mini Cooper with a white top. Unfortunately, Chandee could not find any other car available due to a vast convention for the Arms Control Treaty at that time.

Figure 41 Chandee's forced choice: the Mini Cooper

I smiled and said, "I believe we should be grateful. It could be worse, and maybe you could only find a VW bug available."

She smiled. "It doesn't bother me. I think it's a very cute car."

Chopin said, "Sure, very cute. Try driving that cucaracha with my long legs and see how cute you feel when you feel like you're a sardine in a can."

Chandee said, "Don't worry about it. Sit down comfortably in the back and I'll drive. I have short legs. It won't be a problem for me at all."

Chopin sighed unhappily. He said resignedly, "OK."

I smiled at the unhappy expression and the way Chopin rolled his eyes as he crammed himself into the back of the car, bending his long neck and body into that little car. Once we were all in the car, I said, "This little car reminds me of a little Yorkie terrier puppy I had many years ago. It had a very tiny body, but he ignored it. He didn't know that he was so tiny and wanted to start fights with the big dogs of the neighborhood. He had the heart of a lion. That always caught my attention and made me look at him in admiration. That's why I gave him the name of So Big, even though he was tiny. His personality grew into that name. He had a very big heart."

Chandee pressed on the accelerator, and the Mini Cooper jumped. I looked back at Chopin and rolled my eyes a little. I held on to the handle above the door. Chopin returned my smile as he reached up to hold onto the handle above his door.

He said, "I believe Chandee has discovered another little lion with a big heart like your Yorkie."

Chandee replied, "You've seen nothing yet as to what this lion of a puppy can do." She turned sharply around a corner, making Chopin roll around in the back seat.

Chopin yelled, "You made your point, OK? Slow down, girl! It's too early in the morning for an adrenaline rush. If you need them, I have some Formula 303 pills in my backpack. You know, our secret weapon to mellow out our systems."

Chandee smiled mischievously but reduced her speed. "Remember, Chopin—very expensive perfume comes in tiny bottles. Poison, too. Look at the effect on people both have. That means you should never measure anything in this life by its physical size if you don't want egg on your face."

Chopin smiled and mumbled, "I don't understand how you Asians always are so sensitive and take everything so personally."

Chandee said, "The same way the majority of you blacks want to make us responsible for what our great-grandparents did to your great-grandparents when they were slaves. OK? There nothing sensitive in this at all. Remember, Chopin—who rented the car? You're indirectly blaming me. Unfortunately, this was better than the only other option I had, which were motorcycles."

Chopin shook his head in displeasure. "Motorcycles? What were you thinking, girl? If you showed up with motorcycles, that would have been over the top! If that was the case, thank you for your selection! I would rather crawl into this back space than expose my head to all the bugs on the highway."

I nodded and smiled. "Believe it or not, motorcycles can be a lot of fun."

Chopin shook his head and grunted. "There's no doubt in my mind that you guys are the same type of personality and character."

Chandee smiled again. To mess around with him, she said, "If I have to tell you the truth, I did consider the motorcycles. The only problem, though, would have been our luggage and how to bring two or three motorcycles at once. To keep you guys from having to deal with that, I decided to go with the Mini Cooper, which you've only been complaining about."

I said, "OK, guys, mellow out. I'm fine with the Mini Cooper. You, too, Chopin?"

"Yeah, yeah."

We pulled up outside the hotel and went into the lobby. I asked Chandee to register us in the hotel while I called Dr. Zayas-Bazan from the courtesy phone to save some time. That way we could be at Location 33 at the time we had agreed upon. We checked into our rooms and left at once towards our meeting in the Mini Cooper after I had verified with Dr. Zayas-Bazan that he was already waiting for us. We established the signal he was going to give me to identify Mr. David Walker. Even though we had his picture, and I had my photostatic memory, we wanted to be 100% sure without any possibility for error. Since he had known Walker for a very long time, going back to when they did some work together for the Secret Service in Miami, Florida, he would recognize him immediately in the restaurant. On his way out he would touch him in a friendly way on the left shoulder, which would give us the green light to proceed with our plans.

We arrived at the Jewish café and split up to avoid looking like a group. Each of us was going to sit in a strategic location in the café. They would be in place ready to back me up in case something went wrong. After we got ourselves situated, I established visual contact with Dr. Zayas-Bazan as we nodded to each other slightly. He proceeded with his part of the plan, standing up from his table on the pretense of going to the restroom. He slowly walked by the table of Walker.

He said in surprised joy, "David Walker? How are you? It's been so long since I've seen you!" Walker smiled. He hesitated at first, but then recognized Dr. Zayas-Bazan. "Don't you remember me, David?"

He was sitting with two other muscular men who looked like bodyguards. He stood up. "Dr. Zayas-Bazan?" He held out his right hand, and they shook hands.

Dr. Zayas-Bazan gave him a friendly pat on his left shoulder. "You look very well physically. What have you been doing? You even look younger. What is your secret?"

Walker said pleasantly with a big smile, "A lot of work. It looks like the more work I do the better I feel. It keeps me in very good shape, both physically and mentally." He preened a little proudly. He clearly loved the compliments from Dr. Zayas-Bazan and wanted to brag about his good condition like some kind of thug or bully.

I had to hold back my laughter at how that old fox, Dr. Zayas-Bazan, using his knowledge of psychology, fed the ego of our enemy and achieved distracting him with the compliments. I was dressed in a black jogging suit with white stripes down the sides. I wore a long-visored black baseball cap and dark sunglasses. I didn't want to give him the slightest opportunity of recognizing me in any way or form. Since he wasn't alone, I didn't want to ruin the most important factor in this operation: surprise.

As they spoke, Dr. Zayas-Bazan put his left hand over his abdomen. "I'm sorry, this conversation is very pleasant, but I have an urgent call from nature. I stopped to say hello, but Nature continues to scream to me."

Walker was still standing by the table. "I have to go, too. I'll go with you so we can keep catching up. I've been holding on, waiting for our food. It's past lunchtime already, and I'm hungry." The two bodyguards stood up, but Walker waved them back down as the waitress arrived with a tray of food. "Wait here. This is my old friend. You don't have to worry. The food is here, so don't let it grow cold. The pastrami sandwiches are great when they're hot, as are those crispy French fries. I'll be right back. I'm just going to take a quick leak while I talk to my buddy."

The bodyguards relaxed, glad that they don't have to leave the sandwiches, which did smell wonderful. As soon as I saw that I got up and walked slowly behind them to avoid calling attention from the bodyguards. They were very distracted by the food, and I didn't want to draw their notice. In his impatience, one of them took some French fries before the server put the plates down.

One said, "Hey! Those are my fries!"

"I'm sorry," the other replied. "I only took a few. I thought it was mine."

Dr. Zayas-Bazan and David were at the door to the restroom and walked inside. Without looking back, I opened the door and turned slightly as I did to see if my presence had been detected by them. I could see that they were ignoring me entirely, forgetting completely about David as they focused on their food and drink. I smiled and thought to myself that nothing less could be expected from mercenaries.

I walked into the bathroom. The only people at the urinals were David, Dr. Zayas-Bazan, and a tall man wearing a yamaka with a Star of David. He finished and washed his hands, drying his hands before the sinks with paper towels. I went next to him and turned on the faucet, keeping an eye in the mirror on the man as he dropped the used towel into the trash. I did not put my hands in the stream of water and watched the movements of Dr. Zayas-Bazan and David as they kept their backs to me. I could see them finishing up and turning around as they zipped their flies. I took some towels from the container and acted as if I was drying my hands. As they came over to me, I removed my sunglasses and gave him a slight nod as I made eye contact with him as a go-ahead signal. He returned the signal and exclaimed, "Dr. del Marmol!"

I turned and said, "Yes—who wants to know?"

He said, "What a coincidence! Two friends I haven't seen in many years in the same place."

Walker turned suddenly, his hands still soapy and wet from the faucet. He looked at both of us and said, "Coincidence my ass, you son of a bitch! You sold me out!" he reached for his gun. "Traitor!"

I jumped on him and grabbed a wrist in each of my hands, his right hand first before he could draw his gun. I shoved them up as high as I could with all my strength. I looked him straight in the eyes. "Murderer! The only traitor here is you. To your country, your family, and to the religious principles and morals that you swore to defend!"

I dragged him to the last stall with a handicapped sign, large enough to be wheelchair accessible. As I looked into his eyes, squeezed his wrists, and pushed him back, he stopped resisting. I slammed him up against the wall over the folding table for the diaper changing station. I leaned in to whisper in his ear. "Watch my vision—this is what will happen to you if any of your assassins try again to hurt Brenton Cooper, his family, or anyone of my friends or associates. This will be your destiny if that happens." I released his wrists and clapped my hands forcefully over his temples. His arms dropped to his sides numbly, heavily, as he entered a trance, though his eyes remained open, looking at me in terror. He started to drool.

I continued whispering in his ear. "Your guys can make all the immoral arrangements you want, but in the end, you will be the one Divine Justice will be looking to for a clear accounting. In this process of covering up your corruption and hiding your horrible intentions from the public, you tried to assassinate innocent people only on the assumption they could blow your cover. You were only concerned about the barbarities that you guys want to keep hidden and silent from those who have deposited their trust in you as leaders. You will be the first ones I will unleash this beast on so that it swallows your heads. I can assure you with my blood and life that this is the first and last warning that I will give to you. You and your family will be the first ones, followed by your accomplices." Walker started to urinate all over his shoes.

I released him and he slid slowly down onto his haunches to sit on the tile floor in his own urine. I leaned down and removed from his right leg a small pistol he had concealed in a leg holster. I handed it to Dr. Zayas-Bazan, who smiled and said, "Sneaky little guy."

I then took his regulation pistol from his shoulder holster and murmured in his ear, "I'll put these two pistols with the binoculars I still have in my safe. The day you change your ways and decide to have a more friendly approach and come to me in peace, harmony, and with no more violence, I'll return them. Until then, I leave you to live another day."

He said nothing but continued to look at me as if he had seen a ghost, extreme terror in his expression. Dr. Zayas-Bazan watched in silence, and asked, "What did you make him see that left him in this state of complete shock?"

I nodded. "I showed him Mini O.B.'s parents and what they did with the mercenaries that tried to intercept us during the trip from Montauk to MIT, when we visited you in your labs. You conducted those tests on the little creature and assured us that the creature did not belong to this Earth[26]. Remember?"

"Oh, yes! I recall—but I only saw the little one. The parents were so bad and frightening?"

I nodded. "You have no idea. I can show you, but I don't want you to go through that. They were over seven feet tall with bear-like claws, shark-like teeth, and were capable of ripping into pieces a human being's body in seconds like you were shredding documents in a machine."

He waved me away. "Thank you, I don't want to see that. If those are the side effects, I don't want to see." He pointed at Walker, who was still shaking in terror, his eyes staring out of their sockets.

I pointed to my temple and said, "I have the film right in here. I can transmit how these creatures destroyed all these mercenaries who might even have been associated either directly or indirectly with Walker. You know birds of the same feather always flock together, or at least in association."

He asked, "Do you think its secure for us and our team to leave this assassin alive and free behind us?"

I shook my head gravely. "What do you recommend doing? Whatever you recommend, I advise you to do it quickly, or in a very few minutes we will have those gorillas we left sitting at his table breathing down our necks looking for their master."

He looked at the ring on my right hand. Then he pointed and said with a sorrowful expression on his face, "I believe this will be one of the few occasions that your ring is an acceptable solution. We might repent later at leaving this murderer alive. It's very possible this is not the first time he tried to assassinate you and God only knows how many more. Take into consideration the political power he possesses, having the ear and attention of the most powerful man in the world, who is capable with just an executive signature of destroying a nation in less than

---

26 As related in *The Lightning and Montauk: Reality vs. Fiction.*

seventy-two hours. You remember Libya and Muammar Khaddaffi? I believe these are the most powerful reasons for not leaving this man alive. Especially with him knowing all of us and us knowing what he is capable of doing with his mercenaries to achieve the sinister plans, political agendas, and personal ambitions in order to perpetuate their power."

I had remained silent for a few seconds, deep in thought about the suggestion. It didn't make me very happy, though I knew how right he was. There was a great deal of truth in what he had said. Taking the life of another human being unless it was absolutely necessary was, to me, repugnant. I usually took extreme precaution so when the time came that I had to decide to let someone live or die, even our enemies, I had an option open to me. But especially in this case there was no need to defend the lives of any of us who were in danger at that particular moment. Taking Walker's life on the assumption that my lecture to him had not worked and he went back later to repeat his criminal acts was a step I was unwilling to take, especially on an assumption. It was the same reason Walker had sent his mercenaries to assassinate Brenton Cooper: an assumption that Cooper could expose his plans to relocate bin Laden. As a possible prevention, if he found me by his side, I would be assassinated as well to avoid their secrets from being exposed. They only wanted to protect for their own interests the most wanted and macabre mastermind of the murder of over 2,977 American human beings along with 225,000 non-fatally injured. Walker's superior wanted this solely for his political ambition to impress the public and pretending this man had been captured and brought to justice in order to earn the sympathy and votes of the citizens in gratitude. Such a façade was something the American people had anxiously waited for years to see; whatever side of the political spectrum the entire nation cried for justice.

I went over to Walker, asking the Supreme Architect to give me a signal, no matter what it might be, before I proceeded to take his life. As if in answer from

Providence, the door to the handicap stall burst open. Three men with Mira Safety CM-7M military gas masks dressed in civilian clothes were outside, pointing pistols at us. I immediately reached for my pistol, as did Dr. Zayas-Bazan. The leader of the group recognized me and lowered his pistol, gesturing to the others to do likewise.

He removed his mask. "We're not here for you." He turned to his men. The other two obeyed and removed their masks as well. Dr. Zayas-Bazan and I also lowered our guns.

I said, "If you're not here for us, who are you here for?"

He pointed at Walker. "For this mercenary and traitor to Israel as well as the security of his own country."

I looked at Dr. Zayas-Bazan in confusion and shrugged in amazement. He also shrugged, but his manner approved of the new situation. The leader of the group put his pistol away in a leather shoulder holster beneath his jacket. He held out his right hand to me. I took it and shook hands with him. He said, "My name is Adam from the Mossad, Israeli intelligence. This is my buddy Bram and Alon." He gestured to the man to his right and then to his left. The other two men smiled and also held their hands out to us. We shook hands all around and each of them told me what a pleasure it was to meet the Cuban Lightning.

I smiled and nodded. "The Cuban Lightning is very pleased to meet you guys from Mossad. Of course, I know what the Mossad is. I'll be very happy to offer you my package. To be truthful, I had tremendous indecision whether to leave him behind dead or alive before you guys arrived. My irredeemable optimism was fighting with my conscience about what to do, and you guys have relieved me of that burden." Adam and his men handed their ID cards and badges to prove their identities to me. "That's not necessary, guys. If you weren't who you said you are, there would have been a shower of bullets and some strange people from the coroner's office would be called to examine those of us who didn't survive the encounter."

Adam smiled and removed a syringe from inside his coat. He injected something yellow in color into Walker. He ordered the others to change Walker's clothing and put a hospital gown on him. The other two pulled a wheeled gurney over and put on medical robes over their suits. They put Walker's body on the gurney and draped stethoscopes around their necks. Adam held out his hand to me again. "It's been a great honor to get to know the Ghost that possesses the most divine radiant light over the Earth: the Cuban Lightning."

I smiled uncomfortably. "Thank you. Humble and great is the man who can give glory to others and not himself. But I want to ask you a question before you leave. What is the reason you guys were wearing gas masks when you broke in here?"

Adam smiled and winked at me. "When you guys leave here, you'll understand the reason for these masks." He pulled two masks out and handed them to me. "You might want to put these on unless you want to take a long nap outside. Everyone in the restaurant will be asleep for the next several hours. Our friend put enough gas for the whole day since we didn't want to harm any innocent individuals here during this operation. Thanks to you, everything went smoothly, a lot better than we had expected. We had anticipated, because Walker has such a dangerous reputation, a most violent reaction, especially with two professional assassins guarding him twenty-four hours a day. You managed to put him out of commission without a single shot being fired. I really appreciated that, and I am indebted to you. You did an excellent job in baiting him into the most peaceful place in the restaurant: the restrooms. He's an advisor the President that has been considered for many years to be the worst enemy to the people of Israel and democracies around the world. This President is a militant for the movement of the extreme left wing, the international organization that advocates global communism. It was founded in 1919 by Lenin and succeeded by the Communist Information Bureau in 1947 formed by Stalin. This organization's sole mission consisted of penetrating the heads of states and young senators with ambition to become President of this wonderful nation of America with the objective of not only controlling the monetary system but also destroying the global economy using different conniving ways to create chaos. Doing so will accomplish their primary goal: convert the modern world into one totalitarian regime under the Marxist-Leninist communism. This is why we consider him so dangerous."

I smiled. "Not on my watch." I patted him on the shoulder. "I don't believe on any of your watches, either, if I'm not mistaken."

Adam smiled and stepped forward to give me and Dr. Zayas-Bazan hugs. "You can be sure that you're not mistaken. To prove this to you, I'm going to give you this token. It makes you one of us. I do this in gratitude for your cooperation and assistance, this token will identify you to any member of our organization as a loyal, good friend of the people of Israel."

I nodded. "Thank you very much for this great honor. I really appreciate and will hold it very close to my heart, brother."

"This is the least I can do for you, considering the great service you rendered us today but also for all the things you've done for all your life. I know your file. All I ask is one more favor, please. Wait here for a few minutes so you give us time to put this mercenary into the ambulance we have outside waiting for us to transport him to our interrogation place and then send the package for complete processing and identification."

"How much time do you need?"

"Five or ten minutes, max."

I looked at my watch on my left hand. The three men, Adam leading while the other two wheeled the gurney, left the bathroom. I examined the token Adam gave me in my left hand. The center of the coin was stamped in the fashion of Roman times with the stamp "Imperatore" (which translates to "Emperor") and the number 188-217 AD stamped on one side.

Figure 42 Mossad token

Dr. Zayas-Bazan smiled in satisfaction and wiped his forehead with the index finger of his forehead in relief. "I believe that not only you made three new friends today, but like always you also managed to resolve an awfully hard, indecisive problem we had. I know your personality is noble and optimistic, and how difficult it is for you to take another human being's life. It looks like, as always, the Supreme Architect, knowing you better than anyone else, took that heavy load from your shoulders and gave you an option. On top of that, he sent you as presents new friends in our fight against evil."

I smiled. "It looks like that, my friend." I handed him the token. He examined it in surprise and handed it back to me.

"I'm not an expert in coins, symbols, or tokens, but it appears to be an ancient Roman coin from just after the time of Jesus Christ, the Son of our Supreme Master, when He walked among us in Nazareth accompanied by his

Apostles. I believe Adam truly must have a strong motive and powerful feelings that make him so impressed about your personality in order to give you such a valuable present."

"Well, as for values you know it all depends on what you refer to. If you're referring to material value, of this I'm not very sure. Also, you know that's not of any importance to me. That's not what I'm looking for at all. But if you're referring to moral, patriotic values of great benefit to our line of work, this coin has an incalculable price, not just for me but for all those on our team. It can take us out of a very difficult jam which we encounter such situations when we have to prove or identify ourselves as friends of Mossad. Remember, this is an extremely powerful organization to the global intelligence, as powerful as the CIA." I smiled. "I wouldn't even be surprised to find it more powerful, taking into consideration the extreme efficiency and wisdom Mossad works with. See how its members have conducted in the past in every operation they display around the world. They have built an excellent reputation of five stars in the international intelligence community that they enjoy today. That prestigious reputation can cover us when we hold that coin in our hands. It's not important to me if that token comes from Jesus' time, from a fancy car wash, or a restaurant in bankruptcy."

Dr. Zayas-Bazan smiled in amusement and shook his head. "Your mind and the way you analyze everything never ceases to amuse me, Dr. Julio Antonio del Marmol. The funniest thing is that all your comparisons you use frequently your friends and associates have started to call 'Marmolisms.' But 99.9% of the time they prove to be accurate. Not even close to be wrong no matter how crazy and bizarre it sounds at the time." He smiled and shook his head again. "What I'm going to tell you now is that I wouldn't be surprised at all that your suggestion about that token in the long run can become as you suggested, of no material value."

I looked at one of my wrist watches and checked the time again to see if the ten minutes Adam requested were up. "OK, let's get out of here. I'm a little worried for our friends, Chandee and Chopin. Remember, they are there supposedly guarding our backs."

We left the restrooms into the main dining area. What had looked like a bee swarm before looked like a frozen piece of time. Everyone, including our two friends, had been transported to anesthetic dreams induced by the gas our new friends from the Mossad had sprayed for everyone to enjoy their afternoon siesta. Some had pastrami sandwiches and golden French fries sitting before them, but the customers leaned back, right, or left in their slumber. I noticed the two bodyguards for Walker had disappeared. Their food, however, was left on the table.

As we walked over towards Chandee's table, Dr. Zayas-Bazan said a little agitatedly, "What an embarrassment! Can we still call them backup?"

I said, "Please help me get them out of here before the local authorities arrive."

We got them out of the restaurant and into the Mini Cooper. I said to Dr. Zayas-Bazan, "Remember, the same weapons we use against our enemies they use against us. In this case, by our closest allies. We all have the same arsenal. The same surprise we used to take advantage of Walker, Adam and his friends used to surprise all of us. Don't be so judgmental of our friends for getting caught by surprise. After all, they surprised the two of us as well. None of us had thought for a single second was that the Mossad would be interested in our package. But it looks like that Mr. Walker has been very busy lately screwing around with the wrong people around the world. To our benefit, since everything ended even better than I had planned. To return to talk of embarrassment, I believe the true embarrassment, if we are to be fair, will be to David Walker, when he finds himself naked in some undisclosed location in the middle of nowhere in the Middle East, waterboarded by our new friends, Adam and his buddies. You should realize they were extremely opportune in their arrival and freed me of the tremendous weight of something I will never enjoy in my life: taking the life of another human being." We finished putting the seat belts on Chandee in the Mini Cooper and returned for Chopin. "Remember, my friend and first mentor, something you taught me once you told me there's only one destructive weapon so powerful that not one of us can defend against it and all be at its mercy. Very few times can we survive it. That is—"

We finished together, "surprise."

We both laughed, and he shook his head. "It's incredible how you memorize in such clarity things that are decades old and I've even forgotten telling you myself." He nodded seriously, a little remorsefully. "Please, don't tell Chandee and Chopin what I said when they wake up. What I said, to be honest with myself, was inappropriate and not right. I know from your own words and references before of the loyalty they've always conducted themselves towards you and the other members of the team."

I smiled and patted him on the shoulder. "Don't worry about it. I never repeat any comment between friends to avoid wrong interpretations. The only comments I repeat are those of my enemies with other enemies so that I manage to confuse them and cause them to attack each other."

He gave me a small smile, a little more relaxed. "I believe strongly, Julio Antonio, that I'm getting a little old. I'm starting to make mistakes that I've tried to teach you to keep you from making later in life. Like life itself is a circle, I'm starting to think I'm coming back to the beginning."

"Yes, you're right. Life is a funny circle. That is why I'm here to amuse you with your old memories and remind you what you've taught me to keep you from putting your foot in the dark, deep hole that you taught me to avoid always."

He looked at me gratefully. "Thank you very much."

"You don't have to thank me. I'm only doing my duty and responding to your teaching."

"OK. Follow me to the lab at MIT. I will inject an antidote to Chandee and Chopin that will accelerate their recovery from that gas in their bodies and brains. It will reduce the effect, so they don't sleep for so long. Then you can go back to your hotel without drawing attention and return to your place of origin as soon as you want."

"Thank you. That will be ideal. You know, in our kind of work, that there is never enough time. Saving a few hours will be hours of tranquility that we can find a way to use in case something unexpected happens. Especially when we have to improvise with our plans."

Dr. Zayas-Bazan replied, "You're right, my son Julio Antonio. Follow me and I'll prepare a fine cocktail that will get your friends to dance the hula."

I smiled. "That is OK, of course if the hula doesn't do too many hulas. Remember, Chopin is our pilot. I don't want your cocktail to make the hula go in his brain and make him so confused that instead of landing us at John Wayne Airport in Orange County, we wind up in Jose Marti International Airport in Havana. That will be my last hula dance, especially a surprise to all of us without a single disguise among us. It would be a tremendous travesty."

He smiled and shook his head. "Remember, I'm a pharmacist and a chemist, not a drug dealer."

"I'm' just joking with you. Where's your sense of humor?"

We exchanged smiles and I followed him until we reached MIT in Massachusetts several hours later. We drove inside the parking lot outside the building that contained the labs.

He said, "Wait for me in the car. I don't want to draw attention after hours by having you bring in our friends in that poor condition. They might think we're making zombies somewhere in the labs."

He left and went inside the building. A little while later he returned carrying a Gladstone bag in his right hand. He sat down inside the car and opened it. He removed a rubber tube and tied it onto one of Chandee's arm. Once he found a vein, he injected a solution already mixed in the syringe. He pulled the needle out and placed a cotton ball on the injection site, instructing me to hold it for a while. He did the same for Chopin. After a few minutes, he said, "Let them rest for a while. In about seven or eight hours they will be ready for whatever you guys want to do, maybe less."

We exchanged hugs. I said, "Thank you very much for everything."

"It's a pleasure and an honor that you reach out to me for anything at all and never hesitate when I can be of help to you. Drive carefully—remember, you have a long drive ahead of you and we've been very stressed."

We said our goodbyes and I drove back to D.C. To not call attention to us as we arrived in the hotel, I parked the Mini Cooper in the self-parking in the underground garage. I parked strategically in the left corner, the darkest place I could find in the entire garage. I wrote a note for Chandee and Chopin to read when they woke telling them I would wait for them in my suite and to wake me up if I had fallen asleep, no matter what time it was. I left it on the dashboard and cracked the windows a little, so they had sufficient ventilation inside that little car. I took a couple of blankets from the trunk and covered them. I calculated they would probably sleep the rest of the night, easily, even though Dr. Zayas-Bazan had told me that they should be ready soon to travel. I knew that was only a speculation from him to make me feel better and more relaxed. In medicine, it all depends on the metabolic system of the individual person and also the amount of gas they had inhaled. Without those factors on hand to make an educated diagnosis, he had only injected my friends an amount approximated to his calculation of the amount of time we had spent in the bathroom, and such calculations are always made conservatively low. The worst thing you can do with chemicals and drugs is to administer too high a dose. This can be fatal and cause a cardiac arrest, killing the patient, especially when not absolutely sure the type of chemical sedative that they had inhaled. All human bodies possess similar immune systems, but at the same time much different in their physical and neurological reactions. That of course is what makes us similar while different and extraordinary machines.

I smiled to myself, thinking of the beauty of that great miracle the Supreme Being created and no other creature ever could compare to our human bodies. Only the Supreme Architect was capable of making this fantastic masterpiece: fragile and balanced between life and death. Many of us can never understand or appreciate that and its magnitude. I looked at my friends Chandee and Chopin, completely unconscious, and my medical knowledge informed me that only a small portion extra that others signified harmlessness for others could be mortal, never waking up from that state of unconsciousness. I could only think that they both were there because of me. If I lost one of them, the weight I would carry on my conscience for the rest of my life I would be immense. I could not avoid growing emotional and my eyes grew moist. I took Chandee's hand in mine and kissed it. I crossed myself with my right hand and began to pray. "A man that hath friends must showeth himself friendly: and there is a friend that sticketh closer than a brother. Friendships are important but it doesn't matter how many friends you have. It matters more what type of friends you have. And you are the best friends I ever had. Please God, don't take them away from me. Amen."

I crossed myself three times and said the blessing in three different languages, closed the door of the car, and walked towards the elevators. As I walked in, I realized someone must have called the elevator from the lobby, as that light was on. I didn't give it much importance, thinking that no matter what this was not an hour in which much was moving in the hotel. It was a strong possibility that someone in the lobby wanted to go either up or down at that moment. Due to what had recently happened over the past hours, I couldn't convince myself that this was simple coincidence, so I readied the ring on my right hand for action. I didn't let myself grow completely paranoid; I just wanted to be ready in case something happened. Something, perhaps my subconscious, told me that something wasn't right. I began to become untranquil. It wasn't intense, but some kind of bad energy was floating around me, persuading me that elevator was not the right place to be.

The elevator stopped at the lobby, and a tall man, and very well dressed in a trendy black coat, black tie with peach and white flowers and with an unlit pipe in his mouth, entered the elevator. As the doors nearly shut, a very young girl in a wheelchair asked desperately for the elevator to be held. At once I followed my reaction and with my left foot first and then my left hand, I stopped the doors from closing in time for her to wheel herself inside. I stepped back a little to give her more space as she entered while I held the door with my left hand.

A few seconds later I glanced at the man and noticed that he had a cane which had occult symbols on the handle. I also noticed he made not the least effort to help that handicapped woman. Looking at his cane, I thought he might also be mildly handicapped, and so excused him to myself as being apathetic without assuming anything. I turned my head as I heard the voice of the desk attendant call my name and gesture to me.

"Dr. del Marmol, I have several messages for you here. Do you mind?" She held up several small notes in her right hand.

I raised my right arm and gestured for them to continue without me in a friendly manner. "You two have a good night," I said to them with a smile.

I turned and walked to the front desk where the beautiful, blond girl with brown eyes waited for me. As I came close, she said, "Mr. O.B. has been calling you all day, several times. He asked for me to please look for you when you got here and give you this message before you go to your suite. He said he needs to speak to you immediately, that it's urgent."

I took the messages and saw they were all the same: "Call me immediately. Urgent."

She said, "You can use the house phone. It's for the guests."

I thanked her and said goodbye. I ignored her suggestion to use the house phone. I walked to my right over by the restrooms, where I had seen public phones before. I hurried, thinking there might be a possibility for my bad feelings and negativity felt earlier. I entered the cabinet and dialed a different number and area code. A woman's voice answered. "ID code, please."

"Black Tears in My Eyes 71."

"Please wait."

It sounded like she hung up. "Hello?" I asked. "Hello?" I could hear a ringing on the receiver.

After two rings, O'Brien's voice came on. "Thank God! Where is your package?"

"Hello. How are you doing? I have no package with me."

He ignored my customary comment. "Thank God."

I asked, "What happened? Change of plans?"

His voice was agitated. "Yes. Please do me a favor and multiply all your precautions. Prepare to leave the city immediately. I'll be in the bar of your hotel in half an hour. Tell your friends to open their eyes and watch their backs." I smiled and chuckled. "Why are you laughing?" he asked in irritation. "This is life or death. There's nothing bloody funny about it."

I didn't like this tone of voice. I didn't like a thing about him at this moment, much less the patronizing tone he used in correcting me. I let some of my irritation show. "I just recommend you keep your pants on. I don't appreciate your tone of voice. You better calm down. Then you'll understand the damned bloody funny reason I'm laughing."

O'Brien said, "I'm sorry. I'm very, very stressed." He understood my irritation and calmed himself. "Don't let your Cuban temper get the best of you. It's not my intention to offend you. I didn't believe I would find you alive."

"Is the problem that serious? You don't have to apologize. I know you're a grumpy old man."

"More than you can imagine. Be very careful, OK?"

"Very well. But you'd better take a Valium or a shot of Grand Marnier before you see me, OK?"

He chuckled briefly. "OK, see you."

We hung up and I went towards the elevators. I boarded one car and pressed the button for the underground garage. When the doors opened, I walked briskly towards the Mini Cooper, worried for my friends, my heart in my throat and hoping I would find them alive. I opened the driver's door and saw both friends were still sleeping like angels in Paradise. My soul returned to my body. I sat down in the driver's seat and picked up the note from the dashboard, ripping it up. I wrote another note: "When you wake up, please find me in the bar next to the lobby of the hotel. Under no circumstance go to the suite until you talk to me. We've got Code Blue there." I signed it and put it on the same place in the dashboard. I checked their pulses to make sure they were still alive.

Once I realized they were fine, I got out of the car, locked it, and walked back to the elevators, checking my surroundings as I did to make sure I was unobserved. I got on the next available car and pressed the button for the lobby. I got out and walked to the bar where I was to meet O'Brien. As I walked into it, I saw that it was completely empty, only a music group, the bartender, and two maintenance men from the hotel working on the light and sound system. They were changing some light bulbs and adjusting some speakers. A lady past her prime was sitting at the piano with a small group comprised of a young, long, straight haired man sitting on the drums, a man of middle age on the bass, and a young black man on the tenor saxophone. They were playing Elvis Presley songs, at this moment "Suspicious Minds."

I ordered a glass of cognac heated. The bartender, as he saw O'Brien approaching me, asked me if I wanted my drink brought to a table. I nodded.

"Whatever you want to eat or drink with your gentleman friend, let me know. As you can see, we're not busy today." The bartender was a young man with a shaved head and a corpulent body.

O'Brien replied, "Thank you for the 'gentleman.' There's very few of those around." He pointed at me. "Whatever my gentleman friend ordered. Make it two of those."

The bartender turned to prepare our drinks while we left to go to the farthest table at the extreme left end of the whole place situated in the darkest corner. O'Brien leaned back. "Where are Chandee and Chopin?"

"Under a very strong anesthetic gas, sleeping off whatever is left in their system. They're inside the Mini Cooper in the underground parking garage."

O'Brien looked at me in surprise. "Oh, that's why you laughed when I told you to tell them to keep their eyes open! Are they OK?"

I nodded. "I believe so. Our friend Dr. Zayas-Bazan injected them with an antidote to accelerate their elimination of these chemicals from their bodies as fast as possible. They had inhaled that gas for a while during the ordeal today. After all, what was supposed to be a tremendous fiasco wound up being a successful and fantastic operation. Unfortunately, we were all caught by surprise, but Dr. Zayas-Bazan and I were not in the same room, and so were saved from being in the same state of unconsciousness. For Chandee and Chopin, the surprise was a major one. We didn't have any opportunity to warn them about the gas. They ended up being sedated like the rest of our enemies along with the innocent bystanders of the restaurant."

O'Brien asked in confusion, "Where have you hidden David Walker?"

I shook my head. "I don't have him in my possession. Like I told you on the phone, I don't have the package. Which I'm really glad for."

O'Brien looked a little irritated. "Then who has him? He's disappeared. They're looking for him all over the place. Who in the hell has this guy now?"

I leaned back. "Mossad. And you'd better control your emotions, or you're going to drop dead at any moment, not from a bullet but from a heart attack."

O'Brien was livid as he listened to me. If he wanted to prove what I was saying and what he had heard in complete consternation he looked at me and asked in a low voice as he saw the bartender approaching us, "Mossad? The Israeli intelligence?"

I looked him in the eyes and nodded. His eyes opened wide in disbelief at my words. He grabbed the glass of Grand Marnier and swallowed the whole thing in a couple of sips. He said to the bartender, "Please repeat the dosage."

The bartender smiled and left to do as asked. I took my glass and smelled it for a few seconds and then took a tiny sip. "What is wrong with you today? I cannot explain to myself what the reason for your attitude and the tremendous stress is that you're displaying. I believe even before I proceed with my story of what happened today, I need to stop and begin with you telling me what's been going on over the past hours that have made you so stressed and, to be completely honest with you, completely terrified. I've never seen you in this condition in all the years we've worked together doing this nasty job."

The bartender returned with two glasses of Grand Marnier. "Do you guys want anything to eat?"

I said, "Please, bring me one of those trays I saw earlier in the lobby outside with salami, prosciutto, and mortadella and bring it to me for to go."

"Sure." He turned and left.

While I spoke to the bartender, O'Brien picked up both of the new glasses and looked to me for permission. I nodded and he poured one glass into the other and put the empty glass next to his previous one. He took a big gulp of the liqueur. "This makes me feel better. From the very little you've told me, I'm very happy that you don't have Mr. David Walker with you guys. In the last report he made to his accomplices and associates in the State Department, he advised the President to get rid of Brenton Cooper and any individuals associated with him. According to his report, he considered them double spies, trying to interfere with our intelligence and putting at risk secrets to national security. This happened in the middle of the day today before he left his office with his security detail. He never returned to his office." O'Brien was still agitated. "The President has ordered an immediate search nationwide and sent a high priority alert to law enforcement for this strange disappearance of not only him but also his aides. Nobody, even the restaurant employees, has seen them. They've disappeared as if in a magic act in front of over twenty people in the restaurant." He paused. "Doesn't it seem strange to you? Everything?"

"No, nothing strange about it to me at all. Remember who the owners of that restaurant are and the majority of the servers there. Jewish, no? And who are the agents of Mossad?"

"Of course, Jewish."

I held up one hand. "Claro, chico! It's very possible, and I'll explain to you in a little while what happened. It's a great plan, well-coordinated by Mossad. Remember, this President isn't friendly to Israel. If you think a little bit about everything, when you leave only thorns in the road you walk on behind you, if you have to return down that same road and someone stole your shoes, I believe it's going to be *pobrecito*[27]. Very painful and difficult to even imagine it, especially for all the extremists that love all the extremes and are good and happy as long as they don't have to be part of those extremes. They are good to others, but not for themselves."

---

[27] Poor baby

O'Brien said with a long face worriedly and a little scared, "You know that we're not in the best graces with this President. You also know unfortunately his ideas are the extreme Left. I don't have to remind you that he took Cuba off the list of the worst terrorists around the world, giving them a green light to continue the atrocities they've committed for decades, including sending armies to other countries and killing our agents. On top of that, he's in the process of reestablishing economic and political relations with Cuba, opening an embassy in Havana, thus allowing them to validate themselves around the world. You also know that he's not a great fan of the Cuban Lightning. They might try to implicate you and your team in all that just happened, or maybe even something worse: they might use their secret muscle that are on their side in the CIA to assassinate you and your team, making it look like an accident."

I smiled. "That will be very difficult if not impossible. They will be limited in their methods to make it appear so. In the end, they will be victims of their own conniving ways. You know all the members of my team are very highly skilled. The only thing going against us is the factor of surprise. To avoid that is why we have you. From now on, you have to keep your eyes open with dilated pupils to keep us informed of every single move they make against us from the individuals infiltrated inside our government to destroy our freedom and family, and worse yet to take our God away through the imposition of fear and totalitarian ideas. Now you've given me a completely debrief of what you know, let me tell you what happened today. This way, you'll understand what our next steps will be to proceed to be able to take out all these Left-wing Marxist radicals from the White House like you pull a rotten tooth out of your mouth. We will send them so far away, politically handicap them, take the power they so much crave, and finally let them eat each other like piranhas."

O'Brien asked, "How is it possible that your friends have come to be knocked out by that gas but neither you nor Dr. Zayas-Bazan were affected?"

I took another sip of Grand Marnier and started to relate the details of what transpired that day in the Jewish restaurant. I also gave him the other details of the exchange I had with Adam and his two associates from the Mossad. When I finished debriefing him, O'Brien's nervous stress and near terror had changed completely, perhaps because of my state of mind and calm narration, reassured that everything was under control, even expecting the worst that anyone would accuse me or my associates with anything that had transpired in the restaurant. There was no evidence at all that could incriminate me of anything or anyone who was with me because we were all in disguise, there were no cameras there, and even if they were there, the people with Mossad would die before pointing a finger at any of us. I put the coin in front of O'Brien. "I'm one of them now."

He picked the coin up. "What is this?"

I said, "You're talking to one of the collaborators and friends with Mossad now. Which I've been for many years, since I help them indirectly all the time."

He grinned broadly. "You're something. How do you manage do to these things? You should have been doped and brought the same route as David Walker right now. But you managed to get out of that situation and made a friend. Unbelievable!"

"I see you've changed your demeanor completely, night and day change. Was that me, or my favorite medicine, Grand Marnier relaxing your nervous system?"

He shook his head. "I think it's a little bit of both. But the most important thing now that we have to consider right now is that we eliminated a very powerful enemy. I have to congratulate you for your superb skills in dealing with people. From what you told me he had tried to assassinate Brenton Cooper as a potential whistle blower in their mind, but you in the process as well. We would never find out how many more victims he could have claimed in his career. Now that you're a friend of Mossad, maybe we'll find out after he's gone through an intense interrogation. Will you please let me know all the details from your friends in the future what becomes of him? And what is the tremendous interest Israel and Mossad have in getting him out of circulation? I don't know what kind of danger this Secret Service agent represents to the nation of Israel, but it must be something extremely important to conduct an operation of that magnitude in our country."

We had nearly finished our conversation when Chandee and Chopin appeared in the doorway of the bar. They signaled to me with their hands, but out of respect did not approach our table. Instead, they sat a table not too far from us. O'Brien looked at me with again and stood up. He gave me a bear hug and said in my ear, "I'm sorry for my doubts and worries earlier. Remember, I love you as the son I never had always. Maybe it's because of that sometimes I overreact like a typical father that wants to protect his son."

"Thank you very much for your sincere love. But remember what you told me years ago that the Devil loves his son, but for no reason at all will poke his eyes out."

O'Brien smiled and patted me on the shoulder. "You and your elephant-like memory always use my own words to silence me."

We said goodbye. On the way out he waved goodbye to Chandee and Chopin. My friends came over to my table and sat on either side of me. I gave them the details of my meeting with O'Brien. They explained to me what had happened in the restaurant: three men had shown up and dropped cylinders of gas which rolled all over the restaurant floor. The masked men yelled that everyone should stand still and that the gas would only put everyone to sleep for a while, and that if no resistance was offered everything would be OK a few hours later.

Chandee added, "It all happened so rapidly that we could do nothing. When we reacted to what was going on, the gas was already having an effect on us, and we lost consciousness."

Chopin corroborated what she had said. "I reached for my pistol, but one of the masked men yelled at me not to move or they would have to shoot me. They explained they didn't want to shoot weapons or innocent people could be wounded or killed unnecessarily. He repeated that they were there with one purpose only, and after they were done, they would leave the same way they came in without hurting anyone." He looked at me with a long face, ashamed. "I'm sorry, Dr. del Marmol, but I understood we were at a grave disadvantage, and I didn't want to be the reason for those maniacs killing innocent people in the restaurant. If what they told us was true, I assumed there would be no reason for us at all to lose our lives."

I patted him on the shoulder. "I salute you and respect both of you now more for maintaining your equanimity and containing your emotions by not acting recklessly. If you hadn't, that restaurant would have become a funeral home. As I told you guys before, the men from Mossad were not kidding. They wouldn't have stopped for anything or anyone because that was the mission they had: retreat, kidnap, and bring David Walker in dead or alive. We all know very well what exactitude and discipline these men work with and how they plan and take their missions, especially when it's a powerful enemy to the people of Israel."

The bartender returned with the tray of appetizers I had ordered. It looked beautiful, and they had added some jumbo shrimp, scallops, and other seafood to the selection I had requested. I asked my friends if they wanted to order anything else to drink or eat. I noticed both of them looking at the tray hungrily. I realized that we hadn't eaten anything all day long. They looked at the exquisite cold cuts, cheese, and olives along with the variety of seafood.

I asked, "Are you hungry? I haven't eaten anything since yesterday evening."

Chandee replied, "We haven't either. But with the nervous tension we've endured food hadn't even crossed my mind until I saw this wide variety of appetizers before my eyes. Now my brain is functioning at 100 mph and I've realized I'm not hungry—I'm starving."

I asked Chopin, "What about you, my good friend?"

Chopin touched his stomach and rubbed his hands together. He crossed himself. "Thank you, God, for someone mentioning food. I believe if you put me in a cage with a hungry lion, unless he ate me first, I would eat him, starting with the tail. That's how hungry I am!"

"I'm sorry, my friends. I've been so worried and preoccupied that I not only forgot to eat for myself, but I also haven't even asked after you guys."

Chandee said, "Well, to be fair, food hasn't even been mentioned up until this point. The closest we came to it was arranging to meet at the Jewish restaurant."

After the waiter took our drink orders, I told him to bring a menu so we could order some food. If we were going to confront death in the next few hours, we might as well do so with a full belly and enjoy a great pleasure. I uncovered the tray and said, "Guys, dig in until we get the food we want to order. Don't eat too much of this stuff; I want to eat a decent meal before we leave DC."

Ignoring my suggestion, they both attacked the tray of appetizers while we waited for our drinks and menus. The waiter returned with leather covered menus bearing a French coat of arms from the Napoleonic era in the center, embossed in golden letters with the name of the restaurant: Bonaparte. After he put the menus down in front of us, he said, "These menus aren't from us, but from a French restaurant nearby. It's the same company anyway, but this is in case you want a five-star meal. All we serve here are appetizers, buffalo wings, salads, and other snacks."

I picked a menu and opened it with a big smile. "Thank you very much, sir. I believe you read our minds. This is precisely what we're looking for—an excellent meal."

They opened their menus and exchanged glances with me. Chandee said, "Look at this—nothing less than your favorite soup: bouillabaisse."

Chopin said, "OK, that's what I want to start with."

I said, "How about bouillabaisse with beef wellington or chateaubriand? You choose."

Chandee said, "Definitely beef wellington."

Chopin replied, "That's perfectly OK with me."

I said to the waiter, "Very well, my friend. Bouillabaisse for three and the same for beef wellington."

The waiter said, "The bouillabaisse for three is fine, but the beef wellington we make for two people with a half a filet or a full filet for four people."

"No problem, for four is fine. We're very hungry, and whatever we don't eat we'll take on the plane. We have a seven-hour flight back home and this left over could be the perfect survival tool for the trip." Before he left, I added, "Could you please bring a half carafe or a swoon decanter of house wine?"

"Very well, sir." He went to fill our order.

Chandee looked me directly in the eyes and caressed her chin with her left hand. She leaned back with a mischievous smile and asked me ironically, "I believe O'Brien said that it was imperative we leave the city as soon as possible to prevent unwanted surprises. But now I see you're changing it. Either you didn't take what O'Brien said seriously or I don't know what's going on, but we're wining and dining now. You've thrown me off. Which is it: a rush or leisurely departure?"

I said, "Well, if you want to follow the orders to the letter and you guys decide to rush out of here, I only have to tell the waiter to forget out our order, cancel this exquisite meal and wine we ordered, and simply bring me the bill for whatever you guys drank. We'll be out of the hotel in ten minutes."

Chopin and just popped a jumbo shrimp in his mouth and nearly choked. "What are you guys doing to me?" The tail of the shrimp still dangled from his mouth. He sipped from his drink and recovered from his choking fit. His face was long as he said, "Man, why are you teasing me with all these delicious things, and now out of the blue you want to rip them away from me?"

I smiled at his disappointment and raised my arms high. "Wait a minute. Don't blame me." I pointed at Chandee. "Miss Rebel with a Cause is the one who proposed that indecent cowardly retreat."

Chandee gaped at me and slapped my shoulder. "Why are you saying that to me? That's not fair!"

I grinned at her. "Who brought back to me the memory of O'Brien's words? When did you, who always has been a rebel with a cause, converted yourself into an obedient sheep?"

She said, "You know better than I that I'm only joking. Just as I know that you know that if anyone had planned to stop us from leaving the capital that plan is possibly in motion already. Under no circumstance will it make any difference what time we leave here. It will be inevitable. It will be here in the parking lot, in the bar we're eating in now, or the airport. Maybe even on the flight to Orange County. These individuals have all the resources at their disposition." Her voice grew determined. "In other words, fear of what, like you've told me many times. Fear keeps you from thinking properly and make correct decisions."

"Ha! You're doing to me what I do to O'Brien all the time. Using my own words against me, eh?"

Chandee smiled and shook her head. She turned to Chopin. "Don't worry about it, man. I assure you I'm only joking. There's no way, unless you eat too many appetizers before our meal is served, that we're leaving here before we sink our teeth into that exquisite beef wellington."

I smiled and raised my arm high. "There it goes, girl! No fear in our lives. High five!" She and I exchanged high fives. Chopin, overjoyed, also gave us a high five.

"I like that!" he exclaimed.

After we had finished that exquisite meal, I paid and left the waiter a very generous tip. He was so happy with that tip he began to tell us his life story. He was a very charismatic man of Italian origin, Giovanni Martino. He said he was a musician, trumpeter, and saxophonist, and also played with the house group in the bar. He said, "If you guys will hold on a minute, I'll play a song for you before you leave."

We agreed to wait, and he brought his group back to play "La Muchacha de la Valija" by Fausto Papetti. Halfway through the song he switched from trumpet to saxophone. By the time it was finished, the restaurant was full of people, so he said on the microphone, "This interpretation by my group is dedicated to the generosity of Dr. del Marmol." His audience applauded, and we walked to the elevators.

CHAPTER 14: OUR ENEMIES IN THE SHADOW OF OUR FRIENDS

Before I walked into the elevator car, I felt a strange sensation, the same unpleasant one I experienced before. I held the metal tray that all the leftovers had been put into save for the bouillabaisse, and Giovanni also had included a large container of sauce, wrapped in cellophane. Like déjà vu or a rewound movie, I saw the man with the cane, still dressed in black with the same tie and this time smoking his pipe, walking towards the elevator. I straightened my poison ring, anticipating that an attack was being planned. The young woman in the wheelchair yelled from the hallway to hold the door—exactly as had happened before.

I stopped the door with my left leg once more, but this time I didn't leave the elevator. Chandee beat me to it and left the car to help the young woman. Chandee rolled the girl straight into the elevator, so the girl was facing the man in the black suit. It was exactly as had happened before but in a different dimension. The man didn't move a finger to help either the young woman or Chandee, not even an inch from where he was standing to accommodate the wheelchair. The hairs on the back of my neck stood up like a rooster's comb.

I saw that this time, he held his cane in his left hand, not his right like before. I looked him straight in the eyes and tried to keep our gazes locked. After a few seconds he gave it up and stared at the elevator floor. I took the opportunity to see that the young girl couldn't see me and signaled to Chandee and Chopin by pointing two fingers at my eyes and jerking a thumb over my shoulder at the two people behind me. As we made eye contact, Chandee and Chopin gave me small nods to acknowledge my signal. I was really concerned about the man in the black suit, but since the young woman was between us, they interpreted my signal as keeping an eye on both of them. I was later grateful for several years afterword for that.

The young woman in the wheelchair said, "Twelfth floor, please."

Chandee said, "Someone's already headed there, sweetie. That's also our floor."

"Thank you," she answered.

Silence descended as the elevator ascended, stopping at the seventh floor, when a group of young kids, who declined to get in because there were six of them and there wasn't enough room for them all. Chandee was nearest to the doors, and so punched the button to close the doors. We ascended to the eleventh floor and stopped. The doors opened and a middle-aged Asian lady with a tiny chihuahua asked, "Could you please squeeze in a little bit? I'm only going one floor up."

Chandee said, "Sure, of course." She pushed everyone back to make room.

The man with the black suit and cane protested irritated, "No, no! There's no room in here for anyone else!"

The lady asked "Why? It's only one level. You can squeeze a little bit."

He said sternly, "No! This elevator is over capacity. Do you want to kill all of us? We have a handicapped person. Be patient." He turned to Chandee. "Will you please close the door?"

Chandee glared daggers at him and the bullying tone he was using. If looks could kill, he would have been dead then and there due to the authoritarian manner in which he demanded her to close the door. She looked at the lady apologetically. "I'm sorry, they don't want to move. There's nothing I can do."

I realized at this moment that the accent of the man in the black suit was South African. The lady with the dog yelled as the door closed, "That man is a jerk! It's OK, Panchita. We'll wait for the next car, honey." She said to Chandee, "Don't worry about it, my angel. I know his kind of person."

The elevator went back into motion, and we finally reached the twelfth floor. I held the elevator with my left foot because I still held the tray in my left hand. I waited until my friends got out of the elevator and then passed the tray to Chopin, who took it in his right hand while he held the key to our suite in his left. There was no one in the corridor. The young woman in the wheelchair got out last, but nearly ran us over in her rush toward the right side of the corridor, while the man went in the opposite direction from her, heading towards the left. The young woman stopped in front of the door to her suite and tried to open the door.

As we got close to her, it appeared she was having difficulties, as if the key wasn't working. She dropped the key to the carpet, and Chopin bent down to pick it up. The young woman, who looked so harmless with her atrophied legs, took a mesh sap she had concealed up her sleeve and hit Chopin over the back of his head. He collapsed onto the floor, dropping the tray, which I managed to catch thanks to my quick reflexes. The young woman now stood up and pulled a submachine gun she had concealed along the right side of the wheelchair. As she raised and cocked it, I threw the tray at her. The cellophane flew with the rest of the food and hit her just below her chin. The container of bearnaise sauce opened, throwing the sauce into her eyes.

She could not see and began to fire indiscriminately. Chandee and I dove to the floor, one on either side of her wheelchair. Chopin began to stir groggily, trying to get close to her. Chandee crouched and moved as close as she could to the girl from the left, near the wall. I jumped and grabbed the now-empty tray of pure silver, thinking to use it to render her unconscious. The young woman heard me and blindly pointed the gun in my direction and opened fire, firing five shots. I saw the dents in the tray from where the bullets hit the tray. Some bullets fell at my feet, but others ricocheted into the wall, and one hit the fluorescent lights in the ceiling, spraying me with plastic and glass in my hair.

I took one of my Rolex Oyster Perpetual watches off, spun the heavy watch over my head like a sling, and hurled it full at her. It hit her in the forehead, making her lose her balance. She dropped the weapon, which fell heavily onto the carpet. Chandee took advantage of the opportunity of her blinded and dizzy condition to kick her so hard in the face that the woman rolled a couple of times over the carpet. She grabbed the woman by the hair, dragged her over to the nearest ice machine, perhaps forty feet away, threw her inside it, and then grabbed a mop to slide the haft through the handles of the ice machine door.

However, our ordeal wasn't over. The man in the black suit was still in the hallway. He pulled out a pistol with a silencer attached. I saw him point it at us and threw the tray like a boomerang. It flew through the air and hit him in the forehead, cutting him deeply. Blood flowed into his eyes, blinding him. He released the pistol, which flew down the hall, landing luckily right by Chopin, who was clearing his head. He picked it up and saw the man bending over and, using his cane as a support, pulling another weapon strapped to his leg: a snub-nosed revolver. As he aimed it towards us, Chopin shot three times, hitting the man in the chest. He fell backwards onto a column in the corridor from the impact of the bullets on his chest, smashing his head against it before he could manage to pull the trigger.

I yelled to Chandee, "Bring something to tie up this woman. Go into the suite and call the front desk. Tell them you heard a violent commotion in the hallway of this floor. Make sure they call house security and tell them you don't want to leave your suite because you're afraid of what's going on."

"OK," she replied.

I asked Chopin for the pistol and cleaned it with my handkerchief, placing it next to the man after I removed the magazine. I said to Chopin, "Please come with me."

We went to the ice machine and pulled the woman out. We proceeded to tie her arms with the telephone cord Chandee brought from her suite. We dragged her next to the body of the man, placing the submachine gun next to them as well after I checked to be sure the magazine was completely empty. I searched their pockets and found three business cards from different individuals: one from the Department of State, one from the Department of Justice, and one from the White House. I looked at the man's passport and saw that I was right on the money: he was a South African. The woman was Venezuelan. Both were permanent residents of the US since 1970. I picked my watch up from the carpet.

I said, "These individuals are like contagious and infectious bacteria. Most of the time, you don't know where they come from, but you find them everywhere. When you least expect it, they hit you."

The woman was conscious. Chandee looked at her. "Who are you? Why did you try to kill us?"

The young assassin was around 35 years old. According to her passport, her name was Margareta Cordoba. I put the cards I took from them into my pocket. I repeated, "Who sent you?"

Chandee repeated the question, adding, "You don't have much time. You'll be gone if you don't answer our questions."

She said, "No one sent me. I work on my own. I'm a freelancer."

Chandee said, "Yes, you're a freelancer that is now going to be disavowed because you got caught. You'll be rotting in jail. That man is dead, and you're responsible for the whole thing."

She smiled cynically in amusement. She spoke in Spanish. "I don't even know who he is. I'll be free in a very few hours, you stupid Chinese bitch. You better find a bodyguard for yourself and be careful in your sleep. Next time you will not wake up in the morning." She must have figured Chandee wouldn't understand her.

Chandee slapped her and then backhanded her. She said in Spanish, "The only bitch here is you, and you will go directly to the Inferno."

Magareta smiled again as if she hadn't felt the slap. "Why don't you hit me harder? I'll tell the authorities that you guys were the ones who killed him. That's the truth. I don't even know him and never touched him."

Chandee looked at me seriously, and Chopin asked the question of me with his eyes. "What are we going to do with her?"

I looked at both and nodded as I heard the bell of the elevator ring near the back of the corridor. I stung her with my ring. I said, "Die, then. You won't be able to talk to anyone. This poison is strong enough to kill ten elephants, deadlier than you can imagine. You'd better pray to your idol, Satan, to prepare a bed for you in Hell. You will be visiting him permanently." I looked at Chandee and gently took hers in my hand. "You see this face? Look at her very well and be careful since you've offended her several times. This will be the last face you see before you start your trip to the Inferno."

She began to convulse a little bit and her attitude changed. Her eyes bulged in terror and began to beg me as she stared at the ring on my hand. "We can negotiate. If I tell you who sent me, you can give me the antidote I know you have for what you injected me with."

I stood up. "I know who sent you. I believe you're too late for negotiations."

She grabbed my left wrist and tried to pull me down. "Please. Bring your ear to my lips. Please." I bent over slightly, and she whispered a name in my ear. "Please, don't let me die like this. I can be very useful for you. I have a lot more information. I'm sorry. I underestimated you."

The security guard from the hotel was already walking towards us with the Asian lady with the dog. She yelled as soon as she saw the man with the black suit, "That is the bad man who didn't let me into the elevator."

I turned my ring around and quickly gave Margareta the antidote. I said, "If I see you again in my path, unless I'm looking for you, that will be the last time you see light." I took Chandee's face again in my left hand. "Remember this face and protect it, if you don't want me to become your ghost in your worst nightmares." I said to Chandee, "Take the cord off."

Chandee rapidly untied it, pulled it out behind her, coiled it up quickly, and put it in her pocket. She said, "You're not worried about what she'll say?"

"She won't say much for several hours. She'll start convulsing and vomiting, and they'll take her to a hospital where they won't know what's wrong with her. It will be several hours before she can say anything. After this experience, she'll keep her mouth shut for her own safety."

The guard came over with the lady. We stood up watching the four guards approaching us to where we had once more a confrontation with new enemies. He finally got to us and asked, "What happened here?" He looked at the submachine gun and pistol. "Don't touch anything. This is probably a drug deal turned sour. It's not the first time we've encountered something like this in this hotel."

I said, "We didn't see anything. We came up in the elevator, and the shooting started as we got out of the elevator. They shot at each other. We were bringing some leftovers from the restaurant, which as you can see got wasted. We stayed in the elevator until everything finished."

"Is that man alive?"

"I don't know."

Chandee said, "I took his pulse. I think he's dead."

"What about the woman."

"I think she's in shock. Maybe unconscious."

Margareta opened her eyes abruptly and began to convulse and foam at the mouth. We breathed a quiet sigh of collective relief. The lady with the little chihuahua crossed herself. "Lord, you love the righteous and you despise wickedness. Thank you for being a righteous God and not a God who loves war, murder, and death. Thank you, Lord, for not allowing me to get in this elevator." She crossed herself again and called her little dog, "Let's go, Panchita, away from this scene from Satan." She leaned down to pick up her dog and walked down the corridor to her suite.

I said goodbye to the guards, saying, "Please tell the authorities that we have nothing to add to this since we saw practically nothing."

The team leader said, "No, don't worry about it. You guys go. We can handle this."

We walked to our suites and when we were a prudent distance from the guards, I said, "Prepare your suitcases immediately and meet me in the garage. What Margareta said in my ear, it looks like our enemies are closer than I had imagined, and maybe will be a great surprise even to O'Brien. I already checked out over the phone and gave the credit card to the front desk. Everything is ready to go. I'll be by the Mini Cooper in a few minutes."

The acknowledged and I went to my suite and picked up my garment bag and carryon, and then left the suite. As I did, I saw medics coming out of one elevator and got into a different car, pressing the button to go to the garage as I did so. When the elevator stopped in the lobby, I could see FBI agents dressed in civilian clothes and possibly some other federal intelligence agents there. I went to the car and put my luggage on the ground and waited for Chopin by the left side of the car to make sure he could check the car for any additional surprises.

A few seconds later the elevator bell rang, and I was happy to see Chopin and Chandee with their luggage running towards the car. Chopin gave the car a quick check from the bumpers to the hood, making sure nothing was suspicious and we didn't have any explosives waiting for us there. He even squirmed under the car to check the undercarriage before looking at the trunk. Finally, he checked the doors and brushed his clothes off.

He gave us a thumbs up and said, "Everything is clean. Let's go."

We piled into the Mini Cooper and as we left the underground parking structure, we were shocked to see the man with the black suit walking out of the hotel in handcuffs, escorted by the FBI. We looked at each other in astonishment. Chopin said, "I shot this man three times!"

I asked, "Where did you shoot him?"

"In the chest."

"There you go—he was apparently wearing body armor."

"Son of a gun! Oh well—this will be fresh meat for the next chateaubriand entrée because I will never forget his face."

"I will never forget his accent," I said.

Chandee said, "I'll never forget his eyes."

We took off towards the airport. A little while later we pulled into the private plane section of the airport. Chopin told Chandee to return the car while he prepped the plane for takeoff. "I will check the plane extremely carefully, guys," he said. "Remember the presents they left for us at South Coast Plaza."

I said, "I'll never forget that one. We have to give credit to our enemies. With the new technologies, they have evolved in their criminal careers into skilled, sophisticated professional killers."

Chopin started to work on the plane while we sat at a table nearby that the employees of the hangar used for lunch breaks. Chandee stood up and went over to the Pepsi machine near the table. She looked at me affectionately. "You have something shining in your hair. Stand up and come over to me." She picked up the plastic pieces from the broken fluorescent bulb. She tried to fix the hair she had mussed up in digging out the pieces. As she did so, she discovered more pieces and glass from the bulb. She shook her fingers through my hair, and the pieces tinkled onto the metal table. She said worriedly, "Why don't you go to the bathroom and check your hair in the sink? When you go to bed, without even feeling it one of those pieces could cut your scalp."

I smiled and put my head down. "Why go to the bathroom? I can't even see what I might have gotten in my hair. If you don't mind, why don't you do what monkey mothers do with their little babies and check me out? You can remove any strange aliens from my head."

"You're just a big baby. Come over here, and I'll do that with pleasure." She began to pick the tiny particles out of my hair, depositing the pieces in an ashtray in the middle of the table. A little while later, she finished and the ashtray was virtually filled with pieces of plastic and glass. She smiled. "I think your head, like a vacuum cleaner, sucked up all that debris." She shook her head. "Thank God that they were all small pieces, small enough not to hurt you. Could you imagine what it would be like if they were large pieces like the one that landed on the floor? They could hurt you very badly and give you several cuts along your skull."

I crossed myself. "Let's thank God for that. Every minute and every second of our lives we have to thank Him for protecting us."

Chopin yelled, "Bingo!" We both turned and saw Chopin removing from beneath the plane some cables that looked like a timer connected to a bundle that he very delicately and slowly brought over and set down on the table. "I'm no expert in explosives, but this looks like C4." He looked disgusted. "It looks like these sons of whores really wanted to send us to the Inferno. These were placed over the fuel tank. It took me a while to find it. It was so perfectly concealed that I didn't notice it at first; then I saw a single cable that they had neglected to properly conceal. I pulled on it and saw this bundle." We looked at each other in a blend of depression and happiness at Chopin's find. It would certainly have done the job. He said, "This diabolical black President wants to get us out of his way, no doubt about it. It's unbelievable with the tremendous security we have at this airport, now more than ever, how anyone could come here without being seen. Unless the person who did this was one of the mechanics that serviced our plane. Most of the people who work here work for the government. A lot of the time, they're even undercover agents for either intelligence, the FBI, or some other government agency. They don't trust leaving any of the planes unattended for their covert operations. How the hell did this happen? These people are specialists in counterterrorism. Somebody has to be on the take."

I tried to be optimistic and give them a morale boost. We had to look reality in the face as we looked at the bundle of explosives and timers on the table before us. "As you said a few seconds ago, most of the time. Of course, that is far from being all the time." I smiled. "I don't want you guys thinking that because we have an irresponsible, arrogant President with the Utopian Marxist dream that it means the entire government sympathizes with what they're doing or even remotely in agreement enough to be their accomplices. Most of the people in this country's government are honorable people, believers in God, and hate the extreme Left wing just as they hate the extreme Right wing, as do the majority of the men and women in this country. This nation was formed by men and women from different races and colors. Most of them came to this country fleeing persecution by totalitarian regimes. Marxists and Nazis, it's the same whether that ice cream comes in a cone or a cup. I assure you guys that these men and women prefer to die thousands of times than to submit to the Utopian dream this President wants to impose.

I pointed at the bundle on the table. "I believe the first thing we have to do is to thank God and our great friend, Chopin, for being blessed with the wisdom to be able to detect these explosives. And thank you, my friend Chopin, for saving our lives once more and allowing us to continue in our fight against the enemies of humanity and their friend Lucifer. Many times, our enemies dress like sheep and get close to us without our noticing. There is no reason for us to think all the real sheep are bad and vindictive. Once more, we discovered them, and we are still alive. We will continue to fight these extremists until we rip the mask covering their hypocrisy off their faces."

Chopin stood up and gave me a brotherly hug. "Thank you for your words, my friend Dr. del Marmol. You pulled me out of my depression with them." He started to wrap the explosives, detonator, and other components. "I believe I'll save these in a safe place. When the moment comes, maybe we can use them against our enemies to defend ourselves, giving them a taste of their own medicine. We can leave now anytime you want. The plane is clean and ready for future fights."

I said, "OK. Let's get out of this unfriendly city."

Chandee, who had until now been quiet, stood up and came over to me. She kissed me tenderly on my lips and said with moist eyes, "Please I'm only going to ask you one thing."

"What do you need, sweetie?"

She took my face between both hands and looked me deeply in the eyes. "Please, never change. Never stop being the Julio Antonio of Rio Cristal in Havana, Cuba. You continued to be him today in Washington, D.C. OK?"

I smiled. "For a little while, you scared me. I thought you were going to ask me to go back to the restaurant and bring you the beef wellington we wasted in the battle at the hotel."

She bit her lip and hit me in the shoulder. "Can you not be serious for at least five minutes? You never take anything seriously."

"Don't you think that what we've gone through in the past few hours was enough seriousness so we can take a break and treat the rest of the day as a joke? At least for our little trip?"

"A little? Seven hours?"

"I believe we all deserve that joy."

She nodded. "OK. All right. I ask your permission to be able to joke for the next seven hours."

"Permission granted."

We all smiled while Chopin shook his head as he climbed into the pilot's seat. We took off and flew back to Orange County, California. Seven hours later we landed at the John Wayne Airport, and I went to the public phone and called O'Brien to tell him that I needed to talk to him immediately on a matter of extreme urgency, that I needed to debrief him on what had transpired after he left the hotel before I left the country. I also needed to give him my reading and advice about how we needed to move forward with this sophisticated enemy we had in the White House. We set to meet the next day at Location #9, my office in 151 Kalmus Dr, Suite 100-# in Costa Mesa, where I had recently established my new business D'Marmol Communications International, with offices in Newport Beach and at 15476 NW 77th St Suite 331 in Miami Lakes, Florida.

Figure 43 D'Marmol Communications business card

I went with my friends to the safehouse on Balboa Peninsula. It was near the end of the peninsula where one could see the bluffs of Corona del Mar, in plain view of the other safehouse on the hilltop situated on the opposite side of the harbor mouth. We had been forced to vacate it after the recent events involving Yoko de Coco in order to let it cool off. We sat down with the rest of my friends for a little while and I debriefed them as to what had happened during our trip. Rocco was jumping around and rolling on the carpet, making everyone laugh. He did this whenever he missed my presence for a while—it mattered not if it was one day or ten.

Yaneba said, "You're not going to believe it, but every night he got outside and howled on the deck, looking at the yacht. Until I walked him over to the yacht and all round it to show him you weren't there, he wouldn't calm down. This dog loves you so much, probably more than a woman in love when you are absent from her bed."

I shook my head. "Well, he's just returning my love. I treat him with the same love he offers to me. But I believe, to tell you the truth, the howling is not because he misses just me. He misses our adventures when we go out on O'Brien's yacht during our scuba diving trips. Sometimes we bring this yacht to the bayside of the Balboa Yacht Club in Corona del Mar. By the way, how has Brenton Cooper behaved in my absence?"

"Great trooper," Elizabeth said. "He hasn't moved a muscle out of the Balboa Bay Resort. He is right there, on your yacht, waiting for you. I told him several hours ago you were on your way back after you called me when you left D.C."

I replied, "I'm very happy to hear that and to know that he is disciplined enough to follow my orders to the letter. There's a strong possibility I'm bringing him with me to Venezuela. I don't want you guys to get distracted from the work you're doing right now that's so important along the Mexican border. The only people who will come with me on this trip will be Chandee and Chopin after we rest for a few days. After the commotion in D.C., we all need a little rest to recharge our batteries."

Elizabeth smiled. "And to think you assess this as a very tiny eyelash in the soup. Evidently, after your debriefing, D.C. became a hair salon floor in your soup."

Chandee smiled. "You don't even know how true that is. After all, we all enjoyed one of the best French soups, bouillabaisse, hairless between all that misery. The best gourmet appetizers in my life. Yummy, yummy! Accompanied by the most exquisite beef wellington!"

Yaneba smiled. "Well, well—there's never a dull moment or bad time when in the company of Dr. del Marmol, eh?"

Chopin smiled and put his hands on his knees. "Well, with the exception of that Mini Cooper, which was not really the fault of him." Chandee glanced at him in a nonplussed manner, clearly expecting some blame. He raised his index finger high and smiled to show his white teeth. "Well, it could have been worse if not for the clever and intelligent decision of Chandee who declined the motorcycles and brought us the only option available in that Mini Cooper."

Chandee's demeanor changed, and she smiled. She raised her hand to give Chopin a high five. "Thank you, Chopin, for recognizing that." She smiled mischievously. "After all, the Mini Cooper turned out to be not so uncomfortable or a sardine can, because you slept for over eight hours in its back seat." She turned to Chopin and grinned. "Is that not true, Chopin?"

Chopin's face was long. "Don't push it, little *cubanita chinita.* OK?"

Chandee shook her head. "What? Don't tell me that you don't remember that we slept very comfortably, both of us, in the belly of that little lion."

Chopin nodded in resignation. He mumbled, "Never argue with a woman. They are like a *Jalisco.*[28] Especially if they are Cuban."

All three women turned around and glared at him. "Hey!" They picked pillows up from the sofa and began to beat him with them. Feathers began to fly out of the

---

[28] A city in Mexico where the reputation is that they are such sore losers that they will shoot the winner of an argument with them.

pillows from the force of the blow. He rolled around on the carpet laughing.

I stood up. "Uh, oh! You're on your own, my lovely friend Chopin. Your tongue brought you to the real angry mama lion now. Save yourself however you can. I have to go pick up Brenton. Let me know later how you survive."

As I walked to the door he yelled, "Dr. del Marmol, don't abandon me! Help me! These mama lions are going to eat me alive!"

I smiled and responded as I continued to walk away, "From the rough waves of the ocean I can protect myself. But from calm waters and soft waves, only God can protect you, my friend."

Chopin said, "No, no! Don't abandon me!"

"I'll see you later." I closed the door behind me and left the house, leaving the laughter of my friends as they enjoyed the pillow fight that looked like Chopin was predestined to lose. Outnumbered three to one, he had no chance. Rocco followed me, looking back at the noise. We both got into the Jaguar XJSC with the V12 engine.

Figure 44 The Jaguar XJSC

We drove to the Balboa Bay Club. When I arrived, instead of parking in the valet, I circled around to the back where the executives of the club would park. In case any of the feathers from the birds we had just put in the cage were still floating around, as a precaution I was keeping my guard high, ready to defend myself against any kind of retaliation from that group of extreme Leftists who had been kissing the hand of the man that now was sitting in the White House—the most powerful house in the world. I wondered how it was possible, as I walked from the corridor in back out to the yacht, that this could happen in this nation, the cleanest and most democratic country in the world. I remembered the voice of my father giving me the answer. He had told me many times that the most powerful weapon any man possesses is persistence. Even a single drop of water constantly hitting a rock for many years eventually makes a big hole in it. This is the quality our enemies possess. Communists and Marxists continually indoctrinate and put to sleep the most brilliant brains with their constant rhetoric to the point that they give up and join them.

As I opened the small gate onto the pier that connected to the yacht, I said in a loud voice, "Ahoy there! Permission to come aboard!"

Brenton recognized my voice and came onto deck, smiling from ear to ear. "Captain, you don't need to ask permission to board!" He saluted me. "This is your ship."

"Yes, normally I don't do that. But due to what I just went through I found it very opportune. A dead captain is no longer a captain. He just becomes another cadaver and member of the crew."

Brenton smiled. "From me you have nothing to worry about. I'm not trigger happy, like our friend Esquivel, who shoots first and ask questions later."

I raised both arms. "Please, please, don't remind me of that triple zero! Just thinking of that bully makes my stomach churn and I become nauseous. To think that a human being could stoop so low due to his inferiority complex to become a terrible abuser and such an unscrupulous individual."

He raised both hands high. "I'm sorry, my friend. I don't want to bring you bad memories. To make it up to you, I'll bring you a couple of your Negra Modelos that Elizabeth brought me. I've learned to like them, and we can drink them together."

"How have my friends treated you in my absence?"

He showed me the beer. "I don't think that I'd have noticed I left my house if it weren't for the absence of Massile, Sunset, and Dark Chocolate. They not only filled the refrigerator with food but also beer, wine, everything else you can imagine." He smiled in gratitude. "Thank you very much, my friend Dr. del Marmol. Elizabeth relayed your message to me that the carnivorous bird is already in the cage."

I nodded. "Yes. And it looks like this has become an exception to the rule. Though normally not everything comes out the way we planned, this came out to be even better in the end. We had to tie up some loose ends at the last minute with a little violence. But there were no major problems with no losses to our side. In this case, there were some personal attempts against someone, but we always left an emergency exit just in case something transpired at the last minute unexpectedly. If this comes out flawlessly the way you planned, which is very rare, it finishes without finding a single eyelash in the soup."

Brenton smiled. "You're right. But when this happens, we have to forget our scruples and take the eyelash out of the soup and continue to eat it to the end to achieve our objective which is of course finish the soup before it gets cold without allowing this particular incident to distract us."

"You're right, my friend. Even though I don't think we'll have any more feathers in this case on the plate from this bird because of the distance he will have to go is extremely far away for him to even consider coming back from his migration. I advise you to double your security measures, not just for yourself but also for your family.

Even though my friends have their eyes on them, at least for a little while until we both have the assurance that the bullying assassin leaves no birds of his feathers behind him to finish the job."

Brenton replied, "Don't worry. I always take extreme precautions for me and my family. Thank you not just for this but for everything you've done for us. When did you want to leave for Venezuela?"

"In a couple of days. I need to tie up a few things with O'Brien and my team before we leave."

"OK. I'll be ready."

"I believe that I have to ask you a little favor if it's not an inconvenience. I'm going to take you up on your offer to leave my great friend Rocco with your family." I patted him on the head, and he nuzzled it enthusiastically. "I don't know how long this trip will take, and my friends said that Rocco is getting older. All he has done for the past few days was to howl all night until Elizabeth took him on a tour of the yacht to show him that I wasn't there."

Brenton smiled. "That has nothing to do with age. My dog, Dark Chocolate, does the exact thing, according to Massile and Sunset when I stay away for a while. Let me tell you, my friend Dr. del Marmol, that this has a name: unconditional love. These beautiful pets offer it to us which has incalculable value to us as human beings. We need that feeling to live our lives in peace and harmony."

I nodded in agreement. "Unfortunately, your old boss in the Secret Service is the exception and doesn't need any of those feelings in his life. Otherwise, he would not have conducted himself with you in the manner and ways that he did."

Brenton smiled. "Yes, until he found the ghost of his worst nightmares in the Jewish restaurant. He probably saw in a mirror, as you told me, in the bathroom the reverse of himself since you are the opposite of what he is. That scared the Hell of out of him! I can say one thing to you, my friend, for I give thanks to God to put you in my road."

I replied, "Everything in life is like night and day: for the one to exist so must the other. The difference between the first and the second is that your happiness and joy are the only ways we can compare the two. We can pick and choose from the beautiful plentitude of a splendid sunny days to a frightening and terrifying dark, cold night filled with foggy mist."

Brenton replied seriously and a little sadly, "I agree with you 100%. That is the meaning of life itself. The difference is minor, as you and I know very well since we both experienced both sides of the coin. It makes those like us more appreciative of what we possess. Happiness, peace, and harmony—our enemies can take them away in just a few seconds." He scratched Rocco's head, who now sat between us in the same chairs we had sat in when the sniper had attempted to assassinate us.

I shifted in my chair and stuck my index finger into the bullet hold in the chair backing. "Many times, it can be measured in fractions of a second how quickly we can lose our lives. The worst is when we don't even expect it." I raised my bottle of Negra Modelo and said, "We have to be happy, both of us, because we're survivors, and we survived a new aggression. And we're still right here, surviving loco to be able to tell the tale to other people at a later date."

He raised his bottle and clinked it against mine. "Amen to that and thank God for it."

We stood up and exchanged a brotherly hug. We dropped both bottles into the trash basket near where we had been sitting. Followed by my great friend Rocco, we took extreme precautions as we left the yacht on our way to the Jaguar. As we walked through the corridors of the Balboa Bay Club, checking around us continually on our way out, I was wondering what life would bring us next. After we got into the Jaguar, I drove out of the club. I could see not far away the Lancia with my two friends Elizabeth and Yaneba who had been sitting keeping watch over the car.

I drove towards the Pacific Coast Highway on our way to Brenton's house at the border of the Newport Beach and Costa Mesa area. As we approached his residence, as expected Brenton's family received us with tremendous joy, including her dog, Dark Chocolate, who ran in circles around him and submissively urinating all over the place upon seeing her master. Brenton stroked her head and belly for a few seconds. Her ecstasy didn't last long as she became distracted by Rocco's presence, a more important subject to her as a male of her species. A few minutes later they were running playfully around the patio, one after the other, showing us without any shyness how great they felt at seeing each other.

Brenton smiled. "Do you see them?"

I nodded. "Yes. She's ignoring you and Rocco is ignoring me completely. They don't even notice us."

Brenton asked, "Why don't you leave Rocco from now until we leave, like you planned? That way he can get accustomed to my home."

I smiled. "I don't think he'll need that. He's been accustomed since I brought him here. He's in love with your dog." We watched Rocco enjoying the company of his female companion. "I think it will be a great idea to leave him here now in case for any reason he starts to howl at night and disturb your neighbors, we can bring him back and leave him in Elizabeth's care on the peninsula before we leave."

Brenton asked, "I thought your house was in Corona del Mar.'

"You know how it is. When you're a spy, you have houses everywhere and nowhere. That makes us both ghosts and homeless."

After Massile brought us a large jar of fresh lemonade as was her custom, we enjoyed some peace. A little while later, Massile gave me a hug before I left and a very convincing kiss of gratitude on my cheek for my diligence and intervention in her husband's behalf. "Thank you," she murmured.

"Don't worry about it. It was a pleasure for me, especially for a family like yours. You're great people." I said goodbye to them and left towards my other refuge, the house on Lido Island.

I parked the Jaguar in the garage and entered the house, turning on the intercom stereo system as I did. I played the CD I had recently recorded in my little free time, "Encoded Deceptions."

Figure 45 CD cover

I left to the master bathroom and turned on the jacuzzi. Taking my clothes off, I donned a bathroom and headed to the bar next to the kitchen. I made myself a mimosa and prepared a snack tray of olives, prosciutto, Brie, and other cheeses along with crackers. I took both to the master bathroom and set them down on the edge of the jacuzzi. I took off my bathrobe and opened a drawer beneath the sink to get a bag of lavender Epson salt. I emptied the bag into the jacuzzi and got in, listening to the sixth track on the CD, "Surviving Loco." I snacked from the plate and took a few sips of the mimosa, relaxing as I listened to the music.

After a while, the next track, "Extreme Intolerance," began to play. I thought about the motive that made me compose these different songs. After a few hours of physical and mental relaxation, I left the jacuzzi. The disc had repeated and was now playing the second track, "Nobody is Like You." I took a cold shower to rinse the salt off my body, dried off, covered my body with an aloe vera gel, and got dressed in a black tuxedo with a long, white scarf. I got into the Jaguar and drove towards the Balboa Bay Club, leaving the car in the valet parking. One of the guys said, "We haven't seen you here for a while!"

"I've been coming in, but from a different route." I made a circle with my arm.

The valet said, "I get it, I get it."

Inside the club I walked towards the John Wayne Pavilion through the long hallways, sitting in the seafood restaurant and ordering a Bloody Mary cocktail. As I started to sip, I turned slightly in my seat. A tingling sensation on my neck told me someone was watching me. I noticed that my senses weren't wrong as my eyes locked with a beautiful blue-eyed woman. She had a body like a character like a Playboy centerfold with long, wavy red hair. I had encountered her several times in the lobby and the hallways of the club as I came in and out on various occasions. Something else had previously caught my eye—the beautiful Bentley convertible she drove.

It flashed like lightning through my mind the profound look she gave me at the entry of the club with her long eyelashes. Those beautiful big, blue eyes had been burned in my memory for a long time. Now I had her right behind me alone and a beautiful, elegant black and white evening gown accessorized by a broad-brimmed white hat with a black bandana. She raised her champagne flute to me, and I raised my Bloody Mary to return her greeting as we sat in the left corner of the bar.

My order arrived at that moment: lobster thermidor, a French dish with lobster meat cooked in rich wine sauce stuffed back in the shell, the whole browned in the oven. I was distracted for a few seconds by the waiter as he served me, and when I looked to my left once more for the woman, she was gone. She had apparently finished her meal and disappeared like a magic act, leaving behind only the flute with a little champaign at the bottom and some intense red lipstick on the edge.

A little while later, I was nearly finished with my meal when the waiter surprised me by coming over with a small envelope and said, "The Countess la Vita Dolce." He pointed at the table where she had been sitting. The last name rang a bell: Marguerite in Italy that I had saved from being assassinated, years ago. He added, "She asked me to not interrupt your meal and not bring the note until you finished. I see you're almost finished…"

I gave him a small smile. "It's fine, OK. Thank you very much." I opened my wallet to give him some extra compensation for the extra service, but he held his hand up and shook his head.

"No, please, Dr. del Marmol. This is part of our service."

"Thank you very much. I'll add it to your tip because I consider this not part of your regular service. I think you're acting almost as a very delicate diplomacy between us. I don't think that's part of your job."

"Yes, it is, actually. But I very much appreciate it. Thank you for your generosity. For your tranquility, she already compensated me generously. That's why I'm refusing you. It wouldn't be proper or honest, especially when both of you are so generous to serve you whenever I have that pleasure. It's very little all the service and diligence I've managed to be able to do for you would never be enough. Whatever I can do to please you is a pleasure for me to reciprocate."

"Thank you, Federico."

"Did you want anything for dessert?"

"Yes, please bring me the flan with fresh strawberries, and as always baptize it with Grand Marnier."

"Of course, Dr. del Marmol."

As soon as he left, I opened the envelope, which contained a small note on perfumed paper. The envelope was addressed "To Dr. del Marmol, Urgent." I remembered at once the same note I wrote to the lady in Palermo. The perfume smelled of jasmine and the paper held the red outline of a rose for a watermark on the peach paper. The note read, "Dr. del Marmol—you don't know me, but you know my family in Palermo very well, especially my sister, Marguerite. My name is Faviola and I have something very confidential and of extreme importance to discuss with you. It is of great urgency. I believe I have given you enough to deposit a small token of trust in me. Come to me at the Rusty Pelican in Newport Beach, only a few blocks from the Balboa Bay Club. I will wait for you in the parking lot. To refresh your memory, I will give you just one name: Teatro Massimo. All my family hold a great debt of gratitude to you because of your great unselfish gesture in risking your life to save my sister's life. I believe from my heart I can now return that favor to you. Please be absolutely certain you are not followed. I will be waiting patiently for you. Please do not disappoint me. I know this sounds strange to you, but this is extremely important for your security as well as mine. Again, do not allow anyone to follow you. Take your time. I hope you enjoyed your lobster thermidor, which shows me your excellent, refined taste. It is an excellent choice on the menu. Your friend, if you allow me to call you that, Faviola la Vita Dolce."

I saw a note in large letters on the back that instructed me to burn the note after reading it. I pulled a lighter out of my pants and burned the envelope and note in the ashtray on the table. The memories of the Teatro Massimo in Palermo when the assassins led by Hiro during that ordeal flooded back to me[29]. It made me devour my flan without ever really tasting it, gobbling it rapidly. Clearly, her sister must have explained how much I enjoyed good food for her to give the waiter the instruction to wait until I had finished eating before handing me the note.

---

[29] As related in *The Lightning and Montauk: Reality vs. Fiction*

CHAPTER 15: UNMASKING THE DOUBLE-EDGED TRAITORS

The Countess certainly had successfully opened my curiosity, and even though I had no idea at all what this was all about, I rushed to get out of there. I thought of those brief moments when I passed her in various places in the club. I started to think as a spy does, even though she appeared to be friendly, like a tropical day she could transform in a moment from a sunny day into a violent storm with strong winds, even a deadly hurricane. I immediately left the restaurant after saying goodbye to Federico while insistently leaving him a generous tip and went to a club phone to deliver instructions to Chopin along with the location for meeting the Countess. I told him, "Arrange the team in an urgent manner as preventive medicine in case this Countess isn't what she says she is, of blue blood and maybe only a cheap Beijing copy of her sister and her supposed last name. How long do you need to be in place?"

Chopin replied, "Ten minutes." That wasn't an exaggeration—they were only between 3-5 miles from the location.

"I'll give you more than that. I'll give you fifteen to be in place."

I got in the Jaguar and drove around the club parking lot at a slow speed, taking my sweet time in departing. I checked one of my watches and drove slowly to Balboa Island to board the ferry. I crossed the harbor and then returned, circling back to the Pacific Coast Highway. Seeing everything was in order, and no one was behind me save for Elizabeth, Chopin, Chandee, and Yaneba situated in different vehicles strategically, I entered the parking lot for the Rusty Pelican.

Figure 46 The Rusty Pelican

As I drove in, I saw the beautiful Bentley Faviola drove. I drove slowly in, signaling to the valet that I was coming in just to circle around. Faviola came out from the bushes and tried to open the Jaguar door. I saw her face, unlocked the door, and she jumped quickly into my car. I could tell she had been trained. I was going to slow down to let her get in, but she insisted I keep going with some excitement in her voice. "Don't stop, get out of here. Turn right on the PCH. We're going to Coto de Caza. Do you know the way?"

"Of course. It's like I was born here."

"Did anyone follow you?" she asked in concern.

"I believe you can be absolutely, personally sure that no one followed me. If you knew me a little bit from your sister, you would know that I very seldom make mistakes. I took all precautions to make sure we are alone, and I took the disinfecting route—the ferry from Balboa Island to the Peninsula. If you have any fleas on your clothes, I assure you the ferry will make it show its teeth. If by coincidence you realize there's a flea around once you enter the ferry, all you have to do is circle around to cross on the ferry once more. I assure you that this is 100% bulletproof, since I've been doing that for many years. I share this with you because I like you. I don't tell my secrets to everyone."

She smiled and held out her hand in a more relaxed manner. "My name is Faviola la Vita Dolce. It's nice to meet you."

I smiled and kissed her hand. It smelled of an excellent quality of perfume. Still holding her hand in mine, I replied, "Do you have an aphrodisiac for a perfume? The smell has caused my spirits to rise like a ghost floating up into the air." She smiled as I released her hand with its well-groomed nails, painted in black and white separated at an angle. The nail polish she used must also be excellent quality. Everything about her I found fascinating. I said, "My name is Julio Antonio del Marmol, and the pleasure is all mine. Your beauty captivated me since the first time we passed each other in the lobby of the club and again several times in the hallways. Today for the first time I saw you after wishing to see you again, in the restaurant and never before."

She replied in a pleased tone at my compliments with a little blush and a large smile and a shake of the head, "You've made me blush like a teenager. I'm too old for that!"

"If you're old, I wish all the women I meet in life to look like you. I won't ask you your age, I don't care."

She tapped me on the arm. "You're too nice. Believe it or not, my taste and palate are extremely demanding. On only a few occasions have I been able to find any local restaurant that was able to satisfy my demands. That is why I would rather eat at home with food cooked by my own chef who knows my palate better even than myself. Sometimes he surprises me with things I had been thinking of eating."

I smiled. "Are you sure your cook isn't a spy?"

"I also eat in the privacy of my home. It's a lot safer and less risky. Unfortunately, we're very spoiled, and even with the best things in life when we repeat them too much to become a daily routine, then we try something else."

"Well, it all depends on the quality of what you repeat and the creativity of those who repeat it for you."

She smiled mischievously this time. "Well, maybe you're right, but not all of us possess that extraordinary gift of creativity."

We were approaching her residence, her guiding me and giving me instructions. Even though I knew the place very well, I allowed her to take the lead to make her feel more comfortable. As we spoke on the trip, Faviola managed to keep her concentration on the conversation while evidently noticing the presence of my friends. "Do you know the girl we've passed on the motorcycle a couple of times? And the one in the Italian sportscar?"

I smiled. "They are part of my team, but I will tell you something—having you spot them will hurt their egos, because they are professionals."

She put her hand in her purse and held up a CIA identification badge, putting her left index finger to her lips. I hadn't expected that, but at the same time it wasn't a great surprise. She made me feel a little more relaxed with that; at the same time, I also was a little worried by it. On what side of the CIA was she playing? What did the CIA have in their hands that could not be communicated to me through O'Brien? It crossed my mind that the badge could be a fake. She noticed the change in my face from friendly to a little more reserved.

After we passed the checkpoint at the entrance to the community, which required even residents to provide a photocopy of the ID of any guests, I asked her, "Where are you taking me? I feel like I'm coming to see the President of the United States."

"Don't even consider the idea of being close to the President we have right now. That's my personal advice, but I don't want to get into that until we get to a secure place and can talk." I became silent as we passed the guard shack at the entrance to Coto de Caza, so she added with another mischievous smile, "I think I managed first to surprise you. Now I managed to get you to think. You're probably not accustomed to women who can do that."

I looked at her. "Do you really want to play this game?"

"No, no—I'm just saying from what little I know of you and found in your records, I can tell that you are not only a huge question mark but also a ghost from great dimensions that I've never encountered in my life and all my professional career. You don't exist in any records. Your addresses are all PO boxes, and of course all the paperwork in government agencies state you are a ghost since 1971, homeless, which makes no sense, since you're an educated and intelligent man. All that can be seen by the way you dress and the cars you drive; I know you're not a simple man."

"Thank you very much. I will tell you one thing: when I saw you, it didn't even once cross my mind that a beautiful woman like you could have even a minimal interest in trying to find out who I am, especially a poor, homeless man. Taking into consideration that you are, apparently, a very wealthy woman, from the way you dress and the car you drive."

She smiled again. "Remember, nothing is the way it appears to be, and you are a vivid example." We were now at the entry to her own home, which was more an estate than a simple residence. She said with an ironic smile, "Does this make sense? Now you're on your own. Your friends cannot escort you or protect you anymore. They can't come in here to follow us."

I smiled ironically myself. "That's what you think. Of course, I won't do anything to change your mind. Remember, the spy that shows all his weapons, including his friends and associates, that is the spy who is the first to die when any conflict of interest between them occurs."

Faviola raised her right arm high, smiling as well. "I am the last person you have to worry about even when any conflict of interest arises. I am the most loyal person you can ever meet to my family and friends. I know how I can keep gratitude in my heart for those who exposed their own lives for one of my people. In the end of our meeting later, you will prove it for yourself. Facts and actions are a lot more convincing than any beautiful words anyone could utter."

"I agree 100% with that. People can tell you anything; action is what counts." I parked the Jaguar in front of the mansion, and we walked inside. A man of medium height, balding with white hairs on his temples asked for the black overcoat I was wearing over my tuxedo. He said in an exquisitely polite manner, "Good evening, welcome to the home of the Countess la Vita Dolce."

I smiled. These were the kind of high-class manners from the 30's, 40's, and 50's that made life so pleasant that we had lost over time. In our modern era in which we now live, it appeared the Countess had preserved those values and manners even with her servants, even though she was still a very young woman, likely in her early 30's, and very updated in fashion from the way she dressed. She handed her coat and my overcoat that the man took in his hands. In a very respectful voice, Faviola said, "Thank you, Alberto. Please, I don't want to be disturbed by anyone without exception. I have a very important matter to share with Dr. del Marmol and want absolute silence."

Alberto replied with a small bow of his head and a smile, "Very well, Contessa. Your wishes will be fulfilled." With a slight bow he said to me, "It is an extreme pleasure to meet you, Dr. del Marmol. I shall be at your service for anything you need."

Faviola said, "Alberto, talking about service, why don't you bring something to drink for Dr. del Marmol?"

"What would you like to drink, sir?" he asked me.

I held my right hand high. "Nothing, I'm fine right now."

Faviola held up her right index finger. "Alberto, even though Dr. del Marmol doesn't want anything to drink, please bring us a bottle of champaign with two glasses, a bottle of Dom Perignon Brut 1971. Unopened. The bottle should be sealed and opened only in front of Dr. del Marmol."

I smiled because I knew what she meant without actually coming out and saying it. I had no intention of drinking anything there, even if I saw it opened before me, because I knew that a virgin bottle could still be violated with a sedative or poison very easily. The bottle could be opened, the substance introduced, and then reseal it with the necessary equipment. I had seen people die without the experience I've had after opening a supposedly fresh bottle, paying the ultimate price.

We continued to walk through this impressive mansion. She asked me to follow her to what appeared to be the master bedroom, which was combined with a huge, beautiful atrium with a massive meditation pool, tropical plants, and a lovely waterfall that ran from the upper floor down three floors into an Olympic swimming pool at the bottom. The master bedroom had a jacuzzi and sauna with a high ceiling and plants hanging from it. It gave the feeling of a tropical jungle, an aviary with several kinds of birds like guacamayas and cockatoos. It looked like a natural glass cage. There was surround sound speakers concealed in the tree trunks. Even as you listened to the music you could look around and not find the speakers. The music she had playing at the moment I walked in was the song, "The Velocity of Love," by Suzanne Ciani.

A little while later, after she showed me around the place and that gorgeous master bedroom which was something out of a surrealistic dream, she asked, "How do you like my humble chateau?"

I replied with a smile of surprised satisfaction, "If I have to tell you the truth, you not only managed to surprise me twice in one day, but your chateau I don't like it—I love it. It's such a beautiful place that I have no words to describe it. If this is the master bedroom, I don't want to see the rest of the house. It will give me a great deal of sadness to return to my life as a ghost and drifter, going from town to town and country to country around the world."

She gave me a big, mischievous smile. "This house is yours. To prove it to you, as we Italians say," she opened her purse and pulled out a keychain with the same heart design on her stationary that had her name engraved on it and placed it in my hand."

I said, "What is this?"

She leaned over and gave me a tender kiss on my cheek. She whispered in my ear, "If I only had gratitude and affection before I knew you, after such a short time after meeting you, you are fascinating me. I would like to have you as my intimate, close friend, the one I've never had that I've been looking for all my life." She leaned in as if to kiss me on the lips, but there was a knock at the door.

"The champaign, Contessa," Alberto said from the other side of the door.

"Come in, Alberto."

He opened the door and pushed a rolling cart with a chrome bucket with gilded handles and a vase with red roses, jasmine, gardenias, and other tropical flowers recently cut from their garden by the fresh fragrance they emitted. In the center two buckets of ice sat with two bottles of champaign. Alberto took one of the bottles and held it out to me. "Doctor, could you please check the bottle to make sure it's still sealed before I open it?"

I looked at them in embarrassment but checked the bottle briefly as he asked. I returned the bottle to him. Alberto opened the bottle. Faviola said, "Alberto, Dr. del Marmol may have accepted my invitation to be a guest for a while. I ask you to offer him all the attention and facilitate to him your best service and the optimum all the time it pleases him to stay with us as one more member of the family la Vita Dolce."

Alberto smiled splendidly. "Yes, Contessa. I will provide my best attention to the Dr. del Marmol to the point that he probably will never like to leave our chateau." He poured a little champaign in both glasses and handed one to Faviola. She tasted it, nodded, and handed it back for him to pour more fully. He then handed each of us a glass. She held her glass, looking me in the eyes for a few seconds, a mischievous smile around her lips, waiting to see if I was going to drink. We held the gaze for a few seconds, then she nodded her head and drank the entire glass. She handed her glass to Alberto for a refill. After seeing that, I had no other option.

As she took her second glass, I said, "Hold it. Let's make a toast. From the special gratitude I have in my heart for your beautiful, generous gesture to not only make me feel at ease but also offering me your hospitality, and I believe your sincere friendship, let's toast to a long, solid friendship."

She smiled and clinked her glass to mine. This time, she took only a sip with an expression of satisfaction as she nodded. "Thank you for at least showing me this small vote of confidence, Dr. del Marmol. I'll make sure you never have to repent of it, even if I have to bleed in order to fulfill this."

Alberto asked, "Contessa, if you don't need me anymore, I will return to my normal duties."

Faviola nodded. "Yes, Alberto, you can leave." Alberto left at once, closing the door behind him. "Well, the first thing I'm going to ask you, and I'll test you with, I need you take all your clothes off." She put her glass down on the rolling cart. I gave her a look of incredulity, my glass still in my hand. I couldn't believe such a beautiful woman could be so forward. She looked at my frozen attitude. "This is not a sexual advance after offering you the key to my residence, much less sexual harassment. Neither you nor I need it in order to have sexual contact with anyone to use that method. This is only a security measure for your benefit as well as mine. What I intend to tell you in a bit can not only cost me my life but also yours." She raised both hands high impatiently. "I don't know about you, but I don't want to leave to my enemies this beautiful world for them to break into pieces and make millions or billions of people suffer for the rest of their lives."

She went into the bathroom and returned only in her underwear and bra, her clothes hanging over her left arm. Over her right were two bathrobes, one of which she handed to me. I took it without moving, and she began to put her clothes on hangers. I still stood there, champaign flute in my right hand and the robe in my left, contemplating that beautiful woman who moved rapidly around like she had springs in her legs. After she put her clothes back in the closet in the hallway between the master bedroom and bathroom. I remained frozen in my position.

She returned to the room and without hesitating removed her bra and underwear before a mirror, giving me an angle of her magnificent body from several angles like Venus di Milo, though this one with both arms in place. Faviola looked at me mischievously once more, picked the bathrobe up off the bed, and asked, "Do you like what you see?" She winked at me with one of her beautiful, big blue eyes. I could only nod.

I downed the glass of champaign in several sips. After she saw me do that, Faviola wrapped herself in a bathrobe. "What are you waiting for? Take your clothes off. This is the process we have to follow so you don't have the most minimal doubt that either of us have any recording devices on our bodies. Neither of us, whatever happens from now on, won't turn against each other. The conversation we will have in a moment will tell us also if we without knowing it have carried a bug on our clothes or bodies. Any bugs in the water will be drowned and inevitably die."

She looked at me as I started to remove my clothes, handing hangers to me as I did. "I'll put them in my closet. It's soundproofed, that way if anyone has a bug on there no one will hear anything we say. It doesn't matter how advanced the technology they have. I have the best of the best here." She handed me a gown with her initials monogramed on it. "Please follow me to the dry sauna."

We walked through the glass door to the steam room, removing her robe and putting a towel on. She hung her robe on the wall, and I followed her action. We sat down on the wooden bench. She bent down to me, removing a bandana around her hair. "Check my hair."

I checked through it meticulously. "You're clear."

"OK, now let me check you." As soon as she cleared me, I straightened up, and I could see her jaws were clenched., showing her tension to me. "You and all your team will be assassinated in the next seventy-two hours. After we go through the cleansing, I'll give you all the details about who is behind it all, and the way you'll avoid this taking place. I will tell you now how you will use O'Brien as a weapon to defend yourself."

What she said took me by surprise, so I asked, "What does O'Brien have to do with all of this?"

Faviola shook her head. "Nothing. But at the same time, a lot. He is forced to deal with all these mercenaries and their double faces on a daily basis. Using their antiquated psychology, O'Brien could perhaps manage to put tremendous fear into our enemies' minds as a strategic plan to stop whatever they want to do with you and your friends." She looked at me and reached out to take the wrist of my left hand. "I heard an elaborate plan to eliminate all of you guys from the lips of the Secretary of State because you could endanger what they are trying to do by blowing their cover. She presented her plan to the President himself and a group of his advisors. It looks like she wants to make it appear like an accident by sabotaging the oxygen tanks on the small submarine you guys use in the Marine Research decoy location in Corona del Mar, using the logo of the Oceanographic Technology International."

I stopped her. "How do you know that?"

"Be patient. You'll know how I know everything in the end. You'll know what I'm telling you is the truth—you guys use this location as an undercover base to facilitate infiltration operations all over Central and South America as well as the Caribbean Islands. Sometimes even in other parts of the world."

I shook my head and smiled. "You are too well-informed. That is starting to make me nervous. Of our activities, to my knowledge and have been reassured by O'Brien, nobody has any knowledge of, even at the highest levels of the CIA. Until now, I had believed that our operations only went through the highest levels of our intelligence. Believe it or not, maybe it will seem funny to you, but this made me sleep better for many years. I've been betrayed once, which forced me to abandon my family and my country, and at the same time nearly cost me my life and did cost the life of one of my dear friends. But it looks like, from what you just told me, that we're all in the open in our operations. This is a great disappointment for me. In the end, I believe strongly that my tranquility and sleep has been flushed down the toilet a few minutes ago after listening to you. You spoke of fearmongering before? You've put some fear in me now."

Faviola raised both arms high. "Don't take me wrong! What O'Brien has told you is the absolute truth. What you guys have been doing is off the grid. No one in the Congress or anywhere else has any idea of what you guys are doing. You are the ghosts of the intelligence community."

I looked at her in confusion. "If that is true, how do you have so much knowledge of where we launch those operations from? Which is it? It's one or the other."

She looked at me with a small, mischievous smile. She stroked my cheek with the back of her hand. "The only reason I know these details is because I've been having an intimate relationship for many years with one of the ex-Presidents of this country."

I looked at her very seriously and in surprise. "With whom?"

Her smile had not faded. "Bill Clinton. The husband of our current Secretary of State."

I leaned back on the wooden bench of the sauna and wiped the sweat from my forehead with a sauna towel. "Oh, my God. There's no doubt in my mind that this day has been one full of surprises for me."

She grinned. "If you think this is a lot, I'm telling you now that it's only the beginning. I can guarantee you that you have a lot more on the plate. In my opinion, the Cuban Lightning can handle them."

I shook my head again. "I don't want you to put your expectations for me so high. What you've confessed to me so far, I think it's sufficient to fill me and be difficult to digest. Now you're telling me this is only the beginning! I hope the main course is not a chateaubriand for four! With this appetizer, I'm already full!"

Faviola smiled and leaned back. "Come on, you don't fool me! I know it takes a lot more than what I've been saying to you in order to fill your stomach."

I smiled and replied, "Taking into consideration all you've just told me and to speak frankly, I've been wanting to give you the benefit of the doubt. I've been thinking that all you've told me is 100% true. Do you have any idea the tremendous danger that you've put your life in by telling me all of this? At the same time, as a spy, it should not surprise you that I ask myself why you're taking such a great risk, not just with your life but the lives of your entire family." She was about to speak but I held up a hand to stop. "Please, before you answer, I ask you only one thing: whatever you've told me or at least led me to understand, until now if you're doing all this because I saved your sister's life, don't repeat that anymore. That might be *a* reason but it's very difficult for me to believe as you know well, with all my respect Countess Faviola, that it is the *only* reason. Whatever you have to say to me in the rest of this conversation, at least try to be more specific and clearer in your real motive for doing this. There has to be more to this than what you've told me. You will make me understand and put my spy mind at ease while at the same time you will give me a great satisfaction to my curiosity. Maybe you'll even put to rest any doubts in my mind that I've had about you up to this point. At least on a minimal level of trust about you personally. I want you to understand that besides everything else, if you consider my position and what I've been doing all my life and analyze how we met personally for the first time you have to understand that my instinct for preservation is on the highest level of alert right now from every single thing you just communicated to me. And this is only the beginning! That is why I ask you, no matter what my instincts are telling me that you are a trustworthy, loyal, good person and have extraordinary goodwill in your intentions, but they are also screaming loudly to me that you're not telling me the entire truth. This fact, that you're not being completely truthful with me, even before you've completed saying everything you want to divulge to me, puts at risk everything else you've told me."

Faviola irritably shifted her position on the bench, moving from me a little. She stared up at the ceiling of the sauna for a few seconds with a displeased expression on her face. I kept silent for a while. She understood the logic of what I had told her. I gave her the time to think about and digest it, since I could see she was an intelligent woman. Finally, she turned towards me and forced a small smile. "I didn't expect any less from you. Besides being a spy, you are a very intelligent man. You and I don't know each other enough. I don't expect you to simply take my words as twenty-four karat gold. You're 100% right. This is not my only motive for my actions. It's not just gratitude; there are other factors existing that impel me to share with you as we move ahead in this conversation. I can tell you and guarantee to you this: if the gratitude for what you did for my sister is not my primary motivation, it is the most important one. It told me a lot about your character, regardless of my other motives. I think by the end of our conversation everything will be clarified. If this doesn't happen, I invite you to question me as much as you like until I clear up any doubts you have."

"Very well," I said. "We'll do that. Please continue with your debriefing of information. I'm sorry to have interrupted you, Faviola."

She smiled, and her attitude softened to a more friendly one. In a pleasant tone, understanding the reasons for my doubts, she continued, "You have nothing to apologize for. If I were in your shoes, I would do exactly what you're doing. I might not even agree to meet with you. I really appreciate your sincerity and candor to meet with me. That makes me feel better. I like your bluntness, since that lets me know that you really are searching for a reason to believe what I say, but you want to verify it. That's logical:

believe but verify. It has to all make sense, so let me start from the beginning once more in a different way.

"My relationship with the President started way before he had been elected. Even though I knew him from one of the political fundraisers and all of my friends warned me that he was a sexual maniac, a chauvinist pig with no respect for women, I could not control my curiosity and was physically attracted to him. He practically persecuted me, calling me virtually every day and night. I always asked him if his wife knew what he was doing, and he always said there was no 'wife,' just the appearance of a marriage. He said they had certain disagreements after she got pregnant and that he no longer wanted to have sex with her but agreed that their marriage it could continue forward as a political convenience. Believe it or not, the first time we had sex was in his office. Later, we continued at his house in the master bedroom. I knew the relationship with him wasn't going to get me anywhere; it was a pure sexual addiction. I saw him whenever I wanted, with no attachments. If I didn't want to have him around, I could disappear for months, which probably enticed him more. As time passed, evidently my uncaring attitude converted him into an angry man, possessive to the point of becoming a control freak. He wanted to know everything I did. When I tried to cut our relationship off because it started to make me feel filthy, he offered to take me to orgies and threesomes with his wealthy friends. These were very sadistic, dangerous, and perverse sexual acts he wanted to indulge in. They were violent, and I didn't see him for months. I began a relationship with a prominent New York attorney named Gabriel. When he found out, he threatened that if I didn't drop that relationship, I would be responsible for his death."

Faviola took a deep breath. I saw tears in her eyes, a sign of her emotional state. In a cracking voice, she said, "Three days after Bill told me that, Gabriel was found dead in his office of an apparent suicide with a bullet in his temple. His head was on the top of his desk in a pool of blood." Faviola gestured in pain and frustration and said in a revulsed tone, "Nobody can tell me that Bill didn't send someone to do this. Gabriel never went to the office at night, and the day before he asked me to marry him." She held out her hand to display an engagement ring. She could no longer contain her tears and began to weep. "He had been killed by the Clinton family, and I will know for the rest of my life that Bill is behind my fiancé's death." She looked into my eyes. "Do you think this is a good enough reason for me to hate the Clintons?"

I nodded. A few seconds passed in silence as I waited patiently for her to pull herself together. I asked, "Forgive me, but you just said, 'the Clintons.' What does Hillary have to do with this? He was the one who threatened you, or did I hear wrong?"

"No, you heard right." Her face grew red in anger. "They are identical: cynical, liars, corrupt to the bones. Together they indulge in sexual orgies. She covers him, and he covers her. Both of them are members of the Satanic group established in Montauk with his best friend, Mike Thompson. They inducted the current President Obama and his wife Michelle into their rituals. They eat recently born or unborn babies. Their belief is that this maintains infinite youth, mental and physical strength and the power to control the will of others. Their goal is to become together masters of the universe."

I put both hands over my ears as if in pain. I turned towards her a little, nodding. "Do you have proof of that?"

"No, but I saw it with them."

"I have proof of it. Some of my friends took a video of one of these gatherings, and I have several copies in security boxes in one of my banks in Newport Beach."

She said emphatically, "I know."

I looked at her in surprise. I said worriedly, "How do you know this?"

She said firmly to alleviate my worry, "Your cousin Antonio in Palermo. I just got back from Italy, and he told me that you have proof that incriminates all these people, including the President and Secretary of State, in your security box. All the rituals they participated in as members of that Satanic cult. He was the one who suggested bringing that film to put fear into their brains and give it to O'Brien. The plan is this: you give it to O'Brien, and he will show it to the President. I assure you that all they are planning to do to you and your friends will evaporate in a single second. The one thing these people fear is being publicly exposed. Your cousin also told me to tell you to watch that video again meticulously, because in it you might find the faces of the current President at that large table they're sitting around. If you can find it, even his profile, then you'll really terrify them. If you possess *that*, what else might you have? Based on Antonio's description of the last conversation you two had in Palermo, that would be more than enough to take these guys off your back as well as those of your friends."

Now I knew how she got all this information. I raised my index finger and said, "Now I feel a lot better. Everything makes sense to me. I have only two questions for you, and I believe I will be satisfied."

She looked at me and said pleasantly, "OK, what is your first question?"

"What does the CIA have to do with all of this?"

She shook her head ambiguously. "Nothing at all. I just happened to be in the right place at the right time. As an agent for the intelligence community, of course my resources are extremely convenient. I can obtain any information that is classified or confidential, like the marine research station at China Cove Beach in Corona del Mar." She dried some sweat from her face and added seriously, "I think Providence picked me to not only punish this bunch of political assassins by providing you with this vital information to bring justice to my fiancé Gabriel, a great, young, intelligent, well-educated man with beautiful Christian principles that lost his life in his youth without even knowing why. These people have no respect for human life." She raised her hand to show the engagement ring again. In the dim light of the sauna, the ring glittered in the steam and diffracted into rainbows along the ceiling.

We stayed in silence as we watched the pattern. She asked, "What is your second question?" I looked at her sympathetically. She understood the compassion with which I had been watching her and put her right hand over my eyes. "No, no—don't look at me with pity. After all, maybe I deserved all this after so much time departing from God. Maybe he sent me this punishment to open my eyes and look at life in a different way. Only those who suffer the intense pain of losing someone very close to their hearts are capable of appreciating the miracle that we all take superficially and don't appreciate. That gift is the most beautiful treasure from the hands of the Creator, which is our lives."

I shook my head. "No—God never punishes anyone. He is a being of forgiveness, love, compassion, happiness, and joy. We are the ones who make our destinies. Many times, Satan the Destroyer takes us off our rails. He is the only one that takes joy in our suffering and agony." I shook my head this time. "Believe me, I've been able to observe him close enough to smell the pestilent odor of sulfur. He goes around the world, recruiting men with no heart or feelings, filled with jealousy and anger, in order to destroy humanity and rip us all from our peace, happiness, and joy." I looked deeply into her eyes. I could see her sincere respect and joy that my words had given her. I realized that her intentions were to help me and the others while destroying our common enemy. That enemy was here, there, and everywhere, always unexpectedly waiting to watch for our weakness, for us to make any mistake in order to use that weakness to destroy our lives. We looked at each other. She saw that I had, unwanted, allowed two tears of gratitude roll down my cheeks. I said, "Thank you. Thank you very much."

She took my face between her delicate, refined, and very well-kept artistic hands. She brought her face to mine and kissed my face tenderly. It then escalated to a more passionate one, several times over my cheeks as she tried to swallow those tears on my face. She knew they came directly from my heart in gratitude for her generosity and sacrifice she made to warn me against the attempt on my life and my team. She stood up and dropped the towel onto the floor. She invited me to stand as well, extending her hand to me. She removed my towel, allowing it also to drop onto the floor. We embraced with our naked bodies in the middle of the sauna, kissing passionately for several seconds. Then she put the towels on top of the wooden bench and lay down on it, inviting me to climb onto her. She took my hand in hers. Looking into my eyes, she said, "I want to make love to you."

I smiled. "And I with you, *bella* Faviola."

She returned the smile and I lay down on top of her. We embraced and enjoyed a mutual pleasure that ended a while later with our bodies covered in sweat not just from the heat of the sauna but from the physical exercise we had as well.

When we finished, we wrapped ourselves in our bathrobes and walked to the giant shower in her master bedroom. We entered it and embraced as the freezing cold water hit our bodies, relieving us of the intense heat and the steam rising off of our skin. We left the shower and walked to the jacuzzi, wrapped only in towels. It was covered in red roses during our absence. Faviola told me that was one of the assignments Alberto had. She liked the smell of fresh cut flowers, and he did that religiously each day in case she wanted to use the jacuzzi.

She said, "With few exceptions during the week, I love to sink myself into this rose water nearly every day." She took my hand. "I want to clarify something for you. It's not fair for you to make any assumption about something that is not in reality what it is. I want you to understand that I'm not in any danger. You and your friends are, but nobody has knowledge of where I got this information and its details of how this assassination attempt will take place. The only people who know about this are two people I have complete trust in. one of them is you, and the other is your cousin Antonio in Palermo. I trust him because he's been loyal to me all my life."

I looked at her in surprise. "What about the person who gave that information to you?"

She smiled. "That person doesn't even know how I obtained it from him."

I shook my head in confusion. "That is my second question I didn't get to ask because we started to have a wonderful encounter in the sauna."

She smiled. "As you see, with patience and time, all the fruits from the tree eventually ripen and fall into your hands from their own weight." She caressed my cheeks again with the back of her hand. "Is that your last question?"

"Yes. It's my second, but it's my last, since I have no others."

"OK. A few months ago, I found Bill in a reception at the White House that I had been invited to. He said he needed to speak to me in private about something I left with him that he wanted to return to me. He took me to one of the conference rooms. I didn't want to be impolite or create a scene at this big reception. Without being seen even by his wife, we left the ballroom from different exits and met again in the Situation Room where he had told me to meet him. I believed he wanted to impress me. He showed me pictures of bin Laden, who had already been relocated to Venezuela, even before they told the public about the supposed capture and killing of him. Also, he showed me photos that would be used in the deception operation for political reasons of the double they would use. They had conducted thorough research and carefully calculated more than once by the experts that Obama would not be re-elected, so Hillary came up with this idea to restore the popularity he had lost. Without doing this, they believed he would not get re-elected for a second term. According to Bill, and I don't know if it's true or not, Hillary is the one who prepared the whole thing with the backing of the leaders in intelligence."

I thought about the time Brenton had mentioned this before. It was exactly as he had described to me. Faviola continued, "Everything had been going well until Bill tried to have sex with me, and I resisted several times. He turned violent, grabbing me by the shoulders and pushing me down on the conference table there. I hit my head on the edge of the table, and that blow made me woozy. He tried to get under my skirt, even in that state. I had no strength to defend myself anymore, and thank God Hillary appeared in the hallway at that moment, yelling his name in a loud voice. He hurriedly pulled an executive chair from the table and pushed me under the table, adjusting the chair back at the table. He opened the door, and I heard Hillary say, 'What have you been doing? The President wants to talk to you—what are you doing here with the doors closed? Do you want to get me into trouble? Do you have another woman in here?' She pushed her way into the room, knowing him very well. Fortunately for me, before she got where I was under the table, Obama showed up in the doorway. He said, 'Come on, guys. We've got something very important I want to discuss with you two. I need your opinion.' Hillary turned around and smiled hypocritically, and the two of them left me alone. I started to leave, and as I walked down one corridor, I heard their voices coming in my direction. I tried to open a door to one office, but it was locked. I tried another, and it opened. I dashed inside the office and as I heard their voices getting closer, I concealed myself in the closet among some coats, hiding in the back of it. My heart was in my mouth as I tried to find a reasonable excuse for being there. The bump on my head made me dizzy, and I thought I would be arrested, accused of being a spy, in the best scenario a Taliban spy or in the worst a Chinese spy.

"I broke into a cold sweat that ran all over my body as I identified not only Obama and the Clintons but also the voices of Director of National Intelligence James Clapper, Vice President Joe Biden, and CIA Director John Brennan." She breathed deeply. "This is where I heard all the details, point by point, as I told you before. Not even Bill realized I was in there. It will never cross his mind that I listened to all the plans they made, not only with bin Laden but on another subject, of extremely relevant importance that I will communicate with you when you need it.

She continued, "That is the reason you should not worry about me absolutely. You only have to worry about you and your friends. Put this plan into action immediately and get that information into O'Brien's hands. I'm only going to ask you one extremely important thing: I don't care how much trust you have in O'Brien, I don't care if you consider him like a part of your family, please, no matter how much pressure he puts on you, please don't mention my name, for the love of God. Bill is very conniving and astute. If it reaches his ears, he'll put one and one together. It won't be long before he figures out that I'm the only one in that particular area which could be the source of that information. Then my life will be worth less than a young cactus in the desert. Do you understand?" She was deadly serious.

I replied, "You don't have to worry about me at all. I never opened my mouth, even when they burned my testicles with boiling water. You know about that, don't you? You probably know very well that you can sleep very deeply with Antonio, my cousin. You've known him and he has my same genetic makeup."

She said, "I don't know much about your past, but from the little I Know, you are an exceptional man. You give respect and consideration even to those who don't deserve it and live your life with dignity, based on respect and good principles and actions, the most important values we human beings can possess as a rule. The Golden Divine rules." She smiled broadly. "For that, and from my feminine instincts, I told you today a lot more than what I shared with Antonio in Palermo about that personal ordeal I had in the White House with Bill Clinton. I believed it necessary to take that worry from your mind. By the time Bill returned to look for me in the Situation Room, assuming I was still unconscious, I had already left the White House. I never, never took a phone call from him and moved my residence, leaving strict instructions to all my servants that if he located me or anyone tried to find me, tell those people that I had left for Europe and had no idea when I would come back. Finally, he gave up and stopped looking for me." She crossed herself. "Thank you, God, for taking off my back that diabolic creature. For many months in Europe, I could not even sleep in peace. I had horrible nightmares of his grabbing me, gagging me, and tying my hands and legs to take me to one of his orgies with Jeffrey Epstein. Probably Bill received some cut of that lucrative business. In those nightmares they raped me on top of a conference table with almost twenty-five men who beat me up and, still conscious, stripped me naked, put some condiments on top of my body like one does a pig, everyone naked in a diabolic ritual, and shoved me into an industrial oven to roast me and eat me, consuming my body while I was still alive. That nightmare haunted me for so long that I didn't have sex for a long time with anyone. Every time I tried to, even the thought of it, made me break into a very profuse panic attack with sweats, nausea, vomit, and severe diarrhea.

"That is why I want to give you my most profound thanks. From the very first moment I saw you in the hallways of the club, you caught my eye, and I felt a physical attraction to you, but you also brought me a beautiful sensation of trust that I have not experienced for a long time with anyone. Then, later when I sent my sister the picture I took discretely of you in the club to Palermo, and discovered what you had done for her, I investigated you more deeply and again discovered who you really are. I started to have not only sexual fantasies about you but also beautiful dreams that I haven't had since I was a teenager. Now you can perhaps understand better why I cannot allow those diabolical beasts that now possess power in the White House to harm you or kill you as they plan to do." She smiled, now in satisfaction. "And now, more than before or ever, after a beautiful experience in the sauna, somebody who wants to harm you has to come over my dead body."

I smiled. "Do you think my performance was to the level of your expectations in your dreams? I don't know, because we did it so quickly in the sauna."

She took one of my arms and drew close to my face. "Oh, yes, Mr. Lightning. You exceeded greatly my imagination, my dreams, and surpassed expectations. She kissed me on the lips tenderly several times. "These are kisses of gratitude." They grew to more passionate ones that lasted a lot longer than her smaller kisses. She made a move and turned her legs over mine. Her left hand searched under water to accommodate herself to sit slowly onto my lap with an expression of satisfaction. She took my face then with both hands and kissed me again passionately. Breathing rapidly, her nostrils flared open and closed from her near hyperventilation in time to our heartbeats, uniting as tympani in a symphonic orchestra during the grand finale, coming together with the rest of the percussion of the orchestra without losing rhythm or melody.

After a little while, it appeared that the Countess Faviola had completed what she called a sexual marathon, that allowed her to catch up for the longest period in her life for which she had been deprived of the most beautiful need of a human being to satisfy: the internal screaming of physical sexual ecstasies.

She asked, "Did you have any previous plans for tonight?"

I replied, "Nothing that can't be postponed. Why?"

"I would love for you to come to the theatre with me tonight to celebrate a beautiful first encounter, the beginning of a great friendship. I have two tickets for the last performance of the night for the musical *Mamma Mia!*. I would very much love for you to serve as my escort, because I will have the opportunity to introduce you to my dearest friends." She smiled mischievously. "I want to show you off. Of course, I won't put you in any compromising commitment. I will introduce you as a great friend of my family, and your cousin Antonio Barriety's in Palermo, who is very well known to my friends. Nothing more than that."

This time I was the one to smile mischievously as I caressed her chin. "What, is there anything else between us that I don't know about?"

Faviola smiled broadly and came close to me. She gave me a tender kiss on my lips. "I don't know. That is up to you."

I wrapped my arms around her neck and returned her kiss tenderly. "Remember, it takes more than one to make a promise, but it only takes one to break it. This is something we should never play with and take seriously as a love relationship because everything in life involves risks. This risk should therefore be mutual. Unless you've been very sure that you can take that risk with that person, you should stay still. Don't you believe so?"

She replied, "I'm ready to take any risk as long as it is with you."

"Thank you for your vote of confidence. Are you sure?"

She took me by my neck with both hands and gave me a long, passionate kiss. When she finished, she said, "Does that convince you? You haven't given me an answer about being my escort tonight. You already have the appropriate attire for the occasion."

"Yes, I will accompany you with pleasure. That is the reason, believe it or not, that I'm always prepared for all occasions to be overdressed rather than be underdressed. You don't know how many times that has saved me embarrassment, as I have learned in the past."

She smiled. "That is one of the things I like more about you than any man. The others have been courteous, lovely, and respectful. But dressing elegantly is to me the most important thing for the whole package. I believe I'm lucky, because I found in you the complete package. You also know how to pick your colognes. Believe it or not, that was one of the things that first caught my attention in the club lobby. You fascinated me with your aroma. By the way, how many colognes do you use? Now, after I've had intimate relations with you, I can identify you have different fragrances in different parts of your body."

I smiled. "You see? That is the secret that only a woman like you knows, because you've been with me."

"Do you have a specific reason for this? I'm curious. Is it your trademark?"

I nodded. "I believe all human beings are very similar in our anatomy. But we are extremely different in personalities and character. That is why I also believe that all of us should look for the way to make ourselves different in our tastes, just like choosing colors, to avoid being confused one for another. I decided a long time ago to use three different fragrances in different parts of my body. Something very few people do, so I use for my face and neck Monsieur de Givenchy; for my torso, belly button and abdomen, Pasha de Cartier; and for my pubic area and the rest of my body down to my legs and feet, Burberry London." I smiled mischievously. "I believe that this is not only stays impregnated in your memory for a long, long time but also makes me different from everyone you've made love to before, like everyone else I have had an intimate relationship with. I leave a great memory that establishes me as completely different from any other intimate relationships. As you said before, leaving also impregnated in your soul my trademark."

She looked at me in surprise. "Yes, you're right. Something different and completely exquisite, which is hard to forget." Faviola smiled. Still with her arm around my neck, she said, "In my opinion you have tremendous reasons because this is a very pleasant surprise, especially in you, the male sex that normally don't put too much detail like we women do. But I want to tell you, love, that you with or without cologne, using just the natural gifts you were born with for free, are sufficient to live a great, long impression in the most demanding of women." She smiled and kissed me tenderly on the lips once more. Her smile became mischievous. "Please don't abandon your colognes just because of what I just said. This is like the cherry on top of the cake. They make a beautiful compliment."

I smiled. "Thank you very much for your reassurance and beautiful words."

The Countess stepped back. "We'd better get out of the jacuzzi before we turn into prunes. I need a lot more time than you to get ready. You don't need makeup, and I do. I don't want to show myself in public with my own face and then the other women will be talking about me behind my back."

"Come on, you don't need makeup. You're a natural beauty."

"Thank you love." We got out of the jacuzzi. "Remember, as your colognes enhance your presence, my makeup enhances my beauty."

We wrapped ourselves in our bathrobes and walked towards the huge shower in the center of the master bathroom to rinse ourselves before getting dressed. We were supposed to go to the theater in South Coast Plaza at Segerstrom Center for the Arts in Costa Mesa. We got out of the shower and dried off and walked towards the bathroom. I was surprised to see two scuba diving wetsuits on the bed, black but of very thin mesh material with a hoodie attached by a zipper to cover the hair.

I recovered from my surprise. "I didn't know you had any plans after we go to the theater to go to a scuba diving adventure."

She smiled. "This is not what you imagine. This is a very new technology of body armor. This new fiber," she said as she picked up a suit to hand to me for closer examination, "is not only capable of stopping a bullet but also a knife or any kind of acid that our enemies could try to use against us. This is like having a double skin suit of stainless steel, bulletproof, with titanium that is resistant but able to support all types of temperatures. This was perfected from the suits astronauts would use when going into orbit. It insulates you against both cold and hot temperatures. They explained to me that the fibers were implanted in the material for that purpose to maintain your body's metabolism."

"This is an extreme technological advance. I have suits made of similar fabric, but not this thin and not this advanced."

She added, "This not only protects you from hot and cold temperature extremes but also offers you a great advantage when you confront our deadly enemies. It clings to your body like a vacuum seal or suction. You don't wear this on top of your clothes but under them."

"How can such a thin material have so many technical components built into it?"

She shook her head. "The marvels of modern technology." She gave me a kiss on the lips and picked up one suit before walking towards her vanity in the master bedroom where she kept her makeup. "Put that one on, OK? Just in case we encounter an unexpected situation."

I replied, "Thank you for thinking of me. We never know when we can encounter one of those unexpected situations, especially with what has transpired over the past seventy-two hours. I believe you have the right idea following your debriefing, I should be extremely prepared for the worst and not be an easy prey for our enemies. Thank you again." I began to put it on as she did her makeup.

A little while later, she with an elegant evening dress and I in my tuxedo left her mansion in her Bentley convertible had retrieved from the Rusty Pelican restaurant. She told me that Alberto had been instructed to take a taxi there to bring it to the house. Before we left, Faviola left further instructions with Alberto. We drove out of her development of Coto de Caza. As we reached the Pacific Coast Highway, she looked into the rearview mirror. She smiled mischievously. "I hope the people following us are your friends. If not, they'll force me to shake them off my tail. Please take a look and let me know."

"I don't have to look; I saw them before you did. Yes, they are my friends. Like you, I don't like anybody to know where I'm going or where I'm coming from. In our line of work, that can be very dangerous. For your tranquility, they are my friends."

"You didn't even look!"

"I told you—I saw them before you did."

"Do you still have doubts about me?"

"Doubts never disappear, but that's not the reason. The real reason is that we'll stay for hours in the theater and leave your car in the parking lot. I believe that that it is always prudent to have a few pairs of eyes watching our car. Even though I have a great, tight relationship with the mall's private security, not too long ago right under their noses in the special assigned parking area for them, our enemies managed to put enough explosives under one of our cars capable of blowing a great portion of this beautiful shopping mall to atoms." I shook my head and said ironically, "I believe it would be a tremendous waste to not only lose your very expensive Bentley but also our lives in the process. On such a glamorous night of celebration of our first romantic experience, that might be a possibility of becoming a solid and very fruitful association. I hope it lasts for many years."

She smiled with a beautiful expression of surprise. She turned towards me sharply and reached out with her right hand to squeeze my left in a sincere gratitude for what I said. "Really? Is that the way you truly feel?"

I smiled again, more broadly this time. "It's very good to get to know each other a little. So I have to tell you that I always do exactly what I say and feel here." I tapped my breast with my right hand. "Only to my enemies do I never show that aspect of my character. You are very far away from being one of them. That is why I should tell you that one of the most difficult, despised but necessary metamorphoses that a man with my principles and character suffers daily in our profession." I shook my head in clear displeasure. "There's nothing I despise more in this life than hypocrisy and lies. Unfortunately, these two are the most powerful weapons a spy possesses. That is why, even though I manage to master my profession, there's not a single moment in my life in which I don't despise the circumstances or maybe it was my destiny to be converted at such a young age into something I never wanted to be: a master spy." My eyes grew moist in my emotion. "This is one more reason or maybe the most powerful reason to despise with all my heart communists and Marxist ideologies. They are fully responsible for stealing from me the most beautiful gift that any human being can possess: my childhood and innocence."

Figure 47 Segerstrom Center for the Arts in Costa Mesa

CHAPTER 16: THE ANGEL FROM THE SKY

Faviola was driving along Bristol Street, close to the Southcoast Plaza near Paularino. She abruptly turned into the driveway of the Hilton Hotel, a location used frequently by my team for our meetings. She stopped the car, taking me completely by surprise. She didn't turn off the engine.

I asked, "What happened?"

Without losing a second, she took her seatbelt off and opened her door. "Please, get out of the car."

I slipped my right hand inside my jacket, searching for my pistol. I saw a short distance away Chopin and Chandee had stopped near us, and also reaching for weapons. To my surprise, Faviola walked around the Bentley and came to me, giving me a vast bear hug and a small kiss on each of my cheeks with teary eyes. "You are the most adorable man I have ever met in my life. I'm sorry if I scared you with my abrupt reaction to stop here spontaneously. I think it's necessary to express to you at this particular moment the magnificent impression you created in my mind with your words filled with sincerity and pain that you suffered in your youth, how that makes me admire you more for your integrity and sincerity that you've entrusted in me to tell me that you despise what you are. This important revelation of your most intimate feelings demands my immediate stopping on my side to recognize and memorize with gratitude your trust in me." She smiled and hugged me once more. "Now we can continue our trip."

"A very short trip. We're not even half a block from the mall."

"I believe that every single minute I spend by your side I like you more to the point that I believe I'm falling in love with you, even though that sounds ridiculous in such a short time. I think I've been in love with you since you passed me in the lobby of the club that first time when you captivated me with the scent of one of your foreign colognes."

I smiled and shook my head. "You're not far behind. You're not only an exquisite woman and beautiful, but you're also extraordinary and never thought you would be working with the intelligence community. But I also love your spontaneous personality. You are a box of surprises, and they're all beautiful and pleasant."

She looked at me in gratitude. "Thank you for your beautiful words and compliments." She squeezed my left hand in her right in a gesture of affection. We had already entered the mall. After we stopped right in the parking lot of Nordstrom's, she looked at her wristwatch. "We have almost an hour before the function starts. Do you mind if we come in here for a little while into Nordstrom's? I want to buy some feminine clothing so that I don't have to come back here tomorrow. I've been putting off this shopping trip."

"Remember, I'm here for you to accompany you. To me, it makes no difference where we go. I'll be by your side with great pleasure."

She smiled. "Well, I didn't want you to come with me to the women's negligee department because that will ruin the element of surprise. I want you to see me later in my intimate apparel that I buy and show you my best in my new clothing. You can wait for me in the men's department. Maybe you'll find something you like for yourself. I know you have great taste, and this is one of the best stores in the entire mall, and you probably frequent it."

"Yes, you're right. I've been looking for white dress socks, but because it's winter, normally these stores remove everything white from stock. White is taboo in winter, and that's one of my favorite colors. Nothing worse than wearing white shoes with black socks!"

She smiled. "Well, maybe you'll be in luck and find your white dress socks here today."

We entered the store, and I was taken aback as we entered by the lack of Christmas music playing over the speakers, which was normal at this time of year. None of the symbols of Christmas were on display, either. A young woman that had an employee tag on her blouse with the name Lisa greeted us with the beautiful manner characteristic of Nordstrom's. Her tag also identified her as a manager. They were distinguished for their courtesy nationwide. I said as I walked in, "Ho! Ho! Ho! Merry Christmas to you and to everyone here today! And a peaceful and prosperous New Year ahead!"

I saw Lisa's face reflect fear and panic as if she saw a ghost. With a small smile that could not be more fake and forced, her jaw clenched and said respectfully, "No, no, sir—Happy Holidays. That is not politically correct, and we should be considerate of others to avoid offending those who don't believe or practice Christmas."

Faviola looked at me in surprise. After I recovered, I said, "Excuse me, with all respect, Lady Lisa—that's your name, yes?"

"Yes."

"Can you please clarify something for me? Who can I offend, with all my respect, Lisa, by wishing them Merry Christmas, peace, and prosperity? This is not just a holiday—this is the motherlode, the beautiful Christmas that we celebrate without offending anyone when we celebrate in peace and joy for many years in this beautiful nation, the birth of the baby Jesus Christ, the Son of God." I reached into my pocket and pulled out my money clip like soldier reloading his weapon and pulled out a $1 bill.

"Sir, with all my respect as well, some people don't believe in Christmas, and those people can be offended when you say, 'Merry Christmas.' Don't you think it's fairer to say, 'Happy Holidays' in general?"

"No, ma'am." I held out the dollar bill before her. "I don't think it's fair to *me* or to my lady companion here, and I'm going to tell you why. If what you say is true, this bill that pays for every single item we buy in this store, put food on our table, pay your paycheck to fill your necessities at home could also be offensive to anyone? It says very clearly here 'In God We Trust.' Is that not offensive? Should we then burn all these bills?"

Supervisor Lisa looked at me very seriously. "I'm sorry, sir. I'm only doing my job. I repeated what they've instructed me to tell all our customers without exception."

I shook my head in obvious disgust and disdain. Faviola and I exchanged glances. She said indignantly, "I never believed that this extreme atheist horrendous ideas would come all the way to this beautiful USA. It never crossed my mind."

I said, "Don't let it ruin this beautiful night that is still young. Go and buy your feminine clothes you came here for. I'll wait for you like I said before. These big monopolies are becoming so ignorant and greedy for money and profit that not trying to offend a small minority of extremists supported by the current President that supports their ideas they don't even know they're offending those of us who are in the majority. They don't even know that they'll destroy not only our traditions but will themselves be decapitated this beautiful, prosperous nation from the productive capitalist to the grinding poverty of the communists filled with hunger, calamities, and miseries."

The young supervisor looked at me, stunned into silence. She could finally only say, "I'm sorry, sir. I'm sorry."

I shook my head. I noticed a very large group of people surrounding us, listening to what I said. I hadn't noticed them before, but now they applauded me. A beautiful, distinguished woman in a red dress, took a sprig of jasmine from her hair and walked over to me. "Do you mind?" She put it into my lapel of my tuxedo. "This is my present for your beautiful and brave words defending Christian principles and the right of free expression that we all should possess and respect to death without fear of anyone." The beautiful, young woman, after she finished putting the flower in my lapel turned to Faviola. "Congratulations on having by your side a man of this caliber. Defend him and stimulate him. There's not many of him left."

Faviola grinned and nodded. "I know. I know. Is he not a great man? Is he not a brave man?" She spoke with pride.

The lady gave her a hug. She held out her hand to Faviola and held her other one out to me, which I kissed as my mother had taught me when I was little. She said, "It's nice to meet you." She said to me. "Especially you." She turned to Faviola. "No offense." She said to us, "My name is Andrea Segerstrom. We own all of this. Our ancestor left this that they built with the sweat of their brow and enormous sacrifice in 1898 when they lived in Chicago. They expanded to Wisconsin and Minnesota. The family would eventually include ten children that eventually migrated to California, settling here in what is now Costa Mesa. They farmed on leased land and then bought forty acres to start. That is the way all of this began." She waved her hand to include the entire Nordstrom's store. She reached into her wallet and gave each of us a business card. It was beautiful with golden borders and the family crest. "I am at your service. Whatever you need, please don't hesitate to call me. People like you we need here in this place and around the country, that are capable of fearlessly defending the values of our ancestors and not allowing our traditions to be stolen by these elements of extremists with totalitarian ideas. You make me very proud today to see people like you still exist."

"Thank you," I said. We gave our goodbyes. Lisa remained rooted there as if she had seen a ghost.

Faviola went to the ladies' department. I looked at Lisa indifferently and walked away to the applause of the group surrounding us. I went to the men's department and found a very nice, light grey suitcoat with a matching set of shoes to purchase. As Faviola rejoined me with her bag of lingerie, I found it amusing to notice Lisa no longer welcomed people with 'Happy Holidays.' Instead, she was greeting people with "Hello, good evening, welcome to Nordstrom's." I had no idea if she switched greeting because of my words or if she was intimidated by the presence of Andrea Segerstrom.

As Countess Faviola walked towards me with a big grin on her face, she gave me a great hug holding her bag over my shoulder. She said in my ear, "You made me so proud of you I don't think I'll ever experience this again in my life. You stimulated me so high sexually that I had to visit the lady's room to clean off the results of that excitement. I can tell you if we weren't in a public place, I would ask you to make love to me right now on top of this counter."

I smiled. "If you continue to tell me all these things in my ear, I'll be the one who will be in trouble. We'll both be arrested in Nordstrom's for public indecent exposure."

She drew back a little upon hearing that with a mischievous smile. She took my face in both her beautiful hands and bit my bottom lip gently. "Let's get out of here before we get in trouble. I believe we won't make it like we planned to the theatre. Do you not think so?"

I smiled. "Remember, I'm at your disposition tonight to the point I've allowed you to take the wheel of my life, something I've never let any other woman—or anybody else, for that matter—violating all the security rules I've been taught since I was a little boy and starting on my crazy life as a ghost spy. We were outside the store in the parking lot. She stopped and kissed me again.

She looked straight into my eyes. "Is that true what you just said?"

"Of course."

She kissed me on the lips passionately in the middle of the parking lot for a few seconds. We separated and she said, "I believe it's a lot more prudent if we walk to the theater and leave the car parked here in front of Nordstrom's. I think if we both get inside that car now, Mama Mia will be left behind in history. Let's walk in this cool, beautiful night to cool our sexual instincts while we walk in the cold night breeze to the theater. Getting in that car tonight is too great a risk with our volatile sexual appetite we both have right now."

I smiled. "As you wish, Countess."

We opened the car and put the bags in the back seat. Then we walked across the parking lot towards Bristol Street and the theater. As I crossed the street at the signal light before the mall, I could see Chandee and Chopin following us between the cars, leaving Elizabeth to watch the Bentley. Even though Faviola hadn't noticed them in her sexual excitement, I saw them not far away inside one of our cars.

A little bit later, as we arrived at the theater, we approached the refreshments bar and ordered two glasses of champaign since we still had some time to kill. The first bell of the three calls had not yet rung. As we enjoyed our beverages, we watched the multitude coming in and out of the bar and lobby. We were both scanning the area in order to see if we could detect any enemy faces or something that could put us on our guard.

The Countess breathed a sigh of relief when we had completed our scan of the area. There was no immediate danger, and she felt more at ease after that first assessment. A young couple came by near us and said hello very affectionately to Faviola. After they exchanged kisses and hugs, she introduced me to them. "Let me introduce you to my special friend, my escort tonight, Dr. del Marmol. He is the cousin of Antonio Barriety in Palermo, who you know very well."

The gentleman held out his hand. "It's a great pleasure to meet you, Dr. del Marmol. I am Virgilio Benzanillo." He was a very tall, thin man but clearly very fit. He was mostly bald but held himself with an aristocratic air. He handed me a business card which read "Benzanillo, LLC: International Records and Films."

I replied, "The pleasure is all mine. Whoever is a friend of Countess Faviola is always a friend of mine."

His companion held her hand out to me as well. She was a gorgeous woman with long eyelashes over her large, green eyes. She had lovely olive skin. She smiled in a friendly manner and said, "You caught my attention because you look very nice in your tuxedo."

I smiled, took her hand in my right, and kissed the back of it. To my surprise, instead of the reaction I usually got from that greeting, I received no compliment and her smile disappeared. Her expression grew horrified, as if I were a leper. She snatched her hand away and took a step back. Maintaining some distance between her and I, she returned to Virgilio and looked at him in embarrassment, as if she should not have allowed that to happen. An awkward silence fell on us. I looked at Faviola, who glanced back at me in confusion. The woman looked as if she felt guilty with an expression of sadness and confusion. She said, "I am Soraya Papadopoulos."

I replied, "Nice to meet you, Soraya. That's a nice, Biblical name. Please forgive me if in any way or form I offended you with the gesture of respect I always use whenever I meet a woman. My mother taught me to always do that since I was a little boy."

Soraya looked at Virgilio fearfully with a small, nervous smile on her face, as if trying to plead with him for approval. She had not made the slightest flirtatious gesture, only complimenting me on my tuxedo. Virgilio looked at her a little ashamed. He looked at us, still showing his shame and guilt in his eyes. He shook his head and said with a small, forced smile, "I know, I know. This is a very common thing in Spain and other countries around the world, a custom. Soraya, you have nothing to be ashamed about what Dr. del Marmol did. It's just a demonstration of respect, affection, and courtesy."

Soraya, caught in the middle, was now doubly embarrassed. She looked at me, the moist eyes showing her distress. Finally, two tears escaped her control. She forced a smile and looked at me. "I'm sorry, Dr. del Marmol. I didn't mean to be rude or discourteous. I'm simply not accustomed to that kind of gesture, and you took me by surprise. I don't want to it to cross Virgilio's mind that I gave you any reason, not even with a look, for you to show me so much affection without our even knowing each other."

Virgilio was clearly irritated at hearing her use him in her apology. He grabbed her by the arm to pull her towards him. "Soraya, why did you have to include me in that? You made me look like Othello, filled with rabid jealousy, misunderstanding every gesture and drama into some kind of irrational sexual excuse. I think you'd better shut up. Instead of trying to fix what you did wrong, now you're trying to blame me for it and so creating a worse situation by turning me into a jealous villain that has a chain of horror on your soul."

Faviola and I exchanged surprised glances. We now understood that the reality why Soraya had reacted the way she had. She was plainly afraid of Virgilio. It was as if she were submissive towards a sexual tyrant. Obviously, Virgilio maintained over her some kind of fear. They had probably had several confrontations before just because she looked at a man the wrong way or in a way he didn't like. Now, filled with shame, Virgilio was trying to persuade us that he was not like that at all. Instead, he made it very obvious to us that it was exactly that way.

Another group of friends who knew the Countess came over, giving her hugs and kisses in greeting. I noticed how Virgilio used the opportunity to look despitefully at Soraya, grab her by the arm and pull her away in a hurry from our group and the embarrassing situation there. I saw as they left out of the tail of my eye that she was protesting with him as they made their way to the lobby. Evidently, he was unhappy and continued to drag her out of the public eye, where he might be able to return to being a bully in private. I shook my head as I watched that abusive man get away with his prey.

Faviola noticed my demeanor that showed my disapproval of the unnecessary attitude of Virgilio. After a few minutes, she introduced me to her friends. The first bell rang, calling us to go inside and take our seats. A middle-aged couple approached Faviola. She introduced them to me as Dr. Jack Tirbol and his wife, Mola. He was a short man, nearly bald, in his late 50's. His woman was very beautiful and evidently much younger than he, with a beautiful Andalusian accent. They pleasantly invited us to lunch the next day at the Balboa Bay Club.

He mentioned that I had an extraordinary and great personality and intelligence, and he wanted to have the opportunity to get to know me a little better. The second bell rang. One more call, and they would turn the lobby lights off with the auditorium lights darkening shortly after.

We said goodbye to Dr. Tirbol and his wife and headed towards the area where our seats were located, Faviola told me that Dr. Tirbol had been her physician for many years. "He possesses a strange personality which sometimes is inappropriate, with abrupt reactions without any justification at all. He owns several medical clinics in the Costa Mesa Santa Ana area. He is honorable in his professional conduct towards me, but he's not very sociable, much different than his wife Lola. Sometimes, he reminds me of the Grinch. To be fair in my assessment to you, he's not a bad person. He has integrity and can be a good ally and friend in our clandestine fight."

We were passing in front of the bathroom as I assessed what she had just told me. I thought she described him quite well from my brief observation of him. The door to the women's bathroom suddenly opened, taking us by surprise. Virgilio, with an angry face, nodded abruptly to us without saying hello and walked right by us. It appeared he was leaving the theater. If our surprise was great at that moment, it grew more when we saw coming out of the same door Soraya. She was sobbing as she tried to cover her face with a small lady's handkerchief which failed to hide the black eye she now had. A small trickle of blood rolled from the edge of her bottom lip.

Faviola held me by the arm. "Don't get involved. This man is dangerous. That's all I can tell you. Please, give me my ticket. Find our seats and wait for me. Let me speak to her by myself."

She let go of my arm. Before she left, she added, "Trust me. I know the best way to handle this. This is not the first time I've seen this happen with them. This guy is not only a bully, but he's also a tyrant. He's been terrifying his poor girlfriend for a long time."

Faviola virtually ran behind Soraya. When she caught up with her, they stopped in the middle of the hallway and began to whisper in Soraya's ear. I stood there, watching what was going on. Soraya initially was refusing what was being said, but eventually Faviola managed to bring her back to the women's room, cleaning up the blood running down Soraya's chin.

I located the door on the ticket and went inside the theater. The attendant took my ticket with a big smile on his face. Using a small flashlight that projected a red beam and guided me through the dimly lit auditorium and used it to point to my seat. He kept the beam there until I sat down.

Shortly after the play had started, Faviola sat down next to me. She whispered in my ear, telling me everything I had already imagined indeed what was going on between the two. Virgilio was a clandestine federal contractor, but a little different than Faviola. He was the team leader in charge of making anyone he was assigned to disappear. He was a hitman, licensed to kill.

I murmured in her ear, "Nothing you say surprises me. I could see in his eyes the evil in his mind."

Faviola nodded. After the play finished, we left the theater, walking towards the Southcoast Plaza Mall. I was very unsettled in my spirit and mind. Faviola tried to find Soraya after the play, because she had arranged for us to take her home to her apartment since Soraya had said she didn't want to return with Virgilio. Faviola assumed that maybe Soraya, still ashamed before me, didn't want to face me with a black eye and fat lip and so at the last minute had decided to take a taxi to go home rather than wait for us and experience even more humiliation. According to what Soraya had shared with Faviola, she had already decided to leave Virgilio once and for all. That is what she had told Virgilio when they left us, because she was afraid to death of him, and the relationship would never work. Soraya said he had a tantrum and turned violent as if her words were the small wire that blew the fuse in Virgilio's mind. He had followed her to the women's room where he indiscriminately beat her up.

While we were waiting by the street for the pedestrian crossing light to allow us to cross Bristol Street, the women and men in charge of the janitorial staff at the theater tried to open one of the stalls in the women's room. When they finally opened it, one of the women screamed as she saw Soraya Papadopoulos, the beautiful Greek friend of Faviola, seated on one of the toilets decapitated, her hands holding her head in her lap in a demonstration of sadistic revenge. That scream was heard throughout the theater, and the executives ran to the horrific scene. At the same time, one of them called the Costa Mesa Police.

Back at the signal light, we were given the green signal to cross as the oncoming traffic stopped. As we stepped off the curb onto the street, a huge white cockatoo flew out of the dark night, hitting me squarely in the chest, its wings open and pushing me back. I landed on my rear on the concrete sidewalk. Its wings blocked most of my vision as it sat on my chest, but in some gaps, I could see a car blow through the red light, hitting Faviola only a few inches away from me. Faviola's body flew through the air, landing heavily on the pavement. The car didn't slow down or stop. I tried to push the bird away from me and levered myself up from the sidewalk with one hand. Another car ran the red light at the same speed, running over the Countess Faviola's body. This time, Chandee, who had recovered from her surprise, shot at the driver of the second car from the other side of the street, hitting him and causing him to lose control of the car. He ran squarely into one of the light poles.

My friend ran towards the car while I ran towards the convulsing body of the Countess. When I reached her and lifted her up from the pavement, she tried to speak, blood coming out of her mouth. She opened her eyes as I lifted her up. She stopped convulsing and looked me in the eyes, noticing the cockatoo that now rested on my right shoulder. She said, "What a beautiful angel you have on your shoulder. You'd better take care of him, because he saved your life." With a small grimace of pain, she tried to smile. "Please, if I have to go because it's my time, don't forget me. Never forget this beautiful romance that evidently died before it was born. Take care of yourself." I felt as if someone had punched me in the stomach, and I tried to control myself, so I didn't start weeping openly. She closed her eyes as if losing consciousness, so I shook her gently.

"No!" I pled with her. "Fight, please—don't give up. Do it for me."

Her eyes partly opened, but it seems to take all her strength to do even that. "Goodbye, sweet prince." Her eyes closed, and I repeated my pleas to her and shook her, but her hands let go of my arms and dropped limply by my side to rest next to her legs.

I checked her pulse and found none. I pulled her onto the sidewalk and began to administer CPR. She didn't respond. The cockatoo jumped onto her chest and began to nuzzle against her chin. The bird bobbed and closed its eyes. When I saw that, two tears escaped my control to roll down my cheeks. I gave her a tender kiss on the cheek. "Goodbye, my beautiful princess. Rest in peace."

The paramedics gently pushed me to one side and began resuscitation measures, lifting Faviola onto a gurney and gave her an intracardial injection, but she remained lifeless. Chopin came over to me and handed me a wallet with a badge inside. It was a CIA badge.

He asked, "Do you know this man?"

I looked at the ID. It belonged Virgilio Benzanillo. "Yes. I just met him inside the theater. He was supposedly a friend of the Countess."

"Well, no more. This is probably the last illicit game he'll play in his life. He's dead now. He fractured his skull on the wheel of his car. It's truly a pity, because we cannot interrogate him to find the truth behind all of this."

The paramedics had taken Faviola, but another pair of paramedics arrived to attend the dead body in the wrecked car. I looked around in confusion. I felt like things were off balance, a little dizzy. I watched them put Faviola's body in the ambulance. The cockatoo had returned to my shoulder. As they lifted the body up into the ambulance, he released an eerie cry as if he were in agony or mourning. I put my right hand up to protect my ear from that shrill, piercing cry. I must have scared the bird, which flew into the open doors of the ambulance where the paramedics were still working on Faviola with a defibrillator. I walked towards the ambulance, motivated by something deep inside me that something here wasn't right. I wanted to find out why the bird flew over into the vehicle.

As I got over there, I saw one of the paramedics trying again to shock her. There was still no reaction from her. Something strange happened then. Something like electrical power shot from my feet to my shoulders, and back down, right side to left side. It was very similar to the convulsions I had felt when I lifted her body from the pavement. I began to shake. I could not understand what had just happened—it was so quick. I also didn't know why the bird was there or where it came from.

To my surprise, I saw the bird was perched on one of the open doors, watching the paramedics work. Every time they shocked her with the paddles, the bird also reacted. I looked at the bird and then at the paramedics. The one holding the paddles looked at the other one shook his head sadly. The bird flew inside of the ambulance and landed on her chest, digging his claws as he landed. A few seconds later the bird flew back to my shoulder, and

Faviola sat up like the snake in a can prank. Both paramedics looked at her like they had seen a ghost. She looked at me and said, "Julio Antonio, are you OK?" Then she fell back onto the gurney. The paramedics immediately checked her pulse and reconnected her to the telemetry.

I said, "That's me—Dr. Julio Antonio del Marmol. What did you just give her?"

"A combination of Coramine and epinephrin."

"Take her clothes off. That will make her feel better. She has an undergarment that will maintain her body temperature."

One of them said, "Thank you, sir. Thank you very much."

"You're welcome. Where are you taking her?"

"Hoag Memorial Hospital, Newport beach," he answered.

"Thank you very much."

"What's her name?"

"Countess Faviola la Vita Dolce."

"Anything else you can tell us?"

"No."

"What happened?"

"She was hit by a car and then run over by a second."

The other paramedic exclaimed, "My God—it's a miracle! I thought we lost her. I don't know what that bird did, but you should take good care of it. I had lost all hope for your friend. Something inexplicable happened when that bird jumped on her chest that worked better than the defibrillator. You should breed that bird and consider training it as a paramedic."

I smiled. "Unsolved mysteries, my friends." I shook my head and caressed the back of the bird's neck with one finger. I smiled slightly. "The most logical conclusion is to call this miraculous, because this beautiful bird is not mine. I don't know where he came from. The only thing I can say for sure is that he didn't just save her life. He also saved mine."

I said goodbye to the paramedics and rejoined my friends. We walked to the Bentley, caressing the cockatoo the entire way. He appeared to like it as he purred like a cat. I said, "Wherever you came from, my friend, I give you my sincere thanks and a warm and lovely welcome."

Chandee handed me Faviola's purse. Chopin likewise gave me a travel bag he had taken from the assassin's car. It looked like a bunch of tools that sat in the front seat of the car, but the impact had thrown them onto the floor. He said, "I believe whatever is in this bag will give us a clue or evidence in case you don't know the origin of this hit man. You might use whatever he has in these tools to decipher this mystery and motive behind this well-planned attack. Evidently the first car executed the first hit and then he came behind to finish the target off to complete their mission in case the victim, in this case you and Faviola had not been killed by the first one."

I smiled. "It looks like our enemies don't know any of our defense methods because they abandoned divine energy that protects us. Let me tell you guys that the Countess is alive and on her way to Hoag Hospital. They'll probably put her in observation for a couple of days, for at least the next twenty-four to forty-eight hours to make sure she doesn't have any internal injuries. The most important thing was that she regained consciousness and recognized me, so there's no brain damage. I believe she'll be OK, and I'm fine, as you can see. Just a little sore butt from where I fell onto the sidewalk. That means our enemies failed again in their intent to eliminate one of us and in the process, they lost one of their own. This is a little too much. Based on the last information I received from the Countess as well as other reliable sources, this makes me change our plans completely immediately. We will all leave the country together. It's not just me that's in danger—I believe all of you guys are targets as well. We're all in imminent danger of losing our lives. For that reason, I've come to the conclusion that all of you need to pack your bags. We're out of here until I can decipher what's going on. Cancel all the operations we currently have in motion with the intelligence community. Tomorrow morning I'll have a meeting with O'Brien, and afterwards we'll meet in the lab at China Cove in Corona del Mar. I don't want to take any more chances or unnecessary risks and wait for another attack in our own homes."

I turned to Chopin. "Change every single oxygen tank and filters in the sub. Don't reuse any of them. My information is that they'll try to poison us with our oxygen supply, and I want one of you guys to stay in the sub on guard. Or you guys can take turns so someone is awake at all times and prepared for the worst. We have to be sure that tomorrow morning when we board that vessel we don't wind up in a deadly trap, giving them the opportunity of eliminating all of us in one stroke."

Chandee replied, "I can stay all night while Chopin does all the work."

Chopin said, "That is not necessary. I have to be there anyway. I have to make sure not only to replace those tanks and filters but to inspect the entire sub step by step to make sure everything is in order. We're going to have a long trip and I need to be certain that none of you blame me for being negligent. I'm very meticulous what I do." He saluted me. "I'll make sure you have a safe trip to La Guaira, Venezuela, my Captain."

Elizabeth said, "Excuse me guys, but I think it will be more prudent and safer, especially if your information is so reliable that all of us should stay tonight on the sub. Not only can we help Chopin, but we can watch each other's backs. When we get tired, we can take turns so that someone is fully alert the entire time until our departure. In case a new attack is planned or already in motion, they won't find any of us in our safehouses, which is where they probably expect to find us."

I nodded. "I believe that Elizabeth has the best idea. If you guys have no objection, let's proceed with her plan."

The others nodded with approving expressions. I said to Elizabeth, "Go to Brenton's house and let him know we're leaving tomorrow morning, so he should be aboard tonight. Don't do it over the phone. Be sure that he spends the night with you guys, for his security since I need him as the link with Abdul's family. By the way, Chopin, be absolutely sure to pack Abdul's head and hands in dry ice when you take them out of the freezer in the lab."

"Very well," he said. "Please, before you open any doors to this car, since Elizabeth had to abandon it, let me check the car out. I don't want to take any chances tonight."

"Go ahead," I said.

Chopin gave it a thorough bumper to bumper check, lifting the hood to check the engine—everything was clear. We said our goodbyes, and I put the bag of tools into the trunk. I got in and drove towards Hoag Hospital with only one thing in mind: be sure, before leaving the country, that not only the Countess Faviola was in good hands but also protected against any new attempt. I had developed a plan for that in my head. I left the cockatoo inside the car before entering the hospital.

I entered the lobby and asked for my friend, Dr. Martin. The young girl at the front desk informed me he had already left for the evening. I said, "Please page him. I have an emergency and I need to communicate with him immediately."

The girl already knew me very well, so she didn't hesitate to page him. She pleasantly asked me if I wanted to wait in the lobby or in the room where Countess Faviola was resting. She paged Dr. Martin even though it was two am. I let her know I would wait in the lobby.

A little while later she called me to the front desk, where she put me on the phone with Dr. Martin. His voice was drowsy and still half-asleep, but with his usual rich humor he asked, "What? You have new wounds from your *vida loca*? You only call me when I have to patch you up and you don't want anyone to know about it. What are you doing at the hospital at this late hour? Why didn't you come to my house?"

I smiled. He paused, so I finally had a chance to make a reply. "I'm sorry to bother you so early in the morning, but I need your help urgently. Please, get dressed and meet me at the hospital as soon as you can. This is life or death. I don't want to say any more over the phone. When you arrive here, I'll give you more details. Ask the front desk for the room for Countess Faviola la Vita Dolce."

"OK. I'll be there shortly."

"Thank you. I'll be waiting for you. Please—time is golden, and it could be vital to save the life of my friend, the Countess."

"Very well. You know I live a few blocks away; I'll be there in a few minutes. Let me talk to the front desk nurse on duty, please."

"OK." I handed the phone to the young woman. "Dr. Martin needs to speak to you."

After a brief conversation, the nurse hung up and called on the intercom. "Will the Chief Nurse come to the lobby?"

She arrived a few seconds later. She came over to me. "Dr. del Marmol?"

"Yes."

"Nice to meet you. Katerina Arnaud." She gave me a splendid smile. She had a clipboard with notes pertinent to the Countess' case. We walked into the hallway. "It looks like your friend will be OK. I don't think you need to worry too much. Definitely plenty of bruises and muscle pain. She's currently under sedation to minimize her muscle pain with muscle relaxers. We've conducted X-rays and no fractures. It looks like she has a concussion, which is why she initially lost consciousness. She probably will have a severe migraine until the swelling on her brain recedes. Thank God for that fantastic body armor—I've never seen anything like that before."

I smiled. "And you'll probably never see it again. It's a new technology, and it probably saved her life."

We arrived in Faviola's room. She showed me the suit draped across one of the chairs that plainly showed the mark of the tires on the chest. "It's unbelievable she's still alive. Unfortunately, she didn't have the same protection on her head, which is why she has the trauma there. By the same token, the tires didn't run over her head. If they had, I don't think she'd be alive now. The most important thing now is that she gets a lot of rest to allow the medication to release the tension in her brain and restore it to normal function. Let's pray that this trauma won't cause any degeneration or complications like a clot forming in the brain. Since she is under medication to prevent that, such an occurrence is unlikely." Katerina was in her mid-forties, very attractive, with a pleasant personality and an aristocratic look. She affectionately stroked Faviola's hair away from her eyes with her right hand. She smiled slightly. "What a pity for such a beautiful, young woman. We don't want to lose her. She's in the prime of her life."

At that moment, Dr. Martin walked into the room. He greeted us and I said, "I'm sorry again, my great friend and colleague to take you out of bed at this hour. What happened tonight was not an accident. It was an attempt on our lives." Katerina's eyes widened and she pulled her glasses down slightly. Dr. Martin knew my lifestyle and so was unsurprised. "I'm sorry to tell you that we cannot leave her in this room. We have to take her name out of admissions, as well. Unfortunately, she took the worst of the hit. I took the best, only a sore butt. My feelings are that whoever is behind this attempt might regroup and come back to finish the job."

Katerina shook her head in distress. "I'm sorry, Dr. del Marmol, but the Chief Surgeon gave strict orders to not move this patient under any circumstance. That could be fatal for her until her brain damage heals. She is in a very delicate condition."

I reached into the inside pocket of my tuxedo and pulled Faviola's ID badge out. I showed it to Katerina. "I'm showing you this in complete confidence. With all respect, Katerina, if we don't move her, she's as good as dead." I remained pleasant but firm. "This beautiful young woman is a clandestine agent for the CIA. If you don't want her to die tonight with a bullet ridden body, I suggest with tremendous courtesy to move her as soon as possible, not just to another room but another ward on a different floor to a place they cannot find her. At least until she can get on her feet and disappear on her own. These assassins are very professional and very well paid, probably by rogue agents in our government. My worst fear is the elements even as high as the White House are involved in this attempt. If we leave her here, she will not be alive in the morning. Of this, I am nearly completely certain, which is why I bothered Dr. Martin at this hour. He knows I'm not kidding. I don't do this unless it's absolutely necessary."

Martin said to me, "My friend, I know everything you say is 100% true. I know you very well and what you've been doing for many years. I've had to patch you up for bullet holes, broken bones, even plane crashes." His worry was plain in his face. "Are you absolutely certain this was an attempt on your lives and that these assassins would repeat what they failed to do?"

I shook my head in frustration. "To be completely honest and sincere with you, nothing in this life is absolutely certain. But I can tell you that 99 3/4% I'm sure of is that the same individual that decapitated the woman who was with him in the women's restroom at the Segerstrom Center for the Arts was one of the ones who tried to kill us. Maybe his target simply was me and the Countess just was an innocent victim. That individual lost his life in his attempt to kill us. My question to you is simple: if the people who sent these people to the extreme of killing us at Southcoast Plaza Mall, what else would their accomplices be willing to do? They want to finish what they started already. If we don't move her, bed and all, she has a greater chance of surviving than leaving her here to her luck while she cannot even defend herself in her sedated condition. I see the bed has wheels, so we can minimize the risk to her if we move her carefully."

Dr. Martin gulped. He looked me in the face, filled with concern. "The problem is if she loses her life in another room in another location in this hospital, the first thing the Chief Surgeon who worked on her will do is blame us for her death. Even if this is not the cause of death, unfortunately in order to watch his responsibility and clean his hands that is what we'll face."

"Well," I said with profound displeasure in my voice, "if you guys don't do this for me, at least do it for your colleagues."

Katerina asked, "I beg your pardon, Dr. del Marmol—can you please explain that?"

"It's very simple. If these assassins nearly killed the Countess in an attempt to kill me, which is a possibility, what would stop them from killing one of your nurses or doctors who happens at that moment to be in the room with her? Anything is possible. They don't want to be discovered or exposed, much less apprehended." I saw Katerina's face change as she thought about that seriously. It pained and worried her simultaneously as she rubbed the top of her right hand nervously. She wiped her brow with the back of her hand for a few seconds. Then she sighed helplessly.

After she digested what I had said, she said to Dr. Martin, "Well, if you'll allow me to suggest a possibility—as Chief Nurse I can authorize moving a patient, going over the medical orders; regulations specifically state that I can do that only when the room is not secure or could incur any abnormality that puts the patient at risk as well as the personnel attending the patient."

Dr. Martin looked at her in surprise. "For example?"

She took a small washcloth and folded it up. She went over to the room's stainless-steel sink and put it over the drain. With a mischievous smile, she opened the faucet all the way. She said, "For instance, the room could be overflowing with water by accident."

Dr. Martin said, "Hm. Of course, by accident. Someone must have forgotten in the commotion the room, ward, or floor where they took the patient. Only her doctor will have this information in the clinical report for his daily visits." He smiled. "Of course, this is one of the sections in the rules when the Chief Nurse has the authority to override any previous orders by any doctor in order to protect the security of the patient and the staff."

Katerina began to disconnect the bed from the various connections to the wall. She picked up a phone and called the nurse's station to inform them that she had disconnected telemetry because the patient needed to be moved due to a sink leak in the room. The sink was already overflowing, and water began to run across the room. She said, "I'll need the help of both of you until we get to the floor and I've gotten the Countess reconnected. Then you can go, and I'll let Dr. Martin know the room number and everything else as to where I've moved her. I don't think she'll be here more than forty-eight hours unless a complication arises."

Dr. Martin said, "I want you, when that happens, to bring her directly to my house or page me and I'll come here and pick her up."

I said to him, "Thank you. I really appreciate this."

"Don't mention it. I'm not going to say no to one of those large bottles of Grand Marnier you bring me every now and then. I'm running out."

"For this, my friend, you'll get a case."

"No, not that much. I'll become an alcoholic if you bring me that much!"

I bent over and gave the Countess a tender kiss on her cheek. I said to Katerina, "Thank you very much."

She gave me a kiss on my cheek. "You're a good man. If I ever have any problem, I want to have you by my side."

"Let's hope you never do, but if you have a problem, don't hesitate to give me a call." I handed her one of my cards.

"Oh!" Dr. Martin exclaimed. "He must really like you because he doesn't give just anyone a card! He's the ghost of Newport Beach."

"Of Newport Beach?" I asked. "Of the globe!"

We had been talking as we wheeled the bed into one of the cargo elevators. We took Faviola to the new place Katerina had selected and reconnected all her telemetry devices. Katerina said to me, "I know you would do this even if it were a member of my family."

I replied, "You can bet your life on that." We smiled at each other as we said goodbye and left the room.

Dr. Martin and I got into the regular elevator and headed to the lobby. I gave him my most sincere thanks for everything and asked, "What do you think made Katerina change her mind so rapidly at the end of our conversation after so long showing herself so strict and reluctant to break protocol or override the orders of the Chief Surgeon?"

Dr. Martin smiled mischievously. "Please don't pretend you don't know." He pointed at me and said, "You. You are the one who convinced her when you said that if we didn't do it for the Countess, we should do it for our colleagues. She realized that it would be true, but what you didn't even know that this happened before. Someone attempted to kill a patient here in the hospital; two nurses and one doctor who were attending that patient died." He grinned. "You put the finger in the wound."

I looked at him innocently. "I don't understand what you're saying and can't explain it. What are you referring to, a finger in the wound?"

We got out of the elevator, and he said, "Katerina has four beautiful daughters. All four work on the night shift. Two of them are doctors and the younger two are nurses, going to the university now to become doctors themselves. She obviously thought her daughters could easily be the next victims of those assassins. Without knowing it, you put the finger in the wound. Or you actually *did* know, and now you're pretending to me." He looked at me curiously. "Did you know that she had four daughters working here?"

I smiled and put on another innocent expression. I shrugged ambiguously, neither confirming nor denying his assertion. I asked instead, "Did you by any chance at the moment we spoke on the phone have them in mind?"

"Of course! That's why I told you to let me speak with the receptionist and pass my instructions on to Katerina. I was thinking that she and her daughters could be great allies in giving preferential treatment to your friend the Countess." He suddenly straightened and said with conviction, "Ah ha! I know what you're capable of doing. I've seen you do unbelievable things with your mind, but I never imagined you could read me through a telephone line." He shook a finger at me. "I know you read me during that conversation—that's why you knew all the details about Katerina's family. Please, for my own satisfaction, don't deny it to me. Am I right? Come on—I know you don't like to talk about the extraordinary gifts you possess, but maybe you'll make an exception this time. If you can do this over a telephone, that is amazing! It will be a great satisfaction for me to know my assumptions are correct."

I smiled. "Remember, 99% of the time when you assume you're wrong." We were walking out of the lobby of the hospital. I put on my innocent face again. "I don't know what you're talking about: reading minds and stuff is too complicated for me."

He looked at me unhappily and with a great deal of doubt. "OK, if you don't want to tell me, that's fine. You're going to leave someone you say is a great friend with that thorn in his foot." I shrugged and limited myself to smile at him again.

We approached the Bentley. I opened the doors, and the cockatoo flew out of the car and disappeared into the darkness of the night. "What was that?" Dr. Martin asked. To distract him, I started the engine with the remote. "Wow!" he said. "You can do that? That's a beautiful convertible. Is that a new acquisition to your collection?" He spoke in sincere admiration as he looked it over.

"No, it's not mine. It belongs to the Countess. Considering you are the best doctor around me, I decided you were also the only one who could offer me the protection I need for her until I return from my trip. I know you're a very brave and dignified man. You've proven that to me over the past several years. When I saw the delicate circumstances around her, the first person I thought of was you. It's until I return from Venezuela. I expect it to be a very quick trip. I have to close the circle I left open behind me from my last mission to that South American country. If this trip doesn't present any unexpected complications, I will be back very soon."

"In your line of work the unexpected is a frequent occurrence." he observed. "Thank you very much for your vote of confidence and trust in me. I hope I will never disappoint you. Take all the time you need, don't rush to close that circle you left unfinished. This could have very dangerous consequences. I know by now that you never leave anything on your plate unless it's absolutely necessary."

I smiled. "I believe you know me by now a little bit."

"Not enough, but I'm working on it. Every time we get together."

I smiled and put my hand on his right shoulder. "Thank you once more very much for what you're doing for me right now. For your satisfaction—don't repeat this to anyone at all, because it will lose its real value, which is the element of surprise—you are right. I received that information very clearly by telepathic means during our phone conversation."

"*I knew it!*" he exclaimed.

"You're concerned about all these women all the same time. It's in your mind when we spoke."

He laughed loudly. "I knew it! I knew it!! I could feel you in my mind, that's how I knew!"

I got into the Bentley and put my finger to my lips and made a zipper motion over them. He returned the same signal with an expression of satisfied gratification. He raised his arm to say goodbye. I returned his farewell and left the parking for the Hoag ER and headed out on the Pacific Coast Highway towards the Balboa Bay Club. I needed to retrieve a copy of the film of Mike Thompson's Satanic cult that included a young President Obama. As Faviola had noted, I had several copies deposited in several key places. One of them was in a secret place on my yacht.

Most of the banks weren't open yet, obviously, and I didn't want to create suspicion by having a bank open its doors for me well before they would be open. I took my copy for my early morning meeting with O'Brien.

CHAPTER 17: THE GREAT BASTARD

I arrived at the Balboa Bay Club, leaving my car with the attendants and instructing them to leave the car there because I would not be long. But I wanted them to keep their eyes on it until I returned. All the attendants had known me for years and that I would recompense them generously, so they always did as I asked. I retrieved my package and left the club, heading towards my safehouse on the border of Santa Ana and Fountain Valley, an equestrian property at 4222 West Regent Drive. That property was far away from our center of operations, and I hadn't used it for a long time. It was where I was planning to rest for the few hours left in the night that in such a short time had come to be of an advanced age, almost at the end of its life.

I took a quiet, restful nap and got up. I took the Bentley towards my office at D'Marmol Communications International in Red Hills where I was to meet with O'Brien. I arrived and sat down at my desk, starting to write my seventh letter to President Obama, in which I scolded him for his lack of courtesy for not responding to my previous letters in which I had offered him the courtesy of my assistance to help him keep our enemies at bay. I also advised him against the liberal policies which he continually lost in court or giving our enemies the ability to destroy this country, which would lead to the destruction of the rest of the world. Even though he had not replied to my previous six letters, his actions made it very clear to me why he had not replied. Once I finished the letter, I folded it and put it in an envelope. I inscribed the envelope "For the Eyes of the President Only." I made a copy, sealed it, and put it in my desk.

949-283-4648
www.spymasterspy.com

April 16, 2015

President Barack H. Obama
The White House
1600 Pennsylvania Ave. NW
Washington, DC 20500

Dear Mr. President,

Until now, I've been trying to excuse you to my friends and associates and blame your indecision on your youth and political inexperience. In my last six letters, which you had neither dignity nor decency to acknowledge receipt of, I have been respectful in addressing the mistakes from the point of view of my political experience you were making and the inexperience in the team of advisers you've surrounded yourself with. Of course, my basic assumption was that you had the best interests in mind to defend this country from her enemies, both domestic and foreign, as per your oath of office, sworn before God with your hand over the Bible; something you apparently don't value at all. I attempted to advise you, even though I mentioned in my first letter that my friends and associates considered you to be a blatant Marxist with a hidden agenda, and now I have to admit with sorrow that I was wrong to give you the benefit of the doubt. They told me it was not due to your advisers that these mistakes were made, but that they came directly from you because of your narcissism. Your agenda shows me clearly now that, given the opportunity, you would become the worst dictator humanity ever has had with the lowest intentions of destroying this country and her institutions, free society, and if not parallel with Putin's Russia—because you don't accept any criticism or competition—then bringing down Putin's dream of controlling the world by building yourself into the supreme Marxist in the world.

It is not difficult for me to understand now. I've seen men convert themselves into dictators with dreams of controlling the world before once they have a taste of power in their mouths, corrupting their minds to the point of destroying their own people in order to maintain that power. I know your past environment growing up was not exactly rosy; you weren't fortunate as I was to have the bonding and family structure in a great, warm, loving household in which you not only had the love of your mother but also your father as a role model who tried to teach you the very best ways he knew. Even though I had my own conflicts with my father because I didn't follow his ideology, you have the opposite in that, even though he wasn't around, you embraced his ideas and his frustration of not being able to fulfill his dreams. Evidently that frustration was passed on to you, and you have assimilated it very well. I see with no doubts any longer that you have been psychologically damaged from that environment, and are not looking out for the best interest of this country and the established institutions of a democratic republic, instead placing your own interests, your ego, and your legacy-building ahead of these, even before your own family's well-being, without calculating the damage your actions will do to future generations.

I almost fell out of my chair yesterday when I saw your statement on television, deceiving the American people once more, pretending that, because the Cuban regime hasn't supported terrorism for

I

the last six months, they should now be exonerated from the list of terrorist nations they've been on for the last thirty-three years. Your deceitful statement was that Cuba does not constitute a threat to the United States in any way. Mr. President, who do you think you're kidding? Do you think the American people and the rest of the world are idiots, and that you're the only smart man around, when not even a year ago we caught Cuba red-handed in Panama, smuggling nuclear weapons to North Korea? The president of Panama raised a scandal in the United Nations, exposing this most vital violation of non-proliferation agreements that Cuba has been involved in for over fifty years now. I don't think you are an expert in intelligence or this kind of material, Mr. President. I happen to know from sources close to you that you don't even read the intelligence briefing the intelligence community puts on your desk every day. I would like to know how you came to this conclusion? I will give you a comparable example: we have a child molester rapist, and murderer that has been committing these crimes for over fifty years. However, because for the last six months he behaved well under the restrictions you've placed on him, you want to release him into general society, in spite of the fact that there is abundant proof that he has tried to deceive the authorities repeatedly every where he goes. And you want to free him and let him become the director of an elementary school? Would you, Mr. President, send your daughters to such a school under this man's supervision? You need not answer; I already know the answer, if you have a little love and care for your daughters. How could you then expect other fathers and mothers to send their children to that institution and trust that immoral, deceitful criminal?

I ask myself if your humongous ego is more powerful than your common sense or intelligence than any other human being has. If you examine the past, the present, and the likely future, it will show you that Cuba is the absolute worst enemy we have anywhere in the world. Sit down with someone in the intelligence community that has knowledge of this, and you will learn of the barbarisms that Cuba has committed around the globe, every time allied with our enemies in various regions—as they most lately did with Iran, another beast you wish to unleash. God help us and the rest of the free world!

But I tried to excuse you, Mr. President, in the last few months, blaming your outrageous, illogical decisions to be against our friends and extending the hand of friendship to our enemies. I asked my friends and associates how much damage you could do, since you only have less than two years. Their answer has been, "Dr. del Marmol, that is plenty of time. He could do a lot more damage in this short period, because he no longer cares. He doesn't have to show a smiling face to the public and promise to them hope and change. The cat is already out of the bag, and 90% of the people who supported him and voted for him, even in his own Democrat party, feel betrayed by his extreme and irrational ideas." One day, you will be judged not just by men, but also by God, as a direct consequence of the actions you have been taking. I hope this doesn't affect the legacy you are so concerned about.

I want to make clear in this letter that this will be my last one to you. I hereby withdraw every single offer I made to you, to advise you, to support you, whatever is needed to help you succeed in your Presidency. The only thing I leave open is my friendship, which I offer to anyone save for those who act aggressively against me or my family, as your new friends, Fidel and Raul Castro did when they killed my son and attempted to destroy all of my family. As of today, I disassociate myself from you and your Administration, because I don't want to give you any more excuses for something that is so blatantly obvious as you have been doing every day, even occasionally contradicting yourself based on previous promises. I am firmly convinced by your recent actions towards Israel, Iran, and Cuba that you are the closest false prophet after Castro I have ever seen come to this Earth as you hide your lies, deception, and agenda to the American people and the rest of the world behind your smile. You will be condemned by history after your Presidency ends, and even your extremist friends will want to disassociate themselves and run far away from you, because in this world there is room for only one big ego who wants to control the world. I have this vision that you are not going to be the one. I hereby cease and desist any advice to you, and wash my hands of the filth which your outrageous decisions will create with a terrible toll for the future of humanity. I pray that God will have mercy on your soul.

Most Respectfully Yours,

Dr. J. Anthony del Marmol, PhD
International Intelligence Adviser

Figure 48 My 7th letter to Obama

It was 5:45 am. No one had yet arrived for work, which was not surprising. I had my employees keep eleven am to nine pm schedules. I did this in all my businesses to think of my employees and motivate them to do their best. Instead of working eight hours five days a week, they worked ten hours four days a week, giving them three days off each weekend. This gave them a great deal of joy working for me and my associates. Since they didn't have to show up to work until eleven am, they had no traffic coming into work or at nine pm when they left work. They had all morning to run errands, banking transactions, doctor's appointments, etc. These hours helped them avoid all the hassle and stress of juggling work with personal needs. Our people always complimented us on how we conducted our business and encouraged employee loyalty with maximum productivity. My businesses also always had a Thursday afternoon buffet lunch for everyone in the company for free. It was usually a seafood buffet with French pastries. Never had any of my employees seen previous employers offer such rewards. It made me feel proud to be able to offer such compensation to those who made my businesses successful.

I finished opening the mail that had been left on my desk by my secretary. I heard the door buzzer sound and saw O'Brien waiting outside on the exterior cameras. I buzzed him inside. We greeted each other and embraced cordially. He said, "I've been outside there for half an hour because I didn't see any of your cars. I thought you weren't here yet. But knowing you're never late barring an emergency, I figured that beautiful Bentley is your new toy, so I came up and rang the bell. It looks like I wasn't wrong. Since you're the only one here, it must be yours." His satisfied smile disappeared when I replied.

"Yes and no. You're wrong, because it's not my car. But yes, because I'm driving the car. You cannot add it to my collection. It belongs to the beautiful Countess Faviola la Vita Dolce. By the way, I don't know if you are aware, but she works for you guys in the CIA, unless her badge and ID she showed me are perfect forgeries. I had very good opportunities to observe them in detail while she was getting undressed after we showered in her residence following a long jacuzzi bath."

O'Brien raised his thick Irish eyebrows in surprise. Then he grew worried. "Be careful with the opposite sex. Remember what I've told you a million times, and I believe your Uncle Emilio told you *five* million times, that 98% of deaths in our business are caused by the opposite sex. Not from lack of training, but maybe through an excess of confidence which neutralizes the agent when he lowers his guard before that member of the opposite sex as he tries to impress, in this case, a woman, and ends up killed."

I shook my head. "You don't have to tell me that. I know it perfectly well. You haven't told me a million times, probably more than my uncle: *ten* million times. But none of that is important right now. Don't forget that I had experience with it myself with Lauren. A very painful, truthful, bitter experience. This doesn't mean that from now on, because of that bitter experience, I won't believe in anyone ever without giving the other person the opportunity to demonstrate to me whether I can trust her or not. Of course, I exercise extreme caution and take all precautions necessary. We have to continue forward in life because life is pregnant with bad experiences and painful deceptions; but it is also filled with beautiful illusions, great friendships such as yours and mine, and also happiness, peace, and harmony. If you and I stop believing in people because of a bitter experience, life will pass before our eyes and we will, because of the fear of deception and betrayal, never be capable of discovering that sweet and great friendship and love. We will allow the great opportunities to escape and fail to enjoy the most fruitful friendships and joy of discovering loyalty and happiness that brings to our lives the colorful flavors we should never miss."

O'Brien nodded doubtfully. "I admire you because, after all you've gone through in your life, it is very difficult to understand where you get all this optimism."

I smiled broadly. "If you think that it's difficult for me to believe in anyone now, just wait until our conversation is finished and I let you know who is behind all the attempts not just on my life but all the other agents in intelligence. You'll wonder how I'm able to continue to look at life the way I do and with the optimism that I see things. These traitors come to us with friendly faces."

Later, after I let him know everything that had gone on with the Countess, what I had discovered, save for those things the Countess specifically told me to not repeat even to him. O'Brien was struck mute from his shock for a while as he digested all I had conveyed to him. He recovered after a while, shaking his head all the while as he rubbed his fingers along his forehead. He grew enraged and tried to control himself before speaking. "These damned politicians profess love for the USA, but in reality, they're destroying the nation from within! And not just her deepest roots of culture—like good Marxists, they want to establish a social environment filled with hatred and racism, class warfare, and the abolition of religion just to keep themselves in power as totalitarian extremists. At the same time, they make people reluctant to express their views publicly out of fear of censorship, ridicule, or of being destroyed. Their final action would be to strangle all opposition to what they really want to impose on the American people: Marxist communism!"

I observed his rage, understanding perfectly how he felt. I could see his empurpled face that was the exterior symptom of his rage. I handed him a copy of my letter to Obama and a disc which contained the evidence. "I believe, when you finish reading this letter, that I will put a smile on your face. Even though I'm going to mail this to him, my plan is for you to put both this letter and the disc on his desk. We will call this Operation Shock and Awe. We will use their same weapons of coercion, but without violence and with great intelligence. We will be able to intimidate them with this plan to the point of putting them on their knees in absolute fear. You will communicate and show the evidence that we possess in that disc to the highest leaders of your institution, the CIA. If this nonsense doesn't stop, we will expose this publicly. These attempts on our lives should cease immediately or else. Not just to me, but also my team. I will take my team in a few hours out of the country. I want to finish the circle with Abdul the decapitated terrorist, return his head and hands to his wife Hania. To my knowledge she is a Christian, and I believe every human being deserves a Christian burial, especially for the father of her sons. Besides that, this is the promise I made to Abdul when we made a deal before he died. I want to fulfill that so I can sleep at night in the future as well as I do now. Also, I promised him to deliver a certain amount of money to his wife for the support of his family. You already know the story. I want to clarify to you that I will use this opportunity to take my team out of circulation, giving you enough time to execute these plans. I will communicate with you in a few days or a week, and you will let me know if it's safe for us to come back and that you were capable of stopping this nasty game by this new President. If you cannot be able to neutralize this situation, I will use my own resources and put this before the eyes of every single man and woman in the world. Until you give me the green light, I will not come back into the country or expose any of my friends to threats against their lives for no other purpose than for a corrupt, ignorant politician who just wants to be re-elected as President. It doesn't matter which political party he represents. Democracy is being put in danger when individual politicians without scruples use her name to defraud, intimidate, or terrify their own people."

O'Brien looked at me and said, "That's dignified enough to put on a plaque and nailed to the entry to the White House."

I smiled. "I don't believe this will give much joy to this Administration. Without losing my optimism, maybe it will be the greatest thing for the Administration that succeeds them. Of course, this is if we manage to reach the next Administration alive to be able to read that plaque."

He said, "Only God is capable of turning off the Lightning. I don't believe that this one or any other

President will be capable of doing what Castro and his Marxist accomplices around the world have failed miserably to do in fifty-six attempts."

"Well, what I think you're forgetting is that I have behind my back His Son guarding me for so many years every single minute of the day and night. I don't have the slightest doubt of that."

O'Brien grinned broadly. "I don't either. Why do you think whenever I have the smallest opportunity I come and sit down with you for a little while? It's not just because of the extraordinary amount of information you've produced for me all these years and brought me so many promotions throughout my career in intelligence. I have to thank you for that from the bottom of my heart. You are also my fount of optimism in the most depressing moments like right now. You always have the antidote for that venom. That's why I'm convinced that you are absolutely right: it has to be Jesus Christ behind you. If He's not at your back, I'm positive that He's in your spirit. How otherwise could you shake off that seventy-five years and six months of going to jail when everyone, including me, had abandoned you in panic? That will be my worst regret until I die: letting my superiors send me far away from you so I could not move any fingers to at least give you moral support. On top of that, allowing the Secret Service to torture, mistreat you, lock you up incommunicado in that small cell in San Pedro, far away from your family and friends, and interrogating you for weeks like you're the worst criminal they had ever seen. In all that, you never opened your mouth to say a single word to jeopardize a single one of us." He raised his right arm high and pointed at me. "You gave us, including President Reagan, a lesson I don't think any of us will be able to forget, a moral lesson of integrity. That can only come from men like you who have received directly from a Man like Jesus Christ. He never denied once of being the Son of God. He took on Himself torture to death, maintaining his principles, morals, and values with the last breath of His life and preserving His integrity intact to serve as an example to every man of noble spirit and good heart all over the world for thousands of years ahead."

"Thank you for your great support and words of encouragement. You don't have to be ashamed of what you yourself cannot control. It was not in your hand to save me or anyone else. I understood what you could and could not do. It was above your paygrade. Just like now what's going on with Obama, no matter how badly you feel about what he's doing, you cannot control it. I have to thank you again for comparing me to the only Man on this Earth I have admired all my life. I can guarantee you that, even though I went through perhaps the most bitter, black moments in my life due to that ordeal during the Zipper Operation, I'm very far away from even the minimum pain that Jesus Christ suffered and the humiliation He was a victim of. It's something I don't think any other human being should have suffered anywhere on Earth." I smiled. "That suffering I went through I can guarantee you I would never wish on anyone only made me stronger in my spirit. Now that you have knowledge of all I've shared with you and have in your hands the evidence, I believe you'll be able to put in motion a great psychological work with this corrupt and ambitious politician who is capable of destroying this country. Do the best effort you possibly can with your resources to neutralize them and make possible our success. I will be in communication with you and will keep you informed of our progress in Venezuela."

We stood up and exchanged big hugs and said our goodbyes. He said, "Don't tell anyone where you're going."

I made several phone calls to organize my departure and to communicate with my friends I was nearly finished. I left my office and drove the Bentley along the Pacific Coast Highway heading towards Newport Beach. I stopped in at the French bakery, Pandor, to purchase several pastries to take on our trip. I left the Westcliff Mall towards Coto de Caza; I wanted to leave Faviola's car at her house and get my Jaguar. As I drove out of the mall, I saw a Mercedes

Benz with four men inside following me from the mall. It was strange to me because it was too obvious. They were following too closely to me, which was very unprofessional. A few blocks later, they changed from completely obvious to ultra-professional as they disappeared from my rear view like a magic act. It occurred to me that there could be multiple cars involved as my assailants could use government agencies that had the power to utilize multiple cars to throw their targets off.

I kept my guard up and continued checking the rearview mirrors constantly. I didn't see any other car that was suspicious behind me, much less the Mercedes. I drove through the guard shack of the development, punched the gate code, and parked the car on the extreme left side of the drive like she usually did. I took my personal things out of the Bentley and put them in the Jaguar. I was about to walk to the residence when Alberto left the house with a rifle sporting a telescopic site in his hands. He was very concerned as he looked everywhere. He signaled to me with his right hand to come inside.

He looked terrified and like he was expecting trouble. As I grew close, he said, "Don't stop. We're in danger here. Let's go in."

I followed him inside, and he closed the door and double locked it to make sure. His face was full of uncertainty and fear as he put the rifle against the wall. He said, "Two agents from the Secret Service visited me early this morning, about four-thirty am. It was an extremely strange hour. They told me that Faviola had been killed."

I looked at him in surprise. "Where?"

"She was killed by an assassin on Bristol Street right across the street from Southcoast Plaza." I breathed a deep sigh of relief. "But they cannot locate her body. It appears that they took her to Hoag Hospital in Newport Beach. They checked the hospital and it appeared that her body has disappeared. The paramedics said they took her there, but there are no records of her ever being admitted there. Both agents asked me if I received any information about here to contact them so that they could locate her body."

He pulled a business card out of his pocket and handed it to me.

I took it and looked at it for a few seconds. I shook my head discontentedly. "John Benzanillo, Special Agent, Secret Service. This individual must be related because his last name is the same as the individual who decapitated his girlfriend in the Segerstrom. This cannot be a coincidence. Can you describe them to me?" After Alberto described the supposed Secret Service agents, my memory recalled one of the men he described as the one in charge as one of David Walker's most trusted men for Superstar Geronimo. God only knows how many innocent lives were on his list of victims that he had executed in his ambitious rise to power, obeying those corrupt politicians who employed him, using his position within the government inside the Secret Service as a strong arm to repress any opposition to their extreme ideological ideas. At the same time this man had been paid by the taxpayers who were ignorant of all his criminal activities.

Alberto was very worried. "I have everything prepared to get out of the country. Those are the instructions the Countess gave me before in case something like this happens. I am responsible and in charge of protecting her only six-year-old son. I have him upstairs in his room. I already picked him up from the private school little William attends. We call him Willy. The Countess gave me precise instructions to remove him out of the country if something happens to her or anything like what's going on right now."

I took Alberto by the arm. "You don't have to worry about it. She's not dead, but don't repeat that to anyone.."

He placed his left hand to his chest. "Thank God! I have to proceed with my orders to take her son to her family in Palermo, since he'll be in danger of being killed." He spoke with a voice and face filled with profound sadness and despair.

I put one of my arms around his shoulders. I said affectionately, "I don't want you to worry at all about the Countess. I shouldn't tell you this, so please don't disappoint me, but she's alive and I made sure she was left in a secure place. She's wounded, but alive and well. She should recover very soon; I can assure you of that."

Alberto's eyes opened wide in astonishment. "Where is the Countess? Is she OK? Is she fine?"

"Yes. Like I told you before, she needs perhaps a few days or a week to recover fully. She has a small concussion, but she'll be OK. Between us, she'll be back with us very soon. With all my respect, for both your security as well as hers, no one should know this. That way, even if somebody kidnaps and tortures you, there is nothing you can reveal because you do not know it. That's the way we work. All you must worry about now is the little boy, Willy. I think that's more than enough to keep your hands full—it's a very great responsibility. You should dedicate all your attention to that and follow the instructions she left you. Take him with you out of the country where he will be much safer with his grandparents in Palermo. As you said before, he is in danger of being assassinated. This will be a terrible news for the Countess, especially in her present condition. Imagine if, when she recovers, she discovers that she's lost her only son."

Alberto crossed himself. "God forbid!" he exclaimed with a horrified expression. "God protect both of us, especially that innocent little boy, from anything horrible happening to us." He took me by my arm. "Please, follow me. Let's go to his room. I picked him up from the boarding school a few hours ago. I want to take you to his room so you can meet him and get to know him for a bit."

We climbed the marble stairs with a black and white carpet edged in gold covering the center of the stairs. We got to the second floor and walked to his room. As we opened the door, I saw a little boy with red hair, a few freckles on his face, about six years of age. His height was much greater than I expected, perhaps that of a ten-year-old boy. He left the electric train he was playing with in the middle of the room with a smile on his face. He ran to me yelling, "Daddy! I saw you in my dreams and knew you were coming to see me today!" He grabbed me around the legs and hugged me fiercely.

That was an emotional shock to me. The sincere affection he was displaying towards me gave me an electrical thrill up my spine to the back of my neck. The hairs on my neck raised up. This emotional encounter caused me to tremble a little as the memory of my own son, Julio Antonio del Marmol Junior, at that age flooded my memory. Julito had been murdered by Castro's henchmen in retaliation for the damage I had been causing them. My emotional state took me back to Julito's infancy and the beautiful times I had with him and my lovely, devoted wife. I left that dark day in October of 1971 after the bitter news that my cover had been blown reached me and I was forced to leave the country immediately. I had felt the resentment towards the intelligence community for quite some time afterwards. My eyes grew moist at the gesture of love. I automatically raised my arm and put my hand on his head to caress his hair.

My voice thick with emotion, I said, "I know. I knew, little Willy, that we would meet today, you and me. I saw that very clearly in the eyes of a white bird that crashed into my chest only hours ago. Now that you tell me about your dream, I believe that it was not a dream—it was a revelation that you and I would meet today."

His face lit up like a light bulb as he listened to me. Joyfully, he stepped back a little and looked up into my eyes. "Really? Then you already knew that we would meet today? Exactly as my Mommy told me so many times, that you would come one day to stay with us for all our lives."

I smiled as I looked down at him. "Yes, but now for a few days you have to go with Alberto to Palermo, where you will be stay for a while with your grandparents. Your Mommy and I will reunite with you later."

He looked discontented at that for a brief moment. Alberto helped me by saying, "Come on, come on—you have to hurry up and get whatever you want to bring. We don't have any time to waste."

"OK," he replied. He turned back towards me and asked, "What is your name? My Mommy told me many times that it is a very high secret, because you are very important, and she didn't want anyone to know your name or who you really are. Now that I'm meeting you, you can tell me personally."

That put me in a spot. "Well," I said, glancing at Alberto.

He took Alberto by the hand. "Could you come with me for a moment, please? This is a secret." He took Alberto over to the bathroom. Alberto shrugged and walked inside to be locked in, understanding that neither of us wanted to hurt the boy's feelings. "It will only be for a few seconds."

"OK, but hold on, I have something the Countess told me to give him." He reached under the mattress, raising the corner, and pulled a manilla envelope. He handed it to me, and I saw it was sealed and stamped, ready to be mailed. "The Countess told me before leaving with you to the theater to give you this only in a case of extreme emergency like now. I was to put this envelope in the mail immediately to you."

I looked at the envelope in my hand. It was indeed addressed to me. Curiously, I noticed that the address on the envelope was one of my safehouses out of the area. It was obvious that this letter must be sufficiently important for her to take the time and precautions so that it didn't end up in the wrong hands.

Alberto tried to rush Willy to finish packing only the most necessary things, but Willy was not to be distracted and took him over to the bathroom, locking the door behind him. I said to satisfy Willy's curiosity, "My name is Dr. Julio Antonio del Marmol, but my intimate friends call me Dr. JAM. It's a lot shorter and easier to remember."

Willy smiled and nodded with a believing smile on his lips. "I like your name as well as what your friends and intimates call you. From now on I'll call you the same, OK?"

"Very well. Now let Alberto out of the bathroom and let's do what we need to do to keep packing."

After he released Alberto. I sat on the bed to open the mysterious envelope that Faviola had left for me. I wondered what she had put in there that she had not had the courage to relate to me in person after spending so many hours together. I decided it must be something extremely urgent, or something she wanted to confess to me that she didn't have the courage to tell me before. As I read, she explained that, as she had entrusted me before about her relationship with President Bill Clinton, she went on to tell me that her young son, Willy was the fruit of that relationship. To protect Willy, she never revealed his existence even to his father out of fear of Hillary. She knew what the First Lady had done to other people and feared that she would try to hurt Willy. The only people that knew this embarrassing secret were her mother and father in Palermo and her butler Alberto, who also was a witness to the whole tumultuous romance that she had ended for the reasons she had explained previously. Her parents possessed the DNA and other paternity documents that proved that Willy was Bill Clinton's son. At the end of the letter, she said that if anything happened to her or her son, whether a seemingly accidental or strange death, to put all the documentation before the public eye. She knew this would hold the Clintons accountable.

After finishing the letter, I folded it and carefully put it inside my coat. Alberto looked at me with curiosity in his face. Thinking it might be bad news, he asked, "Anything bad I need to know?"

"No. The truth is," I continued to try to satisfy his evident curiosity, "it's nothing you don't already know."

He turned and saw that I was about to leave the room. He said to Willy, "Finish closing that suitcase. I'm going to walk him to his car. I'll be back in a minute. Hurry up, OK?"

I said goodbye to Willy, who affectionately ran towards me to say goodbye. Alberto closed the door behind us.

We walked downstairs, and he asked, "Dr. del Marmol, you're sure Countess Faviola is in good hands and in a secure place?"

I smiled. "Alberto, if there's anything I can say I'm completely sure of, it is that. If it were any different, I would not let her be left behind, even at risk of my life, I would postpone my trip. even though it's of extreme importance and urgency, for all of us, including her."

Alberto smiled, a little more relaxed. "I know you're not only a gentleman but a man of honor. I took my time last night to make inquiries about you and to research your past. Every report I got on you was extremely favorable. Also unbelievable at how you have been able to survive so many attempts on your life."

I smiled and pointed up towards the cathedral ceiling over the stairs. "Not only the Supreme Architect but also His Son has guarded my back all my life. I believe strongly that as long as He finds it necessary, He'll keep me down here. I'll accept that and continue doing His work for as long as He needs me against the dark powers of this world."

Alberto crossed himself with his thumb. "Amen."

Those were his last words as two shots came through the window by the stairs, sending shards of glass everywhere. One bullet went through Alberto's temple, the other into his chest. He rolled down the stairs before my surprised eyes. I glanced out the window and saw it looked out over the driveway. The only thing I could do was to bend over in time to avoid two new shots, which whizzed over my head to hit the bronze metal railing, showering me with sparks. As fast as I could on my knees, I went down the stairs to get the rifle Alberto had left by the wall. I ran into the kitchen and out the back onto the patio. As quick as I could, I went into the bushes that grew along the hills to protect myself in the natural terrain. I worked my way up a small bluff near the house cautiously. I didn't want the leaves rustling to give my position away to the sniper.

From the elevation I was now positioned in, rifle in hand, I scanned my surroundings through the telescopic lens. I saw a man come out of the bushes in the garden heading towards the front door of the house. I took aim and fired, hitting him in a leg. He let go of his rifle and tried to hold himself up. I fired twice more, smashing his rifle into three or four pieces as it kicked up into the air. He pulled a pistol from his waist and fired blindly in my direction. I shot twice more, the first shot going through his hand and causing him to drop the pistol. The other shot went into his right shoulder, making him roll onto the concrete driveway. He still tried to drag his body towards the pistol that had landed not far from him.

I saw through the scope a VW minivan arrive in the driveway. A muscular man got out of the driver's seat to help the sniper into the passenger door. He closed the door after seating his accomplice and went to the driver's side, pistol in hand. At that moment, he noticed the front door of the house was open. He changed his mind and walked towards the house, seeing Willy standing in the front door with hands behind his back. I pointed the rifle at the man's head, not taking any chances with the boy. The man pointed his pistol at the little boy, quickly closing the distance between him and his target. He yelled, "Come over here, boy!"

I put my finger on the trigger, knowing that it had to be a killing shot, but both the man and I were surprised when little Willy pulled from behind his back a small .38 revolver and began to shoot at the man. The pressure on my trigger lessened, as the man he stopped, wounded in one of his legs. He began to limp back towards the minivan, but little Willy didn't stop shooting that revolver, even after the man got into the minivan and turned to leave at a high speed. The back window shattered from one of Willy's last shots as the tires squealed in protest as the van sped off out of the driveway. I smiled at Willy's prompt action that brought back memories of my own childhood and my own actions, growing up under Batista's dictatorship and then the communist regime of Castro.

I scanned through the lens my surroundings. There appeared to be no other sniper in our area, so I abandoned my hiding place and climbed down the hill to rejoin Willy, who still held the revolver trained towards the driveway. Even though he had emptied it, he was still pulling the trigger and eliciting a series of harmless clicks. He was clearly in a mild state of shock. I had counted the bullets, so before I heard the clicking, I knew he was out of bullets.

In a joking way to try to release his stress and emotional shock, I yelled as I approached, "Don't shoot, OK? It's me."

He immediately replied by putting his left finger to his lips. In a low voice he said, "Don't worry, I don't have any more bullets."

I smiled. As I got close to him, I mussed his hair. "You are a very, very brave young man. You scared these bandits clear off. I'm giving you my sincere thanks. Next time, let me give you some advice. Don't use all your bullets. Keep a couple to spare for anything unexpected that happens after all the shooting is done. Especially when they're already retreating."

He said to me very seriously, "OK. I'll do that from now on, Dr. JAM. But those mean men killed my friend Alberto." Two tears rolled down his cheeks. He tried to dry them quickly on the back of his left hand, the gun in his right preventing him from using it. I gently removed it from his hand, and he used both hands to wipe his tears from his face that now abundantly ran down his cheeks.

To distract him, I asked, "Who taught you how to shoot? You did it very well. You put one bullet in the leg of one of those assassins."

He tried to control his sobbing. "My mommy. She taught me and showed me where I could find this revolver in a shoebox in her closet. When I saw Alberto dead as I came downstairs and didn't see you anywhere, I realized I would need to defend myself." He hugged by my waist. "I thought you were dead, too. I'm really glad you're not.

You made them run with that rifle. I was only a small help."

I smiled. "That's not true. You're being very modest. You were a great help. If it hadn't been for you, I would have had to put a bullet in that man's head to prevent him from hurting or kidnapping you. I don't enjoy killing any human being, so I have to thank you for that. God intervened through your hand to keep me from having that man's life on my conscience so that I'll be able to continue sleeping peacefully."

Willy stopped sobbing and looked at me in surprise. "Wouldn't it be better if we killed him? That way he couldn't continue hurting people or killing them like they did Alberto, who never did anything to them. Look, he's dead on the floor of our living room."

We walked inside the residence. I said, "Maybe you're right, Willy, but what if I put a bullet in the head of the man who didn't kill Alberto? What if the true assassin was the other guy, and that man was just an imbecilic accomplice?"

Willy looked at me with a puzzled frown. "Well, in that case, we should have killed both, just in case. That way we don't make a mistake by leaving the murderer alive."

I smiled and shook my head. From a certain perspective, he was right. "This is a little complicated, Willy. When you grow up and as you mature, you'll understand it better. Unless it's absolutely necessary, the life of another human being is something we should respect. Only in extreme circumstances should we take that life with our own hands—only when we have no alternative. In other words, if it's your life or the murderer's."

He nodded, unconvinced. We put a blanket on top of Alberto's body. He helped me to put the body in the trunk of the Bentley. I wrote a note to Faviola to let her know what had happened and informing her that for her security as well as Willy's, I was going to take him with me on my trip. I would look after him closely and would call her in a week or two on my way back. I hoped it wouldn't be a long one, after I made sure that everything had been resolved, and that there was nothing any longer to worry about. I told her not to worry, that Willy and I had connected very well and established a very good friendship. Basically, he had assumed that I was his mysterious father she had described to him as a hero would one day appear to him who would rejoin him to bring happiness ever after. I did not want to break his heart by bursting that bubble of his beautiful fantasy and was going to leave it to her when to decide to break it to Willy and tell him the whole truth. I was not going to be the one to shatter that beautiful dream he had about his father. I also let her know that, on top of everything, he had had a dream that night the evening I came to visit him through extraordinary circumstances I could not explain, he had visualized and idealized his father as someone who physically resembled me and my features. I would give her more details when I saw her and signed it "Love, Dr. JAM."

I left it in a sealed envelope on top of the beautiful baby grand piano right in front of the living room close to the front door. I took a couple of bags from Willy that held his most necessary items, we left the house in the Jaguar, passing through the gate securing the driveway. I realized that the gates had not been forced, which mean the perpetrators of that attempt had in their possession a remote control to open it. That implied the person was either someone Faviola had absolutely trusted, or they were backed by a powerful entity such as the government.

Before we arrived at the gate to the entire development, I drove along the narrow streets between the hills of Coto de Caza. I turned on Via Alondra, and the Mercedes I had seen before when I was leaving Westcliff Plaza was behind me once more with the same four men inside. After a few seconds, they attempted to pass us, the man sitting in the passenger seat started to shoot at the tires of the car. They could not know that the Jaguar's cars were puncture proof Michelin Uptis tires. I told Willy not to worry, that our friends were just trying to scare us and playing games.

Willy looked at me in sheer disbelief. "I'm not five years old, OK? I'm six. If these are your friends, I don't think you need any enemies! Don't worry about me, OK? Keep your focus. I'm not easy to scare. Remember what I said before: I'm not a typical kid. If these for any reason the same assassins, even different ones, don't give them the same courtesy as before, please. We need to put them down or we're going to spend the whole day running from these psychopaths."

I looked him in the eyes for a few seconds. "Are you *really* six, kid?"

He smiled impishly. "No, I'm six and a half. It all depends. In this circle I'm that young, but from other circles I'm probably two thousand years old."

"OK, let's see if what you just said is true." I floored the accelerator. "Hold on, OK?"

The nose of the Jaguar raised up slightly as we sped up. He clapped his hands. "Wow! I like it like that! What do you have under the hood, Dr. JAM?" He turned his head, looking for the Mercedes that was now a few blocks behind us.

We arrived a couple of miles from the central gate, and I pulled over onto the shoulder. "Willy, I want you to do exactly as I tell you, please." He nodded. "Get out of the car and run as fast as you can and dive into the ditch to hide there. Keep your eyes open. As soon as you see the Mercedes in flames, run back to the car and we'll get out of here. I assure you that we will now settle this your way."

"Great, Dr. JAM!"

I pulled over and he did exactly as I had instructed, jumping into a ditch about 200 feet from the Jaguar. I went to the trunk and opened it with the remote control. From a hidden compartment in the lid of the trunk, I pulled out a shoulder mounted RPG. I loaded it and took a couple of spares in my suit pockets. I adjusted the sighting lens and walked down the center of the road back towards we had come from, trying to put as much distance between the

Jaguar and where I would be shooting. I left the engine running with the keys in the ignition.

A few minutes later I turned to check the distance between me and the Jaguar, spotting Willy's little head peering over the top of the bushes by the road. Even though he made no comment before leaving the car, it was clear he didn't want to lose the slightest detail as to what I was going to do. I was another 200 feet from the Jaguar when I saw the Mercedes coming up the road with its four men. I trained the missile to the right of a small hill and fired. The explosion near their car showered them with rocks from the hillside. They slammed on the brakes and came to a dead stop on the road as they saw me reloading the RPG. All four doors popped open as they piled out of the car. Pistols were out, but then they saw it was an RPG I was training on them, and they began to run, seeking refuge in the ditch by each side of the highway.

I fired right at the engine block of the Mercedes, sending the exploding ball ten or twelve feet into the air, dropping pieces of debris all over the highway. I turned around and closed up the launcher, returning to the Jaguar. I yelled to Willy, "Come in, we're done!"

He came running out of the ditch. "Wow! That's it, no more assassins on our tail!"

We got into the Jaguar and to the disbelieving eyes of our persecutors we sped away without their firing a single shot. They were too much in shock at what I had done in the middle of that exclusive and luxurious residential area. I drove away slowly to not attract attention, leaving my enemies behind without a horse to follow us.

Figure 49 The cockatoo, Venus, our savior

CHAPTER 18: 11,643 NAUTICAL MILES BENEATH THE SEA

Willy looked at me with a big smile on his face as he put his seatbelt on. He grabbed my arm in both his. "Wow, that was awesome, Dr. JAM!"

A little while later we descended to the Pacific Coast Highway and arrived at the lab in China Cove. My friends were anxious to leave, and I introduced them to my new little friend Willy, who was fascinated with the submarine as well as participating in our trip. Something out of the blue happened that sealed our exit from California, taking us all by surprise. A ball of snow came out of the sky—it was the white cockatoo with its crest bristled up. If flew in a semi-circle like an umbrella, its wings and tail revealing now in the light of day the lemon feathers that were exposed only while in flight. He screamed melodically his call, which sounded like a symphony to my ears—OK while far away from the human ear but painful when in close proximity. He landed on my right shoulder and bobbed his head down as if exaggeratedly bowing up and down along my neck, seeking for me to scratch his feathers. He was seeking my attention, croaking more softly.

Chandee came over to me and then proceeded to scratch the cockatoo. "I believe we all will have a very happy trip. We're being accompanied by your angels in disguise."

Everyone smiled. Willy was fascinated by the cockatoo and came over for a closer look. "Wow," he said, "that is a beautiful bird! Is it yours, Dr. JAM?"

I smiled. "I think this cockatoo is a free spirit and doesn't belong to anyone. From the moment she crashed into my chest and landed on my shoulder to protect me and warn us of the danger we were in, she has given us love and protection. I, in return, accepted with gratitude that invitation and will take care of her for the time that she decides to stick around. I'll make her my responsibility unless somebody like you wants to share with me a little of that obligation by giving her water, food, and whatever else she needs on a daily basis like you do with guests in your house. At least until the day that guest decides like her to fly to other lands or perhaps other worlds where we can't follow because we're not authorized or fully prepared to enter at this time."

Willy looked at me in surprise. "Do you think she comes from another world?"

I smiled again. "My little friend Willy, I believe in everything, and I believe in nothing until I convince and verify it for myself." I nodded. "If I have to guess, even though I'm not completely sure is that this beautiful cockatoo not only saved my life last night but also the life of your mommy. She came as a blessing from God in the middle of the night with her white, angelic aura and her screams of agony took us out of very immediate danger or certain death." I mussed his hair.

He said, "I will tell you this story we go on the trip. Now we have to get out of here as soon as possible. Very well, Dr. JAM, but I want to tell you something." He put his hand on my shoulder and nudged the cockatoo puckering his lips. The cockatoo shifted and wiggled her way up his arm. "I accept the responsibility; it will be an honor to share it with you. It will be a great pleasure. After what you just told me what she did for you and Mommy, it will multiply the pleasure to pay with my gratitude for her heroic and brave gesture. I'm pretty sure she risked her life doing that."

"You don't even know how much she risked. When I tell you the whole story, you'll understand better the tremendous risk she took. Flying at night, which they don't normally do, and all to save us from a horrible death."

Brenton was nearby. "When you decide to tell this story, please include me in your audience. That's sounds very interesting, and I want to tell Sunset and Massile about it, since they have been extremely fascinated with your life."

"OK. After we're in open sea, we'll have plenty of time for you guys to listen with patience what transpired last night. Not just my story, but also the corroboration of my friends who were witnesses to what happened."

Figure 50 Our submarine

Chopin said to me as he came back from the rear of the sub, wiping his hands on a small towel, "Well, Captain, we're ready for departure." He grinned broadly. "There's only one thing that I need to go over with you." He held his hand out for something from me. "If you will please give me the honor." I reached inside my jacket and handed him the remote control. Like the plane we were in earlier, the sub could become invisible. He activated it, and to everyone's surprise and the extreme shrieking of the cockatoo, the sub seemed to disappear from beneath our feet. "Abracadabra!" He said it again as he pushed the remote, and the sub reappeared. He did these two or more three times and handed the remote back to me. "Now everyone can board. The sub has passed the third safety test. We will be under way shortly, invisible to the eyes of everyone."

Little Willy asked Chopin, "Do you have to say abracadabra?"

Elizabeth shook her head and grinned. "No, Willy. He's just fooling around. The little button Dr. del Marmol has is what does the trick."

"Ah!" Willy said in comprehension.

As we entered the vessel, Elizabeth asked me, "When did you acquire this new submarine? The one we had before didn't have this incredible technology. If the other one cost $20 million, I don't even want to ask how much this one cost!"

I replied, "To please your curiosity, over twice what we paid for the other one. But can we put a price on our lives? To hunt sharks, we cannot bring sardine hooks. Especially in our case—if we want to come back from that kind of fishing alive, we should have the most modern technology and resources in our hands to defend ourselves or the fight will not be effective."

Chandee said, "I love this technology and also our new submarine!" She put her hand on Willy's had. "Do you like it?"

Willy said, "Of course! It's awesome!"

Yaneba said, "Dr. del Marmol, you never cease to amaze me. I know, like everyone else does, that everything you do isn't just for your personal protection but also ours, which was the most important thing you had present in your mine when you ordered this submarine. I know like everyone else the security of our team for you is more important than your own. You've demonstrated that once more now as you bring all of us with you to put distance between the imminent danger that we now are taking on with this new President that's half-communist if not completely communist like his father."

Chopin grinned. "I believe that you're being too gentle in your comments about this President. You don't know all his thoughts—he is a lot worse than a Marxist. He is an individual with no roots that might have had a bittersweet romance with Satan." He turned to me. "You should ask O'Brien, who has been near him so many times, if he smelled the same sulfur that we smelled with Che Guevara. I assure you that no matter how much deodorant or cologne he uses that he will not be able to get rid of that odor."

I smiled. "My friend Chopin, I don't need to ask O'Brien. To my previous knowledge of this man, even though I've been trying to get him out of the darkness during the several letters I wrote him, I knew him before he was even born. I know where he's coming from."

We left the harbor at a moderate speed to not create any unnecessary waves that could catch the attention from any vessels moored on either side of the harbor that would reveal something large was moving under the water. A few minutes later, we hit open sea. The strategic position of the lab was its close proximity to the mouth of the harbor, allowing us quick access to open water. We enjoyed the splendid, magnificent beauty of the submarine world and vegetation. For most of my team, this was nothing new. But for our two new friends, Brenton and Willy, this beautiful panorama resulted in a great fantasy converted in reality.

Little Willy, cockatoo on his shoulder, did not take his eyes away from the porthole that offered us a spectacular view. Chandee sat next to him, giving the names of the different fish, species of algae, and other marine vegetation, keeping the little boy completely absorbed in fascination.

Yaneba came over to me. "Do you think O'Brien has the power to put a bandage on the hemorrhage that this Administration as created for the country? Or do you believe we're all becoming political exiles in the world? What an irony! After all these years of hard work, we all have to abandon ship."

I put my right hand on her shoulder. "Remember, you should never lose faith. Without faith, you're like a parachuter in the jungle with no weapons to defend yourself. To answer your first question, I have the complete assurance that O'Brien will put an end to all this nonsense, not only because he will put his best effort into that but also because of the weapons I put in his hand. All he has to do is use them properly and apply psychological pressure to these corrupted politicians. As to the second question, I don't know how you've felt these past years, I can assure you that I've learned to defend, love, and respect this beautiful USA as my motherland, Cuba. I will also never forget who pushed me to abandon my family, my roots, and that is the reason I never became a political exile. One day, I will be able to go back and see my beautiful Cuba free and independent again of the worst political system that humanity has ever suffered from: the totalitarian communists, that I consider worse than the Nazis or at best the same dog with a different color."

She nodded and tapped her chest with her right hand, "I've been feeling all these years right here the same. We are in the same boat."

To alleviate the tension, I joked, "No—in the same submarine."

She grinned broadly. "You and your sense of humor is exactly like your optimism: it never changes."

"Thank you. Maybe that sense of humor and optimism, even when I'm on the borderline of mental insanity, is one of the reasons I'm here alive still with you guys."

She smiled again. "You know something? You look tired. Your face shows clearly that you haven't had a full night's rest. You should go get some sleep for a few hours, or maybe a few days until we arrive where we're going. Move over. Let me sit in your chair and be the captain for a while. It wouldn't be the first time. Go to sleep. I assure you that this will be a great thing for your body, and you will be able to think more clearly with a mind that is rested and fresh to deal with all the little problems that we'll need you to solve for us. As you just assured me that your psychological weapons in O'Brien's hands will be effective because you entrusted him with the way to disarm this corrupt politician, I think you will be able to sleep better."

"I expect so." I stood up, leaving my seat free for her. I patted the chair with my right hand for her to sit down. I gave her some instructions of the new system for compression and defense that she didn't yet know about. "The rest is exactly like the one we had before. All of you know that one to perfection."

"Yes, I know. Go, don't worry about it, and rest. However, much time it takes your body to recover, not with those dark circles under your eyes. As you rest, I will give those instructions you just gave me to the others, just in case they need to replace me."

"Thank you." I turned and went straight to my cabin. I entered and lay down on the narrow but very comfortable mattress. I took off my clothes, lay down, and passed out, exhausted not just form the physical exertions of the night before but also from being a little more relaxed, thinking that no matter what when we came back things should be better. The stress had put a heavy load on my shoulders when I found out we were some of targets of certain individuals within the new Administration that now occupied the White House, apparently trying to protect our enemies and clearing the path for the harm they wanted to do to our country.

As I fell asleep, I floated in space as normally I had done before when I traveled in time. This looked like a very far trip for I crossed many oceans and lands until I entered an enormous storm like a hurricane that generated humongous waves. I suffocated as if I were drowning. I landed in the Guipúzcoa Province of Spain in the autonomous Basque country to the north. It was the smallest of the Spanish provinces, situated on the Bay of Biscay between *Biscaya*[30] Province and the French frontier. Alava and Biscaya became one of the autonomous regions of the Basque country in 1980. The name was a

[30] Biscay

geographical entity from the end of the 10th century and as a country Guipúzcoa was unified with Castile in 1200. The beaches near Zumaia were considered the most beautiful places in that province.

Figure 51 Zumaia Beach

I woke up as I landed face down in the sand. My clothes were in rags as if I had been shipwrecked. Debris and pieces of wood, along with the mast of a sailing ship lay in the sand a few feet away from where I lay. I tried to open my eyes, thinking I was blinded until I recovered and realized my situation. I raised my hand and shook the sand clear. I could see by the sunlight was the bare feet of a woman wearing gypsy clothes that were of a fashion from centuries ago. From her back, shoulders, and the tiara on her head, she looked a little like a princess. She had been collecting seashells in the sand and had been poking me with a branch to see if I were dead or alive. My left hand reached to my forehead to shield my eyes from the harsh sun. I noticed something moist on my head and looked at my hand. It was filled with semi-coagulated blood. I noticed that my hand looked like that of a very young man, not my own. There were no freckles or wrinkles, and the skin was too full and elastic. The young woman had red hair, blue eyes, and olive skin.

She crouched down. "Are you OK?"

I nodded. "Yes, yes. I think I'm OK."

She spoke with a beautiful Castilian accent. She tried to help me stand. "Come on, stand up. You have a nasty cut on your forehead that needs to be attended to. You've lost a lot of blood."

"Where am I? What year is this?"

She laughed suddenly. "You are in Guipúzcoa in España. It's nearly the end of May 1800. Don't worry about it. You look OK. Can you stand?"

"Yes. I'm a little dizzy."

"Of course, you've lost a lot of blood. Your mind is probably not functioning very well."

I saw several women who were dressed similarly to her, but not as luxurious. They came over to help me as I staggered. These beautiful women were all very tall and looked very similar to each other, except for the one who discovered me was around my own height. She gave orders to the others, who went to retrieve a wagon that was hooked to two beautiful Paso Fino horses. They assisted me to get over to the wagon. I sat down in the back, and they instructed me to lie down. They covered me with a blanket—even though it was a hot sun, I was shaking with the cold sweat that ran all over my body compounded by the sea water. I was utterly soaked, as if I had been in the sea for several days. The evidence indicate that my ship had wrecked and by a miracle I had survived it, ending up on that beautiful Spanish beach. That woman extended her hand to take one of mine in hers.

She said in her angelic voice with a compassionate smile, "My name is Saraly. What is yours?"

"My name is Francisco del Marmol." I listened to my own words and confirmed that I was indeed in my ancestor's body. I had apparently traveled into it in one of my psychic trips into the past. It appeared that I was now Don Francisco del Marmol, the future governor of the Province of Guaira of Venezuela. The reality was that I didn't know why I had taken this trip to this part of the world. I had no idea why I had returned once more to my ancestral roots. I only knew that this had been a very quick trip, very abrupt with no transition. I least expected it to be eighteen years before my first contact had taken place in 1818.

I felt tremendous sadness and a sour taste filled my dry mouth. I found it difficult to breath, and I started to choke. I coughed two or three times as my right hand raised to my throat. "Saraly, can you please give me a sip of water?"

Saraly turned to the other ladies, one of whom brought me a leather waterskin. She understood that I was having difficulties breathing and she supported the back of my neck and shifted me over to the wall of the wagon so I could sit up. She began to give me water from the skin. She said gently, "Drink it slowly." She patted my back a little.

I rushed to drink more to get that disgusting phlegm in my throat that obstructed my trachea and blocked my respiratory system. I opened my eyes wider to drink more water and saw that they had not noticed behind them, in the woods, an enormous black panther had come out of the brush, slowly advancing in our direction. It appeared it intended to jump onto Saraly's back, who was distracted by the need to hold my neck and assist me. She asked me if I felt any better or stronger. Due to my blood loss, I could not see clearly—I thought it was a panther, but the image was too blurry for me to tell precisely. My vision started to clear as I took a little water in my hand and washed my eyes. I thought in my weakened state that maybe it wasn't truth, but an illusion brought on by my lightheadedness.

I opened my eyes again and saw clearly that it was indeed a panther, and it was close enough to start its pounce. I shoved Saraly to one side, yelling with all my might in an attempt to alert the others, "Be careful!" I drew my sword.

One of the women saw my action and yelled, "A spy for the pirates! Be careful!"

Trying to protect her, another drew her sword and yelled, "Assassin!"

They saw me with my sword out and ready to attack, but my close proximity to Saraly made them think I meant her harm. The panther jumped, now at me since I had shoved Saraly out of the way. The panther landed on my body, skewered thoroughly by my sword. The blade pierced the beast's heart, which died instantly. Utterly exhausted, I let go of my sword as my body lay back, drained completely of the strength I had left in my body. The world turned black as I lost consciousness.

I had apparently slept all night and late into the next day. When I opened my eyes, to my immense surprise I looked out a beautiful, splendid, large window surrounded by mountains and looking out over the Atlantic coast. It appeared I was in a castle. Not far away a big structure that looked like a colonial country warehouse stood. From the room in which I lay in a huge bed I could also observe the vineyards with ripe grapes—the time to harvest them was quite soon. There were so many rows of grapevines that they were lost in the distance. To the right another building looked like a storage for wine bottles. Next to it was a massive winepress that looked like a giant barrel cut in half. Metal bands held the wooden strakes together. Evidently the winepress where the grapes were deposited to extract the juices, later to be fermented into wine.

The sound of peacocks resounded throughout the area. I could see them walking through vast gardens with waterfalls surrounded by bougainvillea. A woman came into the room. As soon as she saw me sitting up in the bed looking out the window, she yelled, "Olivia! Olivia! Go and tell Saraly that her gallant knight is awake."

I tried to get out of the bed, but my head began to spin wildly. I would have fallen down if it weren't for the intervention of that young woman, who prevented me from falling facedown onto the floor by supporting me under my arms. "No, no," she said, "get back into your bed."

I put my left hand to my head to try to contain the tremendous migraine that suddenly erupted inside it. I realized that there was a large bandage over my forehead. The sweet woman helped me up in bed. She said encouragingly, "You're OK. Just be patient. Don't leave the bed until you're completely fine and recovered from that nasty cut in your forehead. You lost a lot of blood and are very weak in consequence."

Saraly's face appeared in the doorway, surrounded by another three beautiful Amazons. She had a broad smile on her face, very happy to see me awake. She said, "Well, well—once more you've demonstrated to me that you're not only noble and brave cavalier, but also that you have in yourself a great, strong spirit that also knows how to offer help to others as well as knowing that in order to provide it one must fight to continue living. You scared all of us. For a moment we thought your tremendous loss of blood would make you perish. When you lost consciousness in the wagon, we wouldn't be able to help you. Now I observe and it gives me great joy to see you've recovered at the speed of lightning." She leaned over me. "Now you don't have to worry about anything. Just concentrate on recovering. Eat all the food and the delicious dishes that we will bring to your bed."

"Thank you very much," I said as I nodded.

She clapped her hands, and two other women entered the room. She said, "Bring food and milk immediately to our guest." She turned to me. "Are you hungry?"

I smiled. "I think I could eat a raw lion." I noticed that their faces appeared frightened and glanced at each other. It might have been offensive to them. I hurriedly added to clarify, "That's only a joke."

Saraly looked at me and forced a small smile. "Yes, yes. We know that you didn't mean anything wrong, but for us here in this region the lion represents Satan, the Father of Devils. Our enemies, the Moors, when they come to attack us, bring with them those trained beasts to intimidate us into submission. Many of our families died at the claws and wound up in the stomachs of those lions."

I raised my arm high, sadness in my expression. "I'm sorry. It wasn't my intention to bring to you bad memories, much less remind you of such crimes."

She drew close to me to fix the pillows behind me to make me more comfortable. She pointed through the massive arched window to the top of a small hill at the foot of the mountains. There was a building that appeared to be a lighthouse, but it was slightly different. On top of it, above the windows the beam of light would shine, was what appeared to be a belfry for a massive bell. "That lighthouse was built by our ancestors to save our ships from the rocks at nights but also to save us from the Moorish pirates who nearly exterminated our race over the past few decades nearly to the point of extinction. They've killed indiscriminately all the men and kidnapped our women and children into slavery." She spoke with a mixture of sadness and resentment in her voice. Still pointing at the building, "That bell is not only to warn of danger but also of terror for our community. That lighthouse contains eyes twenty-four hours a day to warn us with the sound of the bell. When we hear it, we know our enemies are approaching."

"Why running to escape? What not run to confront and kill them? If you prepare yourselves strategically, you can maybe no longer need to run. You give to them a taste of the same terror they've put in you for all these decades and a great lesson to those who escape alive. It will be enough to spread the word that they should never return to destroy the happiness and prosperity you built with so much sacrifice and work. That, to me, is worth defending. Why not do so, if necessary, with your own lives? That way other generations don't have to continue to feel the suffering that all of you have endured for so many years."

Saraly looked at me with eyes moist with tears, and then at the other women surrounding her. She nodded to them. All of the women nodded as well and smiled. It seemed as if they had been discussing something before they came into my room; now they had taken a secret vote in my presence. She took a step forward towards my bed. She took my right hand in both hers and asked in a voice thick with emotion, "You came over the deep ocean waters, arriving in the night on our shores. You came to our land as a surprise, maybe being sent by our gods of the universe. I give you the warmest welcome and now I ask you: do you accept the responsibility of being our leader in our just fight for our own existence? To destroy our dark enemies as you destroyed with your courage, sword, and noble heart the dark panther that wanted to devour me heart and soul?"

I raised my head and nodded twice in exactly the same manner they had when they were voting. I replied with one word: "Agreed."

Two tears rolled down Saraly's cheeks. Bending down, she kissed my hand and stepped away a little. She took her sword and touched the top of my head with it. The other women drew their swords and raised them high, touching at the tips. They repeated after her in solemn voices, "Francisco del Marmol, on this beautiful day in the month of May of 1800, I nominate you with the authority I have been given by my community as guardian of our *acaudalado*[31] to use for your benefit as well as that of our community, to protect it, if necessary, with your life, against our domestic and foreign enemies. We pray to God to give you the wisdom and courage you need to complete your endeavor that you will swear this day to defend, if necessary, with your blood before all of us."

One of the women passed an old Bible with the Old Testament and held it out to me for me to place my right hand over for my oathtaking. "Do you accept it, Francisco del Marmol?"

I placed my hand on it. "Yes, and I swear to my best knowledge and all my strength so help me God."

---

[31] Wealth and riches

All the women yelled joyfully. Saraly said, "Olivia, try the war uniform that we prepared for Francisco."

Olivia was a beautiful blond with green eyes. She left, followed by two other women. She returned with a costume which included the head of the panther I had killed and a white cape with borders of black and gold embroidery.

Saraly asked, "Do you think you can help us tailor this to you personally? Can you get up if we help you? It will only be for a few minutes." She draped my arm around her shoulder, and I made an effort to maintain my dignity. She said, "You will be the most feared black panther in our history."

I smiled slightly with an effort. I helped them by standing up for a few minutes until they got all my measurements for the war Saraly had in mind to declare their independence from the Moorish pirates. After they took the necessary measurements, they helped me back into my bed.

Four women brought a table over to my bed with a variety of food: rotisserie chicken, many fruits, soup—a buffet fit for a king. Even though I had been living a comfortable life with abundant food, this treatment was so special and heartfelt that I felt a little out of place. I was embarrassed by the pampering, but after a few days I grew accustomed to it. It ended several weeks later, and I could say that those days of tender compassion remained in my mind for a long time. I felt a very great debt of gratitude.

A few weeks passed, during which I recovered quickly thanks to the extremely good treatment they gave me, and I started to put into motion a strategic plan using my military training and experience that I had obtained from serving in the Armada of the Royal Guard for King Ferdinand VII, better known by his faithful supporters as *El Deseado*[32] but to his detractors *El Rey Felon*[33]. I had served as his personal chief of guards. I elaborated a plan

---

[32] The Desired

[33] The Felon King

to protect that community from the Moors. The region was so far from the Spanish capital, virtually at the French border, that they had little protection from the King. With their help, I put everyone to work. I constructed in strategic positions large catapults to be used before the Moors even managed to disembark on their coast. Filled with rocks, these catapults would shower them with oil not just with the purpose of burning the ships, but the rocks would also create holes in the hulls to sink the ship. The idea was to sink and burn them before they had the opportunity to lower boats for landings. I explained to them that this would also prevent them from bringing their lions and the rapists who abducted not only their young girls but also stole the fruits of their labor, leaving behind only death and poverty for those who managed to escape from the claws of their persecutors by running into the mountains like they always had in the past.

I proposed to Saraly that we should go to the south of Spain, into Andalusia. My idea was to buy with their tremendous amount of wealth in pearls many female falcons, who tended to be larger than the males. These falcons were very well-trained birds of prey and would not only constitute for them a great defensive weapon but also creatures that would terrify the foes with their massive claws and beaks. They were known to attack their prey in weak places such as the eyes in the first attack, and then subsequently come in for the kill once the prey was rendered defenseless. We purchased 25 of these birds and hired the trainer to come back with us so that he could train others to handle these birds. He would then be released from his contract to return to his family in Andalusia.

When we returned from the trip with our falcons, Saraly assigned the responsibility to her right arm, the beautiful Olivia, to be in charge of assigning to each of their women one falcon each. That way, the bird would respond to only that person, adopting the bird as a weapon like perfectly organized gladiators prepared for battle. Saraly thanked me and said, "You once more showed me that you, without any doubt in my mind, have been sent by the Supreme Being to put an end to the abuse and injustice from these Moors once and for all." She took my right hand. "Come with me. I want to show you a place on the peak of that mountain, a secret place I've never taken anyone to before. I want to share this with you. You deserve to be trusted completely."

We went to the stables with two of her women, who prepared two beautiful white Paso Finos and we left the area under the beautiful sun riding to the top of the mountain. We grew close to the foot of the mountain and stopped to observe from that extraordinary altitude the beautiful, breathtaking view of the Atlantic coast. It was like something out of a fairy tale. Both the horses prevented an accident as the terrain began to grow very rough the further up one went. We dismounted and held the horses by their bridles and walked the rest of the climb until we found a small plateau between two prominences of the mountain that had a large waterfall the fell onto the rocks to form a large lagoon. There were large trees that from their massive trunks and incredible height looked to be thousands of years old. They looked like they were trying to touch the infinite sky as they reached towards the heavens. We could see some of the clouds were nearly level with us, so we were very high up. It wasn't very cold; in fact, the temperature was very pleasant.

Not far from the waterfall and by the shores of the lagoon sat a rustic cabin with stables next to it. They were constructed by pebble rocks that were multicolored, even the roof, mortared with clay. The rocks appeared to be volcanic in origin. The structure of the cabin, like the stables, appeared due to its utter lack of symmetry to be a painting by some Cubist artist, even though that style would not rise to prominence for over a century. The building was so skewed that it looked like it was ready to fall down. Even the chimney was inclined to one side slightly. Majestically, however, it continued to issue a long column of white smoke that got lost in the low clouds that seemed to float just above our heads.

All the landscape had an indescribable beauty that appeared to have been taken right out of a medieval work of fantasy. As we drew near the cabin an unusually large black, white, and gold wolf came out from the ruin, baring its teeth, clearly warning us aggressively to not come any closer to its space. The wolf's teeth were sharp, and it crouched down, ready to attack as it looked us in the eyes, which followed our every movement.

I put my hand to my sword and began to draw it in preparation to defend us. To my surprise, Saraly knelt down to the ground and said, "Jupiter! What happened? Don't tell me you don't recognize me?"

The beautiful wolf changed in a few seconds from an aggressive posture to a more submissive, friendly one. He clearly recognized Saraly and crouched on all fours, his belly nearly touching the ground as he crept forward uncertainly. Cautiously, he made his way up to Saraly. At the same time three more wolves came out of the open doorway, each a different color. The silhouettes of a middle-aged man and woman yelled out simultaneously, "Saraly! Blessed are the eyes that see you well!"

Saraly smiled. From her kneeling position as she scratched Jupiter, she answered, "Blessed are my eyes that see you well and safe." She was now completely surrounded by these four giant wolves, who now fought to receive her affection. Each tried to show Saraly some personal affection, each fighting to be the first to receive her affection in return. She patiently gave a fair share to each wolf. She called them by name, "OK, Saturn. You are so big now since I saw you last, but you continue to be so beautiful!" To a brown and black wolf with a somewhat reddish coat, she said, "Pluto, you haven't changed at all! Always so much saliva in your mouth and your long tongue." She finally turned to a black and white that had a golden patch over its left eye like some pirate. "Venus, you are beautiful like the princess of the universe." Venus was the only female and rolled onto her back on the dead leaves on the ground. She appeared to be the matriarch of the pack.

After Saraly finished greeting the wolves, she stood up and walked over to the couple who had by now come out on the steps of the porch and down onto the ground. She turned and extended her right hand to me, beckoning me forward. I walked forward through the wolves who were now smelling my clothes enthusiastically while they tried to keep contact with Saraly, nearly tripping us as they shoved each other out of the way. She hugged and greeted the couple, receiving kisses and hugs in return, and introduced them to me as her maternal uncle and aunt, who were now her adoptive parents after she had lost her biological mother and father when she was very little due to the Moorish pirate, who had orphaned her by killing them. All the girls who followed her now had similar stories, escaping to the top of the mountain years before.

Pascasia and Timoteo were the only adults surviving at the time of the last attack by the Moors. They told me they had raised and protected the fifty-nine young girls who were the only survivors. They ranged from five to fourteen years of age. None of the boys survived, save for those the Moors took as slaves. Timoteo said, "You can call me Timo, if you like. I don't care for my name that much, and so prefer to shorten it so it's less hungry."

We were invited into that pastoral but comfortable cabin and sat down around a circular wooden table. I looked at it more closely and realized that it was petrified wood, which was highly unusual. It looked like marble of a red color with veins. Pascasia said, "Timo did this himself."

I ran my fingers over it—it was literally as smooth as glass. The workmanship was exquisite. They were both very happy to have me there and see me with their adopted daughter and at the attraction that was clearly between us. We were offered fruit, cheese, beef jerky and boiled eggs along with home-made bread. There were also marmalades made from various berries.

After a long conversation of several hours' duration, Saraly said, "I want to take Francisco to the Canyon of the Screaming Devil." They exchanged surprised glances.

Pascasia said, "My girl, don't you think that is too dangerous, especially for Francisco? He is not accustomed to this altitude. I think you should wait until tomorrow so he can get adjusted. Remember, people who aren't acclimated to these elevations sometimes have difficulty even breathing."

Timo broke in. "You should also remember, Saraly, that the most powerful reason the Moorish pirates never came back to persecute us at this elevation was because most of them got very sick, vomiting like rabid dogs. Not only that, but some of them also lost consciousness and fell off the cliff of the Canyon of the Screaming Devil."

Saraly smiled and turned towards me. "Are you having any dizziness or been feeling sick?"

I shook my head. "No. On the contrary, I feel better and healthier breathing the pure air you have in these mountains."

They looked at each other uneasily. Pascasia reached over the table with her hand and took my right hand. She looked me in the eyes and said very seriously, "I believe that you, like a hurricane, have found your mountain. You are very similar to Saraly. Like she said a little while ago, you might have been sent by God far away from the universe to change our destinies, but also to plant our seed with yours in other parts of the world as one." She turned my hand over and looked at my palm, tracing the lines there with her finger. She smiled. "You have an extraordinary bloodline, probably even more powerful than mine. You can see far away into the future. Your bloodline continues to be the defender of underdogs everywhere. They are warriors and gladiators all along, and you will have many sons, and they will also be gladiators and generals. They will change history, as also will your grandsons and bloodline for centuries ahead. They will follow in your steps for several generations." She smiled once more with some mischief in her face. "You will take Saraly to very faraway lands where you will be very happy together." She spoke solemnly. "You will be responsible once and for all to turn off the voice of the Devil Canyon. It will never be heard again."

Saraly blushed like a teenaged girl. She said, "Please, Mama Luca."

"No, no," Pascasia replied with strong conviction. "I'm convinced of it. I saw it clearly in his right hand. After a very bloody battle with nearly everyone killed, friends as well as enemies, in the end, but not you two, because you, Francisco del Marmol, will finally tether the screaming devil right here, and the canyon will be no more." Her eyes widened as if she had seen a ghost and release my hand suddenly. Her expression was terrified, and she shook violently in her neck and chest. Her eyes rolled back in her head as if she were having an attack of epilepsy. Her voice became guttural, as if someone else were speaking. She clapped both hands to her ears as if she didn't want to listen to someone.

Her hands covered her eyes as if she wanted to avoid seeing a nightmare. She screamed, "Why, Lord?"

Saraly rose and went to her, hugging her close in concern. "Mama Luca, are you OK?"

Pascascia inhaled deeply. She opened her eyes, horror still reflected in them. She tried to stand but staggered and might have fallen if Saraly hadn't held her up. Timo shoved his chair nearly across the room as he stood up rapidly and went to the other side of Pascasia to assist Saraly. As they held her, we could see a wet stain at the level of her crotch and a puddle of urine on the floor beneath her chair. She looked down and looked at me to see that I also was looking. She grew very embarrassed, and her expression was clearly shamed. She shook her head. "I'm sorry. This never happened to me before. You are a very powerful being, a hundred times more powerful than I. But what I saw in your future is so horrible that I don't even to repeat it to you."

I nodded. "Don't worry, Doña Pascasia. Whatever you saw I was already born prepared for the worst. Remember, our destiny can be changed by us with the help of God. Something you might be concerned will scare me when reality is the only thing that scares me. It's in my personality to fear nothing or anyone. As we say here in our land, take the bull by the horns. My good, sweet lady, in other words I'll take the Devil by his horns." She crossed herself. "It's the same as the bull and fear. Life loses its flavor without sugar and is not worth living."

Pascasia put her right hand over her forehead and shook her head. "God, I know nothing. You know better, and that is why you put them together. Unfortunately, I have a horrible headache."

I said, "Why don't you go and rest. Please, don't let anything you saw about me bother you or your daughter Saraly. I promise you I will defend her with my own life. No one will ever hurt Saraly. This I promise you with my honor and the blood of my ancestors."

Pascasia forced a smile. "You are an angel." She shook her head. She muttered to herself, "Why, Lord?" She crossed herself. "Why, Lord? No one deserves such a horrible death. Why does such a good human being have to die in that way, especially one of your best servants."

Saraly and Timo took her to her room while I remained sitting at the table. A while later Saraly returned, a little calmer. "Don't worry too much about whatever she said. Sometimes she sees things that, in reality, never happen. But for her they are real because she sees them. She gets very distressed and profoundly disturbed."

I understood immediately that Saraly was trying to make me feel better and was trying to alleviate the emotional tension as she cleaned the chair and floor of the urine left behind. I said, "Remember, the things she told you before that never happened doesn't mean they're supposed to happen. She might have changed things so that they didn't. You have a very strong and powerful clairvoyant in your family. You probably have some within you that you haven't discovered yet. This is part of your bloodline." I noticed that no matter how she tried to cheer me up, her demeanor had changed from joyful and happy to sad and mournful. She might have been feeling a little guilty at what Pascasia had told me, which had taken all of us by surprise. I hadn't the slightest idea that, when she took my hand, our friendly, pleasant conversation would turn into how it had ended. I also had no idea that she had that tremendous gift of seeing the future in the hands of others. I remained silent for a few more seconds. After I recovered, I smiled slightly and said, "Out of curiosity, I would prefer to know what Pascasia saw in my future that terrified her so. The best way to prevent bad things from happening and be able to change that negative energy is to have previous knowledge of them. Then you will be prepared and not caught by surprise. But let me tell you one thing that's more important to me than my own curiosity. If this involves making your lovely Mama Luca suffer in the most minimal way emotionally or physically, I prefer to ignore everything that was said at this table. Let's go back in time and pretend that she never took my hand. Let's forget everything. It will probably be better for all of us, and we can put this unpleasant incident that made someone you love so much so sad. She doesn't deserve any sadness in her life."

Saraly's eyes grew even more moist at that. She said in a cracked voice, "As I know you better every minute my admiration grows, and I like you better for your great qualities. Even though I know like me you probably want to know not just out of curiosity but to be prepared what she really saw. You don't want to live with that question mark over your future. Even if you can't do anything about it and it's inevitable. At least you have the previous knowledge of what you can expect. This, of course, constitutes a tremendous emotional, mental, and physical tranquility. But if you prefer to forget about everything that she told you which inflicts more sadness and distress in her." She came over to me and put both hands on my face. She leaned in and gave me a tender kiss on my forehead. "Don't worry. She told me about her vision in her bedroom. She asked me to not tell you for the same reason that you don't want to do any damage to her. She doesn't want to worry you." She slowly stepped back with a smile on her face. "I'll tell it to you later. I know that your being aware of it will make it less painful, knowing your character as little as I do know already, leaving you with that uncertainty."

I was the one to smile this time and kissed her cheek tenderly. We looked into each other's eyes. I said, "Thank you for knowing me a little already. You're right in what you just said."

She bent over and kissed my tenderly lips for the first time. "You're welcome. You deserve a lot more for saving my life."

We continued to kiss tenderly some more. It eventually progressed to a more passionate one, but Timo interrupted us by coming back into the room. "She is calmer now after drinking her Tilo tea that Saraly prepared for her."

Saraly and I had separated abruptly at being caught, but the old fox noticed and smiled in embarrassment at his interruption. "Well, I'll leave you alone for a while. I need to unsaddle your horses, feed them, and I'm sure they need currying. I expect you'll stay the night here. We want to make a beautiful dinner of welcome tonight and I will kill one of my suckling pigs for roasting in our oven where I toast our bread every morning."

Saraly said, "No, Timo—Mama Luca's not feeling well. Don't bother."

He dismissed her objections with his hand and a big smile on his face. "No, she gets like that all the time and it never lasts more than an hour. She always gets emotional when she reads someone's hand."

Saraly said, "I want to take Francisco to the canyon. I want him to see for himself that natural wonder and while we call it the Screaming Devil."

Timo said, OK, OK. You guys get out quickly, before she gets back. Then I can tell her you're gone and there won't be anything she can do to ruin your trip or take away your fun. Don't worry. Go, go." He waved us out with both hands.

Saraly smiled and took my right hand. "OK, you heard Timo. Let's get out of here quickly before Mama Luca wakes up."

Like two teenagers holding hands, Saraly virtually dragged me out of the cabin, Timo watching us fondly as he took our horses to the stable. We ran up the hill until we reached another plateau on the other side of the cabin. There I saw something that really surprised me, something I could not describe. Many small holes in the rocks formed a natural jacuzzi with geothermally heated water. Each area had different temperatures. We continued walking around on the plateau and saw a massive cave. It was filled with water, and each time the geyser erupted, it shrieked shrilly, sounding like multiple voices. I noticed that the water was salty, which meant it was coming from the Atlantic. The screaming was like thousands of voices shrieking out their pain. It was cacophonous, and you could not help but be chilled by the sound. I could easily see how Saraly's ancestors would name this canyon so. That powerful stream of water, propelled violently by the force of nature through that throat in the rocks, fully fifty feet above the ground near that high mountain was something I had never seen before. It was spectacular.

Saraly smiled to see my surprise. We were sitting in the mouth of that gigantic natural phenomena which had earned a completely unnatural, diabolic name. For a long time, we sat there, watching it repeat every half hour or so. Saraly removed her boots and began to work on her clothes, leaving only her white linen shift with a lace neck on. She got into one of those natural jacuzzies. The steam rose into the air from the surface of the water. Her wet shift was transparent, exposing plainly to my view her lovely breasts and beautiful body. She held out her hand to me in invitation to join her in the water. I hurriedly took my clothes off, leaving my own undergarments on. I was surprised that, even though we were so attracted physically, she would do this at that moment.

I walked down and entered the hot water. I said with an expression slightly pained, "This water is ready to clean chickens!"

She smiled and splashed water in my face. "It's not that hot. It's just that the outside air is colder. This is only your first impression."

"Remember the first impression is the one that conquers you or kills your desires to continue forward."

She smiled. "You're right, because you gave me a great, beautiful first impression when I met you. From that impression you stole my heart like a bandit."

I returned her smile as she continued to splash me, a little embarrassed by her forwardness. "Well, in this case you gave me a beautiful first impression, too. When I woke up and saw those beautiful, tanned legs naked on the beach, does that also make you a bandit?"

"No, no, no—I was only looking for shells for my necklace. That makes me an innocent victim."

I joked, "*Victim*?" I leapt in and hugged her so she couldn't splash me anymore.

We were close, face to face, and she said, "Yes, and innocent, *virgin* victim."

"Virgin? What does that mean?"

"It means that any of us who fell into the hands of those Moors died or you might not have met me. I swore as a young girl if that ever happened to me, I would slice open my veins."

I hugged her closely to me, gently. "Oh, no!" Our bodies were very close together. I said in her ear, "That would be a devastating calamity, a total disaster. It would frustrate the birth of my sons and grandsons, breaking the beautiful continuity of both our families. I've been looking for you, Saraly, all my life without knowing that you had been hiding in these mountains by the hands of God. He dropped me on the sandy beaches before your mountain by the shore. Now I have no doubt that this involves God."

She kissed me passionately. After a few seconds of kissing, she slowly removed the rest of her clothes as I did mine. We explored each other's bodies with caresses and passion, tender as we grew in our desire for each other. She crawled onto my lap and looked anxiously in the water between my legs until she found what she was looking for. A slightly uncomfortable expression flashed across her face, but it quickly turned into a beautiful smile of pleasure and satisfaction. Sounds of delight and ecstasy and love escaped her lips combined with sexual desire. Those sounds united with my own like a mystic dance accompanied by the music of birds and the water's aquatic rhythms from the waterfall. Our hearts beat faster like the bongos in the percussion section of the orchestra in a folkloric, spiritual sound. It was the rhythm of heart, a beautiful *fruta*[34] rumba in that splendid moonlit scene. It completed the landscape in that beautiful moment when we united our bodies and souls.

We were there, making love for hours. Finally, our bodies were completely exhausted. We got out of the water and lay on the wet grass, the night breeze surprising us both since we had lost track of time. Neither of us really wanted to return to our places of origin. The breeze embraced our naked bodies as we lay there holding hands and looking at each other. We could sense the predestination of our spending our lives together until death finally separated us. Two tears rolled out of her beautiful eyes.

I asked her worriedly, "Why are you crying, Saraly?" I rushed to dry her tears. "Have I hurt you unintentionally?"

She shook her head and smiled sadly, sobbing slightly. "No, no—you haven't hurt me. These tears are of a profound happiness that I've never experienced before in my life. I didn't think I would ever have it. But you, my lovely Francisco del Marmol, have brought to my heart and

---

[34] Fruit or fruity

into my life that happiness." She lay on top of me and leaned down to kiss my lips. "But now we'd better go back before Mama Luca comes with the wolves hunting for us, thinking something bad has happened."

I understood and shared that worry. Like we were waking up, we stood rapidly and began to dress. I said, "Yes, we should get back. I don't want to get on Mama Luca's bad side. Not if we're going to be a family."

We finished dressing and walked back through the dense bushes. I could hear the wolves' howling towards the cabin. I looked at Saraly with a smile. "I thought you were joking, but it appears that Mama Luca is on her way to bring us back."

Saraly smiled. "No, no—why would you think she would do that? She hasn't done that since I was a very young girl. I'm a grown woman, and she knows the kind of training I've had and what I'm capable of doing with my sword. She knows I can defend myself or anyone else from any danger."

We heard the wolves howl again, closer this time. Her smile fell from her face. She raised her head high as if trying to locate them by the howls and distinguish if they were Mama Luca's trained wolves or not. Suddenly, we heard something running in our direction through the bushes. A deep panting sound that didn't sound like a wolf was heard, and we both drew our swords since we didn't know what was there in the dark.

I could see by the moonlight the long white tusks gleaming in the dark, then yellow to red fiery eyes, and then a *jabalí*[35]. He was running rapidly in our direction, more towards Saraly than me. Realizing that, Saraly looked at the aggressive animal, I didn't hesitate and pushed her behind me. Foam ran down its chin, revealing his massive fangs. I held my sword in both hands and prepared to strike at an angle that would, if not decapitate the animal completely then very nearly so.

---

[35] Wild boar

Before I could even strike, a silver bullet jumped out of the bushes. It was the female wolf, Venus. She took the beast's neck, surprisingly in the same location I was aiming for. The boar squealed and the pair rolled over the dead leaves. The boar's squeals became more desperate as he felt the wolf's fangs sink deeply into his neck. Seconds later, Jupiter, Saturn, and Pluto jumped on the boar each on different parts of its body. The boar managed to escape Venus' jaws and sliced Jupiter under his left paw. Jupiter flew through the air, landing heavily in bushes a few feet away.

As I saw that, the boar renewed his attack on the others. I raised my sword high and run to their side. Carefully, to avoid harming any of the wolves, I swung my sword a two-handed blow towards his neck. Sinking deeply into the animal's throat, I zig-zagged through its flesh, the boar squealing shrilly, the echoes ringing through the night. I worked my sword back and forth, the boar squealing twice more, and then it fell silent. The wolves maintained their hold until that point. When the boar died, the simply let go and started to walk away.

Saraly yelled from behind me, "Jupiter!"

The large alpha male limped out of the bushes. He whimpered as he put pressure on his injured paw. She ran to him and looked at his wound. She said in a worried voice, "He has a very deep puncture in his leg, close to his ribs where the shoulder joins the body, his axilla."

Jupiter was losing a lot of blood. I took my shirt off and improvised a bandage, using the sleeves of my shirt as a rough tourniquet to create the pressure to help stop his bleeding. It appeared Jupiter was badly weakened. He lay at my feet on the wet grass. He didn't look like he had enough strength to make it back to the cabin, so I decided to go for help. "We're not far from the cabin, but if he walks, he'll lose more blood. Stay here with him, and I'll go for help to transport Jupiter and the carcass of that wild boar so that Timo can use it to feed the wolves for a few weeks."

She replied, "You're always so practical, thinking of the future. That's a good idea. This animal could be very useful, so let's not let it go to waste."

"I'll go get Timo to help us." I kissed her on the cheek. "Sit tight. I won't take long."

She smiled. "I have no doubts. This is the second time you've risked your life to save mine. Let's hope that next time you'll give me the pleasure to demonstrate to you that I'm capable of doing the same for you. This will make me feel dignified to be in your company."

I shook my head. "This you are asking of me is a very risky thing with your life. I'll never take that risk. If I'm unconscious or maybe with no strength left, nearly dead myself, maybe then"

She smiled. "Very well. Then if that's the way you feel, I am resigned to live with my debt to you for the rest of my life."

We exchanged smiles and I walked towards the cabin to get the help we needed. A little while later, as I came close to the cabin a very exquisite smell of roast pork mixed with fried plantains. That conquered and completely opened my appetite. I saw the beautiful golden roast pig that Timo was rotating in an oven on a barbeque close to the cabin. It woke up my sleeping hunger that I had for several hours and repressed before from the sexual pleasure that had controlled and dominated. Now that it was satisfied and exhausted, it surrendered to those exquisite smells that Pascasia and Timo were offering through their excellent cooking as a token of welcome.

My eyes were glued to the oven as I approached. It was constructed against one side of the cabin and saw the fat from the pig dripping into the fire while Timo turned the carcass on the spit. He used guava branches as a brush to dip into the sauce with savory spices to apply to the meat. He continued adding the condiments over the skin and ribs of the pork as it cooked over a low flame. Beneath the pork the multicolored flames increased in intensity as the fat dripped onto the wood. As he saw me arrive, he greeted me with a splendid smile on his face. He used a knife to cut a small piece of meat and skin from one of the legs, put it on top of a banana leaf, and offered it to me.

He said, "This pork is coming out so good that you will lick your fingers." I proved it by sucking on the hot piece he gave me using my fingers as a fork and knife. He was right—I had to lick my fingers from that amazing sauce that virtually soaked the meat. He asked, "Where is Saraly?"

"Not too far away." I told him what had transpired without going into details and finished by asking him for help.

Timo said, "Let's not make a big deal out of it. Pascasia doesn't need to know until Saraly is here. Don't say anything—help me turn off the flame in the oven. The pork is already done and ready to eat for dinner. I'll go to the barn and get the wagon and pick you up here in a few minutes."

"OK," I replied. I did as he had asked to dampen and then kill the fire with some sand from the ground. A few minutes later, Timoteo approached me with a small wagon that was pulled by a donkey. I jumped into it next to him.

As we passed the kitchen window, he yelled, "We'll be back right away. I'm going to go get some wood for the fireplace."

Without waiting for her answer, Timoteo clicked his tongue and lashed the whip against the donkey's rear to get out of there quickly. Guided by me, we arrived a short while later where Saraly was waiting for us. After we all three had gotten the boar into the wagon, we carefully transferred Jupiter into the wagon, wrapped in a blanket taken from beneath the wagon seat. Followed by the other wolves, we returned to the cabin, but now we found a worried Pascasia waiting for us outside, clearly wondering why Timo had left in such a rush with a bronze oil lamp in his hand.

We stopped before her. When she saw the wild boar and the wounded Jupiter, she clapped her left hand to her mouth in surprise, sadness, and wonder. She asked, "What happened?"

I was surprised at her calm reaction and the way she kept absolute control over her emotions, knowing immediately what we needed to do and giving us instructions how to handle it, as if she had dealt with this before. She gestured for us to bring Jupiter to the stable, where we lay him in one corner that had a rectangular table constructed of petrified wood. She proceeded to examine the wound, immediately telling Saraly to put water on to boil in the kitchen. As soon as it was ready, Saraly was to bring it Pascasia and then to bring her some surgical tools and suturing thread and where it could be found.

Saraly at once went to do what Pascasia had instructed. By the light of several lamps, surrounded by the other wolves, who had not left our sides for a single minute. Pascasia managed at least to clean the wound of Jupiter, applying what appeared to be a home remedy made of *sabila*[36] and other antiseptics. Between all of us, we put the wolf in a rustic chair, resting by the chimney where Timo had stacked with wood while we worked.

Pascasia said, "Jupiter looks like he'll be OK. He was quite weak from his wound and has lost a lot of blood, but it looks like he'll be OK." I breathed deeply at the knowledge Jupiter would live another day. Pascasia put out a container of milk before him. He drank it all plus a few pieces of pork that smelled so good that I salivated at seeing a dog having the privilege of having dinner before us as a courtesy to the courage that nearly cost him his life in the defense of our own. A little later, after we sat down at the table to have a delicious dinner with plenty to eat, we told them the full story of what had happened in complete detail. We sat talking at the dinner table for several hours.

Timo excused himself to go clean and quarter the wild boar. The three of us remained at the table completely fascinated by Mama Luca's story of how they had survived

---

36 Aloe vera

all these years with the painful sorrow of losing nearly every single member of their family at the hands of the Moorish pirates. Pascasia had been kidnapped and raped when she was extremely young by the leader of the pirates, a sinister man named Porfirio. Fortunately, she managed to escape from his clutches with the help of the man who was now her husband, Timoteo, to whom she said she owed both her life and her freedom. She, of course, would never be able to forget the horrible face of her rapist, the man who raped not just her but several young girls, his straight hair, dark skin, and how tall and muscular he was. More than anything she could never forget the name of Porfirio.

Pascasia took once more my right hand and opened it over the table. She said, "If you ever find this man in your road in life, you should take his life for me." She looked into my eyes intensely. "That man is the man I saw in your future, trying to take your life in the most horrendous manner possible. That was what disturbed me so much before. I want to ask you once more for forgiveness for that." She shook her head in obvious disgust. "I never imagined that I would see that man's face again in my life. When I saw in your future his face it took me completely by surprise not only to see his cynical, horrendous, conniving face but also trying to commit another crime more horrendous with someone like you who might come to be a part of our family."

I replied seriously, "Remember, Mama Luca, life lived in terror is no life at all and is not worth the living. Even though my soul is very noble, and I ask God that I never have to take another's life, neither Porfirio's nor any other human being's, there are exceptions to the rule. When the moment comes for those exceptions, I have to defend myself or any of you guys, it will be completely different. Self-defense is permitted, even in the Bible. Even when getting to that point, we all have the obligation to do this with deep thinking before we proceed to take the life of another human being."

Pascasia smiled. "Wait here for a moment, please. I have something in my possession I want to give you, something that could be useful for you in your future with Saraly." She stepped away from the table and walked into her room. A little while later she returned with a leather bag that she put on the table. She pulled out of it a light mint green rock that appeared like a pale emerald. Holding the precious stone in her fingers, it appeared to be polished smooth around it, but cut in an oval shape. It looked like the pupil of an Asian eye. She said emphatically, "You said to proceed with caution and only in self-defense. The only caution I suggest to you to have with this individual if you ever encounter him in your road of life is to not wait until it's self-defense. Be sure that he is dead before you leave his side. If not, I assure you even though you have a noble heart and are a gentleman who doesn't enjoy taking the life of another human being, he will not hesitate to take yours but also the lives of many of your family members." She finished with a disgusted expression on her face, raising her right hand with the stone on her fingers. She looked at it in the light of the lamp and then switched it other. "Through this stone, those who have the gift of clairvoyancy can observe the future and what can happen in the next few hours before it creates a devastating effect on us as a mirror into the immediate future." She added sadly, "But it's stopped working for me. I don't know if it's my age, but maybe my vision is clouded. But I think you have the same gift I have and that it will work for you as it had me in the past. I found this rock on top of the mountains at the bottom of the thermal waters, after we saw one night the light of a meteor crossing over the sky and hitting down on the mountain that completely created that plateau, the same place where Saraly took you today: those beautiful waterfalls."

Figure 52 The mysterious stone

She handed me the precious stone that reflected the light of the lamps. As I took it in my fingers the ovel rock shone, reflecting points of light all around the chimney that looked like stars with different symmetry of spikes on each one. Pascasia shook her head in surprise and frowned in puzzlement. "Hm. Hm—this hasn't happened to me for years." Curiosity burned in her face. "Will you please put that stone to your right eye and say if you see anything through her?"

Saraly interposed, "That stone saved our lives many times for many members of our family. We were able to see precisely when hurricanes, tsunamis, and even on occasion the eruption of the volcano in this mountain."

I nodded my head. "That is good to know, Saraly. Thank you." I took the rock and put it over my right eye before the light of the lamp. At first, I could see not only how the light beams reflected off the wall over the chimney disappeared and returned to the stone, but I saw a movement inside it that looked more like waves of the ocean. I thought initially that I was only seeing an optical illusion. The waves continued to increase in height and velocity, the motion becoming more violent, crashing against rocks. The image changed to a clearer one. I had no doubt that it looked more like a picture before my eye. With complete clarity I now saw the masts and ships of the Moorish pirates right along our coast, lowering the boats on pulleys, and loading them with caged lions. Then they were bombarded by the balls of fire I had constructed for our defense. Even though several ships were sunk or in the process of sinking, more ships continued their approach with the hungry lions, eager to be released to satisfy their hunger for human flesh. Some of the pirates had managed to disembark on the shore. Those evil pirates, already with some of the cages on the sand, prepared to release their beasts. I yelled, "Oh, my God!" My face showed my terror at what I was seeing in that tiny stone, not just the future but now the present. As the scene progressed step by step. That is why I stood up and yelled, "Saraly, the pirates have disembarked on our coast, and your brave warrior girls are fighting them. They need our leadership down there. We must leave immediately!"

Saraly clapped her right hand to her mouth. "Yes, we have to get down there at once. Let's hope we're not too late."

I handed the rock to Pascasia. She took it in her right hand and put it over her right eye before the lamp to see if she could corroborate what I had said. After a few seconds, she said, "Damned old age. I cannot see a thing. My old age has deprived me of my sight." She breathed deeply in frustration. She held the rock out to me, but before I took it, she changed her mind and put the rock this time as a last attempt over her left eye. Immediately it cast beams out, illuminating the whole room like it had done before for me. Pascasia screamed in horror, pulling the rock away from her eye. "Oh, my God! It's him! It's him!" She shook her head in extreme distress. "Porfirio! The rapist! That man is a beast! I saw his face right through the rock!" She handed the rock to me. "Go, go! Go quickly! Please do everything possible to destroy that beast! Remember what I told you before—he will destroy you if you don't destroy him in time."

A little while later, Timo brought the two horses to us. We said our goodbyes and left in a rush back down the hill to the village where our friends were even now fighting our enemies. Unfortunately, the descent took time to avoid an accident due to the steep slope of the difficult terrain in that dark night, despite the full moon. There was a dark cloud that promised rain which covered the moon partially. After an agonizingly long period, it started to sprinkle lightly, which made our descent even more difficult and slowing us further. The wet rocks were a little too slippery for the horses. As we descended closer to the village the horses started to grow agitated and nervous at the sound of the roaring of the lions. Those were noises they weren't accustomed to. Contributing to the difficulty of our journey.

We tried to calm the horses, tapping them on the neck with comforting words, but we weren't getting the results we were hoping to get. To our satisfaction, we could see the falcons we had been training were responding very well to their mission. Now, as the cloud moved off the moon and gave us better light, we saw how the birds were fighting even the lions. We could see down by the coast how the falcons managed to poke the eyes of one of the lions out. As a team, they agitated the lion to draw it to the edge of the cliff, eventually pouncing right off the edge to fall onto the sharp reefs locally called the Dog's Teeth in the ocean below. We saw how one of the lions and managed to catch a falcon by one of its talons in its jaws, which fought the lion with its other talon and buffeting of its wings, but three other lions came and ripped the falcon to pieces despite other falcons coming in to attack.

The catapults continued firing on the Moors, sinking many more of their ships. Beneath the full moon, the scenery looked like a major naval battle had taken place. From the fleet of ships that attacked, only two remained afloat, but they continued disembarking more men. One of the canons from one ship hit the hill while Saraly and I were near the top, causing some of the hill face to collapse beneath Saraly. She rolled with her horse down the cliff down to the underbrush, which fortunately cushioned her fall. She regained control of her fall, sliding instead of rolling. I was surprised how she fell right into the hands of the pirates, who bound her hands and bustled her into a boat, rowing for one of the still afloat ships. I reacted immediately, yelling to Olivia, who was in charge of the catapults and signaling to her, "Stop the catapults! I don't want to endanger Saraly's life! The pirates have her."

The catapults stopped, and I understood the immense superiority of our enemies who had damaged tremendously and killed nearly all the Amazons that defended the coast. Only a small group of them now fought back-to-back with swords against the Moors. I yelled from my horse, "Olivia!" who had just decapitated a couple of Moors attacking her from the back. "Sound the retreat! We're going to go around the hill and head for the shore. We'll take one of their boats by force and will take the ship where they took Saraly. We'll try to get the rest of you alive that survived this attack."

Olivia looked at me with tears in eyes, nodding. "What about Saraly?"

I spoke with determination and conviction, "We will rescue her, even if we have to fight with the Devil himself. We'll take her with us far away from these assassins."

Olivia tried to smile, but only managed a smirk. She took a large conch shell out of her leather bag and sounded the retreat signal. The loud sound echoed up and down the coast against the volcanic rock wall. After she sounded the retreat all the still-living Amazons regrouped. I counted only fifteen. I took the leather bag with my telescope and held it to my right eye so that I could see exactly which ship Saraly was going to be taken to. I could tell they were taking her to the second ship, anchored farther off. It was the mothership of the two and watched them take her on board. I watched for a few seconds and told the survivors to follow me.

We rushed down the hill to the beach. The Moors opened fire on us with their muskets, wounding two of our warriors. Helped by the others, we did not leave them behind and continued down the hill. As we climbed down, we heard a strange buzzing that sounded like thousands of bees in the dark of the night as the cloud had returned to block the full moon completely. This enormous black cloud was not a normal rain cloud. Instead, it was a huge number of locusts, a massive swarm of millions of insects of Biblical proportion. It descended over our heads but not into us. The strangest thing was that these insects started to impact the bodies, heads, and faces of our enemies. The Moors, in panic, dropped their weapons and dove to the ground to protect their faces and eyes. The locusts allowed us to escape as a strong celestial force of defense had crossed right over our heads, not even once impacting against any of us. After panicking the Moors, they continued on to the vineyards, which would then be destroyed. I thanked God that the Moors would not benefit from a harvest of the grapes.

We reached the shore and fought with the boat keepers for one of the vessels. We boarded it and rowed toward the mothership I pointed out. The full moon returned. Very carefully, we approached the vessel and climbed up the anchor lines to disarm and dump overboard the anchor watch. We liberated Saraly, and Olivia and her warriors took control of the ship. We raised the anchor and sailed away from the coast, leaving behind us what had been for many years the homeland that we all loved.

The next day everyone was more relaxed and at peace, knowing the two wounded women would recover. Their injuries were superficial, one of them with a bullet in her left arm, the other in her right shoulder. Olivia came over to me and Saraly to offer me the telescope, pointing behind us in the distance. I looked through it and saw one of the pirate ships, which must have been the Moor Porfirio, who had decided to pursue us. I shook my head regretfully at not having sunk that last ship before leaving. Saraly, noting my long face, tried to give me support. "It will be very difficult for them to catch up with us. This ship is a lot bigger and more canvas than the other. We should be the faster ship. Even if they manage to get close to us, we'll give them a warm welcome." She touched one of my shoulders with one hand and a main deck cannon with the other.

I smiled and saluted Olivia, who left. I gave Saraly a kiss on the cheek. "When I saw you fall from the top of the hill on your horse, I didn't think I would see alive the mother of my children again." I caressed her belly. "But, as I saw from the top of the hill fighting the Moors when they tried to tie you up, I realized with great joy that your wood is like a cedar—you don't even let the termites get to you."

She smiled and replied, "I thought something similar but different. I thought for a minute that I had reached the end of my life, but when I looked up and saw you on the top of the cliff, you looked so regal on your white horse that I recovered my spirit. I felt very sure that you would come for me and would rescue me from the filthy hands of those miserable Moors who had captured me. In my soul I achieved tranquility. For the first time in my life, I had no more fear of the Moors and thanked God for bringing you into my life."

We continued our long voyage over the open sea to an uncertain future. We sailed for several long months at sea with no sight of land beyond small islands or finding the New World that we were seeking. We lost several of our

Amazons in hard battle in naval encounters with the Spanish Crown who fired indiscriminately on us under the assumption we were pirates or corsairs due to our lack of national colors to identify us as belonging to any country. I had ordered the crew to destroy the only flags in the ship, which were all Jolly Rogers. That encounter with the Spanish fleet caused a goodly amount of damage to the ship, forcing us to anchor off a small island we had found during our journey. There we were able to make the necessary repairs to the ship and replenished our supplies of fresh water and food, especially fruit, which we hoped would last for the rest of the journey. We had sufficient wine and preserved meat to survive for several more months, but water and fruit were a grave concern.

We continued in search of the new continent or at least the West Indies. Good luck allowed us to escape alive from the Moors and so made a fool of their captain, Porfirio. Our mothership allowed us to carry more canvas and so speed ahead over the open ocean, leaving him far behind us. I thought that God had certainly been with us on this journey and that we should give Him thanks for our ship still remaining afloat, especially after all the hull damage we received from the Spanish fleet. I thought that very soon my faith was going to be put to the test once more, because Saraly was far along in her pregnancy as she expected our first son. She could not even get out of her bed for the past several weeks. She had contracted yellow fever, developing a high fever that made her delirious and incoherent. According to the natives of the island we had stopped at, it was produced by the bite of mosquitoes on those islands. It was quite common in Africa and spread to South America with the importation of black slaves. It affects the nervous system, causing serious hallucinations and in the process affecting the liver and kidneys, producing dark urine and abdominal pain along with vomiting and bleeding from the mouth, nose, and eyes from the stomach. It had received that name due to how it produced a jaundice in the victim. The patient would have muscle spasms, loss of appetite, and sometimes severe diarrhea. Seeing Saraly in this condition completely devastated me as I watched her gradually become very thin and weak, so far from the beautiful and healthy Amazon I had initially met. All she had left was her swollen belly in which she carried that precious cargo, the product of our beautiful and intense love that we had mutually professed to each other. With tears in my eyes before the large wooden cross on the wall, I got on my knees and asked Jesus' image the son of God to please help us to find solid land soon. On this depended the life of Saraly but also all our lives as we were running very short on provisions. If Saraly died, it was not just my love that would die but also my baby and its opportunity to see for the first time the beautiful sunshine we now ran for. Our water had to be rationed, even after replenishment, because the Caribbean sun was our worst enemy and oppressor.

I had nearly finished my prayer and was crossing myself when a blast of thunder broke the silence and shook the entire ship from stem to stern. I got up from the deck quickly in wonderment. I crossed myself once more and touched the head of the image of Jesus on the wall. I said as I shook my head, "I'm not expecting your answer so quickly, especially in this manner. But You know better than anyone whatever You do. They say in my country You manifest Yourself in strange ways."

I crossed myself and left my cabin, walking up to the quarter deck. Heavy rain was pouring down, and I found that many of the Amazons had been killed when the mizzen mast had fallen, dropped by a lightning strike. The beautiful blonde Olivia, with a handful of survivors, were trying to hoist out the ship's boat, informing me that the ship was sinking. The lightning had split the poop deck, destroying around half of it below the waterline. As a result, she was taking on water too fast to pump out. The rain poured down, and the winds of the hurricane blew the waves into immense size. By the flashes of lightning, I could see that a waterspout had formed, and was bearing down on us directly. I felt at that moment completely helpless, thinking only of Saraly, who was so weak she could not walk without assistance. She would certainly die, so in my desperation I yelled to Olivia, "Please help me get Saraly out of my cabin!"

Olivia, with the help of two loyal women, raised Saraly from her bed and brought her onto one of the ship's boats, just before the demonic waterspout hit what was left of our ship. As we paddled desperately to put some distance between us and our stricken ship, it hit the vessel about two hundred feet from us, smashing the massive object into toothpicks in fractions of seconds. It changed its course so that it started to pass behind our boat. We saw it repeat by the light of the flashes its destruction to Porfirio's ship, still in pursuit of us. I thought this might be the reason for this happening, as it was certain that pirate intended to board us. We had never fully lost him—he had always remained just in sight on the same course as ours. It was as strange irony that this ship would be smashed to pieces by that enormous, powerful force of nature had saved us from Porfirio who had been following us in revenge and trying to recover his hostage, Saraly. He had found instead the hand of divine justice, losing his last ship after many hours of trying to sail in the rough waters of the hurricane.

All night we floated in that small boat in a state of uncertainty. We had fallen asleep and awoke to a beautiful sunny day with the most gorgeous sun I had ever seen. Where it had previously been our punisher, now we could see a coast with a white sandy beaches and coconut trees. It was the most beautiful beach I had ever seen before—the Venezuelan beaches of La Guaira, the country's main port that was founded in 1577 as an outlet for Caracas, fifteen kilometers to the south. Without knowing or planning it, this was the beginning of a new life for all of us. There I would establish my family, have a beautiful life, and where I also suffered a horrible death at the hands of the murderous pirate, Porfirio, just as the old lady Pascasia had seen when she read my palm. At that time, naturally, I had no idea what my own future held.

A little while later, dragged by the currents and waves, we landed on that sandy beach. A small group of natives came over to us to offer help. They transported us to a small Jesuit community. The pastor there delivered my first son that I named Raymundo. They offered medical care using natural remedies for Saraly. Her strong constitution was one in a million, and she became one of the very few to survive yellow fever. Even the lingering effects of damage to the internal organs were escaped by her. After her recovery and regaining sufficient weight to appear as she used to be, I gave thanks to God for this miracle and in gratitude and love we asked the pastor who had saved her life to marry us. Our happiness grew enormously with the blessing of several sons and daughters, but the danger had not disappeared from our lives. Not only had I become very prosperous, but I had been appointed Governor several years later of the whole province.

Destiny put me face to face with the piratical Porfirio after he raped an eleven-year-old girl in one of the villages near La Guaira where I was supposed to enforce the law. The police and the neighbors brought the criminal before me, and I discovered from his own lips that the same night when we arrived years before with our small group of survivors only fifty kilometers to the south that horrible criminal had also washed ashore with some of his men. For years he had established himself in that same region. Now, like some destiny, I was the one who had to send him for several years to prison in punishment for his abominable crime of the same kind he committed as he had during his days of piracy. It crossed my mind that, finally, he would receive his final lesson or at least I would not see him again because he should die in prison due to the length of his sentence. I had been flexible and merciful, as the penalty for that crime at the time was death by guillotine. Once more, guided by my compassion and nobler feelings, I had ignored the advice of Pascasia to kill him if I ever saw him again. That diabolical demon would return eventually to haunt me and kill me as well as several of my loved ones.

Suddenly, I felt an intense heat throughout my body as if I were burning in a fire from some horrible dark hole inside a ditch. Then I felt something like a hand shaking me out of it and I started to hear the fire alarm and Elizabeth's voice yelling, "Julio Antonio, wake up! You have a fire in your cabin!"

CHAPTER 19: SEARCHING FOR A BETTER FUTURE

As soon as I heard that, still half-asleep I jumped out of the bed, still confused. I could see I was back in our submarine. It appeared a short circuit had occurred in some of the electrical cables behind the small sofa in my cabin and had started the fire. Some of the pillows on the sofa were burned, but Elizabeth, acting quickly as always, managed to extinguish the fire before it got out of control. More than anything it was a dense smoke that triggered the alarm, burning only a corner of the sofa and a few pillows. Soon everyone, including Willy with the white cockatoo, attracted by Elizabeth's yell, arrived in worry. The fire control system in that sophisticated submarine was already venting the smoke out of the air system. The burned cushions Chopin and Brenton managed to remove from the cabin.

Chopin returned shortly to have a close inspection to investigate the cause for such a mysterious fire. It looked like it had started in one of the few outlets that served a lamp on one side of the sofa. Because it was hidden in an unusual place, he had overlooked it during his inspection. Chopin opened the outlet and grimaced. "This is very strange."

I asked curiously, "What have you found? Foul play?"

"I don't want to alarm you. Let me double check every single outlet in this vessel." He began to check every outlet with a voltmeter and opened the casings all around the vessel. We looked at each other in concern. Chopin tended to minimize everything as he found logical reasons, but this answer took us by surprise. He never exaggerated, much less have doubt when it came to technical matters. It took him several minutes to complete his check. He came back with something in his fingers which had small wires sticking out from it. He held it up before us and said to me, "Now I can tell you with assurance that this was not an accidental fire due to the outlet's malfunction. This was intentional sabotage of our submarine. It was very well calculated—and I can say for certain from a master."

We were all in the front of the submarine where the windows that looked out into the ocean were, watching the beautiful panorama. This was a shock to us because no one had access to this submarine. What Chopin told us meant only two possibilities: the devices he had found had been installed before the submarine was brought to us or something completely terrifying—that we had among us a traitor in service to our enemies. It was not even something we could ever consider even in the silence of our minds.

Chopin said, "You see this little fuse? It's a magnetic fuse commonly used in incendiary devices for sabotage missions. It leaves no trace. It has a delayed effect, only when the outlet was in use for a long time and with the energy passing through it, no matter what the voltage is, this fuse explodes, creating a short circuit that volatizes insulation to create an immediate electrical fire." His expression grew worried. "The most effective thing of this tiny device is that when it explodes it disintegrates and vanishes without any trace of its existence or foul play. That's why I would place it, as it was in this case, in a very hidden, strategic place. The first one they put in your cabin behind the sofa. What is behind the sofa and that wall? The oxygen tanks for the entire submarine. That one disappeared." He shook the hand with the fuse. "This one was placed right next to the tanks of propane gas for the refrigeration units. That's why I guarantee you that this is exactly what happened." His face grew long, and sorrow appeared in his eyes. "I want to ask all of you for my most profound forgiveness. I checked every single outlet before with the electrical schematic of this vessel in my hands. I completely overlooked them is the only answer. I missed these two because they were very well concealed. This one was in the bookcase in the conference room."

I shook my head. "Remember, Chopin, you don't have to apologize. When we get tired, we all can fall asleep at the wheel. That is human. Don't worry—nobody is perfect. Just remember this incident in the future and learn from this mistake. It's not only our lives that are in your hands, but also yours."

Chopin nodded with a disgusted expression at the mistake he assumed that he had made in such a vital manner that had nearly cost all our lives. I put my hand around his shoulders. To alleviate his remorse, I added, knowing how bad he must be feeling, "Chopin, remember—when something like this happens, don't let it bother you for too long. Ask yourself what would have happened if you hadn't made an effort to find the second one?" I took the fuse from him. "If you hadn't, probably the fire alarm system would sound after we all got blown out of the water in a thousand pieces along with the submarine." I smiled as I put the fuse in an envelope. "Thank you, God, that I decided to sleep for a while in my cabin. And to Elizabeth for checking on me while I was sleeping and discovering the fire before it could get out of control just as the alarm started to sound." They looked at me with small smiles on their faces. I asked Yaneba, "Can you tell me why all of you are looking at me that way and smiling like I said something awkward?"

She looked me in the eyes, grinning broadly. She shook her head. "You don't have the slightest idea of how long you've been asleep, don't you?"

I looked at my right watch, checked it against my left, and answered, "Maybe an hour."

They laughed. I could not understand why they were laughing. I checked my watches once more, and it didn't seem like I could have been asleep for more than an hour and half, based on when I went to bed. I remembered clearly the time I had gone to sleep.

Willy was the one this time, with the small fingers of his right hand and a mischievous smile, held up two fingers. He shook his head. "A lot more."

Still not understanding and more than a little incredulous, I said, "Two hours? No! It's not possible." I checked my watches yet again. It was impossible unless they were both wrong. I was even more surprised was that everyone was now laughing loudly. I started to think that perhaps the oxygen regulation was malfunctioning, and they were high.

Yaneba controlled her laughter, understanding my confusion. "Julio Antonio—two *days*. Forty-eight hours."

I looked at her in disbelief and checked my watches again. "I went to bed at three pm, Yaneba. It's only four pm now."

"Yes, you're right. You went to bed at three pm—two days ago."

"How could this be possible?"

Chandee replied, "This happens when we are completely exhausted, and our bodies need to recharge the batteries because your energy is completely drained."

Elizabeth said, "All of us decided to let you sleep, since we knew that you didn't wake up like normal due to hunger and knew already the trip would take sixteen days. You know better that we cannot use the Panama Canal, so we had to spend twice the time on this trip to go around Cape Horn. Thank God that we all decided to take turns keeping an eye on you. That certainly saved all of us from a certain death. If I had not come to your cabin to check on you, I would not have discovered that fire in time. The alarm started to sound a lot later, after I had that fire under control. That's why I didn't wake you before—I was busy extinguishing the fire. You know as well as I what would happen if those oxygen tanks had caught on fire and exploded inside your cabin."

I shook my head, still confused at how it was possible for me to sleep for a straight forty-eight hours. But now I realized this was why my stomach was growling in protest. I put my right hand over my abdomen and grinned. "That is why my stomach is crying like a dog and cat in a fight for a while now. I am right now as hungry as a lion that's been in a cage and abandoned for a week. Truly, as the old saying tells us, we can live for a long time without water and food, but very little time without sleep. Exhaustion kills you a lot more quickly and in silence. There's no doubt in my mind that God sent to us one of His angels to guard our backs on this trip."

The cockatoo, as if understanding what I said, jumped from Willy's shoulder to mine. Everyone stared in strong surprise as the bird squawked three times and caressed my neck with his little head. He bowed and bobbed enthusiastically as if trying to thank me for my words. The strangest thing in the whole matter was that the bird had remained completely mute, almost sleeping on Willy's shoulder until I had spoken. It occurred to me before that the cockatoo had been so tired and sleepy because it had been with my spirit in that strange dream trip in which I went back to my ancestor for the entire two days during all the crazy nineteenth century adventures. I asked Willy, "What do you think if we call this precious angel that saved both your mommy's life as well as mine Venus, like the planet? This is the name of the matriarch that saved the life of my ancestor Francisco del Marmol."

The cockatoo nodded her head vigorously. Once more she croaked three times. Willy said, "I like it, and it looks like she does, too. Look how she's caressing your neck."

I smiled and asked the rest of my friends. "What about you guys? Any objections?"

They shook their heads, and Yaneba said, "Nope. That's a beautiful name."

Having received democratic agreement from everyone, the cockatoo was baptized with the name of Venus. Chandee said, "Well, I've been eating for two days unlike you, but my stomach is starting to protest, probably in solidarity with yours. I think it's best we all go eat something before you collapse from lack of food. Everyone will go with you since you just woke up at the right time. We'll give you a new welcome and open one of those mega bottles of champaign you brought for the mimosas you like."

"That is exactly what my spirit needs at this moment to alleviate the nervous tension this exotic dream created. I was transported into the past over two hundred years ago during these past two days. I had encounters and tremendous ordeals and wore the boots of one of my farthest ancestors, Francisco del Marmol. He became the governor in La Guaira and died in the most horrible fashion, burned alive by his worst enemy. I not only had the opportunity to walk in his boots but also wear his sword on my waist and find and discover his honor and courage in my heart. That made me feel extremely proud of my last name. I believe, even though this became a painful and horrible experience, it will be valuable and necessary as a perfect and opportune debriefing to alert me and prepare me ahead of the type of diabolic enemy of the kind we will encounter in this place. They won't hesitate to destroy us all. For our own survival, this diabolic enemy must be exterminated without any mercy at all. He has become the representative of the diabolic corruption in today's world." I touched my chest with my thumb. "I'm not going to make the same mistake my ancestor made and simply send him to jail, from where he could one day escape or freed by his political corrupt accomplices." I added with firm conviction, "I will destroy him and send him to the Inferno, where he should continue forever, if necessary, with my own hands, those hands I have tried to keep clean of blood all these years."

We were now sitting around the long table in the kitchen. We raised the mimosas Chandee had served us and toasted to the complete destruction of the enemy of humanity, Lucifer, who was now operating in the twenty-first century in one of his disguises as Osama bin Laden. After a delicious meal which took a short time to serve, since I had been prepared packages of gourmet food of lobster thermidor, duck l'orange, beef wellington, and other dishes for the duration of the trip. I had frozen and vacuum sealed them as soon as I had cooked them to preserve their flavor and texture to the smallest detail. That way our meals, once defrosted in a few minutes, still had the quality preserved of a five-star restaurant to provide not only exquisite flavor but also great nutrition to keep our bodies in good health and energy to be able to function properly in our mission but also be a pleasure to consume. Like I always say, you can die tomorrow so let's eat deliciously and properly today. I had repeated always what I had heard from my Mima since when I was very little: belly full and satisfied, heart full of joy and energy, ready for anything that life put before us.

After we finished our meal, I told Willy and Brenton the entire story of what had happened in Southcoast Plaza, as I had promised earlier, and how Venus had saved both my life and Faviola's, with the corroboration of my friends who were present, adding in their own opinions and points of view in the story. Each of them not only was present while all this was happening but had also observed it from different angles as to what had transpired. I wanted to give them the chance to add in details that I might have missed. This made the story a lot more interesting for everyone, especially once I finished my tale and saw how Willy had been absorbed by it, as well as Brenton, who had listened to every word in silence, which made me wonder and concerned.

Brenton said in a voice choked with emotion, "If I had any doubts before, I assure you that not only you but everyone that's been around your or behind you has been protected by a very superior being. Call it whatever you will, it's not important to me, but to me that only has one name: God Almighty, the only true King of the Universe." He took a couple of steps and caressed the head of Venus. In gratitude she jumped off my shoulder onto his and began to caress his neck with her head. She croaked some more.

We all smiled and Yaneba said, "Brenton, it appears Venus likes very much what you just said."

Several weeks later, after arriving in the port of La Guaira, Venezuela, we looked for a strategic place several miles south for our point of disembarkation. We selected the location based on information provided by our contacts inside the country. Those people had also informed us that a nautical club with a huge marina had recently been constructed with a vast capacity for receiving many tourists with super yachts of multimillionaires, a few of whom were nationals within the regime, but the rest foreigners. They needed this tourism to keep the country alive economically because the new disastrous government of Chavez's socialist regime had already destroyed their society.

We left Willy in the submarine with Chopin and Venus. We used special scuba diving suits and modern electrical underwater sleds used by the armed forces for clandestine operations. The name of this particular vehicle was Seabob, produced by Cayago A.G. in Stuttgart, Germany. It was the world's fastest underwater scooter. We went underwater for a while until we could find the location where we would leave our transportation, which (unlike our submarine) was not invisible. We left Elizabeth on guard of our primary means of exit when we were done. The rest of us changed into elegant European designer clothing to look like rich playboys and their entourage.

We walked into the elegant beach resort with our Cartier and Versace sunglasses. We didn't display any political affiliation, which gave us the upper hand to disguise ourselves and avoid creating problems with the intelligence services of that repressive communist government's agencies. Their regime was nothing less than a photocopy of the Castro's government system. All these people, including the armed forces and the Venezuelan intelligence had been instructed by military advisors in the same techniques the Soviet KGB had trained the Cubans in the past. We had a tremendous advantage and superiority over both our friendly spies and our adversaries of other countries because most of us had been trained in Cuba, receiving the same training by the G-2 as well as Western methods before our defections and knew the communist monster well.

Our plan was to divide into two groups consisting of Chandee and I in the first team and with Brenton and Yaneba as the second team. They were to remain on the beach sipping piña coladas next to the pool. Chandee and I were to enter the resort itself to book a double suite where we would meet later on. As we walked into the hotel area along the beach, a beautiful blonde little girl walking her dog along the sand approached us. She was about eight years old with long, wavy pigtails and a filthy face like a drifter. As always, appearance was far from reality; this little girl walked directly over to me and to my surprise addressed me. "Are you Dr. JAM?"

I looked into the little girl's bottle green eyes. "Who wants to know, little princess?"

She smiled slightly. "My name is Paquita. My mommy is Hania Abdul. My daddy passed away. I think this is enough to identify me to you."

"Yes, sweetheart."

"Then you are who you are?"

"Yes."

"Then I will be your tour guide. This is my dog, Tombo."

I smiled and held out my hand. "Nice to meet you. I am Dr. JAM."

She held out her hand, but instead of shaking mine, she deposited something she had taken out of a plastic bag: four canary yellow wrist bracelets, one for each of us. "Nice to meet you. My mommy told me you're bringing us the most beautiful gift for all of our family. She has been expecting it from you for a while."

"Your mommy is right, Paquita, but that gift is only to be given to your mommy personally. Those are my instructions."

She pouted. "Don't wear these bracelets until after you check in to the resort. They will give you different ones with a light blue color. Those tell the local and national authorities that you are question marks. If you are stopped at any check point on the highway or anywhere else, the yellow ones I just gave you tell them that you are people of very high trust. Sometimes, even working directly for Chavez's communist government." She smiled mischievously. "That is one of the methods the communists keep control of their enemies here. They keep a close watch on the tourists."

I nodded. "Thank you very much for this information. It's very valuable to us in our line of work. I have to thank you again for your taking the risk to bring those to us. I have a small question for you, Paquita, if you don't mind."

She shook her head. "No, shoot. Ask me whatever you want."

"We have two men in our group. My friend Brenton and me." I touched Brenton on the shoulder. "Why didn't you come to him, and instead came directly to me? Why didn't you direct your question to him? You don't know me—what made you think that Brenton wasn't Dr. JAM?"

She looked at me mischievously and shook her head. She smirked and said, "Brenton? No." She shook her index finger negatively. "He might be a great soldier or even a Marine, but I can assure you that he doesn't have the sophistication or class to be a doctor."

"Thank you," Brenton said a little sarcastically, "thank you very much, Paquita."

"You're welcome very much," she answered in the same tone of voice.

Yaneba and Chandee laughed, and both said, "Whoa!"

Yaneba asked, "How old are you, little girl?"

"What does my age have to do with anything? With all my respect."

Yaneba was ready to burst out laughing. "You're right, honey. Your age has nothing to do with our conversation, but it has a lot to do with me in my personal satisfaction.

You remind me very much of myself with your adorable personality when I was about your age."

Paquita grinned from ear to ear, her aggressive demeanor vanishing to a more pleasant one. "I am eight and a half years old. I'll be nine in few months."

Yaneba stepped forward and offered her hand. "I am Yaneba. I can tell you I wasn't wrong about you." She pointed to me. "I was exactly your age when I met Dr. JAM. Even though he's a little older than me, it always angered me when he brought my age up." She took the girl's hand in her outstretched hand and with her other hand caressed her hair.

Paquita replied in surprise, "Really? Wow! You've known him for so long?"

Yaneba replied, "Maybe to you that is so young it seems so long. But to me, it's like it all happened yesterday." Her face softened as she remembered our time together in Cuba. We exchanged glances, sharing the memory telepathically.

As Yaneba released her hand, Chandee stepped forward and held out her own hand with a smile. "I am Chandee. And sometimes it is to us is very sad, remember the past and how the communist regime separated our families and stole from us the most precious gift any human being has: the innocence of youth. I met Dr. JAM, too, approximately a year or two after Yaneba, but I was also around your age." Chandee with Paquita's hand in hers, had tears in her eyes. She was certainly remembering the pain and suffering we had all endured in Cuba at such a young age.

Paquita looked at her. "Why are you crying?"

Chandee wiped her eyes. "Just a little emotional thinking of those times when my parents shipped me out of Cuba out of fear of my becoming another victim of the regime and getting killed. Seeing you now the way you are, I know you'll be another freedom fighter. You are already—look at the great information you just gave us. I want to give you the best advice you should remember for the rest of your life. Don't allow the communists to steal your youth like they did to us, Paquita. Youth flies by. Don't rush to become more mature. All that will do is bring a lot of pain to you but also in the future regrets because you can never go back to the past to fix or patch up the errors that logically you will commit through your inexperience."

Paquita nodded in agreement. She said politely, "Thank you very much for your good intentions and for sharing with me as well your experience. My mommy, Hania, has told me that experience of others, even though it may be similar between different people at different ages frequently are completely different. We always should listen to the advice of people who are trying to help us with good intentions. Be grateful and take those views into consideration, especially when they're provided by people older than us because age in people possesses the most important ingredient of wisdom that helps us to survive and prevent us from making the same errors. That has a name: experience."

We looked at this little girl with her dirty face and smiled. We remembered or saw in her ourselves as we, nearly all of us, had the same attitude and eloquence. After we entered the hotel, Brenton and Yaneba headed to the pool area while Chandee and I went to register. After we reserved a double suite, Chandee took Paquita by the hand and said to me, "Wait for me here for a few minutes. I want to do something for her."

She walked over to the gift shop, where Chandee bought some new clothes and sandals for Paquita. The little girl didn't want to accept them, because, she protested, she was in disguise. Her mother had advised her that this was the best way to pass unnoticed and as well as to ensure that people would be extra nice to her out of pity. Despite her refusals, Chandee pressed the new clothes, so Paquita courteously thanked Chandee.

As we passed the swimming pool area towards the tower in which our suites were housed, I nodded three times to Yaneba and Brenton. That was a prearranged signal to them that everything was in order. They nonchalantly got up and started to follow us towards the elevators at the far-right side of the pool. We then took the elevator up to the penthouse suite we had reserved. We went by the wet bar next to the pool; a man and a woman were dressed in the traditional attire of the Yanomami indigenous tribe. These Indians lived in the forests all over the country, most of them in the rain forests along the border between Venezuela and Brazil. They lived in 250 to 350 villages along the Amazon and represented the true heart of the South American nation as they were the pioneer inhabitants of the area long before the arrival of the European colonizers. They were decorated with feathers and multiple minute Venezuelan flags on sticks picked into their clothing. There were so many sticks in their clothing that they looked quite colorful with all those flags of yellow, blue, and red bars and 8 white stars on the blue bar.

The man had many musical instruments tied to his body as a one-man band playing the Venezuelan national anthem. He had a wire holding the harmonica suspended from his forehead with bongos tied to his waist and a trumpet attached to his shoulder by wires on a brace. The woman by his side held maracas to keep the rhythm exactly to perfection. It was a man and woman orchestra. The harmony between the two was perfect, and they had attracted tourists to them, who deposited money into a plastic bucket with lines around it in the same colors of the Venezuelan flag.

We slowly passed them, a little captivated ourselves not just by the music but also the ingenuity of the performers. I looked the man in his eyes and saw him deliberately wink his right eye at me. I dropped a few bills into the bucket, and he nodded appreciatively. I looked at the woman next to him, who did the same. We continued along the pavement next to the pool by the sunbathing chairs. Finally, we reached the elevators. Once we entered an elevator car, we pressed the button for the 12th floor, which was the penthouse.

Once we entered the suite, I took a shower while Chandee made sure to give Paquita a bath, over her objections. She didn't content herself with a bath for Paquita and dress her in new clothes, she also gave her a new hairstyle, transforming the little drifter into a beautiful and elegant princess. Despite her protests, I think Paquita in the end liked it.

I handed the keys for the Land Rover Defender I had reserved to transport us to the capital where we were to find Hania, Abdul's wife. Brenton held in his hand the medium-sized cooler which held the precious cargo for Abdul's family. It was a modern style, light blue and white, that looked more in its form like a makeup box. We didn't want to call attention to it, and put on top a false tray with various kinds of makeup, so anyone who opened it would only see eyebrow pencils, lipstick, foundation, etc. It was beneath the tray the big surprise was concealed.

We walked away from the suite towards the elevators. We heard the rotors of several helicopters and exchanged worried glances. Yaneba had already punched the buttons to the basement, and the helicopters started to descend. Yaneba asked, "Are those helicopters normal?"

Paquita nodded. "All the time. When they bring tourists from Caracas to here, but also when thc government makes some arrests of very important people."

Yaneba looked at her approvingly. "Well, also very high government dignitaries sometimes bring their mistresses here to take them to exotic places far from the curious eyes of the people here in Venezuela, places like Cuba, where they won't be recognized. On that island, they're treated like royalty." Yaneba smiled and patted Paquita on the head. "Thank you for your information. It's very fruitful, even though it doesn't restore my tranquility much less remove my worries entirely. All we can do, like we always do, is to stay calm and try to handle the unexpected things thrown as best we can."

The elevator doors opened. We saw clearly and were surprised to see many soldiers and men in civilian clothes with radios in their ears and weapons around their waists. They spread all over the swimming pool, securing the perimeter. We slowly left the area and walked along the left side of the swimming pool. As we walked towards the lobby, an entourage of bodyguards and soldiers surrounded their comandante, Hugo Chavez Frias, towards our right. Chavez was in fatigue uniform to imitate the Castros in Cuba. He walked in the same direction as we were going, but on the opposite side of the pool and gazebo, where the wet bar was located, and the Indians continued to play their music.

Chavez stopped when he saw the tourists watching the musicians play. It must have flashed through his mind that this would be a good photo op for his government, because it was unusual to see the Indians come into the cities or other urban areas. He walked towards them; when he was around fifty feet away the couple stopped their dancing and playing cold. Both, like a duet, yelled, "*Viva Venezuela, muera la dictadura comunista de Chavez*![37]"

Before anyone in the escort of Chavez could begin to react, the couple dropped their musical instruments to the ground and each one poured bulbous glazed one- or two-gallon wine jars filled medical alcohol, probably 99% proof, over themselves, creating a pool around them from the excess. As soon as they had finished, they threw the jars to the ground dramatically, shattering them, pulled out lighters, ignited them and tossed them to their feet. They reached out to hold each other's hands as the flames immediately consumed them, yelling repeatedly the word "freedom" as a duet, even as they burned alive.

Several guards finally reacted, dropping to their knees to train their weapons on the pair, but when they saw the inferno found themselves paralyzed in sickened fascination at the grievous scene while the two Indians took hands to

[37] Long live Venezuela, death to the communist dictator Chavez!

die together as they continued screaming their battle cry. Some tourists rushed to take pictures of the scene, but the soldiers this time reacted immediately, taking the cameras of everyone as they told the tourists the cameras would be returned later after they were used as evidence in their investigation of the criminal act.

There were journalists present, who protested and demanded the return of the cameras. The head of the entourage said, "We cannot return your cameras until we review the film, by orders of the President."

Everyone there was paralyzed as the two bodies continued to burn in their graphic protest. This act of rabid patriotism demonstrated by those Indian Venezuelans who preferred to die than live in the immoral, atheist system filled of false promises that some called socialism shocked every person in that crowd who were left with the devastating image for years afterwards. This desperation was imported directly from the Caribbean Island of Cuba to Venezuela by the extreme Marxist-Leninists that had brought to the Cuban people and to the rest of the free and democratic world so much hate and death.

We all of us had tears in our eyes. Chandee grabbed my arm and said in a voice thick with emotion, "Let's get out of here as soon as we can, please."

Her voice shook us out of our shock and brought us back to reality, and we continued our walk towards the lobby, this time at a more rapid pace. The lobby was completely empty, because all the employees had been drawn to the horrific act of patriotism that had shaken even Chavez's soldiers to their boots. God sent us this distraction to help us tremendously, because the soldiers at the door of the resort hotel who were supposed to check luggage had abandoned their posts. With the presence of Chavez there, everyone was utterly distracted. We had no problems at the front with the glass doors completely open and arrived at the Land Rover. We placed the cooler in the back and left that location behind us. Steered by our little tour guide, we slipped on our yellow bracelets and put the light blue bracelets into our pockets. Paquita's dog jumped into that back and sat on the makeup case, which we found very opportunistic, since the soldiers would never search there, not with that intimidating dog on top of the case.

I smiled as I watched the dog settle himself in. I patted him on the head and offered him a piece of one of the beef jerkies I always carried in my pockets during my trips into the unknown and unexpected. This had saved my life several times so that I didn't starve to death. We had no major problems along the new highway to Caracas, encountering only one checkpoint. Like Paquita had informed us, as soon as they saw our yellow bracelets, they motioned for us to continue without even requiring us to stop for a search.

We arrived in less than half an hour later, guided by the astute Paquita. We soon entered the luxury zone of the city, El Rosal. It was very close to Las Mercedes. It appeared that this was a very high-class neighborhood and district, with luxurious residential buildings, condos, etc. We passed restaurants specializing in gourmet cuisine, shopping centers, and finally entering a building's underground parking garage, which Paquita had told us to go into.

We parked inside the garage, and she told us to wait in the car while she got her mom. Those were Hania's instructions. She jumped out of the Land Rover and repeated, "I'll only take a few minutes."

Before I could even reply, she ran over to the elevators, pressing a button there. She jumped into a car and disappeared before our eyes. I said to Brenton, "Move the car after everyone gets out. Park the car far from where we dropped her off." I looked at the others. "Fan out and take up strategic positions—just in case."

Brenton selected a location far from the view of anyone leaving the elevators. We spread out around the garage, Chandee remaining near the elevator, close enough to receive Paquita and Hania when they showed up. We had to depend on Brenton because none of us knew what Hania looked like.

Paquita, as she had said, took only a few minutes to return. She walked out of the elevator with a woman of about forty years of age with a white lock of hair on the left side of her long, black hair. They weren't alone. They were accompanied by two young men of strong build—they looked like body builders. They also looked around nervously for the vehicle we were supposed to be in that Paquita had described to them. They looked everywhere and turned to question Paquita, who pointed to where we had parked previously.

Chandee approached them, noticing their confusion, to establish contact. After Chandee spoke with them briefly, Brenton approached, followed by Tombo, who was very happy to see Paquita and Hania again. We watched to see that everything seemed to be in order, no foul play, so one after another we approached them by the elevator. We introduced ourselves, and the younger men around Hania turned out to be Abdul's sons. I instructed Brenton to bring the cooler and my backpack from the Land Rover. Brenton hurried to get them, and we entered the elevator car. Hania pressed the button marked 21.

After we entered their beautiful, spacious luxury condominium, Hania offered us tea, juices, cookies, and nuts in different plates about the living room. After a few minutes of conversation, I said to her, "I need to speak to you in private."

She made her excuses and led me into the master bedroom. I removed my shirt to reveal the plastic brace I was wearing with bundles of $100 bills. I gave her the total of $1,500,000. She thanked me profusely for the delivery of the vast amount of money Abdul wanted her to have in case something happened to him. She said, "Thank you. Before you do anything else, I have something for you as well." She lifted up a corner of the mattress and removed a packet. As she handed it to me she said, "Here are all Abdul's banking contacts in Australia. He wanted you to have this."

I accepted the packet and tucked it into my jacket. "Thank you. I also have this for you." I took the cooler and with a very intense and emotional conversation, omitting the more gruesome details, and handed it to her. I said, "I believe that I've relieved my conscience by bringing to you all we could salvage of Abdul. He told me you were a Christian, and so you can give him a decent burial. I'm sure you want something from him you can remember."

Still in complete control of her emotions, she thanked me. Then she removed the cover of the makeup box, and an uncontrollable scream of pain and horror escaped her throat as she saw the head and hands of her late husband. The scream echoed throughout the condo, which prompted both sons to rush into the master bedroom. They tried to comfort her. She had already forewarned them of what the unpleasant event that had befallen their father. No matter how hard we try to prepare for news like this, it is next to impossible to accept it when you see it with your own eyes. To see your loved one reduced to body parts is unbearable. Tombo came behind the two sons. Aryan, the younger of the two in his late teens, could not control his emotions and began to cry like a five-year-old boy. Abdul, Jr. kept his emotions under control and reacted rapidly when he saw the curious Paquita poke her head in the door of the master bedroom. He bounded over, took his young sister by the shoulder, and ushered her back to the living room.

I excused myself and left the room right behind Abdul Jr. to give space to Hania and Aryan to mourn and mitigate the pain they had repressed for so long for the death of the man who had been a great father, a good husband, and exemplary friend. Life had left him in ambiguous circumstances and had placed in him in the circle of the most egotistical sadist in our time. As he had confessed to me directly, he had repented for that thousands of times, but no matter how he tried to find an exit from that mistake, he never discovered it until it was too late.

I returned to the living room. Brenton was sitting on one side of the sofa on the corner, close now by Abdul, Jr. He looked at me as I entered with a sad expression and depression in his eyes. I shook my head in disgust as did he. He looked me directly in the eyes and I saw something I hadn't seen before—the expression in his face and eyes were far from genuine. What I read in his eyes and face told me in my psychic reading more guilt than tears. It was similar to the expression I had seen in Abdul, Sr. when he had asked me for pardon when he had confessed to me to being the right arm for a long time and principal financier for all the plans of Osama bin Laden had to attack the USA on 9/11.

I suddenly shook throughout my body internally. It rolled from my tail bone up to my neck, raising as it always did the small hairs on my neck. That took me by surprise. Until now, I had felt completely confident in Brenton's presence. But a small, tiny virus penetrated my mind after we discovered that someone had been tampering with the electrical system on our submarine by placing two different devices that had been successful would have been the death of most of us, if not all of us. It had been created in my mind the suspicions that those who had not been placed in the submarine in the outlets before Chopin's inspection, but after his inspections.

This came into my mind a lot easier to believe. Knowing Chopin as I did, it was not possible he would make this type of error. There is always room for everything, and that was why I hadn't tried to create a big fuss over it. I simply attributed it to the complete exhaustion from many hours of work he had just performed in changing the oxygen tanks and other servicing on the submarine, and so left open the benefit of doubt to everyone. I didn't want to rush to make any type of assumption that could come to be unfair and create in my mind a negative, devastating distrust among us during the operation we were trying to bring to a successful conclusion. Being fair and taking into consideration that Brenton had volunteered to risk his life by coming back to

Venezuela where he had nearly lost his life and had been tortured to the point nearly to death and also taking into consideration that he left his most precious treasure, his family, behind knowing that I needed him to identify and make sure that the woman we were going to meet was really Abdul's wife. Of course, his help I considered essential for us to succeed in our mission. Without his presence, our enemies very easily could put a veil over our eyes by sending someone to replace Hania. We could make the fatal mistake of giving the package I was carrying to our enemies; the last thing we wanted was to give more money for that terrorist organization to commit more criminal acts around the world.

All four of us had remained silent. Finally, I broke the silence. I asked Brenton, "Where are Chandee and Yaneba?"

He shook his head with a smile and pointed to an interior door with a glass circular window that looked like the kitchen door. "They're in there, trying to fix the world."

I shook my head and smiled as well. I nodded and stood up and walked towards the door he had pointed out, leaving Brenton the sole company of Abdul, Jr. and Paquita. As I slowly and gently pushed the swinging door and entered the kitchen dinette, I found my two great female friends who looked like they had been very deep in an intense conversation. I walked over to them and said, "I beg your pardon for interrupting. Will you allow me to sit with you? I promise I will not interrupt your conversation but for a few seconds."

Both looked at me and smiled broadly. Yaneba said, "Come on. You came just in time like a glass of ice water in a desert heat." I pulled a chair out and sat down next to them. Yaneba said, "I want to apologize to you for my negativity, but I don't feel at all comfortable in this place. Something is not right here. I don't know if it's that lately I don't trust anyone, especially those who have been close to terrorists, or if it's simply part of my feminine intuition.

But something gives me the creeps with the older son of Abdul."

I asked, "What about him makes you feel this way?"

She looked me deeply in my eyes and took a deep breath. "His evasive eyes and his unfriendly face. It makes me believe that he knows something he really is trying very hard for us to not find out about him. Maybe it's because he's working directly with bin Laden in disguise. You know very well that he could come to be the perfect subject because he possesses all the psychological qualities of becoming a perfect recruit in seconds, especially not just due to the relationship his father maintained until his death to al-Qaeda's leader, but now his father is a martyr for all of them. You have to remember that only you and Brenton know about his repentance. We all are, perhaps in his son's eyes, the assassins of his father. Especially given the way he was killed. Even though we all know it was just a freak accident, he doesn't."

I nodded. "You're right, 100%. I have to give you a great big point for your intuition. I must tell you that I take very seriously a woman's intuition. I have something more to worry about." I turned to Chandee. "What about you, Chandee? What you really think in your heart, of all that Yaneba's been saying?"

Without hesitating, Chandee answered, "I'm the one who brought this dilemma to Yaneba. I discovered that she has the same worries and feelings I have running in circles in my head. But we withheld them so that we don't give you more worries than you already have. Knowing both of us so well, you must have inside your head not a hurricane but a sandstorm about the unfortunate incident we discovered in the submarine."

I smiled and nodded. I said to Chandee, "I believe both of you know me better than my own Mima, who had me for at least a few hours over nine months in her belly. I even made my own birth difficult. I took this opportunity to talk to both of you alone so that I could warn you to take all precautions and measures not just with Abdul, Jr. but also with Brenton. Don't take me wrong—I don't have any concrete justification or reason to have any suspicions of him. But I just had a strong psychic reading of the kind I haven't had for a while in my brain. Now, when I put it together with your feminine intuitions, this mix can become as tremendous a danger for all of us. Without knowing it ourselves, we have brought to the hands of maybe a wannabe terrorist, Abdul, Jr. Brenton might the fuse to the stick of dynamite he has been waiting for to blow up not just us but also the rest of his family."

They looked at me with profound concern in their faces and eyes. They exchanged glances and then back at me, each nodding her head. Chandee said, "You don't know how right you might be."

I said, "Even though all of this is based only on our own instincts, psychism, and female intuition, I've learned to follow my instincts to the letter, and even more my psychic skills. Very rarely do these come to be wrong. We should all therefore keep our eyes wide open and not lose a single movement or step that either of those two, as the price for not doing so could be our lives if we take our eyes off the ball for those very minimal details. It could be the result of all our doubts."

At that moment the kitchen door opened abruptly, revealing Brenton's form. He had a small smile on his face as he said, as it appeared he heard my last words, "You may be right. We have to pay attention to the most minimal details in everything we do. Those details sometimes are the most important ones."

We exchanged glances and smiled. Brenton came over to us and pulled a chair out without invitation. He looked at me and asked, "Will you allow me to interrupt your conversation?"

We laughed. Yaneba said, "You already did. Go ahead."

"I'm sorry. I have something extremely important I wanted to communicate with you guys."

"What's up?" I asked.

He said, "I just discovered from Abdul, Jr. that the polygamist is not just here in our back yard. He's also been in contact with the man. From time to time, he calls him over the phone so that he can pick up his mail in his P.O. box, since he trusts no one to handle his mail save only for Abdul, Jr., who even has a key to the box only a few blocks away from here. He receives correspondence from his close members of his family and those who have his absolute trust. You have to ask yourself what Abdul, Jr. has done to earn this level of trust."

I said, "Your next mission is to get a copy of that box key."

Brenton nodded. "You know, as I do, that as part of his agreement of relocation he committed to cease and desist his terrorist activities, but he's continued to not only be the leader of this organization clandestinely but also the mastermind of all these terrorist attacks. By the way, Abdul, Jr told me he has planned with the polygamist a major and great attack as a sequel to the multiple bridges and tunnels simultaneously all across the USA to paralyze the economy of the nation. This idea came from Abdul, Jr himself. This idea was received with tremendous enthusiasm by bin Laden. That tells me that this terrorist leader continues to flourish around the world and will continue to do so. The idea the Obamas had to neutralize the polygamist turns out to be fiction and functions only for his own interest in being re-elected and as a sensational photo op before the world."

Chandee, Yaneba, and I exchanged glances. I used the opportunity and decided to ask, "Do you know the motive to why Abdul, Jr. has been entrusting you with all this without knowing you very well, practically only hours?"

"Not hours, my friend Dr. del Marmol. He's known me virtually since he was born. I've been visiting them as I performed my intelligence work with his father."

"Oh, I didn't know that. That makes more sense. Of course, he already has absolute trust in you." I smiled and patted him on the shoulder. "You should go back to his side and convince him that he can place absolute trust in us, since we're on the same team. If you accomplish that, it will make our work a lot easier. Convince him that we'll cooperate with him in whatever he needs."

"OK," Brenton replied. "I'll add this to getting the key to the mailbox. I've been working with him while you guys were talking in here, but I'll go back to the living room to continue my work."

"Remember, we don't have much time. We have to get out of here in the next forty-eight hours."

He nodded his understanding and stood up to leave the kitchen to return to Abdul, Jr. in the living room. After he left, the three of us looked at each other in discontent. Our worries had only increased after hearing what Brenton had to say.

CHAPTER 20: THE MASTER ANGEL OF DEATH CRASHES

I stood up and said to them, "I will go down to the Land Rover. I need my notebook and special pen to draw up graphical representations that I have in mind to put into motion a plan that has been growing in my mind. I got the idea when Brenton mentioned the P.O. Box bin Laden has here to receives all the mail from all his old connections and closest most-trusted people."

Nearly at the same time Yaneba and Chandee stood up. Yaneba said, "We'll go with you."

I shook my head. "No, that's not necessary. No one even knows we're in this particular part of the world, much less this city. Besides you both should keep your full attention on Abdul, Jr. and Brenton like I shared with you earlier. It will only take me a few minutes to go and get what I need. I suggest you also, without going into much detail, put some effort into earning Hania and Aryan's confidence and trust. These two, could be extremely important to us as strategic allies. Even Paquita, in spite of her age, could be very valuable. This family nucleus, as you've noticed, is divided by the older brother who has been conquered and brainwashed by bin Laden himself into al-Qaeda. I won't take long. Just a few minutes."

Chandee and Yaneba acquiesced to my reasons and nodded. They sat back down as I walked towards the living room and the front door to leave the modern, luxury condominium. As I passed the living room where Brenton kept a cordial, pleasant conversation with Abdul, Jr. Both were laughing in satisfaction. As he saw me heading toward the front door, Brenton asked, "Where are you going?"

"To the Land Rover," I replied. "I forgot my notebooks, and I need them to put together some ideas as to how we'll execute our exit plan from this country."

Without making any effort to move, he asked, "Did you want me to go with you?"

I motioned him to remain seated. "No, I'll be right back."

He smiled. "OK." He continued his conversation with Abdul, Jr. They were clearly having a good time together.

As I opened the front door, turned to close it and leave, I saw a multicolored inflatable beachball roll down the hallway to stop at my shoes. I turned around and saw a child about the age of Paquita next to a tall man with bottle green eyes who was apparently playing with him. I leaned over a little and with the metal toe protector of my boot I tapped it slightly to send it back to the boy's hands. He rushed forward to grab it.

"Thank you, sir," he said with a smile of gratitude. He gave me a military style salute with one hand.

I returned his salute and said, "You're welcome, my friend."

I was surprised to see the man stop playing with the boy as soon as he heard the bell chime and ran to virtually jump into the elevator car as I entered. The little boy protested, yelling, "You promised me, liar!"

The door closed, muffling the boy's protests. He looked at me nervously and shook his head. "Kids, they're never satisfied. They want to play with us all day long. They don't realize that we adults have things to do and responsibilities to uphold."

I smiled pleasantly but hesitated to engage him. I nodded in agreement, but inside I wasn't convinced. He appeared to be trying to persuade me of something untrue, that he in fact was related to the boy. My mind flashed back to replay the details in my mental recording. I recalled that, as I had closed the door, I had seen the man give the boy something from a wallet and put it back in his jacket. He clearly was trying to make it appear that he lived there, but as I looked at him more closely, he wore the canary yellow bracelet that identified people who were working with the government. I asked, "Do you live here in this building?"

Still smiling nervously, he answered, "Yes, you're right. Temporarily." He held up the bracelet. As he did so, I saw a leather shoulder holster with a beautifully decorated pistol. On the other side, I heard the crackle of a walkie-talkie. "We're ready here. Are you? Are you coming down?"

He grew even more nervous. He turned slightly and lowered the volume on his radio. "Yes, yes. I'll be with you guys in a few seconds."

"OK," the other voice replied. "We're ready. Out."

I knew at once that this individual not only was a dangerous rival but also a sloppy, very unprofessional one. That unglamorous quality made him even more dangerous, so I decided to immediately put him out of commission.

The elevator stopped at the 7th floor before I could enact my plan against him. A group of teenagers jumped into the elevator. The tallest one had a massive boombox, clearly a very heavy one, over his right shoulder. When I saw him, I realized God put in my path a better way of getting rid of this guy by using these kids. I moved next to the green-eyed man and kicked him in the ankle with the metal toe protector. I yanked on the large boy with the radio, causing him to lose his balance. As he fell, the massive radio hit the man right in the head. I jumped on top of the man, pulled his pistol and radio in each hand, shoved the kids back, and jumped out of the elevator. I ran to the door for the stairs and opened it. As I did, it crossed my mind that this was a well-prepared trap. I took one handkerchief out and turned the radio volume all the way up. I cocked the pistol, firing twice right next to the microphone and yelled, "Ah! I'm wounded! Retreat—

we've been betrayed! Someone must have told them we're coming in!"

I ran up to the 8th floor and yelled once more as I abruptly switched the radio off. I tucked both radio and pistol into my belt and ran all the way back up to the 12th floor. I was soaked in sweat by the time I got up there. I paused and opened the door a crack to see what was going on in the hallway. I checked the walkie-talkie to make sure it was switched off, and then pulled the magazine out of the pistol to check how many bullets were still in it. I looked at the watch on my left hand, checking the time against the one on my right hand. I needed to give my enemies some time to find out what their Plan B was.

I remained hidden for fifteen minutes and heard the ding of the elevator. I saw the green-eyed man limp out of it, favoring his left leg. I considered coming out of hiding to take him prisoner, but as I opened the door, the condo's door started to open. An unknown man came out of the condo. I jumped back into the hall to keep my eye on what has transpired. The man was very tall and muscular with a long, black beard. He came out with Abdul, Jr., followed by Yaneba with her hands before her, bound and covered by a towel. Chandee, similarly bound, followed. Then Brenton entered the hallway, and I was unsurprised to see him shake hands with the bearded man. Four men followed them out into the hallway. Hania was begging them with tears in her eyes not to harm them, that they were good people.

The man with the beard tried to convince Hania that nothing would happen to them if she followed their instructions. He put a finger to his lips and motioned her back inside the condo. Brenton apparently had agreed to something with the leader of that group. It appeared he was to stay in the condo by Hania and Aryan, waiting for me to return. Abdul, Jr. left with the rest of the group. The five men took my two lovely friends, and my heart shriveled in frustrated sorrow.

As they walked to the elevators, my eyes grew moist with tears of frustration. I knew this was not yet the time to act; I would only put their lives in danger. As if the energy from lightning had infused me, I immediately ran down the stairs as they left in the elevator. I was trying to race the elevator to the underground garage so that I could save their lives. I needed to take them by surprise. At every single floor, I ran out into the hallway to press the button to halt the elevator at each floor. By the time I reached the bottom, I was exhausted. But the extra effort gave me the time to enact my plan.

I cautiously ran between the parked cars in case a guard had been left down the garage to safeguard their exit. I approached our Land Rover. Seeing no one around and everything was peaceful, I opened the door and removed from under the seat a Monte Cristo cigar box from Cuba. I opened it and removed a magnetic tracker.

I closed and locked the Land Rover. Making my way behind the cars once more, I searched for a strategic position that would give me full command of the view of the elevators. Shortly afterwards, the bearded man and Abdul, Jr. showed up with my friends and the rest of the group. Two other men were waiting for them by the elevators. One of the men left from the group to go and get their car. I followed him carefully, still keeping between the cars. I moved as silently as possible, shortening the distance between us as I did so. I needed to make sure each second that he didn't notice me. I saw him open the driver's door of a blue Mercedes minibus with multiple seats.

Not wasting a second, I approached the vehicle from the rear, activated the tracker, and put it in a very concealed location under the rear bumper. I saw all the windows of this car had been carefully tinted heavily save for the chauffeur's side, which had a very light tint. I heard him start the engine and moved around by his side. I pulled out the pistol and tapped against the window to signal him to come out of the vehicle. He started back, and I saw it was the green-eyed man. He began to freak out when he saw to his terror that I was pointing his own pistol at his head. His bottle green eyes grew wider, and he looked upwards in resignation as he raised both arms.

I opened the door. As I did so, he slammed his hand down on the horn to send a signal to his accomplices. He left me no other alternative than to use my ring to inject that lethal poison into his neck. I saw he had a new pistol, and I took that from him as well. He managed to say, "Not again, man—they made enough fun of me already." Then the convulsions began. As he did so, I gave him the antidote before disappearing between the cars in the garage.

As I did, I saw two of the men running towards the Mercedes to give help. This threw my plans off and I had to change what I had in mind. I circled the garage, keeping my distance from them. They could not see or find me anywhere as I hid beneath a broken-down Cadillac. They decided to leave. Then I left my hiding place knowing there was no longer any danger. As I walked back into the garage, I saw with sadness the magnetic tracker lying on the ground; it appeared that it had fallen off the bumper of the Mercedes Benz as they left. I returned to the stairs and sat down on one of the lower steps to catch my breath and organize my thoughts for my own Plan B. I needed one that would produce better results than this one in order to free Yaneba and Chandee. I started to go up the stairs, this time slowly in order to reconstruct what had happened in my mind and give me time to digest how I was going to handle the next step.

I reached the 12th floor and opened the door a crack again to check the corridor. No one was there, so I double-checked both pistols I had acquired. I had enough bullets in each one to put all of them down if they returned to mount a surprise attack. I had no idea what their next move would be. I knew one thing, though—they hadn't left anyone behind in the condo. They had taken who appeared to be their accomplice, Abdul, Jr. with them. Now that I had seen Brenton in that cordial goodbye to the team leader, I imagined if he wasn't a completely declared traitor, he was at least playing a very dangerous game. He fit in the prototype of the perfect double spy. Or he could be a typical, vulgar mercenary. The only thing I knew for certain was that whatever he was, he was very good—to perfection, in fact. For a little while, at least, he had pulled the veil over my eyes. Even though I had serious doubts which had been growing by the minute, I could not assume anything. I simply didn't know enough about his persona to be able to render any judgement of where his loyalty lay. I needed to ascertain that, and quickly.

I decided not to take any chances and take him by surprise to put him to a final test. The only way I could do that was to pretend. As I looked through the cracked door again, I saw the same boy playing in the corridor with his beachball. That gave me what I needed to enact Plan B. I left my hiding place and greeted him. I asked, "Would you like to make some bolivars?"

"It all depends. How many bolivars? I prefer US dollars." he demanded of me.

"OK, US dollars, then. What is your name?"

"My name is Andresito. How many dollars are we talking about?"

"My name is Julio Antonio. It could be $20, could be $10. Could be more. Depends on what you do." The boy grinned. "Do you know Paquita?"

"Yes," he nodded."

"Very well. All you have to do is to convince her to come out and play with you and your ball. For that I will give you $10. If she doesn't come out to play with you, you can keep it."

"Really?" he asked with a little more enthusiasm.

"But if you manage to get her to come out and play with you, I'll give you $20."

He looked at me a little distrustfully at that. "That's a lot of money in bolivars!" He looked me in the eyes and asked, "You're not a liar like Alexey, are you?"

"Who is Alexey?"

Assuming I knew him, he answered, "You know—your friend. The man with the green eyes. He promised me twenty bolivars, that cheapskate, and gave me only five as a deposit if I played with him with the ball for a while until one of you guys came out of Paquita's condominium."

"Aha! Is that what he told you?" He nodded, so I said, "Can you keep a secret?"

"Of course! I'm not a tattletale."

"Alexey is not only a liar, but he is not my friend. He is a terrorist, and you have to be very careful with him. He and his friends like to kidnap boys like you and eat them. They're assassins."

His eyes went wide. "Really?"

"Yes, and to prove it to you, but you have to keep this between us. I'm a spy."

"Really?"

"Yes." I pulled my jacket open so he could see the pistols. "I'm a secret agent. International. You can help me catch those terrorist boy-eaters if you want to be my assistant."

"Yes, I do," he said excitedly.

"Shh, lower your voice. One of them is inside. I've been watching them and their accomplices. But you can tell absolutely no one, not even your mom and dad."

He nodded exaggeratedly in his excitement and put his finger to his lips. "My throat is a zipper," he whispered.

"Now that you know I'm not a liar like Alexey, go and do your mission. Are you ready?"

"Yes, I am." His face grew very serious, and he picked up his ball, hitched his pants up, and walked over to ring the condo's bell.

I returned to my hiding place in the stairs. As I thought, Brenton showed up at the door, and the boy did exactly as I had instructed him to do. Brenton called Paquita to the door. Hania called out, "Paquita will be there in a few minutes. I'm finishing braiding her hair."

Brenton repeated that to the boy and added, "Wait here, OK? Don't come in." He went back inside, leaving the door open.

I left my hiding place, pulled out a $20 bill, and put it in his hand. "Good job. Go to your home now."

To my surprise, he gave me the money back. "Sir, it's an honor to serve you. Don't worry, you don't have to pay me."

I smiled and thought to myself that I had at last found a future warrior who was not a mercenary. I pulled out one of the pistols, removed the bullets from the magazine, and entered the condo, closing the door behind me very slowly so it made no noise, double locking it behind me. I walked directly into the living room where Brenton had been sitting with Aryan.

Aryan looked up at me in surprise. "Brenton is in the bathroom," he said. I saw his eyes were reddened with tears from the trauma of seeing his father's body parts that were the only things we could retrieve from that horrible accident in which I had very nearly lost my life as well. Aryan looked me straight in the eyes and asked, "Can you tell me—did my father suffer a lot, or was that an instantaneous death?"

I replied immediately, "He didn't suffer at all. He was already sedated when we transported him because he had previously been injured. I was taking him to Hoag Hospital in Orange County, California. We had this accident in the middle of the jungle, and this death for him was instantaneous. I got that from my friends who had remained conscious throughout the entire disaster. I was apparently dead without a pulse or heartbeat for several hours. I scared the daylights out of them when I recovered many hours later for that coma or whatever it was. But Abdul never even knew what happened to him."

Aryan looked at me in sincere gratitude. "Thank you very much for your words. That makes me feel a lot better to know, even though this was a violent death, he didn't suffer prolonged pain from his death. It was an unexpected but quiet death."

I nodded. "There it goes, exactly as you said. Now I must ask you a question, Aryan."

He nodded. "You can ask as many questions as you like. I don't know how my father managed to send a letter while he was your captive, but he sent one to my mother, only a few days before you left Venezuela, possibly even the same day he died. I assumed it could have been one of the servants in the house. It described you as a very honorable and decent man. Not just you but everyone in your entire team; he practically portrayed you guys as saints sent from Heaven who treated him with tremendous generosity, kindness, and mercy. It made him feel in his recovery like he was with family at home. Your attitude as well as those around you made him feel repentant. He had been wanting to get out of al-Qaeda a long time before meeting you, and this particular encounter with you became the deciding and important point where he decided finally to leave." He spoke with moist eyes as new grief for his father swept over him. "Anything I can do to recover your two female friends from the hands of these criminals you can consider me your ally and a new recruit for your group of freedom fighters." He reached out his hand to me, leaning forward on the sofa. I shook his hand cordially and somewhat emotionally. "What is your question?"

"That's not necessary anymore. You answered my question as if you had read it in my mind. You just confirmed to me something very important to know–who I'm surrounded by. I'm going to need all the help I can get to retrieve my friends from these assassins' hands, but also if I want to get my friends and myself out of Venezuela alive. We will need every hand available."

I noticed Brenton coming from the back towards us. He was smiling cynically when he saw me. He said, "Oh, the Ghost has reappeared."

"I assure you that this is not the first time. The most important thing now, which I'm extremely anxious to hear from your mouth, is how the hell you managed to be the only one of us the terrorists didn't take with them. It appeared, from what Aryan told me, they took Chandee and Yaneba without firing a single weapon." I placed my left hand to my forehead. "Did they find both of them sleeping? My commonsense tells me that is the only logical explanation for them taking both of these women without either or both of them putting up a fight. And where were you when all this happened?" I took one pistol out and placed it on the coffee table before Brenton.

Brenton eyed the pistol but made no move towards it. He sat down next to Aryan as Hania and Paquita entered the room. Both girls were rather cold and emotionless, as if they were intimidated by something. Their eyes showed some confusion as they sat down in two other chairs near me, a little distant from the sofa where Brenton and Aryan sat.

Brenton said, "Well, let me tell you what happened while you weren't here." I nodded. "The doorbell rang while I was talking with Aryan, shortly after you left. Hania told Paquita to go check the door. Everyone is trained to check the peephole before opening the door; that's what Abdul, Sr. taught them to do. Paquita did what she was supposed to, but after she saw one of Abdul, Jr.'s friends by himself there, she opened the door. She had no idea that there were two groups of terrorists on either side of the door. They grabbed her, one of them putting a long, curved knife to her neck. They made her stay silent with the implied threat they would cut her head off. They entered the living room and instructed us that if anyone made a sound, Paquita's head would be a decoration on the coffee table. We decided not to offer any resistance. They didn't hurt any of us."

I interrupted. "They didn't hurt anyone, but they did take two prisoners."

"Yes, they surprised Chandee and Yaneba as they did us. They told them they would not harm Paquita or anyone else if they followed instructions. They came directly from the polygamist, and they were told to take two hostages, especially females, to ensure he could have a one-on-one interview with you. That's why they left a contact number and a location for you to go to. He has some questions he has in reference to everything that's happened. He won't rest until he hears from your lips the details of the last conversation you had with Abdul in reference to the financial links that he formed inside al-Qaeda. He's extremely worried that Abdul might have compromised any of that information. Abdul was not cooperative in the last few years, and he started to have his doubts about him. It will put his mind at ease as to whether or not Abdul pulled the strings or not on the financial movements."

I leaned back and stretched my legs as I sat in my chair, giving him more space if he wanted to reach for the pistol without any problems from me. As we talked, he continually eyeballed the pistol. He didn't dare make the most minute movement to reach for it. This surprised me a little but knowing his character and his training in intelligence as well as the Secret Service, the last thing he would try to do is reach for it. I knew in my mind there was a very high probability that Brenton was a double spy.

If he was, he would try to convince me that he was on my side and his loyalty lay with us, and not with our enemies.

I asked, "Why did they take Yaneba and Chandee, but leave you behind?"

Brenton smirked a little. He knew that this question was not a laughing matter. He knew if he didn't convince me of his sincerity that I would take the pistol up and shoot him in the head. Or, depending on how fast and astute he was, he could do the same to me. That last was the slimmest possibility, since the only weapon he had to do that was the baited weapon on the coffee table. None of us had brought any firearms along for security reasons. He knew that pistol must have come from our enemies, so he had no way of knowing if I had removed its ammunition before placing it there. It was a desperate situation; it was one in a million he would actually reach for the weapon. It was like playing Russian roulette, except this particular version of the game had five bullets and one empty chamber.

Hania had been silent, as had Paquita and Aryan. Her eyes were also red from crying. She interposed, "They took the cooler with Abdul's remains you brought us. They promised to return them later." She began to sob at the end of her last sentence. She tried to recover for a few seconds. "The strange thing is that they saw the money but didn't touch it. They didn't ask where it had come from. I was happy they didn't, but I wanted you to know, because it's all very strange."

I caressed my chin in clear concern with my left hand. I looked Brenton straight in his eyes, trying to discover the level of his complicity in all of this. Paquita spoke up this time. She said to me, "I don't like any one of those men. They all looked like sons of Satan. I don't think any of them ever could cross eyes with Jesus Christ because their eyes are full of deceit and hatred. They will be ashamed."

Hania caressed her hair proudly wordlessly with a small smile of satisfaction. Brenton said, "In reply to your last question, the leader of that group of terrorists told me clearly that the intentions of their leader bin Laden are. He is now under an assumed name they cannot reveal to me but gave me the codename Salty 303. He only let his closest people know, but since he was going to sit down with you to let you know you can call him by it. 303 is his file number in this country. He doesn't want to call any attention at all to himself because it's a transitional country. He'll probably move out of this location within the next few months. They'll hold Chandee and Yaneba until you have the meeting with him. They want to guarantee that you'll meet with him before you leave the country. It's extremely important for him. He assured me that as soon as you meet with him, he'll put both women in your hands safe and sound."

I interrupted him by saying, "It had *better* be like that. If it isn't, the one who won't leave the country alive will be him, and I don't care what kind of deal he made with his friend, President Obama. Whatever his name now is, or whatever his name was in the past, like communists who continually change their names. I want you to arrange that meeting at once. We don't have the luxury to stay here too long—each day is a day in which we play with our lives. Arrange it, if possible, for tonight, with three conditions: 1) Chandee and Yaneba will be released the moment they pick me up to take me to that interview; 2) The remains of Abdul are immediately brought back to Hania; 3) you, Brenton, and you, Aryan, will be with me." I pointed at the two of them. "If it's not inconvenient to you and if Hania authorizes it."

Aryan nodded. "For me it will be an honor to be by your side." Hania nodded in approval to show she had no objection.

I added, "Don't be afraid of the Devil. As we say in Cuba and Spain, the bull by the horns until we put his head down to force him to eat the dust of the arena."

Paquita said to me, "If you take me with you, I'll help you. I'll make the bull urinate. I'll blow hot chili peppers in his eyes."

We laughed at that. I replied, "That will be the next time, Paquita. Right now, we want no violence. Your plan is good, but too violent—if you do that to the bull, he could go crazy and hurt any one of us. But if I need your help, I'll let you know. The most important thing now is I need to know if one of you guys knows where Abdul, Jr. keeps the P.O. box key."

Paquita raised her hand joyfully. "I know where he hides it—it's under the metal stool of the piano."

I smiled in satisfaction. "Bravo, Paquita! Go and bring it to us, please. We need that key before Abdul gets back."

Paquita ran to the music room and returned shortly with a small metal magnetic key box. I took the key and handed it to Aryan. I said, "Go to the closest place to make a copy of this key before your brother gets back. I want to return it to the same place. Get back here as soon as possible. Brenton, you'll go with him to call and make that important meeting with 303. But make sure you do it from a public phone, not from any establishment's private line. Keep in your mind that I need a couple of hours. Don't make it too early in the evening. I need time to mature my plans and put them in motion how we'll handle everything, make our exit from this country, and leave Abdul's family in peace with no more interference from radical terrorist elements. Everything we have just said here I want you all to keep in complete secrecy and confidence. And not one single word to Abdul, Jr. when he returns until we leave Venezuela."

Everyone nodded their agreement. Hania took Aryan and Brenton in her car to make the key. They returned a short while later, and Aryan gave me the copy of the P.O. box key. Brenton said that he had arranged the meeting for eight pm that night in the underground parking garage of the condominium. I left with Paquita who was the only one who knew where the P.O. box was located since she had been there with her brother to retrieve bin Laden's mail several times.

We said goodbye to everyone, and we walked towards the elevator, down to the garage, and into the Land Rover.

A little while later, we stopped at a sporting goods store. I looked around and asked the attendant for the smallest handheld crossbow with a pistol grip suitable for hunting foxes and small animals and some string as well as some steel crossbow bolts. He put everything in a plastic bag, and we left.

Paquita asked curiously, "Are you going to go hunting in the jungles of the Amazon?"

"Yes, I'm going to be hunting, but not in the jungles of the Amazon, but the jungle of asphalt and cement in the city of Caracas. It will be the fox who is ultimately responsible for the death of your father."

She looked at me a little confused at first. After a few seconds, she smirked mischievously and patted me on the shoulder. She nodded. "Very good idea. It's about time somebody killed that fox. This time, for real and for sure. That fox with the jackal has been able to get out alive from the traps we've been putting around. He's done so much harm to innocent lives and is responsible for the deaths of many innocent people, including my father." Two small tears ran down her cheeks.

She made me get emotional in return as I felt a knot form in my throat and my eyes moisten. That little girl was so intelligent, so filled with pain but at the same time wisdom, as she analyzed everything so clearly; I understood her pain and it appeared that she comprehended this without my saying a single word. I had spoken figuratively, but she decoded exactly what I had planned to do with tremendous maturity. It was as if I was speaking with a fully grown and intellectually savvy individual.

She tried to stimulate and support with the same way I had spoken with her figuratively without directly mentioning the name of the individual and was backing me up in my plans. She was a perfect little master spy; like me, who didn't like taking the life of any human being, she understood that in the case of this criminal terrorist we had no other alternative but to do so unless we wanted to allow thousands of innocent people die in more terrorist attacks in the future that this man had already in mind to do.

I caressed her hair with my right hand and patted her lightly on the left shoulder. "Thank you for your moral support, Paquita. You may not be able to imagine how much I appreciate your words. Like you, I don't like to hurt people; at the same time, I feel very proud to have you by my side."

She smiled. "From the first time I saw you, Dr. JAM, I had in my heart the complete assurance that you are a very extraordinary man. Your mission on this Earth is to change evil to good before the battle of Armageddon. That will be your final and real mission, eventually." The emotion in her voice touched my feelings. "I want to be by your side now that I have no father. I need someone like you to guide me, if you'll allow it."

I smiled slightly. "It will be an honor, Paquita, and a great satisfaction. But remember, you have your mom and your brothers. You're still very young, and the last thing I want to see in any way or form is for you to get hurt by our enemies." She looked sad and disappointment. I continued, "Don't take that as a rejection. I would love to have you around me."

She reached out her little hand to squeeze my shoulder. "Don't worry about me. I learned self-defense from my father for many years as well as other things. I promise you when the moment comes, if required, I can defend not just myself but you as well."

I nodded. "I have no doubt of that at all. Paquita, when we are young, we make mistakes, as you did when you opened the door to your house, thinking you were doing something right. You saw one of your brother's friends there." Her face grew long as she pouted. "But when you opened the door, what happened? They put a big knife to your throat." She hung her head and gave me a look that said she didn't like to hear that. "They took you by surprise because of your lack of experience, and my two best friends, Yaneba and Chandee, are now hostages as a result."

In an unpleasant tone, she said, "They didn't take me just by surprise, but they also took your best friends by surprise."

I shook my head with a small smile on my face. "Let me remind you—what you said is true, but if you hadn't opened that door and didn't have that knife to your throat, those terrorists would probably be dead at this moment. Believe me, Chandee and Yaneba would never allow themselves to be taken prisoners. If I can assure you of anything, these two women put together are a nuclear bomb. Simply and realistically, they didn't want to put your life in danger. That is why they are in the situation they're in now, and I'm now under the obligation to meet in a very disadvantageous and dangerous position with that diabolical character, bin Laden."

She looked at me with repentance in her eyes and face. Her pain reflected in her voice, she said, "I'm sorry. I'm really sorry—that as not my intention at all and be so stupid."

I reached out and squeezed her shoulder again. "No, you weren't stupid. You were simply inexperienced. I'll fix it. But that's why I say you have to grow up first before you do what we do."

As we drove, she pointed out a small shopping center. "It's here."

"Here?"

"Yes, the next entrance. In that shopping center."

We pulled in and parked the Land Rover. Before leaving the car, I removed the package and prepared the crossbow to have it handy when I got to that place. Paquita's curious eyes watched every detail of what I did. I put the small, loaded weapon inside the plastic bag and carefully tied one end of the string to the trigger with the cord running around behind the trigger guard for leverage. I asked Paquita to follow me to the location, since I needed her to distract the attendant while I finished my work.

We got out of the Land Rover, walked into the store, and Paquita professionally went up to the counter, picking up a postcard to purchase. It distracted the attendant long enough for me to finish my work, tying the cord to the door of the box, and carefully placing the crossbow inside. Depending on the height of the person who opened that door, the bolt would fire either into the forehead or throat—either location killing shots. Even an exceptionally tall man would catch it in the chest. I closed the box, cutting the leftover of the string, and waited for Paquita outside the store. She rejoined me and we walked back to the Land Rover, leaving the shopping center with our mission completed.

We returned to the condominium where I gave Hania instructions to hide both the original and copy of the P.O. box, destroying them if necessary. Under no circumstance was she to allow Abdul, Jr. to have his hands on those keys. I had changed my initial plans to injure him to my more drastic Plan B, taking into consideration the great possibility that the intentions of bin Laden were not just to get information from me about Abdul, Sr. like he had told his accomplices to say to Brenton but also that his protectors had advised him that we were hunting him. His Plan B could be to either assassinate me first, or the entire team. There was even a possibility that he had come kind of agreement with the Chavez government or directly with the Castro brothers in Cuba to finally eliminate my entire team, once and for all. Brenton was still a gigantic question mark. Up to this moment we still did not know where his loyalties lay. I communicated these details to Hania in the presence of Aryan and Paquita. Brenton was taking a shower at that moment, so I used the opportunity to give Aryan one of my pistols.

It was about seven thirty pm when we got a light dinner of fruit, cheese, cold meats, and bread. We were getting ready to go down to the parking garage of the building. Paquita insisted on coming with us, but Hania wasn't comfortable with the notion. Initially, I only wanted Aryan and Brenton with me, but Hania said, "I should be there, too. There might be more than you expect, and we might be able to help you."

She finally agreed that Paquita could come, but the girl was to remain in the elevator, pressing the button to hold the car for us. Paquita was overjoyed to be the elevator keeper in case of an emergency retreat. If things didn't go as we planned, we had our escape prepared. At ten minutes to eight we went down to the parking garage. Minutes later we saw the blue Mercedes Benz minibus appear. They parked close to the elevators and four men stepped out. The first one out was the green-eyed man. He limped to the back to open the door revealing Chandee and Yaneba, handcuffed together in the back.

The bearded leader said, "OK. Come over here. After we search you and know that you have no weapons, and put you in handcuffs, we will let the two women free."

I removed my pistol. "No. That is not the way it will be. I will give my pistol to Hania, just in case you guys pull anything else. All of us here are armed." I raised both arms. "I will approach you, but you have to do the other way around, or no deal at all. You take the handcuffs off and release them, and then you can put them on me. Take it or leave it."

He rubbed his forehead. "OK, OK." He went and removed the bindings on Yaneba and Chandee the others trained their weapons on us. The cooler with Abdul's remains were given to Chandee and Yaneba to deliver to Hania. I was trying to prevent any harm coming to either of my friends. I took a couple of steps forward, my hands extended at chest level, held out ready for handcuffs. The bearded man rushed forward to place the restraints on my wrists. At the same time, Chandee and Yaneba passed by me, and we exchanged looks. We didn't need to speak—our communication was solely done by facial expressions and eye placement. I shook my head very subtly and glanced warningly at them so that they wouldn't act in a way that would endanger the innocent people present.

I could tell it didn't settle well with either of them from their long faces and disgusted looks at seeing me in handcuffs. They found the situation intensely frustrating to see me voluntarily place myself at such an extreme disadvantage just to set them free. They knew I never allowed myself to be surrounded by my enemies, and yet here I was doing just that to gain them their safety. They gave me subtle nods of agreement to convey they had gotten my message. They knew for certain that my primary concern at present was not just their safety but also that of Abdul's family, especially the young kids. I must have a master plan to get myself out of that predicament, which would logically be why I was offering no resistance. They then realized that this was actually a victory and without knowing it, the bearded man was handing it to me. That told me that his boss, likely bin Laden himself, had previously given him instructions to not use any violence to procure my capture, unless in a last resort.

After they guided me to a seat in the back of the minibus, Yaneba and Chandee already having joined the rest of the group by the elevators, looked at me with sad faces. Suddenly, a car entered at an unusually high speed into the underground garage, its tires screeching against the concrete. Five men in civilian clothes that looked like they belonged to either intelligence or Venezuelan Secret Service got out of the car. They all wore badges emblazoned S.E.B.I.N.[38] Pistols in hands, the members of SEBIN yelled, "Put your hands up if you don't want to be hurt or killed. Immediately!"

---

[38] *Servisio Bolivariano de Inteligencia Nacional* (Bolivarian National Intelligence Service)

Figure 53 SEBIN seal

Everyone had been taken by surprise. I was already in the van, so I didn't comply, and Abdul, Jr. likewise did not. Instead, he drew his pistol and began firing at the intelligence agents, killing three of them, even though the bearded man yelled desperately for him not to shoot. The remaining secret police returned his fire in self-defense, shooting Abdul, Jr. in his left arm. The green-eyes man laughed and yelled, "See? That's what you get for making fun of me! That can happen to anyone!" Another of the men inside the van fell with a bullet in his neck, right on the carpet by my feet. He desperately tried to cover the hole in his neck with his hand. Blood spurted like from a whale's blowhole through his fingers. He pressed desperately, feeling his life fleeing through his fingers.

The others outside fled for the elevator save for Aryan. Courageously, he pulled the pistol I had given him and opened fire. He managed to drop the remaining two men, and continued firing, this time on the terrorists to cover the retreat of his mother, Brenton, Yaneba, and Chandee.

The green-eyed man pushed Abdul, Jr. out of the front seat of the minibus with one foot, saying, "Get out of here, you snot-nosed brat." He closed the door, even though Aryan had not stopped shooting. He decided to get out of there as soon as possible and jumped behind the wheel. He and the beaded man were the only ones left. They sped out of the garage, tires squealing in protest. The bearded man on the way out proceeded to drop the mortally wounded man out as they left, not caring whether or not the man was dead.

That was the last thing I could see, because the bearded reached under the seat and pulled out a black hood. "I'm sorry." He put it over my head, obscuring my view. He yelled, "Alexey! *Carajo*! Slow down, or do you want to screw up for the third time today? Do you want to call the attention of the police?"

Alexey, as he listened to his boss yell at him, all the nervous adrenaline rushes he had endured, combined with the humiliation and frustration he had suffered at the hands of the others for his stupidity at being disarmed twice, at these last words from his boss his cup of exasperation overflowed. This young apprentice terrorist from Venezuela looked like he didn't have much of a sense of humor and even less gray matter. He slammed on the brakes, stopping the minibus right in the middle of traffic. He yelled, "That's it! That's it! I'm quitting this job! You're not paying me enough to take all this crap from you and those other assholes all day long! I've fucking had it!"

I could hear the door open and close violently as the bearded man tried to apologize and pleaded with him to return to the car in the middle of the avenue. More attention was called to us as frustrated drivers started to slam on their horns. I heard both doors open. One of them slammed shut as before, while the other in back closed more gently. The bearded man said in a more persuasive tone, "Alexey, what the hell are you doing? You know that this is part of the job. Why are you stopping in the middle of traffic? Do you want to get caught and all of us end up jail?"

Alexey replied angrily, "This is the last time, OK? I deserve respect! I did exactly what anyone else would do, sometimes even better! But no one says, 'Alexey, you're doing a good job!' Not even you—but Alexey gets caught by surprise by this very well-trained man and now it's all 'Alexey is an idiot, Alexey got caught with his pants down!' I need respect, do you understand?"

The other voice calmly replied, "OK, just remember what I told you before. We'll talk after we deliver this package. OK, Alexey?"

"It's not OK, but I'll wait! I'll repeat it again: this is the last time! I've decided not to take any more shit from any of you guys, especially you!"

The same way we had stopped in the middle of the highway now he abruptly accelerated, and we squealed the tires as we sped out of that place, forcing me to grab with my restrained hands to avoid being flung to one side.

I had no way of knowing where we were when we reached our destination. I could tell the minibus had come to a halt, and the doors opened. They pulled me out of the vehicle and restrained both hands. It smelled like we were near the ocean, and I could hear the echo of a wooden pier beneath my feet and the screeches of seagulls along with the smell of marine algae. It gave me the mental picture that we had boarded a large ship or yacht. I was able to verify that as soon as the black hood was removed from my head. The man with the long beard said, "The boss will be here not very long from now. Do you want anything to drink?"

"No, thank you."

When he opened the door to what looked like a luxury yacht's cabin, they brought me inside and handcuffed me to a metal bar rising from the middle of the table much like an umbrella pole on an outdoor table. It was surrounded by stainless steel swivel chairs bolted to the floor. Paquita's dog Tombo walked in. Though he tried to stop the dog, he came over to me, joyfully wagging his tail. The bearded man kicked him a couple of times to get him out of the room as he tried to close the door. Tombo protested at being forced to leave. When the leader tried to grab the dog by the collar, Tombo growled at him menacingly and then began to aggressively bark. The man took his belt off and began to lash at the dog, but Paquita's dog intelligently avoided the blows. Alexey tried to grab the dog from the other side of the table as the bearded man desperately grabbed at his pants, nearly tripping and falling when they dropped suddenly. As they tried to catch him, Tombo saw his opportunity and darted through the crack in the door.

The bearded man slammed the door shut and said to Alexey, "Let's go downstairs. We have to talk."

They left me bound to the center pole of the table. I could hear the dog crying outside while they kicked him as they left. I checked one of my watches and saw that several hours had passed. I suddenly heard a few gunshots followed by a long silence. They had not taken anything from me. Around midnight, I saw the doorknob move as it opened. A tall, skinny man with a dimple in his chin and refined features like a Northern European asked me in surprise, "What are you doing in my private cabin?" As he spoke, he removed a beige cashmere coat, revealing underneath an expensive European suit and silk tie, all colored light gray. Two beautiful young women entered behind him. One was a brunette with olive skin and hazel eyes, the other a blond woman with green eyes. Both were dressed extremely elegantly, as if they were returning from a night at the theater or a high society party.

One of the women asked, "Oh, did you give us a surprise?"

The man replied, "I don't know who this gentleman is and what he's doing sitting at my table."

I smiled and raised my left handcuffed hand. "I'm not here voluntarily. That is the same question I ask myself: what am I doing here?"

The brunette said, "Oh, Alejandro—I didn't know you liked these kinds of things." She looked at me mischievously. "This is quite a surprise you have on this beautiful night. Quite an assortment of chocolate bon bons. You never have an idea of what flavor is the next you will introduce into your mouth."

Alejandro replied in a very abrupt manner, "Why don't you girls go out on deck and wait for me outside? I have to have a conversation with this gentleman. Don't come in here until I let you know, OK?"

The brunette protested, "Why do you have to have a good time all the time by yourself, Alejandro?"

He grew a little upset and spoke with greater firmness. "Get out of here, I say! Or cannot you morons understand what 'out' means? Do I have to kick you out?"

Both women looked at him in shocked fright. He grabbed each one by the arm and nearly shoved them out of the room. Understanding he was not joking, as he might have done on other occasions, they both voiced acquiescence and hustled outside. He double locked the door, nearly breaking their noses as he slammed it shut on them. I watched everything silently, studying both the physical and emotional demeanor of this man and his body language. He suddenly gestured with his right arm, completely confirming what I had been thinking. He had the correct height, weight, and build, slightly wavy hair. Without sitting, he pointed at me with his right arm, "Are you Dr. Julio Antonio del Marmol, the Cuban Lightning?"

I asked him without replying, "Are you Osama bin Laden?"

He smiled cynically and shook his head as he poured himself a cordial from the wet bar. "No, I am Alejandro Gibraltar." I smiled this time. He looked at me in confusion. "I think you've mistaken me. I'm one of the many associates, yes, of bin Laden. But to impersonate Osama is a long way along a very different road."

I asked again, "Do you know what an analyst of personality and expressions is? It is the art to know and study your physical motions and natural expressions that you use all of your life, from pictures, film footage, whatever exists of you before."

"Yes, I know. Body language, facial expressions."

"Close enough. This has a name: micro expressions. By decoding facial expressions an expert can identify and read an individual no matter how many times he changes his face." I caressed my chin. "You can have thousands of different faces, but something you cannot change is your personality and your expressions. Those are inserted in your brain like the serial number is imprinted on the motor of the car you have as your property. That number is on the engine block but let me tell you something: I'm not here to corroborate or disprove your identity. I don't care. It's not in my interest at all. I came here against my will to satisfy perhaps your curiosity or your boss' curiosity in reference to the man of your trust—or, if you want to keep playing this game—your boss's right arm who was in charge of finances."

Alejandro, with his left hand, caressed his forehead with his thumb and forefinger, giving me the final real proof as to who he was—Osama bin Laden. He turned a stainless-steel chair around and sat down before me with a small cynical smile. "They warned me that I should be extremely careful with you. I told my advisors that I had nothing to fear from you. I told my men not to take their eyes off you or remove the mask from your head. They weren't supposed to bring you here—they were supposed to bring you to another location." He shook his head. "I'm sure that they had a powerful reason for ignoring my wishes and do exactly to the contrary of what I told them to do. There was probably some confrontation, someone killed in the process, even though this was something so simple that I delegated to them—to bring you here unharmed to have a civilized conversation about my friend and confidant, Abdul, Sr."

I nodded. "You're very right. Your men have more than one dead or wounded. That occurred through something very simple and unnecessary. One of those wounded is the son of your friend, Abdul, Jr."

"Oh, no!"

"Yes, together with several other of your men dead as well."

"What happened?"

"Five agents from the SEBIN of the Venezuelan intelligence service appeared like a magic act in the middle of our negotiations in the underground garage. The immature Abdul, Jr. lost control and began to shoot his pistol at him. This of course created an unnecessary shower of bullets leaving a few dead in the process." I paused. "But your men should have already told you this. Didn't they debrief you of it all?"

He shook his head. "No, no. I found both of them dead in a confrontation that looked some kind of duel one deck below. They must have had some kind of argument." He pointed to the floor of the deck. "The bodies are still there—I just covered them with blankets so the girls wouldn't freak out. Fortunately, I was the first one to open the door. I didn't want to have to kill those women as well if they had an anxiety attack and begin screaming at the sight."

I shook my head and smiled cynically. "In other words, when you asked me as you entered this room, you had no idea of who I am or what I had been telling you that transpired a few hours ago."

Alejandro nodded. "As I told you before, they weren't supposed to bring you here, much less remove that hood. This now puts me in a predicament. I have to get rid of you. Being the smart and intelligent man that you are, it's not important what I told you. You know my face now. I cannot take that chance. I assure you that I'm truly sorry. Physically eliminating you was not at all my plan. But with those Venezuelan agents being dead, this seriously complicates things. I'll have to leave this country immediately, especially once the local and national authorities find out that some of these men worked for me and that I was the one to send them to Abdul's building as a second standby team to assure myself that you would come here no matter what. I want to discuss with you in private what you talked about with Abdul, Sr. about my finances. That is extremely important to me."

I nodded, understanding that Osama bin Laden knew his cover was blown. Even though he had a different face, the reality was right before his new face. Perhaps because of that, he threw in the towel. He said, "I don't know if you're aware, but there's an even greater price on your head by the Cuban government and the Tricontinental Union than the USA has on mine. Of course, this is tempting for any mercenary and extremely dangerous for you. But to me, it signifies nothing. First of all, I'm not a mercenary. I follow ideals and convictions. I also possess a strong financial network that is nearly indestructible. My followers, like your friends and allies, now with this Administration and their new political ideology of Marxism not only find in me a link to destroy and corrupt the democratic capitalist society but also a partner and ally, not a friend, as against a common enemy to intimidate and destroy the rest of the world. Of course, this worked to perfection with their plans to plant the seed of Marxism around the world in other nations. I'm not a fan of that at all and don't sympathize, but I let them believe I do because this benefits me tremendously until the crucial moment when the great master leader Mohammed, the real messenger of God, appears. We have 1.9 billion followers, or 24.9% of the world's population, in the Muslim faith. Islam is followed by a majority of the population in fifty-one countries. Eventually, we will be the conquerors. We will be the ones left to control the world in the good or the bad, whatever it takes, by force of our majorities."

I smiled and replied, "I am, with all my respect, in complete disagreement with you and your ideas. My heart and my ideas basically have other principles. They are the principles of Christ, the real Son of God. This message is completely different, full of love for everyone, glorifying life not only here but where we go after death. We don't obligate or force anyone, even if we have the majorities to partake in, and have no ambition to control and dominate the world at all save for in love, without a single stain of blood or cutting off the head of anyone. Followers or infidels, whatever they decide to embrace, even if they want to embrace another religion, can do so without fanaticism, also without terrorism or persecution against any other human being." I could see how upset he was growing as I paused. His face contorted and his jaw muscles rippled as he clenched them. "We are not all equally the same. Nor do we think the same way or even have the same color of eyes or skin, but all united by one single thing, and it's a muscle called our hearts, which should always be filled with love and not hatred for all our brothers and sisters around the world. These should be our principles and our religion: do good to others no matter who he is and never do harm to anyone or anything that we don't want done to ourselves. Respect the rights of every single human being who should be to be free to decide their own destinies and ways of life and religion. This will secure the past, with harmony and happiness in the future that we all in our hearts search for in this temporary trip that we all share over the paths of the Earth. No imposition of any political ideology or religion will ever have deep roots anywhere. God, the Supreme Architect of our universe, created no man to be the slave of another. He created and designed man for the Providence of being a happy being and principally to live in freedom."

Osama looked at me with a very serious expression on his long beardless face and cleft chin. It made him appear in his new face as a sophisticated individual, and with his green contact lenses, he looked like a European capitalist of high society. He was silent for several seconds, listening to me without interruption, only making the occasional cynical expression. He made another of his typical gestures which completely revealed who he really was to anyone who had studied his gestures and mannerisms in detail. One didn't need a PhD in psychology or in behavior and facial expression as a form of nonverbal communication. I could not let that small detail he showed me once more unwanted. I pointed at his face. "There it goes! You just repeated the same gesture involuntarily." I imitated the caress of his forehead with thumb and forefinger over the right eyebrow and thumb over his jaw. He only did that when he was discontented or a little nervous from something that made him uncomfortable. He snatched his hand away abruptly out of a preservation instinct even though he had already admitted the truth to me.

He changed his position and put his arm down on the chair. He shook his head and said, "Now I understand why my advisors suggested that I should not even meet with you. If I did, to be extremely careful if I didn't want to repent of it. But I told them they were all wrong. Look at this, I have you here a prisoner, completely defenseless." He smiled cynically. "In reality, it didn't cost me all that much to get my hands on you, just a few inconveniences that very soon will remain in the past as soon as you cease to exist. Your legend will die with you."

I smiled this time with profound irony. "Are you sure of that?"

"Sure of what?"

"What you just said—that you have me completely defenseless."

He looked at me with surprise and a little nervousness in his eyes. I was getting under his skin as he looked around. I could see he felt alone at that moment. He knew he had a weapon, but he also knew what skills I was reported to have. He knew that his most trusted men were out of commission. The last two looked like personal frictions had led to their deaths. He gave me a look nervously and then at the double locked door behind him. He pulled a Mause P38 9mm Parabellum pistol out. The P38s had replaced the Luger P08 pistols, and I could see it was a semi-automatic Micky Vandorn of German origin. I could see my psychology was working by the look of terror in his eyes. I grinned at him as I looked intensely into his eyes. His terror increased, especially when I said innocently, "What—you're going to kill me on your yacht and eliminate the only tool of negotiation you have at this table, the only one that will enable you to leave this yacht alive? Believe me, you're not going to give me any greater satisfaction than to offer my life in order to ensure the end of yours. I will die in peace and tranquility, knowing that you cannot kill any more innocent people with your distorted, fanatical ideas, using your god Mohammed that I don't believe you've interpreted properly. I don't believe in my heart that any god in this universe—maybe in another—but the one I've been traveling in is a god of death of men, women, elders, and children. We can't call that 'god,' much less a religion. This is simply, clearly diabolic, and a Satanic cult that only sick minds like yours could dare to call a religion. This is nothing more than a blasphemy. The Supreme Architect calls us all with the same love to take care of each other, to not kill, much less decapitate innocent people." I paused and looked at one of my watches. I checked my other watch, taking my time. Osama was surprised by my action—it was as if I was waiting for something or someone with a little impatience. This final act made him step back a couple of feet.

He said ironically, "Are you waiting for somebody? Or maybe your date with death has been delayed a few minutes?" He cocked the pistol and pointed it at my head. "Your time has come. It's over, Lighting."

I said very calmly, "Oh, you've lost your interest in knowing the secrets your most trusted man gave me, and what he truly thought of you and your criminal, terrorist organization? You're not interested anymore, apparently, in what he shared with me before he died. I thought that was why you brought me here. You know why your right arm got so close to me, to entrust me with all your secrets? It was because of the honor and decency that we all treated him with to the last minutes of his life." I looked him in the eyes, penetrating his brain. I could see the hatred in there; but I also saw surprise and profound admiration at my words and character. All these mixed in a strange cocktail which warned me that I was playing with fire. It was getting extremely dangerous, so I said, "Everything we do in our lives has consequences, good, bad, and ugly. It all depends on our conduct and who lives with their hands filled with blood of the innocent victims that perished, who in turn dies by drowning in his own blood as a. divine message that whatever he did to others will inevitably come back to give him at the moment of death a little of his own medicine."

Osama thought for a few seconds about what I had said, staring straight into my eyes. I could clearly read and observe a terror in his eyes and soul reflected in his pupils. Lost in his thoughts, he lowered the pistol slightly and said, "Of course, I'm interested in knowing." He added ironically, "Why take with you such valuable information that won't serve any purpose for you, anyway? It would truly be a waste."

As he spoke, he lowered the pistol even more and took a couple of steps towards his right. He headed towards a large painting behind the bar. He put the pistol down on the counter of the bar and used both hands to remove the painting from its frame and rest it against one side of the bar. Behind the painting was a large wall safe. He reached out with his left and hand and picked up a metal briefcase of stainless steel or aluminum and placed it on the counter next to his pistol. He opened it and then the safe. He pulled from the safe what appeared to be several gold bars, gently stacking them one at a time inside the briefcase. As he did so, he asked, "What happened? Have your vocal cords gone soft as you see death getting closer to you by the second? You have nothing to be ashamed of. I've never met a man in my life that when they saw that ugly individual, the Reaper, who did not urinate in the first category, and some in the second category defecating as he begs to be allowed to stay for one more day in this ugly world."

I could not help but smile as I replied. "Respectfully, I'm in complete disagreement with you in both counts. The first one, it's not my style to beg for anything in life. And in the second, in my opinion this is not an ugly world but a beautiful one in which we all live. Unfortunately, people like you make it extremely ugly. That is exactly what my friends and I have been trying for years to clean up around this world—the filth of narcissists and extremists, as well as the tremendous corruption they leave behind, cleansing the world of people like you to leave to future generations a more beautiful and wonderful place." He stopped what he was doing and turned towards me. He held a gold bar in his hand and threw it at me. Had I not ducked, it would have hit me in the face. I discovered two things from this: he didn't like to be portrayed so unheroically and that he had a short temper. I taunted, "Wow! Bravo!! Trying to hurt someone who cannot defend himself—you are a great warrior of Satan."

He gave me that cynical smile and said sarcastically as he nodded while he returned to placing gold bars in the briefcase, "There's no doubt that you are a very rare species of animal. It's no surprise to me that you live up to the descriptions they've given me of who you are. Definitely, even though I don't like you and had some hesitation before about killing you, there's no doubt you have huge testicles. But more than that, which is why you have so many of my people hate you—you have an extremely good education and eloquence to inflict sharp and painful blows with your tongue. You can continue talking. Be my guest—it just makes putting a couple of bullets in your head to silence that tongue forever much easier for me. Begging or not, you will die before I leave this cabin. Now it's only a question of minutes. Tick-tock, tick-tock, tick-tock." He shook his head angrily as he closed the safe, replaced the painting, and closed the briefcase. "Well, have you decided to tell me or not what Abdul, Sr. told you about financial nutrients for al-Qaeda? Or maybe he, like a great man with integrity, managed to keep his mouth shut and take that information with him to the grave."

I smiled once more and checked both my watches. "Well, you will see discover that in a very short time when you doublecheck your bank accounts—if you have enough time to do that before you get out of here. You said earlier that many men in one category urinate and in the other defecate in the presence of the Reaper; I have no idea which category you fall into. But I can assure you that the moment that you pointed that pistol at me you also put a zipper on my mouth and closed off every single type of information you could have obtained from me. Besides, you're the one who compromised his honor and integrity when you told me that nobody would be hurt if we followed your instructions. Now, you say that in order to protect your identity you have to put me down. That tells me you have no integrity like you expect from your friend Abdul, and your words are trash. You can't even imagine, because it wouldn't cross your mind with such low morals, that you sentenced yourself to death because my friends might be on their way here right now." I shook one of my watches. "Tick-tock, tick-tock, tick-tock. Your only chance for salvation is to remove the handcuff on my left hand, put your pistol in my hand; otherwise, you will not live for very long. Even if you manage to leave this yacht alive, I can assure you that before the sun rises tomorrow, you will be dead and without any doubts in the hands of the Reaper, who is already waiting. Tick-tock, tick-tock, tick-tock. It's up to you, because I don't like taking other people's lives. It is your decision whether you live or die. I've never found any joy in other people's suffering, unlike you and your followers, even with those who are my worst enemies."

I could see his terror was growing exponentially. He nervously reached for his pistol once more. He doublechecked the pistol and picked up the metal briefcase in his right hand and the pistol in his left—proving that he was a left-handed man. My words had completely freaked him out. Outside the cabin, Tombo started barking, and we could hear something like a high-speed boat or a high-performance car engine arriving. He went to the door and slowly opened it a crack to see if he could locate the source of those noises. He watched for a few seconds nervously with pistol in one hand and the briefcase on the floor by his feet. Before he could stop him, Tombo pushed his way into the cabin, forcing the door nearly half-open.

We could hear voices from the deck—one of them was Yaneba, who called out, "We are armed. We are here looking for our friend, Dr. del Marmol. We want permission to come on board. We know he is here; our tracker brought us here. We don't want any violence; we just want to bring him home. If you don't want to get hurt, lower the gangway."

Tombo ran towards me, and I caressed his head with my right hand, slipping some beef jerky to him. He sat down at my feet in a protective stance. Bin Laden's face broke out in a sweat of panic. He pointed his pistol towards my head only twenty feet away from me. As if loaded by springs, I jumped up in my chair, stretching my left arm to its fullest extension and ducking down under the table. I could see he was going to fire, and he did twice. One bullet struck sparks as it hit the metallic pole. The other bullet went into the back of the metal chair, causing the swivel chair to spin wildly.

Bin Laden, seeing the ineffectiveness of his shots, went into a kneeling crouch to start shooting under the table between the chair legs and where the center pole was bolted to the deck. He fired twice more, but luckily for me, one of the bullets hit the center pole, sparking and ricocheting back into him, striking him with extraordinarily precision in the left hand and caused him to drop the pistol, which slid across the waxed wooden floor towards me. I tried to reach it, but it was just a few inches out of my grasp. Osama left the briefcase full of gold by the door and crawled towards the pistol.

Then something happened which took both of us by surprise. Tombo, with a fierce growl moved in front of him, blocking him from continuing towards the pistol. Underestimating the dog and assuming that because the dog knew him from previous occasions, bin Laden said, "OK, OK, Tombo. You and I are old friends."

As he spoke, he tried to move forward again. Tombo, however, bared his fangs and growled even louder practically in the terrorist's face. I was trying to get hold of the pistol with my foot. I knew that if bin Laden reached it before I did, he would shoot me in the face at point blank range. He might even put more than the promised two bullets in my head after all my antagonism.

At that moment, I heard the internal voice telling me to do something. As I always did, I obeyed without question, and said loudly, "Tombo! Kill him! Bad man, bad man!"

As if moved by lightning, to the surprise of us both, Tombo jumped on bin Laden's chest and as a dog trained to kill began biting for his throat. As his leapt, his rear legs kicked the pistol, which spun right into my hand. Seeing this and Tombo's aggressiveness, bin Laden stood up rapidly, wrapped his hands around the neck of the dog, shook him abruptly, and threw the animal onto the table, which slid across the metal surface to land on top of me as I was trying to stand up. Using this confusion, bin Laden snatched up the metal briefcase to shield his head if I started shooting. Tombo recovered his legs and ran at him. Bin Laden violently slammed the door, practically on Tombo's face.

The voices of bin Laden's two female companions could be heard yelling outside. I stretched the chain of the handcuff to maximum extent and pointed the pistol at it. I fired once, breaking the chain. I ran out of the cabin trying to catch up with bin Laden. As I did, I heard the powerful engine of a high-speed boat roaring off. From the upper deck of the yacht, I could see the two women and bin Laden in the boat as it rapidly moved away. I could see him cynically smiling as he waved at me, the two women now in bikinis and topless, flaunting their breasts as if mocking me. Without wasting any time, I lowered the gangway to allow Yaneba and Chandee to get on board. Both were very worried at hearing the shots on board and being powerless to come to my aid. After I calmed them down, I told them, "I'm OK. The only wounded person was bin Laden with his new face. He's wounded in his left hand from one of his own bullets he fired at me when he tried to kill me. It ricocheted." They smiled and shook their heads.

Yaneba said, "I don't know why, but that doesn't surprise me at all, knowing you and what happens around you all the time. We should leave here immediately. We don't know how many contractors he has around following his tail."

"I don't think we have much to worry about with that. He tried to lay low, and all the men he had contracted we already put down. But I agree we have to leave immediately. We don't want the bird to fly, and I believe I have the right information where he's going to fly to, if my source didn't betray me, and to where he'll try to disappear. I'm expecting to catch him in the trap I set for him. I know he's not going to leave without checking the mail, since he's expecting new documents from immigration to arrive there. Even if he doesn't fall into our trap, we have to make sure to put my contingency plan into motion before we leave Venezuela."

"Very well," Chandee said. "In this case, we have no time to lose. Let's get out of here."

I looked around as we got into the Land Rover. "Where's Brenton?"

Yaneba said, "We didn't trust him to bring him. We told him to stay behind and keep an eye on Hania and her family."

We left the yacht followed by Tombo. I said to Chandee, "This dog is fantastic. I don't know what I have with animals, but I owe him my life. He behaved like a Doberman pinscher trained to kill. I'll give you details later."

She caressed his head and smiled. "You certainly have a connection with nature. From the first moment I saw him, I knew this boy was an angel sent to be a standby."

I sat down in the back seat with Tombo and opened a large package of beef jerky to refill my pockets and gave him an entire packet. I caressed his head. "Good dog, Tombo. You did well. This is your reward for your beautiful act of heroism."

Tombo kept chewing his jerky, but apparently loved my words. As he ate, he wagged his tail. I had been giving Yaneba directions to follow the route. We arrived at the shopping center where the PO box was located. Yaneba looked for a parking spot a prudent distance away where we would not be seen in the darkness from the store. At this late hour, the small shopping center was completely empty, and we didn't want to draw attention to our bird by noticing us. She pulled out a pair of infrared binoculars and handed one to Chandee. They silently observed the place.

Not much later, the Mercedes minibus stopped before the glass door. Chandee handed her binoculars to me. "Is this our man?"

I looked at him for a few seconds. "Yes, this is our bird."

The tall slim man with the aristocratic air stepped out of the Mercedes with a set of keys in his hand. He walked to the glass door of the establishment and unlocked the door. We prepared ourselves, Yaneba and Chandee with the pistols I had taken from the terrorists, and I with the pistol I had inherited from bin Laden. We got out of the Land Rover, intending to leave Tombo inside to guard our getaway vehicle.

Inside the facility, the man pulled out the key to the box. He stopped before the box, inserted the key, and hesitated for a few seconds in thought. He turned and looked around. Then he yelled to the women in the car, "I need you!"

The beautiful green-eyed blond, who appeared to be his favorite, jumped out of the minibus' side door and hurried to his side. He instructed her to open the post office box, and stepped back several feet, placing his back against the other rank of PO boxes on the opposite side, about six feet away. The young woman looked at him in fright. He gestured impatiently for her to open the box. We couldn't hear what he was saying, but he was obviously speaking.

As soon as she opened the door, a metal bolt sprung out and impaled her clean through her neck right at her trachea. She grabbed at it with both hands and fell onto her knees in a desperate attempt to try to remove it. Bin Laden was frozen in fear as he looked at her while blood sprayed from both sides of her neck. At that moment, Yaneba and I entered the store and ran towards the PO box while Chandee ran towards the Mercedes to neutralize the brunette accomplice. We had no notion whether or not she had weapons, and so she represented an imminent threat. Chandee pulled a plastic zip tie and restrained her in the car.

Bin Laden saw us approaching with weapons in our hands. He pulled two grenades and pulled both pins with his teeth. He yelled, "Stop, or we all die here tonight!" Yaneba had her pistol braced on her arm, aiming at bin Laden. "This is the time to negotiate!"

However, Tombo had not remained in the Land Rover. With a snarl, Tombo ran into the store and lunged at the terrorist. I yelled, "Tombo! No!"

Yaneba replied, "The only one who will die here is you. No more negotiations." Without even blinking, she shot twice. The first bullet hit him right in the forehead, the second right under his left eye and into the temple. He fell to his knees and then on to his chest. We immediately dove for cover beneath the front counter, but due to his falling on his own grenades, only a few fragments from the explosion struck Yaneba in her arm and a couple more struck me in the face. We could feel the vibration of the concussion through the ground beneath our bodies. The glass door was blown out by the explosion.

Chandee came into the store through the glassless front door. "Are you two OK?"

I nodded my head. "Yes, I'm OK. Yaneba?"

"Yes, I'm fine," she replied.

Chandee looked at both bodies. "Thank God, the polygamist is finally dead." Then she saw what was left of the body of Tombo, which had been torn to shreds by the blast. "Oh, no!" she said mournfully.

I shook my head sadly. "He knew who the real abuser was. Such a loss."

Yaneba looked at the metal briefcase Chandee brought in. She tried to pick it up. "What does he have in here?"

I said, "Open it and see."

She opened it and shook her head. "Looks like these terrorists left behind a fortune in gold and he was cashing out. Not such an idealist after all, like all hypocritical extremists, whether Nazis, communists, or jihadists, all they're looking for is money. He was no exception—he had a great retirement plan here."

We stood up as Yaneba closed the briefcase. I said, "Well, we can put this to good use."

"Indeed," Chandee said.

"Of course, where bin Laden is going, he won't need any gold. He's going straight to the Inferno."

Yaneba said to me, "What now?"

I replied, "Let's go back to Hania's to find out if it's safe for us to return to the USA and put our own house in order with a very serious spring cleaning."

Chandee nodded. "Really! That is going to be a lot more complicated and take much more effort than killing bin Laden!"

The three of us left the premises as we heard the sirens of the local police and ambulance service approaching. We jumped into the Land Rover, put the briefcase in the back, and left for Hania's. When we arrived, we were absolutely shocked to see devastation. All of them—Hania, both her sons, and Brenton—had been killed. The only ones we could not find were Abdul, Jr. and Paquita.

I said, "Before we lose our minds looking for her, let me contact O'Brien. He may have an advisory for us relating to this, or at least we can find out whether we can return home or still need to avoid it." I picked up the phone in the condo and dialed O'Brien's code.

He picked up. "Am I glad to hear from you! You have the green light to come home. I put that package on his desk last night, and guess what? I had a call first thing in the morning that he wanted to speak with me urgently in the Situation Room of the White House. Guess what? Your plan worked perfectly, and he assured me that he would call his dogs off. By the time you return, you'll have a pleasant surprise from him in your mailbox. Speaking of dogs, I want to let you know that when I heard that Brenton's family had all been killed, I personally went and got not just his dog, but also yours, Rocco. They're both in a secure place for your tranquility. Unfortunately, all of Brenton's family are dead. It appears he is working with our enemies, so be very careful with him and keep an eye on him."

I looked over at his body. "Well, I don't think I'll have to do that anymore, nor will you. He has paid the price of his double spy game. I only feel sorry for his family—he didn't deserve them."

"Understood. Are you coming home?"

"Yes, but once we debrief from this, we should go to Australia—that is the financial mothership to the whole al-Qaeda network, according to the information I have."

We said goodbye and hung up. Yaneba and Chandee had returned, their worry plain on their faces. Yaneba said, "No sign of her anywhere, no body, nothing."

I frowned. "This is very strange. Could they have taken her with them?"

A timid knock sounded at the front door. I went and looked through the peephole and saw Andrecito standing outside. I opened the door and he said in a secretive voice, "I have Paquita at my house."

As if to confirm that, I saw further down the hall the door to Andrecito's home open. Paquita stood a little timidly in the doorway. Seeing me, she ran over to me and hugged me. She cried, "Oh, Dr. JAM! They're all dead!"

"Who did this?"

"Those bad men came back and killed them all. I hid under the sofa."

I sensed she wasn't telling me everything. "But who let them in?"

She started to cry harder. "My brother, Abdul! He did it—he helped kill them all! Once they were gone, I was able to sneak out the front and hide with Andrecito."

I turned back to look at Chandee and Yaneba. I said, "We can't leave her here alone, not with that murderous brother of hers somewhere out there. The obstacle to her coming with us is, unfortunately dead, so let's take her with us." I turned to Andrecito. "Thank you very much for your courage to hide her and for helping us."

"It's a pleasure, Dr. JAM," he said.

We packed a few things for Paquita and returned the Land Rover Defender where we had rented it from. Then we walked back to where Elizabeth waited with our underwater transportation. We introduced her to Paquita and adapted the gear Brenton had used to the little girl's smaller size. We then returned to the sub. As we boarded, Chopin remarked, "Either Brenton lost a lot of weight, or something happened on the mission!"

I said to him, "Brenton was our saboteur and God saw fit to punish him for it, using the terrorists as His instrument. Much happened, and we'll have plenty of time for a debriefing. In the meantime, meet our newest freedom fighter: Paquita."

Keeping his face serious, Chopin shook the little girl's hand. "Very nice to meet you. You should meet the other two members of our crew." He turned and showed her to the galley, where Willy sat eating a sandwich with Venus on his shoulder. "Willy, meet Paquita. Paquita, this is Willy. The bird's name is Venus."

I could tell Paquita was still sad about what happened to her family but seeing a boy only slightly younger than she brightened her day a little and she smiled at him. She said, "Nice to meet you, Willy. I'm going to be like Dr. JAM someday—maybe you can be like Yaneba, and we can continue on their work!"

Willy grinned and said, "I like that idea! Nice to meet you, too!! Want some of my sandwich?"

I watched them as she joined him at the table and accepted Willy's offer. I looked over at my friends who were all watching with broad smiles on their faces. I nodded in satisfaction and said to Chopin, "The most important thing right now is that we have the green light to go home."

He grinned and said, "Aye, aye, Captain!" We settled ourselves in around the galley table with our two young friends and Chopin went forward to start us on our long journey home to Orange County, California, USA.

Riverside Drive, Newport Beach
Two weeks later
Post Office, 1 am

I parked my car in the C'est Si Bon parking lot, which was about forty or fifty feet from the Post Office where I had one of my PO boxes. Looking around to make sure I was not being observed, I walked into the building and opened my box. As O'Brien had predicted I saw not one, but two letters from the White House. I opened both envelopes and looked at them closely. I saw that they were dated a day apart. Evidently the President wanted to make sure his message to me was clear so that I would not get more upset than I already was and get me to calm down. I shook my head in a mixture of anger and satisfaction at how many people had to suffer and die in order to twist the arm of the devil.

THE WHITE HOUSE

WASHINGTON

April 22, 2015

J. Anthony del Marmol, Ph.D.
Costa Mesa, California

Dear Dr. del Marmol:

Thank you for writing. The best way to advance our Nation's interests and values is through openness rather than isolation. That is why after more than 50 years, the United States is changing its relationship with the people of Cuba and working toward normalizing relations between our two countries.

Decades of isolation have failed to produce meaningful change, and by charting a new course, my Administration is reaffirming our commitment to promoting the emergence of a more prosperous Cuba that respects the universal rights of all its citizens. To achieve this, the United States is taking steps to increase travel, commerce, and the flow of information to and from Cuba. We will also reestablish diplomatic relations with the Cuban Government, including opening an embassy in Havana. Nobody represents America's values better than the American people, and I believe this contact will ultimately serve to empower the Cuban people. Additionally, I instructed Secretary of State John Kerry to review Cuba's designation as a State Sponsor of Terrorism, and after a careful review of Cuba's record that was guided by the facts and the law, he concluded that Cuba met the conditions for rescinding that designation.

Again, thank you for writing. We must create more opportunities and begin a new chapter among the nations of the Americas. By choosing to cut loose the shackles of the past, we can reach for a brighter future—for the Cuban people, for the American people, and for the world our children will inherit. To learn more, visit www.WhiteHouse.gov/Cuba.

Sincerely,

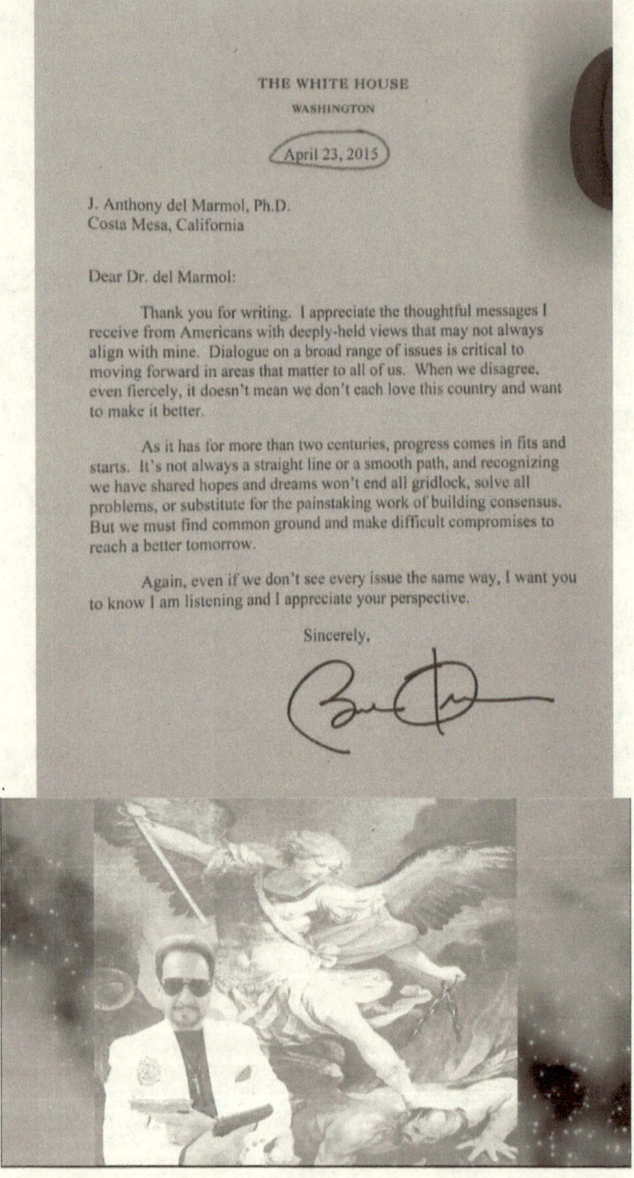

THE WHITE HOUSE
WASHINGTON

April 23, 2015

J. Anthony del Marmol, Ph.D.
Costa Mesa, California

Dear Dr. del Marmol:

Thank you for writing. I appreciate the thoughtful messages I receive from Americans with deeply-held views that may not always align with mine. Dialogue on a broad range of issues is critical to moving forward in areas that matter to all of us. When we disagree, even fiercely, it doesn't mean we don't each love this country and want to make it better.

As it has for more than two centuries, progress comes in fits and starts. It's not always a straight line or a smooth path, and recognizing we have shared hopes and dreams won't end all gridlock, solve all problems, or substitute for the painstaking work of building consensus. But we must find common ground and make difficult compromises to reach a better tomorrow.

Again, even if we don't see every issue the same way, I want you to know I am listening and I appreciate your perspective.

Sincerely,

Those in life that take the effort to find the truth know that in that pursuit they can even lose their lives. They are the only ones that never lose their way, maintaining their dignity intact and defending freedom with their hearts.

Without losing their moral perspective, they keep their integrity intact and find at the end of their lives the shining true light and their real purpose. Without that truth, life itself loses its meaning, leaving only the massive darkness of a lie.

Dr. Julio Antonio del Marmol

OTHER WORKS BY THE AUTHOR

The Cuban Lightning: The Zipper
Cuba: Russian Roulette of the World

<u>Rites of Passage of a Master Spy Series</u>
Cuba: The Truth, the Lies, and the Coverups
The Havana Conspiracies
The Dark Face of Marxism
The Deadly Deals
The Evil Rituals
JFK: The Unwrapped Enigma

<u>The Saga Behind Montauk</u>
Montauk: The Lightning Chance
The Lightning and Montauk: Reality vs. Fiction

<u>ISIS: The Genetic Conception</u>
Lack of Judgement
The Lightning and Bin Laden: Genetic Trail of the Lightning

www.ingramcontent.com/pod-product-compliance
Lightning Source LLC
LaVergne TN
LVHW050908080826
845145LV00001B/17

* 9 7 8 1 6 8 5 8 8 0 3 2 3 *